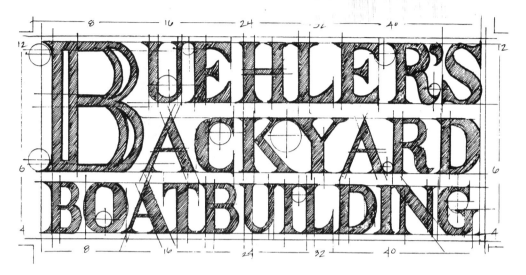

BUEHLER'S BACKYARD BOATBUILDING

George Buehler

 INTERNATIONAL MARINE
CAMDEN, MAINE

Published by International Marine®

10   9   8   7   6   5

Library of Congress Cataloging-in-Publication Data

Buehler, George, 1948-
    Buehler's backyard boatbuilding / George Buehler.
        p.   cm.
    Includes index.
    ISBN 0-87742-257-5
    1. Boatbuilding. 1. Title. II. Title: Backyard boatbuilding.
VM321.B94   1990   90-47667
623.8'223—dc20   CIP

Questions regarding the content of this
book should be addressed to:

International Marine
P.O. Box 220
Camden, ME 04843

Typeset by TAB BOOKS
Printed by Arcata Graphics, Fairfield, PA
Design by Kathleen Collier White
Illustrated by George Buehler
Production by Janet Robbins
Edited by J.R. Babb, Dorothy Chocensky, and
Tom McCarthy

To all people who aren't afraid to do or think things for themselves, and thereby keep this world from becoming too boring.

The years thunder by. The dreams of Youth grow dim where they lie caked in dust on the shelves of Patience. Before we know it, the Tomb is sealed.

Sterling Hayden

BeBOP it!

Charles Mingus

CONTENTS

ACKNOWLEDGMENTS

A thanks to John Van Ameroggin, editor of *Alaska Fisherman's Journal*, who by paying me just enough to force me to write the next article, got me to rewrite my whole shop manual as a monthly series of articles that evolved into this book, *and* who is a far easier editor to get along with than at least *one* I know.

And a tip of the glass to William Garden, whose incomparable designs and good humored writing I discovered in my very early teens, and who, as a result, is probably responsible for me not becoming an accountant or a minister or something.

PREFACE

Mose Allison sings a song that has the refrain: "A young man ain't worth nothin' in the world these days." Well, that just isn't true, unless you believe it yourself. Sadly, many folks don't seem to know that.

Things is so damned *serious* anymore! Back even 20 years ago it was common to see folks out *doing* things, or at least *trying* to do things. Now too many folks just sit home and watch the toob.

Somewhere our culture seems to have lost that spark of imaginative energy that created it. I was thinking recently that I can't remember the last tree house I've seen. Why don't high school kids build 'rods anymore? And why do so many people stand around with their mouths open, afraid to try anything unless they first take a socially-approved class to tell them how?

How, in just a few generations, did this country's soul go from folks who walked, rode horses, and dragged wagons clear across our continent, to a majority who spend most of their time staring at tee-vees; whose feeling of self worth is based more on income than on personal accomplishment?

One reason is that the monthly magazines have pretty much stopped showing things people can do for themselves. Bought out by conglomerates, their old-time greasy-knuckled editors replaced by MBA types with no background in the subject, the American hobby-oriented press is, for the most part, pretty damned dull. Where's the inspiring stuff like "How to Build 20 Boats?" Stuff like Atkin's articles in the old *Motor Boating & Sailing*, and those by Hanna, Chapelle, Farmer, and Garden? And what about all those boat plans and airplane plans and cabin plans and stuff you can really build from the *Mechanix Illustrated*, which is also gone. Gone? How could that happen?

Unfortunately, a boring media results in a boring citizenry, because there's little stimulus around to feed the imagination. Back in the 60s, it was tritely written that, "the medium is the message"; yet the fact is that when the message is mediocrity, well, so are the people.

Figure I/1.
Oh it's salty I is I yam I
arr, and when I spits, I
spits tar. (Cutter *Juno*)

Anyway, it was thoughts like these that made me write this book. Of course, there *was* the wishful fantasy of financial gain, but that wasn't the whole motivation. Nope.

This thing was also written for *fun*. Yup! It's a finger-in-the-wind spread-legged hands-on-hip shaggy-haired and loud-voiced PHOOEY to all those who believe in personality-free boats. It's an UP YOURS to the marine press who drone on so seriously about the dramatic advantages of their advertisers' newest products. More importantly, it's a plug for individual accomplishment: building your own oceangoing boat. There's nothing quite like it, you know—

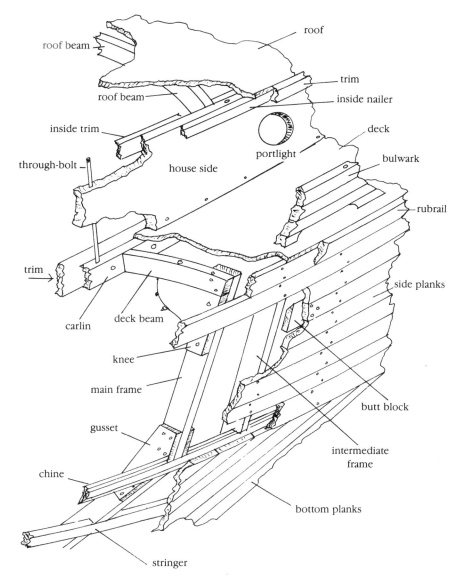

roof beam

roof

roof beam

trim

inside nailer

inside trim

through-bolt

house side

portlight

deck

bulwark

rubrail

trim

side planks

carlin

deck beam

knee

main frame

butt block

gusset

intermediate
frame

chine

bottom planks

stringer

Figure I/2.
This cutaway of a typical hull, deck, and cabin (with apologies to Sam Manning) will help orient you when I start tossing around nautical terms later in the book. If you can't visualize a carlin or something and where it fits into the scheme of things, flip back here and stare at this drawing.

building it yourself, then heading out in it and being completely dependent on your skills. It makes you feel *alive*.

This book is about basic, rugged, and simple construction, borrowed not from yachting's hoary traditions, but from the infinitely more ancient world of workboats, which had to be not only gimmick-free and affordable, but rugged enough to withstand all sorts of abuse and stay out in weather that most of us would just as soon avoid.

Using the techniques described in this book, large boats can be built in practically anyone's backyard, as long as the builder has the cajones to just try. Nowadays a lot of my design work is for fancier stuff than described in this book, but this sort of construction is my "roots." I like it, and I'll probably always do it when building for myself.

There's nothing particularly original in this other than the way it's presented. Although I did my best to lighten up what has all too often been treated as a heavy subject, so to speak, this stuff is all tried and true, and boats have been built as this book describes since well before I was born. I didn't make it up, in other words!

Those of you new to boats or whose experience is just with contemporary production boats may find my harping on brute strength, simplicity, and basic seakeeping ability a bit archaic. You've read the ads and you know that The Current Idea in yacht design has little to do with what I'm talking about here. But there's nothing new about the sea, greenhouse effect or not. Mankind has built boats and sailed on the oceans for aeons; what works well was figured out long ago, perfected in the early 1900s, streamlined and sleekened through the 1950s.

Damn but I like to see folks doing stuff! I like seeing guys hop up cars or kids building tree houses, and the rare sight of a half-built boat next to a house in a WASP neighborhood makes me feel positively *good*!

So, Mose, you're wrong. A brave, young-in-spirit Man or Woman, be they 16 or 90, is worth *plenty* in the world these days! It's just that most don't know it. If you wanna build a boat and sail off to join The Happy Campers of Pogo Pogo or wherever, there's only one thing stopping you: Here's how you can build the boat. The rest is up to you.

See you there maybe.

THINGS TO THINK ABOUT WHEN CHOOSING A BOAT TO BUILD

Although this book will tell you how a large boat can be built inexpensively, the fact remains that a small boat can be built even less expensively. But before we go any further I want to assure anyone who wants a large, grand yacht that I like you too. My continual cautions regarding economy by no means reflect an obsessive identification with the proletariat. It's just that I've never seen any sense in throwing away money, and I pay attention to what I get for what I spend.

Costs have an alarming way of sneaking up on you. Several feet of extra length often results in a bit more beam and draft, heavier rigging and anchors, maybe a larger engine. It all depends on what you want, of course. Sure, larger boats are more comfortable to be aboard, but there's something to be said for having a smaller boat, paid for and in the water, especially if you compare it with a large boat, unfinished and in the driveway.

It's amusing how we tend to forget this with age. Back in '72 I built the original 26-foot *Hagar* (her plans are in Appendix B) for about $3,500, without an engine, and spent two years cruising Mexico and Hawaii. Today, as I add yet another piece to my new 50-footer, I sometimes pause and wonder just what happened to that youthful mind that was so contented with a small boat. Yet I know I could never go back. I *like* big boats.

Building a boat is simple. Believe it or not, the hardest part is just to stop talking and actually start. From that small step, all you need do is fasten one piece to the next and eventually you'll finish. You just have to keep plugging away at it. If you've ever remodeled a house, tended a large garden, written a Ph.D. dissertation, raised a child, or anything else that didn't offer instant gratification, then you certainly can build a boat. If you've never carried through a large project you can still build a boat, of course. But I'd suggest you start smaller, say under 35 feet. This way things keep moving, and you run less risk of getting bogged down.

The first step, obviously, is to choose a design. But before you do that, it's important to decide just how you want to use your new boat. Although a 60-foot schooner sounds romantic, perhaps a 28-foot powerboat actually would be more useful for you. I suggest you think about these points:

- *Size*. The smaller the boat you can be happy with, the quicker you can build it and the less it will cost.

- *Complexity*. Choose a design you can finish. A simple boat can still be an attractive, strong, and good-performing one.

- *Design*. Build what *you* want. It is still socially acceptable to think singularly, even egocentrically, about boats.

Given a choice, I for one always go for the fantasies. There used to be an old man who floated around Seattle's Lake Union in a 14-foot, full-rigged ship—three masts, square sails, the whole bit. Practical? No, but what a fantasy!

A SHORT COURSE ON NAVAL ARCHITECTURE

So many people are saying so many different things about hull shape these days that sifting through it all can be terribly confusing, even amusing. So before we go any further I'd better point out that I'm as opinionated—maybe even bigoted—as anyone else. At least I admit it. That being said, however, I believe the following observations are just common sense.

There are three basic types of sailboats: the racer, the cruiser/racer, and the cruising boat.

The racer is the easiest to define. Its purpose is to win races, so handling ease, accommodations, appearance, and expense are secondary.

Most of the new production boats are cruiser/racer types. They usually have borderline racing sail plans; ease of handling becomes more important, but it still isn't a major issue. A successful cruiser/racer will be a good-sailing boat, ideal for light and moderate wind. It won't be as weatherly or as fleet as the racer, but it will be steadier and easier to handle, and the interior will be comfortable for a group of people to hang out in.

The straight cruising boat is just as specific a design category as the racer, yet it's the hardest to spot; you're likely to see practically any watertight shape out cruising these days. Just look through the cruising literature and you'll see what I mean! For example, back in World War II, a really fearless Aussie vowed that if he lived through that South Pacific insanity he'd do something spectacular, so he took an amphibious jeep around the world. Someone else took a craft made of oxhides across the North Atlantic to duplicate the voyage of Saint Brendan. Thor Heyerdahl has sailed several improbable bundles of weeds and logs across the oceans—not to mention multihulls.

All the same, "true" cruising boat design is a specialized field in itself. Although we've seen that with a bit of luck and a good grip you can take practically anything cruising, there happen to be features that can be designed into a boat that will make it safer, more comfortable, in fact preferable, for cruising.

In my opinion, a proper cruising boat must be well balanced so it steers easily and predictably. The hull should have a smooth roll rather than so much initial stability that it jerks back and forth. It should be able to take a grounding without breaking off a fin or rudder. The sail plan should be versatile, and simple enough to be handled by one person if needed. The interior should be set up for the convenience of the owner's family rather than for the comfort of occasional guests. And it should displace enough to be safely and strongly constructed and still be able to carry the weight of provisions and gear.

What about "performance"? This is a word you'll see a lot in the boat ads, and I'd like you to pause for a moment and think about just what performance means.

I define a performance boat as one that consistently fulfills its design goals. A race boat that loses constantly is *not* a performance boat. The cruiser/racer is the hardest type to pin down. Its very nature stops it from keeping up with the racers, or from being as comfortable and easy to sail as the true cruiser. Maybe cruiser/racers should be called "compromise" boats. They aren't the fastest, the easiest to sail, or the most comfortable, but they move easily in moderate winds and are fun places to take out a group of people on weekends. But if you want to race, or go cruising on open water, maybe do some real, long-term cruising, you'll be far better off with a boat designed specifically for that purpose. A performance boat, in other words.

If you haven't spent enough time around boats to be able to visualize them readily, it might help to think about something more familiar. Comparing a Ferrari, a Chevy Camaro, and a Mercedes station wagon would be similar to comparing race boats, racer/cruisers, and a dedicated cruiser. Like the racer and the cruiser, the Ferrari and the Benz are total opposites. The Camaro is a lot of fun to mess around in—it's sorta fast and sorta comfortable and it sorta corners—but if you're really going to race, or if you plan on doing a lot of highway cruising, you'd pick one of the others.

I'm not really criticizing the compromise boat. If you're interested in weekend racing, if you're gung ho about sailing and like a boat that turns quickly, points very well, and maybe even starts to surf in strong winds; if you have no great interest in ocean cruising or long-term living aboard, then perhaps the compromise boat is just what you need. But I do get so bored listening to the grand claims some designers and production boat manufacturers make about boats that I *know* are simply not suited for the purposes described in the ads. No one type of design will do all things perfectly, regardless of what you hear!

This may come as a shock to you, but the truth is that nobody knows all the secrets of designing sailboats. A visit to any large marina will show such a variety of design ideas that I sometimes think the bottom line boils down to whether or not the thing floats right side up. There are no absolutes regarding what will keep your feet dry, you see, and many designers don't consider how each feature they draw relates to others.

Take a good, stiff midsection, for instance. Sounds good, unless it's a cruising boat, where you want a smooth roll rather than an abrupt, jerky roll. Of course a boat that stays on its feet is desirable, but a boat that is overly stiff will be uncomfortable to live aboard, because its stiffness will give it a quick, snappy rolling motion. This will make you seasick, and can even make movement on deck dangerous.

Or take an exceptional ability to go to windward, based on a powerful, high-aspect rig and an asymmetric, light-displacement hull. Incorporating this into a weekend cruising boat that won't have a lot of people aboard to handle it makes little sense. Sometimes we even see a high-aspect ratio sail plan on a hull that would need a 6-71 Jimmy diesel to go to weather!

There are about as many approaches to yacht design as there are yacht designers. Many start off with a beautiful interior, then wrap a hull around it to make it float—never mind whether or not it sails. Others have engineering backgrounds and can quote all sorts of coefficients and ratios, but there's a problem with this approach, too: Practically all the math in boat design is based on assumption. Somebody assumed something, made up a calculation to prove his assumption, and since then all the engineering types have felt comfortable because they can calculate something just like the book sez.

On symmetry

My own years of observing and using boats have made me a "symmetrical-end" man. Those of us in this school believe that the single most important rule of displacement hull design is that both the front half and the back half of a hull should have about the same volume. Symmetrical. For a simple illustration, roll a whiskey bottle on the floor. Because the bow and stern both have about the same volume, it rolls in a straight line. Now roll a light bulb on the floor. It has a nice, fine entrance and a big transom containing a cozy aft cabin. But when it heels, because it's an asymmetrical shape, it pivots on its fat tail and forces the bow to rotate around in a circle.

A boat hull works just the same. Your boat has to deal with all sorts of forces when it's moving. The wind is trying to push it one way, but you're steering it another way. Swells lift it up and down and roll it left and right, and this makes the underwater area change shape constantly.

An asymmetric hull can't deal with all this very well. Rather than rolling or heeling on a line parallel to its keel like the symmetrical hull, it rotates on its wide stern and tries to force its nose into the wind and give up. This is the main cause of heavy weather helm, and can cause steering difficulties in very light wind and heavy swell. If it isn't reefed down in time or if it's hit by a sudden squall, an asymmetric hull can become completely unmanageable and actually whip around into the wind.

Of course, you can still go cruising on one. In fact, most of the production yachts *are* out of balance. But you'll have a far easier time if your boat is well balanced and not bothered by shifts in wind strength or direction. When you're cruising, especially shorthanded or alone, you have enough to do without bothering with a hull that doesn't want to go straight. I used to cruise on a boat that was so steady you could tie the helm going due down wind, when the breeze was steady. Still, after several weeks the strain of taking four-hour shifts at the helm would exhaust us. I admit things would have been easier with a wind-steering vane, but even then the symmetrical hull is better. Its easier-steering hull eases the job for the often temperamental wind vane. I believe that anyone who disagrees with how important predictable and easy handling is for a cruising boat has never gone for a long sail.

The handling advantages of the symmetric hull are *fact*, by the way; even most of the asymmetric crowd admit it. But they say they know a mathematical calculation that tells them where to put the sailplan's Center of Effort (push), and this overcomes the problem.

Well it just isn't true. The rule for locating the Center of Effort is based on four big assumptions: 1. The hull is sitting exactly on its waterline and not heeling even one degree. 2. The sails are sheeted in exactly midships. 3. There's no shape at all to the sails. 4. The wind is coming exactly broadside.

Since it's a rare thing indeed for any one of these things to happen in real life, and completely impossible that two or more will happen at the same time, I wouldn't put a great deal of faith in the calculation if I were you.

So why are some boats designed with asymmetric hulls? What you commonly hear is that a broad stern gives a bit of "bearing," which helps keep the hull from squatting in stronger winds and lets it go maybe a little faster than hull speed. If it's a light-displacement boat with a flat or dinghy-type bottom, like many of the new designs, it might even get up and plane, if you can keep it from broaching! Other reasons are to get a big cockpit or squeeze in an aft cabin.

How can you tell if a hull is symmetrical or not? First, locate the Center of Buoyancy. The CB is the place where the hull teeter-totters when it bobs up and down. Imagine a boat floating. A wave hits the nose and the bow teeters up; a wave hits the stern and the bow teeters down. The CB is the fulcrum the hull teeter-totters on, and the closer this point is to the middle the more symmetrical the hull.

Now then, the CB is a useful thing to know, *but* because it only measures underwater area, the calculation is accurate *only* (natch!) when the boat is tied in its slip.

The next thing you want to look at is the deck view. The symmetrical hull will look about the same in the front and back. Although we tend to think of double enders as being naturally balanced, many new ones aren't because they're too full in back. A lot of boats with small transoms are symmetrical. In fact, full-bowed boats with big transoms, like Slocum's *Spray*, can be, too!

The final thing to look at is beam. Take a basketball, for instance. It's perfectly symmetrical, but it isn't a very good shape for a boat. All fast and decent-handling displacement boats are fairly trim. This is why most of the world's little working boats used in open water are relatively narrow, trim, and often double-ended. Believe me, mankind has been trying to keep its feet dry upon the oceans for aeons. There is nothing new in marine architecture regarding the basic principles of design. Symmetry and moderate beam are essential ingredients for a decent-handling cruising boat.

HULL MATERIALS

The most practical materials for building a custom, meaning a "one-off" boat, are wood, plywood, steel, and aluminum. The order of preference depends on your familiarity with the material and its availability. In the Pacific Northwest, wood is readily available. As a matter of fact, at this writing I know where I can buy 40-foot long 12 × 12s for 140 bucks. But if you live in Kansas where there ain't any trees, you might want to give plywood or metal a serious look.

Of course, there are many other ways to go. Ferrocement works fine, but it's very labor intensive. Fiberglass works fine, too, but again it's very labor intensive, and it smells like the New Jersey Turnpike. Both of these materials are difficult to fasten an interior into and require insulation to keep moisture from condensing on the inside surfaces.

People build boats in all kinds of different ways. I've heard of boats that are steel to the waterline and wood up from there; boats built of epoxy-saturated papier-maché, boats built of oxhides, balsa logs—you name it, somebody somewhere has done it. All materials have their place, but take my word for this: Wood, plywood, steel, and aluminum really are the best materials, either for home building, or for hiring someone to build you a boat.

Wood

Listen. Picture the ideal construction material. First we'd want something easy to work. We'd want something that glues and takes fastenings easily; something that flexes and bends easily without weakening. We want something that looks good and, since we're just imagining, lets throw in smells good, too. Believe it or not, there is a material that does all this. It ain't manmade! It's wood!

Wood is really a marvelous material. It's naturally insulated, so moisture doesn't condense on its inner face and drip on your face while you're sleeping. It smells good. It's the most fun to build with. It's the easiest material to repair. It's easy to find almost anywhere. And it can be used in any number of ways.

Regular plank-on-frame construction has been with us since Noah nailed up the Ark. Plywood works well, and it's stronger than steel for its weight. Cold-molded laminating is ideal for a strong, lightweight hull. Strip-building with an outer layer laminated on is good for heavier displacement, round-bottom hulls. Strip-built, cold-molded, and plywood boats can all be covered with epoxy, which, advocates say, "encapsulates" the wood. By keeping moisture and air from it, epoxy protects wood from deteriorating, yet still allows it to retain its natural insulating qualities.

There's a lot of B.S. around about maintenance problems with wood, but it really isn't true. What requires maintenance is brightwork! All that varnished teak gingerbread on the Taiwan Baroque boats takes a lot of time to keep up. But caring for a wood hull just involves painting it once a year and checking for leaks, which is far more pleasant than waxing and buffing a fiberglass hull. With good air circulation inside and the liberal use of preservatives, wood will last just about indefinitely.

Metals

After wood I like steel and aluminum. Steel is easy to learn to work, it's fast to build with, doesn't require a great many tools, it's readily available, and it's very strong. It's probably the best material for hiring a hull built because of the speed of assembly. But it must be insulated to keep down condensation and to keep it from sounding like an oil drum inside, and it just isn't as pleasant to be around as wood.

Aluminum has many of the advantages of steel, and it's much easier to shape. Normal woodcutting tools will saw it, but it's a little trickier to weld. Although aluminum is ideal for light-displacement boats, so is plywood, and plywood's cheaper and easier to work.

HULL SHAPES

Although fiberglass and ferrocement can be molded into any Kansas City stylist's twist-and-curve fantasies, wood and metal are different. Not that they can't be tortured into embarrassing shapes, too, but they don't like it, and you'll need all sorts of gymnastics to twist or wrap them to extremes.

That's alright. In general, the longer and trimmer the boat is, the easier it goes through the water, the more spread out the interior can be, and the easier it will be to build.

Take what I call Big Little Boats. Many production boats fall into this group. They are beamy and full for their whole length, and get the maximum interior possible for the length. But their full ends and abrupt curves make them hard to build, they pound in a chop, and they don't slip through the water easily.

The other side is what I call Little Big Boats. Here, for instance, we take the same volume of a fat 30-footer, but stretch her out to 35 to 38 feet, leaving the beam and draft the same. Now we have a hull where the curves are flowing rather than forced, so it's easier to wrap the material around. We can have the same amount of usable interior space, but everything won't be so crammed together. It will feel more spacious, and have more storage area.

Its trim shape will allow the boat to move more easily through the water, so it will both sail and motor faster with the same power. It will cost little more to build than its fatter cousin, because most of the expensive components will be the same. The trimmer boat will need just a bit more hull material, which actually is the cheapest part. If you're hiring it built, the hull might even cost less in some cases: It will be faster to build because the material will flow on more easily.

The trim hull is a better, safer boat on open water. Do you remember the '79 Fastnet race? A bunch of modern production boats were racing off Britain when the weather turned nasty, leaving many of them capsized, dismasted, or broken up, in some cases drowning their crews like rats.

This caused a bit of consternation among designers and yachtsmen, of course, and some interesting literature came out of it. Tank tests were done that showed that the average modern-type hull, which is beamy, very shallow-bodied, and relies on a fin keel for stability, is actually more stable upside down than rightside up. Assuming a boat like this survives a capsize structurally (and many won't because of the light construction), it will just sit there upside down until another wave recapsizes it.

You see, it all depends on what you want the boat for. If you're not going out in open water then who gives a hoot! But if you think you might want to go cruising, that's another matter. As I've said before, there's a reason why all the world's little open-water working boats, from whale boats to salmon trollers, were built trim. They slip through the water easily, they're hard to capsize, and if they do, they come right back up. The few that weren't trim, like the Scandinavian rescue boats, were built very deep for stability, and so solidly that they were practically indestructible.

A term you hear these days is "Displacement/Length Ratio." This is an attempt to describe a hull's actual volume. For instance, a 30-foot canoe and a 30-foot tugboat will be completely different, and describing them with a ratio based on their weight and length gives you an idea of how big they actually are. Boats with a D/L of 350 or more are considered "heavy" displacement, 220 to 350 are "moderate," 150 to 220 are "light," and less than 150 are "ultralight." In general, the shorter the boat the bigger the D/L ratio it needs to give it the volume to carry provisions and still allow for sturdy construction.

The "average" D/L for a mid-thirties-foot cruising boat is probably between 230 and 280. The boat I'm building now—a 50-footer—has a displacement-to-length ratio of only 218. She has about the same interior as many new 35-footers, but everything is more spread out. Because she's so trim, she'll move through the water very easily, and won't require a larger engine or more sail area than a smaller, fuller-bodied boat. Her long, narrow shape makes her very hard to capsize, but if she does, she should roll right back onto her bottom. Long, trim shapes don't like to float upside down, unlike wide, shallow shapes, which often are more stable upside down than rightside up. And of course, she was easy to build. Her 1½-inch-thick planking flowed easily around the hull without steaming or using undue force. She's a good example of the advantages of a Little Big Boat.

An ode to chines

Now you know you want to choose a design that will move, but you also want to choose one that's within your ability to build. The two *are* compatible!

The simplest hull form to build in wood, plywood, or metal is a trim, single-chine hull. Cold molding or strip-plank construction doesn't make sense here because plain old plywood or planking is easily wrapped around the simple planes, and the framing system is straightforward and easily built from commonly available materials using readily understandable techniques—none of this "steaming fresh-cut white oak butts grown in a swamp on the north side of the hill cut at the full moon" stuff.

Many people who aren't used to something are agin' it, be it people from a different country or a new breed of dog, so the single-chine hull is looked down on by a lot of folks, few of whom have had any real experience with it.

To many people used to the flowing lines of traditional, round-bottomed yacht construction, chine hulls often look awkward. But that's a fault of the designer, not the hull form itself, and it's easily avoided by keeping the chine below water the whole length of the boat, and by keeping the freeboard moderate.

To avoid the boxy look of a chined hull, and, some claim, to get a smoother water flow, many boats are designed with two or more chines—a *multichine* hull—or the chine might be rolled in a curve, called a *radius* chine.

The multichine hull has a wider floor area because the sections are sort of rounded, but cutting all the extra panels, and the resulting waste, adds both to the materials cost and the amount of labor involved. By eliminating the multichines and instead increasing the length of a single-chine hull, you accomplish pretty much the same thing, and the extra length will yield a better-performing, more comfortable boat.

The radius chine is a purely cosmetic affectation, and won't do a thing for the interior. Advocates say the "soft" chine creates less turbulence, and the hull will move a bit easier. Maybe so. But how much easier is debatable, and certainly not worth the extra work and time in building it. And again, assuming the same beam and draft, a hull 32 feet on the waterline will not move as easily as one 38 feet on the waterline, even if the short one is round bottomed.

Unlike a ski-boat that skims on top of the water, a "displacement" boat that goes through, not over, the water has a speed that is governed by its length *in* the water. Briefly, displacement speeds are around 1.25 times the square root of the waterline. To show how this works, a friend of mine once cut a 60-foot steel boat in half and added 20 feet to the middle. The new boat would go several knots faster, burning 20 percent less fuel with the same engine! So why burden yourself with the extra labor and expense of building the more complicated, shorter hull? Instead, build a trim, simple, single-chine hull, and use the money you're saving to buy extra material to build a larger boat. In my opinion it will be more satisfactory all around.

The *Thunderbird* is a 26-foot racing sailboat originally designed in the 1950s. Thousands have been built worldwide, and they're still an active racing class. They're all simple, single-chine plywood hulls—and they're one of the fastest boats around for their size. Boat for boat, few can keep up with them. And if you compare price and building time, *none* can.

The great ocean racer *Ragtime* is a simple, single-chine plywood hull. David Lewis circumnavigated Antarctica in a single-chine steel hull. Harry Pidgeon, one of the first circumnavigators, used a planked chine hull for his famous *Islander*. Tristan Jones sailed and dragged a plywood chine boat *across* South America, setting the "altitude sailing record."

Practically all the working watercraft in the Southern U.S., from little skiffs to huge offshore trawlers and shrimpers, have chine hulls. I even saw drawings in a museum in Denmark of chine hulls used by the Vikings! Whether in a racing, cruising, or working fleet of boats, you'll often see a single-chine hull successfully having a go of it.

One of the main reasons for building the single-chine hull is the ease with which it can be planked, especially the bottom. You can *cross plank* these hard-chine bottoms, which means laying the planks from the keel to the chine, rather than parallel to the keel, as is usually seen. Cross planking has an honorable tradition behind it, too. It has been used in the Chesapeake Bay area just about forever.

Cross planking the bottom has some very definite advantages over the fore-and-aft method: It's cheap, because it uses shorter, easy-to-find pieces; there's practically no spiling of the planks, so there's little waste; it's so simple to do that it's actually boring, requiring virtually no skill; it's simple to repair if damaged, and it seems more damage-resistant.

Of course you don't have to cross plank a chine hull. If you want to do normal fore-and-aft bottom planking all you have to do is install more bottom frames and find longer planking stock. Each plank must be spiled to shape individually, which will waste far more material and be much more difficult to do than cross planking. The ease of planking is a chine hull's most notable advantage. It makes no sense not to take advantage of this unique quality.

Since the chined hull is the simplest and least expensive to build and will give you the most boat for the buck, I suggest you consider it. That's why the lofting and hull construction sections of this book specifically refer to single-chine hulls, although the rest of the information will be of value to you regardless of what you're building. Interiors, engine installations, rigging, and so forth are the same problem for all of us.

Of course, there's nothing wrong with a round-bottom hull. Just be aware that it is more expensive and complicated to build. Cold molding, or what I think makes more sense for heavier cruising type boats, strip planking covered with two layers of veneer and a layer or two of glass cloth and epoxy, is a very strong and simple way to build. But it's laborious and expensive. If you want a round-bottomed hull, traditional plank-on-frame is actually the cheapest construction, although it requires a bit more skill than the laminated versions, and much more time and skill than the chine hull.

For those of you interested in numbers, and who may want a little more convincing about the validity of chined hulls, Figure 1-1 shows the hull lines of two boats, one a conventional cruiser/racer, and the other a more substantial cruising boat. I've shown each one as a single-chine, a multichine, and a round-bottomed hull. The sectional shape of each version has the same beam and draft. The numbers show how they compare. Taking the same lines and leaving the draft and beam the same as the original version, I've lengthened the

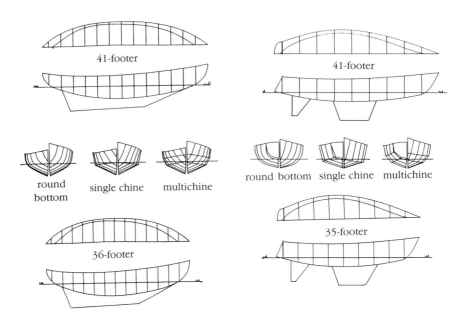

Figure 1/1.
A substantial, long-keeled
cruising boat (left), compared with a typical
cruiser/racer (right).

41-footer

41-footer

round
bottom   single chine   multichine

round bottom   single chine   multichine

36-footer

35-footer

single-chine hull 15 percent, and figured its numbers. The results are interesting. The draft is for the body only, not the keel.

Cruiser/Racer: Beam: 12.15′ Draft: 2.2′

Hull Type	Displacement	Displ./ Length Ratio	Wetted Surface
35′ round	14220 lbs.	199	230.5 sq.ft.
35′ single chine	17025	239	265.1
35′ multichine	12803	180	214.5
41′ single chine	19596	181	304.1

If you are after a light-weather, high-performance boat, at first glance the multichine hull is the one to pick, as it has less wetted surface (friction) and less displacement. But hold on. If you'd be happy with the 35-foot multichine, look what happens when we lengthen the single-chine hull 15 percent. Suddenly our D/L ratio drops down into the low range, and with a waterline that's 15 percent longer and a lower length-to-beam ratio, the hull will move through the water more easily and have a faster hull speed to boot. Although now a light-displacement boat, she still has enough weight to allow her to use a sufficiently stout construction to have a chance at surviving a capsize. Her interior will be more spread out and comfortable since it will have more elbow room, and if you use the same rig and engine as you would on the 35-foot multichine or round-bottom version, the actual construction costs will probably be less while yielding more boat, because of the simplicity and speed inherent in single-chine construction.

Here's the same comparison with the all-up cruising boat:

Double-Ended Cruiser Hull: Beam: 12.5′ Draft: 3.13′
(body only)

Hull Type	Displacement	Displ./ Length Ratio	Wetted Surface
36′ round	21519 lbs.	321	270 sq. ft.
36′ single chine	21686	339	273.26
36′ multichine	21088	325	256.9
41′ single chine	24942	256	314.25

This type of hull has similar numbers regardless of hull form. Just the same, it's interesting to see how they stack up. Once again, the 41-foot, single-chine hull will be a more satisfactory cruising boat than the shorter, more complicated versions. It will be little, if any, more expensive to build than the more complex shapes of the smaller versions.

One final comparison. Remember what I said earlier about a displacement boat's speed being dependent on waterline length, and recall the example of the stretched steel hull; now let's install a 25-h.p. diesel in the light-displacement boat. Allowing a bit of slack for continuous duty, the calculated speeds look like this:

35′ round hull: 7.88 knots at 21.9 h.p.

35′ chine hull: 7.66 knots at 19.4 h.p.

41′ chine hull: 7.85 knots at 17.6 h.p.

Of course, this is a very brief and incomplete analysis of the three hull forms, but it does show that the single-chine hull form is "legit," and offers some very real advantages over more complex shapes. At the risk of redundancy: Boat for boat, when the basic dimensions are the same, the single-chine hull is quicker to build, and because materials are used more efficiently, it's also cheaper to build. All this will allow you to go for a longer boat than you thought you could afford, and the larger boat will cost little if any more to build, be easier to build because the curves are more stretched out and the basic structure is simple, and again, will be more satisfactory to own because of its larger interior and a longer boat's general performance superiority.

Perhaps now you'll understand why I enjoy poking fun at that 4½-foot couple who sail around the world, writing about the virtues of little boats. You see, they don't have a little boat, they have a Big Little Boat. It may be short, but it's full-ended, heavy, and deep for its length, with reverse curved frames, which is one of the most difficult types of hull to build. They could have built a 40-foot, single-chine hull easily in less time and for less money. A boat most of us (probably them too, I suspect) would be much happier with. A Little Big Boat!

One final plug for single-chine hulls. If you tow a round-bottom skiff and a vee-bottom skiff of the same beam and length, you'll note the round one will be squirrelly, and the chine one will go straight. It appears that the turbulence developed by the chine helps keep the boat tracking straight, and the same thing seems to happen on large boats, too.

DISPLACEMENT

Displacement means weight. When a designer draws a waterline, he figures the underwater volume, and the result is what the boat must weigh to sit on that waterline. I briefly discussed this earlier; however, to refresh you, the term "Displacement-to-Length Ratio" is used a lot these days in ads, and many people judge a boat strictly by that. It's said that a D/L over 350 is "heavy," 220 to 350 is "moderate," 150 to 220 is "light," and less than that is "ultralight." When you see a displacement figure, it rarely means the boat weighs that. Instead, it means that's what it will weigh sitting at that point, after being loaded down with provisions, gear, fuel, water, and so on. As a matter of fact, if the boat weight equals its waterline displacement at launch you're in trouble, because it will go over its "marks" when you load her up.

A cruising boat needs some displacement, although the larger you go the lower the displacement can be in proportion to the length. You must have a hull with sufficient volume to support scantlings that will take it through adversity (remember The Fastnet!), and be able to carry enough gear to go away from land—comfortably, by the way.

My new boat has a shelf for my *Encyclopedia Britannica*, a small hold for tools and maybe a motorbike, plus a full galley, a diesel heater, and plenty of storage for cassette tapes, musical instruments, a shotgun, and all the other bits and pieces I like to have around me. She has a low displacement/length ratio—only 218. People who follow these numbers would say she's a light-displacement boat. But look at her! She's 50 feet long, has 2½- by 5-inch frames on 12-inch centers, and 1½-inch planking. This makes her hull 6½ inches thick every 9$1/2$ inches at the frames. Narrow and trim she may be; light-weight and fragile she ain't.

The shorter you go, the heavier in proportion to its length a boat needs to be just to be able to carry things and be built tough. Period. For an example I'm reminded of some friends of mine who used to cruise a small trimaran. Weight was so critical that they only carried 12 gallons of water, hardly any books, few clothes, and minimal food. The hull's scantlings naturally had to be quite light, too. Like all gambling, it caught up with them eventually, and they disappeared on their way back to Seattle from Hawaii. Perhaps they're at that mythical Island in the Sun where hard-core trimaran people believe Arthur Piver went when he, too, disappeared at sea.

Displacement meaning weight, and weight meaning volume, and volume meaning surface area, a heavy D/L boat will have more friction from the water than a light boat the same length, so it won't accelerate as easily, and it won't move as easily in light and moderate winds. But once she's rolling, the heavy boat doesn't like to stop, and will "ghost" along, coasting on momentum, when the light boat is sitting still. Of course it's also harder to stop it from bashing the dock, but with practice you learn when to throw it in reverse!

I've used this momentum performance feature (see what I mean about that word "performance?") to sail straight into the wind up narrow channels. You fall off on a reach, build up some speed, then point the nose into the wind, let the sails flop, and the boat coasts along.

In strong wind, surface friction makes little if any difference in speed. *All* hulls of the same waterline length will only go so fast (displacement hull speed usually equals the square root of the waterline length multiplied by about 1.25 to 1.34, depending on whom you talk to), so when you have a good breeze the heavy boat and the light boat will be about equal—unless they're pointing into a chop, where the heavy boat can bash through stuff that will stop the light boat dead in her tracks. On the other hand, if the light boat is flat sectioned aft she might get up and surf off the wind, leaving the heavy boat in her wake. But that stuff ain't for me. I'd be scared to death worrying the thing would run into a log or broach around and capsize. I like a bit of bulk around me when I'm farther from shore than I care to swim back.

Keels

People concerned with D/L ratios often don't care for long keels. In fact, if they see a long keel they'll dismiss the boat as being "slow," regardless of her shape. But that doesn't make much sense.

Practically all boats these days, regardless of section shape, have "canoe bodies," similar to the examples in Figure 1-1. The beautiful "built-down" reverse-curve hull is rare these days because it's harder to build. This means that most boats have fin keels hanging down below the body; some fins are just longer than others. I doubt that a fin that extends back to the rudder generates much more friction than a shorter one. If I didn't intend to go racing, I wouldn't be concerned with it at all.

I like long keels! The boat, especially when it's symmetrical, may not have that "sensitive response" you read about in ads, but it also won't be squirrely or whip around immediately if you let go of the tiller. The rudder and especially the prop and shaft will be protected if you run aground or hit something, and you'll be able to stand her up on her keel and lean her against a dock if you want to paint the bottom.

I once went out on a boat that had such "sensitive response and ease of maneuvering" that, when motoring at 6 knots, if you let go of the tiller the boat whipped around fast enough to pitch people off the foredeck. A friend of mine was sailing a short-keel boat in a strong wind, heeled way over, going like hell, when BANG! He stopped cold. He looked over the side and found that the boat had bumped over a huge log, which had then wedged itself between the rudder and the short keel. He got loose by pushing on the log with a boat-hook, but his prop and shaft were ruined, and he worried about the rudder all the way back to the boatyard. No thanks!

Light-displacement boats certainly have their place. However, they also require light construction, particularly in smaller sizes. And even at their carefully engineered best, that expensive, light-displacement boat can be cut in half by a heavy-displacement wood or steel boat, which will be cheaper and easier to build.

Anyway, that's what I think about that. Just keep in mind that regardless of what you read in the ads, no one type of boat will do all things perfectly. You have to decide what you want to use the thing for, then pick a "performance" boat for that use.

You know, there's nothing particularly new happening in boat design, anyway. Once in a while something like that winged keel them crooked Aussies used to temporarily snag our America's Cup comes along, but in general, every new design is just a rehash of an existing idea. It may be the most beautiful boat ever designed, but it's highly unlikely that it features any new breakthrough. For instance, in the 1970s the sailing speed record was set by a cat with two masts, mounted side by side. L. Francis Herreshoff drew that up in the 1930s. Or take fin keels and separate rudders. We saw those in the 1800s. Nothing new there. But what *is* new are refinements on exist-ing ideas—like fin keels. Now we have skegs and "NACA" airfoil-shaped keels, although some people think the relationship between what's good for water travel and what's good for air travel is still open for debate.

Again, it all depends on what you want. No one idea is perfect for all uses. A good weekend racer isn't necessarily a good cruising boat, and vice versa. That doesn't make one a better boat than the other, just more suitable for a particular use. Decide what you want to use the boat for, then build what will be suitable.

Many people eventually decide that they want a "cruising boat," even if they aren't planning a voyage. You see, a good cruising boat won't surprise you with funny behavior. It's solid and comfortable; its deck doesn't flex when you step on it; you rarely hear people on a cruising boat screaming at one another, unless they're trying to stop the thing from bashing a dock!

Many people enjoy owning a cruising-type boat even if the only voyaging they ever do is in their imagination. I never did get into that macho "Man Against The Sea" mentality so common today. I go out to take it easy. I like to lay about the foredeck while the boat sails itself. I like a boat with predictable behavior, strong enough not to scare me, and capable of carrying the stuff I like to have around. A cruising boat!

CHAPTER 2 · *SETTING UP SHOP*

Before you start building a boat, you've got to get together some sort of shop. It doesn't have to be much, but some sort of covered shelter is essential to protect your project from the weather and at least provide an illusion of security for your tools.

A PLACE TO WORK

No matter where you're building, selecting a site takes careful consideration. You have to worry about wind exposure, power availability, distance from your home, security, and on and on. Also, think about getting the finished boat out. Although you can always hire a crane to lift it over obstructions, it's a lot simpler and cheaper to build in a spot that a truck can back into.

Be especially careful if you're building in a city. Hiding from strong winds is important there, too, but hiding from city bureaucrats may be even more so. These folks are much worse than strong winds. You see, they feel threatened by anyone with the energy and imagination to do anything requiring unsupervised initiative, and seeing someone actually building a big boat drives them wild. Where I used to live in Seattle, there's actually a law that says it's illegal to build a boat bigger than 25 feet long in your own yard.

So, before you rent a space to erect a shop, case out the neighborhood. An industrial area is best. If you put up a neat structure that blends in with the area, the odds are no roving inspector will harass you. If you'll forgive my sounding like an anarchist, I wouldn't bother with a building permit if I were you. You'll understand my feelings if you go down to your local building department and tell them you want a permit to put up a temporary structure in which to build a boat. Just don't give them your right name, and don't tell them where you want to do it. If you walk out in disgust you don't want them to track you down.

The next thing to look for is protection from the wind, if at all possible. It's terribly disheartening to see your Visqueen roof blow off in a storm, especially if, like some folks, you're also camping out in the shop while building the boat. Try to find a site in the lee of a building or some tall trees.

Electricity is absolutely essential. Your power company will come set a temporary pole, although some want to see a building permit first. You might try for the pole before you build the shop, so you can tell the power people the pole is just for building a boat. If not, I've run in power using several 100-foot extension cords. You can also buy a 250-foot roll of 10-gauge house wire cheaply at an electrical supplier. Put a plug on one end and a socket on the other. If you're running a long wire like this, it's best if you can run it down as 220 volts, and split it down to 110 volts in a small breaker box at the shop. This is very simple, but I'd rather not give directions! If you do it wrong you can burn down your building, so if you don't know anything about wiring, ask a pro to show you the principles. Most places that sell the parts will sketch out a diagram showing you how to hook things up.

Building a temporary shop

A surprisingly sturdy shop can be built quite cheaply from 2 × 4s and roll plastic (Visqueen is the best-known brand). A 24- by 55-foot building, with lights, shelves, used plywood sides, and workbenches, seems to cost from $400 to $600 to put up, depending on how fancy you make it. The shop I'm working in now is covered with a 30- by 60-foot blue plastic tarp, which I picked up for about a hundred bucks from the local "Tool Town" store. The framework is made of 2 × 4s, and the walls are covered with clear Visqueen plastic.

  If you're building in an area that gets heavy snow you'll need a

Figure 2/1.
The quintessential back-yard workshop, constructed simply and cheaply of sheet plastic over a light lumber framework. Note diagonal cross bracing at corners.

Figure 2/2.
Shelves and workbench not only hold tools and small parts, but brace the frame as well. Note plywood gussets connecting studs and rafters, and diagonal bracing between pairs of studs.

sturdier one, maybe framing on 2-foot centers, so the costs will be a bit more.

After building all sorts of lean-tos, I think this is the simplest and strongest way to build a large shop (see Figure 2-3). Basically, the wall and rafter units are assembled in one piece on the ground and erected as a solid unit.

At a minimum, the building should be a few feet longer and 12 feet wider than your boat, and it's nice to have standing headroom over the centerline, although 4 feet is enough to work in comfortably. The walls on my shop are 10 feet high, and each rafter piece is 14 feet long, coming to a peak 6 feet higher than the walls. The forms are held together with gussets cut from 1/2-inch CDX plywood. If you're putting plywood on the roof, use a gusset on each side of the form. With a tarp roof, one gusset per joint is enough. The forms sit on top of a 2 × 4 mud sill.

Before you decide on your shop's final dimensions, you need to decide what you'll use for a roof. Roll plastic and the popular big blue tarps come in standard sizes. You may put up your shop framework and find that no available tarp or roll of plastic matches it.

Clear Visqueen lets in the most light, but it really cooks you in the summer and doesn't last long in the sun—about one year before it breaks down completely. UV-resistant clear plastic is available from

Figure 2/3.
Typical stud-rafter unit.
Erect on 4-foot centers.
Use 2 × 4s for studs and
rafters; 2 × 6s on shops
wider than 20 feet.

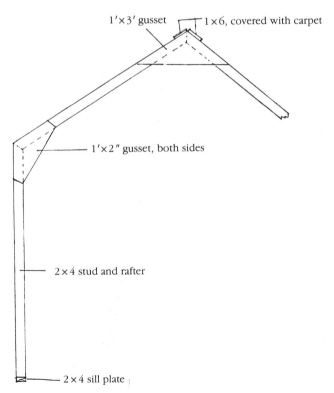

1′ × 3′ gusset   1 × 6, covered with carpet

1′ × 2″ gusset, both sides

2 × 4 stud and rafter

2 × 4 sill plate

Buehler's Backyard Boatbuilding

greenhouse supply companies. (Look for Greenhouse Wholesalers in the Yellow Pages, or ask the folks at a local greenhouse where they get their plastic.) A better alternative is to use clear side walls, with a black roof (which is more UV-resistant than clear) and electric lights. Use 6-mil thickness on the roof and 4 mil on the sides.

I really prefer the big blue tarps. They stand up to the sun much better than Visqueen, and that blue light really is easy on the eyes. In fact, I read somewhere that if you see the devil, you'll be safe if you just close your eyes and think of Christ on a cross, bathed in blue light. I've never had occasion to test this, but there are certain boat-building operations where it might come in handy.

After losing several roofs to wind storms, I learned that if I leave a large hole in the front and back walls, the wind whistles through the building shed and the roof stays put. Apparently, if the building is closed in tight a vacuum builds up that sucks the roof right off.

If you're in an exposed area plagued with high winds, another good thing to do is rent the longest extension ladder you can find, and nail one or two 1 × 4s right on top of the roof tarp, parallel to the centerline. With a hole in each end and two battens on top, my last roof stayed up all year, weathering several good storms.

If you're planning a long building period, or if you're in an area subject to frequent hail or heavy snows and have some extra cash, you can nail longitudinal 2 × 4s 2 feet apart up the rafters, then lay down cheap 1/4-inch plywood like big shingles. You *can* use 1 × 4s if you're really strapped for cash, but you have to climb on them to nail them and the plywood down. I'd use 2 × 4s myself because I'd rather drown than break my neck. Cover the plywood with a large tarp or tarpaper.

So, after you've figured out what size building you'll need, and what kind of roof you're going to use, you can lay out the forms on the ground. Draw them out if you're on pavement or wood; pound in a stake at each corner if you're on bare ground. Make them a minimum of 2 feet narrower than the roof tarp you're going to use, and make the whole building at least 3 feet shorter than the length of the tarp. This way you'll have enough tarp hanging over to allow you to fasten it down securely. The 30- by 60-foot tarp on my current shop, after allowing for the pitch of the roof, gave me a building of 24 by 56 feet.

These building forms are placed 4 to 8 feet apart, and sit on top of a 2 × 4 mudsill laying on the ground. Put the mudsills in place, mark on them the location for each form, and nail a 6-inch piece of 2 × 4 at each point. (This makes it easier to position the forms accurately.) As you erect the forms, "X" brace them together with 1 × 4s. If you can afford it, nail plywood to their sides. This really stiffens up the building and makes your tools a bit more secure. If you don't use plywood walls and a roof, use lots of 1 × 4 diagonal bracing.

Cover the roof with one piece of plastic if at all possible. If you must use more than one, position the pieces so that the seams are overlapped facing the direction the bad weather comes from. For instance, where I live the strong winds come from the south, so I'd put the first piece on the north side of the building, then put on the second one overlapping the first by 6 feet or more. That way the strong winds won't get under the "lap" and rip off the roof.

I like to cover the sides with plastic first, so the roof hold-down battens will overlap all joints. If you're using a tarp for the roof, unroll it on the ground beside the building, throw three to six ropes over the roof, and tie them to the tarp. Get several people to each grab an end, and slowly and gently pull the plastic over the roof. Now, take a long 1×2 or 1×4, staple the edge of the plastic to it, roll it up until you're even with the edge of the building, and spike this batten into the sidewall studs. Roll the plastic away from you, so the roof runs in a smooth line to the edge. If you roll it toward you, there'll be a crack that will leak at every nail. Do one whole side first, then do the second side, pulling the tarp as tight as you can before nailing the batten down. Then do the ends the same way, again pulling as hard on the tarp as you can.

If the weather is hot, do the roof only in the very early morning or late evening. Otherwise the trapped heat will lift the tarp like a hot air balloon and you won't get it as tight as you could.

Make the place into a real workshop by putting up some shelves for tools and supplies, and put porcelain light sockets and plug-ins all over, using 12-gauge house wire. Back when I was single and fancy-free, I had me a couple of really nice shops. The last one had a kitchen, a sleeping loft, and a secret shower that drained into a 4-foot square hole in the sand. With a wood stove in the corner, an easy chair, and a few pinups on the wall, it was quite comfortable.

TOOLS

It really doesn't take a huge assortment of exotic tools to build a wood boat. If you've built bookshelves or a dog house and are now considering a yacht, you probably already have most of what you'll need.

You'll need the basic hand tools, such as a hammer, tri-square, a few chisels, a crosscut saw, a crescent wrench, a plane, a level, and whatnot. A few more specialized tools, such as a bevel measure, a ripsaw, and a block plane, make things easier. Nothing too fancy.

A few power tools are just about essential. The first one to buy is a portable circular saw—a minimum of 2 h.p. with a 7-inch or better blade. You'll use this saw all the time for just about every job. A strong one can even saw curves if you bend a little extra set into the teeth and raise the blade until the teeth barely peek through the wood. You'll use your portable circular saw to cut the keel rabbet, rough-fit planks, build the shop—everywhere! If you nail down a

board to serve as a guide, you can even use it to cut straight lines for cabinets.

I can't imagine building a boat without a table saw (10-inch minimum). This doesn't have to be a big industrial model; the regular model from Sears is fine. You'll use this thing constantly: to resaw wood to smaller dimensions, clean up the edges of used wood, make perfect caulking seams on the bottom planks, precisely cut bevels and rabbets when making hatches and doors, beveling all the frames and floor timbers, and even cutting up scrap for the wood stove. If you don't already own one, buy a good used one. You'll be able to build the boat and then sell the saw, probably for more than you paid for it. Big power tools hold their value better than anything I can think of.

A big, powerful bandsaw is handy but expensive. A small, powerful one works about as well. Like the table saw, either can be resold when you finish the boat. Considerably cheaper and even more versatile is a top-quality sabersaw. If you're pressed for cash, get one of

Figure 2/5.
A table saw will be used constantly on any boat-building project.

these instead of the bandsaw, but get a good one. My $90 sabersaw can cut through 3½-inch-thick fir. My old $40 sabersaw was straining in ¾-inch plywood. Get one with a full 1-inch cutting stroke and a scrolling head.

You'll need a ⅜-inch reversing electric drill. If you buy two of them, one with a variable speed trigger, you can use the first for drilling holes and the second for driving screws. With a little practice you won't even scratch the galvanizing.

When buying these portable power tools, anything but the top-quality industrial line is a waste of money, except perhaps the drills, if they have long warranties. I buy all my power tools at big chain stores, because most of them have great store warranties in addition to the manufacturer's. Ask first, of course, but one local chain offers a full year over-the-counter exchange on everything they sell. I've used it!

There are times when you'll need a heavy ½- or ¾-inch drill motor, a chain saw, and an electric plane. These are all expensive tools, and it's far cheaper to rent them for a day than to buy them, unless you're going to be doing a lot of this building stuff. I did finally break down and buy an electric plane. You can live without it, but they're really handy and will save you a lot of trouble.

You can't have too many clamps. At a minimum you'll need eight C-clamps, big enough to cover both the frame and a plank plus a couple of inches; twice that many would be nice. You'll need at least three (better yet nine) sliding pipe clamps, 4 feet long. One or two "deep-throat," 2-foot bar clamps come in handy practically everywhere. You can make clamps out of threaded rod, wing nuts, and whatnot, but the store-bought variety saves an awful lot of screwing around.

Unless you own no tools at all, the thing to do is just start building with what you have. If you find you need a specific tool, then buy it. Just keep your eyes open; like everything else, the best time to buy a tool is when you don't need it. I always stop at yard sales, swap meets and the like, and over the years have collected quite a variety of strange tools, all at good prices. Some of the exotics will sit in my box for years, yet once in a while that dusty old tool will be exactly what I need to do something. In fact, I have some whose purpose I haven't figured out yet! But someday I know I'll need 'em. You can practically always substitute another tool for the right one for a job, but things are simpler with the right tool. You know, a big part of good woodworking skill is owning the right machinery.

On craftsmanship and standards

This a hard subject to discuss. The true craftsman is a rare bird. He's no more in tune with the cosmos than you are, but he has the picky, meticulous, and patient personality that allows him to concentrate hard and always do a neat job (plus he usually has a whole stable of tools). They're quiet, calm, peaceful people, although sometimes a little, well, boring.

Carpentry work is really quite basic stuff. All it involves is measuring and cutting accurately, so you'd think it would be within anybody's grasp. The basic act of using a tool is quite elementary. You either move it back and forth or beat on it—nothing to it. All it takes is practice in controlling the hand that moves back and forth. There's nothing mystical about it. Just practice.

The higher the degree of finish you demand for your project the more skill you'll need, the more time it will take, and the more wood you'll ruin. A naturally finished hull must have neater caulking seams and a better sanding job than a painted hull with a bit of trowel cement in the gouges. A rounded, varnished cabin or cockpit coaming must be perfect or it looks sloppy; a painted rectangular one can have a touch of Bondo in the joints and still look clean and neat.

Of course, the perfectly assembled boat looks marvelous, and it's the goal you should aim for. But to be realistic, in most parts of the boat a joint can be "not quite perfect" and still be just as strong. And when it's filled with something and painted, it will look just as good.

I'm not praising sloppy construction. But I want you to understand there is a big difference between *good* construction and *perfect* construction. It's important that you understand this, because it will make the difference between your being able to build the boat or simply quitting in frustration.

Before you start building, spend a good month really looking over finished boats. Go to a few brokers and pretend you're in the market. They'll fall all over themselves showing you boats. Inspect a fishboat. These guys go out in open oceans and must be strong. Look closely at how it's built. Inspect top-quality yachts. Try to find an old cruising warrior like a Tahiti Ketch that's been to Kingdom Come and back. While looking at all these boats, think honestly about what kind of boat you want to build and how you plan to use it.

With a cruising boat, you're going to be rafting up at commercial docks, possibly beaching the boat for painting, catching fish from it, dragging skiffs up on it, and so on. This is far harder use than the highly finished yacht—sailed one weekend a month and kept in its slip the rest of the time—ever sees. A cruising boat's construction and degree of finish should be simple and stout; otherwise you'll break your back keeping it up. I follow the old workboat rule of painting her once a year, whether she needs it or not. The rest of the time I'd rather be using it.

There's nothing wrong with simple, neat construction and a painted finish. It will cost less money, and the required level of craftsmanship is within reach of most folks with a little energy.

So do the best you can. Sometimes an extra few minutes of fitting a piece will save hours of trying to trace down a leak. But at the same time, be realistic. Decide before you begin whether you're building a shrine or a *boat*.

MATERIALS

WOOD

Anyone who likes wood boats enough to actually consider building one knows about all the traditional boat woods. Every building and design book ever written lists the same old standbys: white oak for frames, African mahogany or Port Orford cedar for planks, and teak for trim. You know as much about all that as I do.

What you may not know is that many of these materials are practically extinct; when you can find them at all they cost a fortune. Teak, in particular, today is apt to be pretty poor quality. Unless you've watched them cut the tree, the white oak you're paying for very possibly is one of the innumerable varieties of red or gray oak, many of which don't hold up as well as white oak.

So in this chapter I won't simply parrot the traditional yacht-building materials; instead, I'll make you aware of some of the readily available and less expensive ways to go about boatbuilding.

If you study working boats, such as tugs, ferries, barges, and fishboats, you'll discover that practically all of them were built from the woods that grew locally. Here in the Pacific Northwest we have lots of Douglas fir boats. Farther north in Canada they used cedar, fir, and even spruce and hemlock when they had to. In Atlantic Canada they used spruce, hackmatack, and even beech and birch. In New England they used the local oaks and cedar. In the Southern states they used cypress.

Now, some of these materials are very good for boatbuilding, and some aren't very good at all. But they all work, especially in the climate zone where they grow. If you take a softwood boat to the tropics, it probably will rot out more quickly than one built of the standbys, but with good ventilation, preservatives, and good bedding compounds, how much more quickly is a good question. A solid fir boat I built has been in Hawaii for 15 years now and is still floating. It lived through a hurricane when it was 12 years old.

Hemlock—especially hemlock—and probably spruce really shouldn't be used. But if that's all that you can get at a price you can afford, I'd use it rather than not build a boat at all. Most of the boat-construction money goes into outfitting anyway: the engine, sails, hardware, anchors, portlights, and so on. I'd consider hemlock if that was all I could find or afford. When the boat rotted out I'd strip off the hardware and build a new hull.

I knew a guy who built a boat of eucalyptus. It started getting pretty sick after 10 years, but he'd had 10 years to use it. If he hadn't used eucalyptus he would have had no boat at all.

Ask yourself this: Just what sort of boat are you building? If you're putting together a very simple boat, regardless of size, in which you just plan to mess around locally, you can use slacker standards than if you're building a more expensive cruising boat with an eye towards resale value down the line.

Finding wood

One of the best sources of wood you're likely to find is the Building Materials section of the classified ads in a big-city newspaper. Excellent wood is salvaged daily from old warehouses and such. Wood from salvage dealers costs a small fraction of new prices, and often is of higher quality. You might have to plug a few bolt holes in large timbers, and planks might have some nail holes, but these things can be dealt with. A table saw is just about essential for dressing this stuff up, by the way.

You can use salvaged wood for practically the whole boat, although it's hard to find planking that doesn't have nail holes. I've used old rafters that had holes in one edge. I filled the holes full of wood preservative! Of course this isn't the best, but it was the only way I could afford to build a big boat.

The framework, keel, and house sides of a 35-foot boat I built used to be an army camp. My new boat has a keel that used to be a dock; the frames were rafters in a mill; and the rudder, the deck beams, and a lot of the planks were found in a salvage yard. It was all passable quality fir, and the price was 15 to 20 cents a board-foot, compared with 27 cents to $1.50 (depending on grade) for new fir.

A lot of salvaged wood in the east is southern yellow pine or oak—both good building woods. In the northeast you might run across some white pine or spruce. Here on the West Coast, most salvaged wood will be fir, which by good luck happens to be a top-quality boat wood. Hemlock, being pretty much just a weed, wasn't used for much besides firewood until our corporations found they could sell all the fir they could cut to the Japanese, who were too smart to buy hemlock and willing to pay more than us for fir. Now the domestic lumberyards are full of hemlock. The lumber companies dye it an orangish color and call it "Hem-Fir," but it's still hemlock. It can be hard to tell the difference between good hemlock and fir, but hemlock will always have a tinge of purple showing in areas around knots, and sometimes in between grain lines.

The best wood in a boat will be the planking. I've learned that guys who run small sawmills generally like wood boats, and if you give them time, will keep an eye out for the best logs and mill them into planking material for you. I'll go into more detail on planking later, but briefly, it pays to use good quality wood, and a small sawmill seems to be the best place to get it nowadays.

Although you'd never guess it from looking at many boat designers' construction plans, you can use normal dimension stock right off the lumberyard shelf for the whole boat. In boats to 30 feet or so you can use 2 × 4s for frames. On boats to 40 feet or a little better use 2 × 6s. On bigger boats use 3-by or 4-by stock.

Lamination gives you real freedom in making stuff. You can rip 1 × 4s or 1 × 6s in half and glue them up for deck beams. You can make chines, stringers, rubrails, trim, shelves, cabin floors, cockpit floors, dish racks, hatch tops, and whatnot, from 1-by stock, either ripped, glued, and laminated, or just as it comes.

Plywood

Plywood is pretty handy stuff. A plywood deck is fast to lay down, will never leak on you, and for its weight it's as strong as steel. A plywood interior can be built in half the time of an all-natural wood one, although it doesn't look as fancy. But I like the look of the whole inside painted white, maybe with a little natural wood trim here and there. It feels spacious and it's easy to keep clean.

Plywood makes a great countertop when covered with Formica. It greatly simplifies the building of bulkheads, tables, seat tops, and especially frame gussets. Several layers glued together with overlapped butts is a simple, strong, and quick way to build decks, cabin tops, or even hulls. It also makes good hatch tops and can be used for cabin sides.

Plywood is graded by the smoothness of its faces. The best grade (and most expensive) is *Marine AA*, which has two perfectly smooth faces, waterproof glue, and no voids in the (usually all-fir) interior laminates. *Marine AB* is just as good, but one side will have a few imperfections.

Plywoods made for house construction use the same glue as marine plywood, but their interior laminates, which often are of a short-lived "junk" wood, may contain voids. These can cause problems when bending the plywood to shape and can be a good place for rot to start. The best grade, *Exterior AB*, has one perfect face and one almost-perfect face. *Exterior AC* is the same stuff, except one face may have splits or knot holes up to about 1¾ inch wide. These flaws only run the depth of the outer laminate, and present no problem in thicker pieces.

A good compromise material for a hull is *MDO* (Medium Density Overlay) plywood. This stuff (made for sign painters), like marine plywood, has a core of fir or some other good rot-resistant wood, has practically no voids, and comes with a resin-saturated paper face. I've glued two pieces of this stuff together with epoxy and found it as hard to break apart as plywood without the paper face. Just the same, if I was building a hull and using three or more layers of plywood, I'd feel funny gluing the paper faces of MDO together.

Since MDO costs a good third less than marine ply and is still solid fir or other rot-resistant wood, I'd be tempted to disk-sand off the paper face in a few places to give the epoxy some bare wood to grip. Or maybe I'd use an AC- or AB-grade plywood for the inside layer. Try gluing together a sample of these overlay faces and see for yourself how well it sticks, then do what you think is best.

You can buy MDO with one overlay face, too. This is not only cheaper, but gives you wood-to-wood faces if you're gluing two layers together, such as for a cabin side or a smaller hull.

Which grade should you use for the hull? Well, first, let's look at prices. These are 1990 quotes for 3/8-inch stuff from a discount lumber yard in the Seattle area. The prices will increase proportionately with thickness. Marine AA costs so much this particular dealer doesn't bother with it, since Marine AB works just as well.

Marine AB	AB	AC	MDO (2 sides)	MDO (1 side)	T-111
$31.84	$20.48	$12.80	$23.52	$17.60	$12.48

Let's say we're building a 28-foot boat, and we want the hull to be 3/4 inch thick. If we use two layers of 3/8-inch plywood with over-lapped butts we'll need about 28 sheets. This works out to:

Marine AB	AB	AC	MDO (2 sides)	MDO (1 side)
$891.52	$573.44	$358.40	$658.56	$492.80

If money is no object, use marine plywood, since it really is the best. It isn't absolutely necessary, however. The point is, you'll be using multiple layers of plywood for several reasons: Heavy plywood is hard to handle and hard to bend; and several layers of plywood, glued together with overlapped butts, essentially becomes a solid, continuous piece. Building this way, the odd void won't hurt anything, and lower grades of plywood can provide satisfactory results.

Since AB and AC supposedly have the same core standard, if I was building on the cheap I'd use two or more layers of AC. The only time I use marine plywood is when building a small skiff that requires

1/4-inch plywood. Since this is so thin, you want good stuff with no voids, and I think Marine AB is essential, unless you want to bother using glass cloth and epoxy.

I know a plywood-boat builder who never uses anything but a single layer of AB-grade plywood, with no fiberglass coating. He builds fishing boats to 24 feet for commercial fishermen in Alaska, and says his boats last an average of 15 years—with very heavy use: being dragged up on beaches, banging into stuff, and whatnot. The plywood doesn't fail; the boats are just beat to bits.

Of course, it's different with a larger boat. If I were building a sizable plywood hull I'd seriously consider using MDO, but I'd still probably use AC grade for decks, cabin tops, and most of the interior. I don't know. As I'll be saying frequently throughout this thing, we all make our own compromises. MDO is really good stuff and if I had extra cash I'd be tempted to use it on the deck, too. I also might use MDO for big bulkheads because the overlay takes a nice paint job.

As I said, you'll be gluing several layers together, so the odd void won't hurt anything because it's backed up by another layer. After completion, I would probably coat the entire hull with epoxy resin and glass cloth to keep the water out.

Recently I built a small storage building from 3/8-inch T1-11 fir siding, without the phony tongue-and-groove finish. This stuff has one C-grade side, and an unsanded A side that looks like an unplaned board. In fact, the C face didn't seem as rough as that of normal AC, but that could have been the luck of the draw. This stuff was interesting because it's cheap, its core apparently is fir or some similar-quality wood. It has hardly any voids, it's made to fairly rigid specs for the housing industry, and so it seems as if it might be worth using on the inner layers of a plywood hull. You'd have a rough face inside the boat, but since the inside of the hull is almost completely covered by cabinetry that wouldn't matter.

One of these days I'm going to sample glue two layers together, A to A, and see how they hold. If you're thinking about plywood planking you might try this, too, and see for yourself how it works. An option might be to use an outer layer of MDO single-overlay to get the smooth exposed face. You'd have a good-quality plywood hull for far less than the price of marine grade. It's well worth trying, I think.

Planking

The best wood used in a wood boat should be reserved for the planking. *VG-grade* (vertical grain) wood is commonly used because it finishes smoothly and swells more across its thickness than across its width. This is an especially desirable characteristic for the topsides planking. The finish will look better, and the boat's seams shouldn't open up too much if it sits at anchor in a hot climate.

Flat, or horizontal-grain wood is considerably cheaper than VG, however. It also has better abrasion resistance, and is often used for planking on workboats. I see no reason not to use it for underwater planking, and it can be used for topside planking as long as it's good and dry and you don't use very wide strakes. (I'll get into more specifics on wood for planking in Chapter 7.)

The best way to get good planking wood is to scout around and find a small mill that will custom-cut it for you. You'll probably get green lumber, but if you stack it on sticks to let the air get to it, it should dry out enough to use within a year. There are also a number of "boat lumber" dealers around the country that will sell you ready-to-use stuff—for a price.

You can go straight to a lumberyard, or better yet, a lumber wholesaler. Many yards will let you pick through stacks, and it's often possible to find a good deal of planking-quality lumber in the construction-grade pile. There's also a grade called *CPO*, or Clear Pull Outs, that is construction-grade but has no knots. I've used plenty of this. And of course if all else fails you can buy V.G. select.

Unfortunately this stuff has really climbed in price in recent years, and you can actually buy from a boat lumber dealer for about the same price as you'd pay at a lumberyard. But sometimes that's all you can get, and I've built several boats with it.

All plywood, and all top grades of lumberyard wood, will be *kiln dried*. This is considered bad for boat wood because the kilns generally are cranked up really high, and the wood cells get sort of cooked. As a result, KD is less flexible than air-dried wood, and it rots faster. Again, with lots of preservatives, good ventilation, and good bedding compounds, it works fine. As a matter of fact, the kiln does kill any rot spores that might be lingering in the wood! This is another advantage of salvaged wood, by the way. It's all been properly air dried, and nails or bolts have kept it from warping. No less a guru than L. Francis Herreshoff himself specified KD fir for planking several of his designs.

I know some of you with purist backgrounds are going to disagree with what I've been saying here, but consider these points: First and most important, salt water is a preservative. Rarely does a boat rot below the waterline. The damage is caused by fresh water from deck leaks and showers that drain into the bilge. Second, rot is caused by moisture and lack of ventilation. By being sure not to build in dead air spaces, not sheathing over the frames, cutting good air vents in all cabinets and lockers, and installing good deck vents in each end of the boat to insure a constant flow of air, you'll make it pretty hard for rot to get started.

To further stave off the onset of rot, I soak down the whole interior of the hull with several doses of preservatives. I have a plastic pump garden sprayer that does this easily. I scatter handfuls of rock-salt along chines, stringers, and other potential water traps—just as the old-timers did when they built wooden ships. Once a year I take a hand-pump spray bottle (an empty container of Windex, 409, or the like) and spray preservative in all the corners.

And finally, remember that if rot does start, the boat doesn't dissolve instantly or roll over and die. If you poke around once a year or so (while spraying preservative) you'll discover any problem spots and be able to fix them before they get bad. Actually, with the treatment described here it's unlikely you'll find any problems, at least for a long time.

It all boils down to balancing availability and your pocketbook. I know people who consider the use of less-than-perfect lumber to be heresy. Most of them will never be able to afford a large boat, either, but they feel very self-righteous about their allegiance to yachting's hallowed traditions. Personally, I'll be out sailing.

FASTENINGS

Practically every type of fastening can be used somewhere or another on a boat. I use *screws* for planking because they go in quickly and easily with an electric driver and they seem to hold better in softwood frames. Yet plenty of people prefer square *boat nails*, and say they hold better. But you're supposed to screw the butts if you're using nails, so that seems to imply that screws hold better.

Common galvanized nails and *finish nails* are used all over. Bronze or galvanized *ring nails* are used in plywood decks and hulls. *Carriage bolts* are used whenever you want to secure two pieces of wood together absolutely, such as in the gussets, deck beams to frames, hand rails, and so on. *Machine bolts* are used to fasten steel to wood, such as deck hardware, mast steps, motor mounts, etc.

Homemade, or *bastard bolts*, for want of a better name, can be made from pieces of rod. Since the bolts holding the keel together are all odd and extra-long sizes, you'll need a lot of these. You can have them custom-made for you, but the simplest and cheapest way is to buy 20-foot sections of galvanized rod from a good steel supply joint, and cut your own to length.

You can hand-thread them yourself, although 5/8 inch is about as big as you can do comfortably by hand. A good hardware store, pipe-fitter, or machine shop will thread them cheaply, too. Thread one end just enough for a nut, and thread the other end enough for a nut plus a little extra to cinch her down good (you can buy simple thread-cutting equipment at any tool supply house, or find it used).

These types of bolts will be used all through the boat. You'll use them to hold the ballast and floor timbers together, bolt the mast partners through two deck beams, and bolt the cabin to the deck. Make one whenever you need a long bolt.

Although it's tempting, never use *all-thread rod* for any bolt that will be under water. They leak, and there's no way to seal them up. In fact, some carriage bolts are sold with all-thread instead of the traditional bolt design. Never use these on the outside of the hull, for the same reason.

Lag bolts are just big, heavy screws that have a head meant for a wrench instead of a screwdriver. I'm not sure when a screw becomes a lag; maybe when it gets to be 1/4-inch in diameter.

Drift bolts are sort of like big nails made from pieces of rod of just about any thickness. You'll use lots of 1/2-inch drifts in a keel and deadwood, for instance. One end is rounded on a grinder or pounded over on an anvil; the other end spreads out to make a head as the bolt is being driven. You should put *clench rings* or washers around drifts before driving them. These will support the head.

Drill a hole for drifts 1/16 inch smaller than the rod, then ream it out to the same diameter as the drift for about 2/5 of the length, or through the piece of wood that is being drifted to another piece. When driving more than one drift in a piece of wood, put them in at different angles. The wood will never come apart. Drifts are used all through the keel assembly, and are handy for fastening floor timbers.

Any drift, lag, big screw, or long bolt, will go in a lot easier if you first rub a bar of Ivory soap on it.

Without considering such exotics as titanium, you have a choice, in order of preference, of bronze, stainless (only non-magnetic, 300 series), or galvanized steel. Brass, because it dissolves in salt water, and electroplated or cadmium-plated steel, are worthless. Bronze is the traditional fastener, but it happens to be very expensive. Stainless steel is becoming the fastener of choice of many yacht builders. It's stronger and cheaper than bronze, and there's no galvanizing to scratch off.

Personally I don't use stainless much, and never in fastening hull planking. I don't trust it, you see. As mentioned earlier, only the 300 series is suitable around salt water and you can't be positive what you're getting these days, with so much of this sort of thing being imported from the Orient. Also, electrolysis sometimes makes it do weird things, and it's expensive, although not as bad as bronze.

The last time I did comparison pricing was in 1973, and although these prices are dated, they're still proportionally accurate, which is why I haven't done it since. I bought 3,000 dipped galvanized screws for $5.85 per 100, or $175.50 for the lot. The same size screws in bronze were $28.50 per 100, or $855.00. If I had gone to the bother of buying plain steel screws and having them dipped at a galvanizer, it would have worked out to $3.80 per hundred.

But there's more to consider. You simply can't mix metals in a hull. If a boat has bronze screws it *must* have bronze keel bolts and lead ballast. There's this thing called electrolysis that lies in wait for boats with mixed metals. When it finds one, it eats the metal—really! So, instead of the $830 I spent in 1973 on 5 tons of scrap metal and concrete for that boat's ballast keel, if I'd used bronze I would have had to shell out about $2,500 for lead (I didn't check the price of a cast iron keel). The lead ballast would have needed bronze bolts, and a 1-inch bronze bolt back then was 9 bucks a foot, or probably close to $500 just to hold on the ballast. Another 200 feet of miscellaneous carriage and drift bolts would have brought the cost for the bolts, if bronze, to over $1,500. The galvanized bolts cost $160 for the whole backbone and ballast. Remember, these are 1973 prices. Figure on about double those prices or more these days.

So, take your pick. A boat with bronze fastenings and lead ballast will certainly have a higher resale value, but so what? Can you afford to build it just to get the higher resale price? And are you building it to sell or to use? A conservative guess at the price of all the fastenings and ballast in that 35-footer, excluding deck beams and frame gussets, was $1,200 for galvanized steel fastenings and scrap-iron and concrete ballast, compared to $4,800 for bronze and lead. The difference between the two was enough, at the time, to buy the working sails and the engine.

And if you're going to spend the money for bronze and lead, you really should be consistent and buy top-quality, air-dried boat wood. If you've done that, it would be totally out of place to use galvanized rigging wire and turnbuckles. There's several grand just to *support* the mast (never mind building the mast itself) instead of $200. With all that fancy stuff, I never could have used a tree for a mast, so the mast would have been another $3,000 or so instead of the free fir I cut.

If I had gone yacht-grade, that boat would have cost an easy $30,000 to build, instead of the $12,000 to $14,000 I actually spent. I think I sold it for $30,000. If built to yacht standards, it would have been worth $55,000 to $60,000. Of course, I wouldn't be finished with it yet. I couldn't have come up with all that extra cash, and to be consistent with the first-rate materials, the joinery and degree of finish would have had to be much fancier (which means slower to do).

I do use stainless screws in places where I'm laminating up thin stuff and want to drive screws to hold the wood together until the glue sets, without having to bother to remove them. For this use they're ideal, because there's no galvanizing in the slot to get in the way.

But for all other permanent screwing or bolting, I always use hot-dipped galvanized steel fastenings. They're stronger than bronze, more flexible and predictable than stainless, and by far the cheapest. Most commercial boats and many yachts are galvanized-fastened. You have to be careful driving a galvanized screw so that you don't scratch the coating, but that's no big deal. You might have to refasten the planking in 20 years, although the thicker the fastenings the longer they last.

It's getting difficult to find dipped fastenings, but if you live in a city, buy regular bright-steel screws and bolts and take them to a galvanizing joint that has a centrifuge, which will dip and spin them dry so the coating doesn't clog the threads and slots. This is the cheapest way to do it, too, although to pay off it must be done in quantity.

GLUES, PAINTS, BEDDING COMPOUNDS, AND SUCH

Wherever two pieces of wood touch one another, the joint should have glue, bedding compound, or at least wood preservative in it to help prevent rot.

Modern glues are really something, and will be used all through the building of the boat. You can use them to laminate smaller pieces of wood to make larger pieces. These will be stronger and less wasteful, and can make it possible for you to build up heavy chines, rubrails, and so on without resorting to elaborate machinery or steam bending. Cold-molded boats are built completely of laminated wood, from the keel right through to the planking.

Personally I prefer solid wood for the larger pieces, such as the keel or stem. To me, solid wood is more fun and quicker to work with, it looks better, and it's considerably cheaper here in the Northwest, where a good supply of big timbers is available from salvage dealers. Besides, I'm never completely comfortable with glue unless there's a bolt through it, although that's an emotional issue and not, according to glue manufacturers, a practical one.

There's quite a variety of glues from which to choose. Up until the 1970s, *resorcinol* glue was the best glue available, and it's still good today. It was certified by the U.S. Navy as being absolutely waterproof (defined as glue that will hold up in boiling water for a certain period of time), and it really works. Resorcinal consists of a purple liquid and a powder, and its distinctive purple glue seam is commonly seen in the layers of built-up masts and laminated frames.

Resorcinol has a proven record of durability, but it's a little harder to work with than epoxy, for instance, and requires that joints be fitted more closely. Temperatures during gluing should be maintained around 70 degrees—not always easy to do in the winter, unless you cover the glued part with sheet plastic and stick an electric heater inside.

Epoxy glues have pretty much taken over as the favorite glue of boatbuilders, even though they cost more than resorcinol. Epoxy has become the wood butcher's salvation, because unlike resorcinol glue, which must have perfectly fitted surfaces to hold, epoxy actually likes a few gaps and sets up better when the two surfaces are just a bit open. It even works well in end-grain joints. Also, the better of today's epoxies aren't temperature critical, and will set up in weather from 35 to 95 degrees.

A variety of epoxies are available, but all require mixing a hardener with the resin in accurate proportions. Personally, I prefer the 2-

to-1 and 1-to-1 formulas over the 5-to-1s. According to the chemist who owns Titan epoxies (Titan is in Lynwood, Washington, and sells wholesale rather than directly to the public like the others. Most hardware and marine stores in the Pacific Northwest carry it), which makes both a 2-to-1 and a 5-to-1 mix, the 2-to-1 is better because it's less brittle than the "thinner" mix. Titan, System Three, and other companies also make a 1-to-1, slow-setting mix, and this would be good for hot weather work.

I've found that epoxies have a far longer pot life if you use a wide, shallow pot. The deeper the can of mixed epoxy, the hotter it gets and the faster it sets up in the pot. A paint rolling tray works well. Pour in the epoxy after you mix it. A paint roller is the easiest way to apply it, too.

Epoxy isn't without its problems, though. It's expensive, it's toxic, and other than the specially formulated slow kick-off ones, it sets up too damned fast—often no more than 20 minutes after mixing. But it sure does stick, it's supposed to waterproof wood, according to the manufacturer, which in theory effectively prevents rot, and it's good for coating metal parts to protect them from corrosion.

Good old *powder glue*, such as Weldwood Plastic Resin or Wilhold, is also used all throughout the boat. Although it isn't completely waterproof, there's still lots to be said for it. It's the cheapest and the easiest glue to use: Just mix it with water. It isn't bothered by temperature extremes. If you use it on a cold day, it might take a week to set up, but eventually it will. If you're using it on a hot day and it starts to thicken, you can add a little water and thin it out. If you mix too much, you can stick it in the refrigerator and use it the next day.

I use powdered glue when laminating plywood decks and cabin tops, for most of the interior cabinetry, and for laminated deck beams, chines, and stringers. The only place I won't use it is for keel and stem laminations. For the rest of the boat it works fine, and it's considerably cheaper and easier to use than epoxy. Parts glued with it should, however, always be painted to protect them from the elements.

Like resorcinol, the powder glues require good fits and lots of clamping pressure. I've had a couple of failures using it to laminate deck beams because I used inadequate clamping pressure and took the beams off the forms too soon. For economy's sake, I still use it for making deck beams, but I leave it clamped for two days and drive long screws or nails through the top of the beams to hedge my bets.

Bedding compound is a thick, putty-like goop that is used to keep moisture and air from getting into a joint, or for keeping water from going past a joint. It's used all over the boat, anywhere you aren't gluing two pieces together, and is supposed to stay semi-soft forever. Many different brands are available, but only a few really do what they're supposed to do.

One of the very best, and also fortunately the cheapest, is regular black roofing tar. This stuff is made with either an asphalt base or a petroleum base. I've used them both, although I prefer the pe-troleum-based product because petroleum is a wood preservative.

Asphalt-based roofing cement can be painted with an aluminum paint, meant for trailer roofs, that seals the asphalt, which can then be painted over with regular paints.

The petroleum-based product will bleed through anything except epoxy, so if you're using it in a place that you want to paint, use the asphalt-based product. Both of these roofing tars seem to stay flexible forever, and are perfect for bedding keel timbers and butt blocks because they're cheap, and marine borers won't touch them.

They're both messy as hell to use and will get all over you. Before using them, take a trip to the Salvation Army and load up on disposable clothes. Tools and hands can be cleaned with kerosene and waterless hand cleaner.

By the way, I hear in South Florida, workboats and low-rent plea-sure boats cover their decks with three or four layers of tarpaper smeared with the asphalt-based roofing tar and covered with alumi-num or white "Cool-Dry" trailer roof paint. They call it "Miami Teak," and it seems to last quite a while. The tar preserves the wooden deck underneath the tarpaper. Just a thought.

Dolphinite Fungicidal Bedding Compound is another good product. It stays flexible, contains a wood preservative, can be painted over, and is much easier to clean up than tar. To add to your knowledge of true nautical language, shipyard workers call black roofing tar bear shit; Dolphinite, which is green, is called monkey shit.

If you're building a planked hull, you'll need to cover the seam caulking with *seam compound*, of which there is, again, a tremen-dous variety on the market.

In the underwater seams, commercial boats use a paste made of cement and water stiffened up with asphalt roofing compound. I use this myself. It's cheap, super sticky, stays flexible forever, and marine borers won't get into it. You can use this on the topside planks, too, but regular compounds are neater and easier to paint over.

Now, there's all sorts of new "miracle whips" on the market promising all sorts of superlatives, but I stick to a straight oil-base seam putty, like Interlux Seam Compound, which works well and is relatively inexpensive.

I once "payed" the seams of a new boat with a seam compound that was supposed to be the living end. It came in tubes that said: "It swells! It shrinks! It's the BEST seam compound you can get!" Well, it started separating from the wood while my boat was still in the building shed. It took me two months to cut the stuff out of all the seams with a razor. You see, it separated from one edge, but not the other. It did stick very nicely to the cotton caulking, however, so the whole boat had to be recaulked. That was enough for me.

I'm sure many of these products work well, at least for a while. But they seem to have limited shelf life, which I think was the problem with mine, and the old fashioned oil-base seam compounds are foolproof and cheap. They always work, period, and will last indefinitely on a boat that stays in the water year around. I'll never use anything else.

To protect all these wood surfaces from the weather, you'll want to *paint* your boat, of course. You have to use one of the poison paints below the waterline to keep down marine growth, but above the boottop, it's a different story.

Any number of authentic marine paints are available, but I use oil-based exterior house paints, myself. They're considerably cheaper than so-called marine paints, and appear to last as long. I use porch-and-deck enamel on the hull, and a kitchen-grade paint for the interior. Some fishermen swear by exterior-grade latex paints on their hulls, but I've never tried it myself. Some folks like epoxy paints, which can sometimes be bought very cheaply from surplus dealers. I wouldn't use them on a planked hull, where the wood's swelling and shrinking might exceed epoxy's ability to flex. It should be OK on decks or plywood hulls.

You'll use gallons of *wood preservative* in boatbuilding. I coat everything with it. I paint the end grain of all the planks, I soak the frame tops and deck beam ends, and I soak the whole hull, inside and out, with several coats applied with one of the plastic-pump garden sprayers before painting.

Quite a few different wood preservatives are on the market, of varying potency. A chemist who makes them told me to use the green ones for boat work because the clear ones are water soluble. You'll need several coats of paint to cover the green preservatives, but that's OK: A "virgin" board needs a good three coats of primer and two coats of final topcoat anyway. Keep the green stuff off any wood you intend to finish naturally; use the clear stuff there.

Many preservatives are made from copper napthinate and "petroleum bases;" the amounts used are listed on the side. I prefer the Jasco brand, which contains the most poison of all the brands commonly available. I've always wondered if you could buy copper napthinate from a chemical supplier, mix it with odorless kerosene, and get the same thing for a fraction of the cost. One of these days I'm going to try it, and if any of you do, please write and tell me how it worked out.

By the way, these preservatives might have the opposite effect on you, so I always use rubber gloves when handling them, and never spray them in a mist form. I usually apply it with a brush, but if I do spray, I use one of those pump-up garden sprayers and adjust the stream so it's sort of like rain. A toxic mist mask would not be a bad idea, either.

Well, I said at the beginning of this chapter that I wasn't going to parrot the traditional boatbuilding advice; I hope I've at least made you stop and think about other ideas—many of which are used routinely by folks who are out earning their living on the ocean. And I hope I've impressed on you that it isn't necessary to use traditional yacht-grade material to build a perfectly satisfactory wooden boat—despite what you may hear from some of the cultists. I hope I've made it clear that your locally available woods often are very good for boat use, and your local workboats show you that these materials last well too.

Have you ever noticed how nobody likes "local" wines, musicians, or woods, while a thousand miles away everybody says, "Outasight! That's from wherever." Well, John Coltrane *lived* in New York and was a local musician. Douglas fir grows where I live and it's a good wood. Sometimes, if you look, you'll find some of your local talent, or materials, ain't so bad, even if they are easy to get.

Personally, I love wooden boats, although I neither worship nor derive sexual gratification from them, and I'd probably never own anything else. Although traditional yacht standards have their place, many designers specify all the traditional materials for all types and uses of boats, with never a thought about how normal people are supposed to afford the material, nor any consideration that less expensive and easier to find options often will serve just as well.

This probably stems from the fact that a "yacht," which can be defined as a boat that doesn't earn its keep, originally was something built only for the very wealthy. The yacht builders of the day used the best of everything. Why not? They could afford it! But the peasants trudging off to the mines and sweatshops saw these beautiful craft floating about and wanted one, too. Well, as wages went up and credit was invented, many of those peasants found themselves able at least to consider the idea of owning a pleasure boat.

But for some reason, rather than being inspired by simple, no-nonsense commercial boats and proven, commonsense ways of doing things, far too many people are caught up in the traditional idea of "Das Jacht." This "just-like-de-rich-fokes" mentality makes them go thousands of dollars into debt, forces them to build smaller boats than they'd really like—or maybe even go without a boat at all—just because they're afraid a boat built to "workboat" standards can't possibly yield the same performance (there's that word again) as a gold-plater trimmed in teak.

Listen. There's nothing wrong with using the alternative methods and materials mentioned in this book. Simple, neat carpentry and painted finishes can make a beautiful boat! Read this following sentence twice. The awareness of, and selective use of, the many inexpensive materials easily found around you may well make all the difference in whether or not you'll be able to build a real cruising boat.

LOFTING

The first step in building any boat is *lofting*, which is simply drawing the *lines plan* of your design full size. This is important because it guarantees that the dimensions given for molds and whatnot will be accurate. It also allows you to make full-size patterns for the keel pieces.

For some reason lofting scares a lot of people; as a result, some designers and kit builders make good livings selling "full-size" loftings and patterns. There's nothing to be afraid of! Lofting, especially with a chine design, is the simplest part of the whole boatbuilding process. All you do is measure out the lengths and connect the little dots with lines.

It's true that some professionals do know quite a few tricks about lofting, and can draw out each piece of the boat in three dimensions. This can look quite impressive, until you catch on to the concept, of course. Personally, I believe the home builder must approach the lofting, in fact the whole of building, with a slightly less organized attitude. Since you're probably new to boatbuilding, you can't possibly do as complete a lofting job as a pro: You just don't know what goes where when you start. But you'll be able to figure out what goes where, and how to get it there, when you actually get to it. So relax. The procedure described here shouldn't take you more than two full days.

Before you begin, look around to see if you can find the timbers specified on the keel construction plan. You'll want to loft and make the keel patterns based on the material that's available. For instance, if the plans call for 8×12 timbers and all you can find are 8×8 pieces, then you'll have to make patterns based on that. If you can't find the widths specified, try to go wider and cut them down to size. As a last resort you can laminate up the keel, but I really prefer heavy timbers.

Another thing to remember when lofting is that timbers rarely are finished to the same dimension by which they're sold. A 10×12 may actually be $9^{1}/_{2}$ by $11^{1}/_{2}$ inches or even $9^{1}/_{4}$ by $11^{1}/_{4}$ inches, so when you draw the body plan, remember to make the keel width equal to the actual width of the timber. Again, it's very important to buy, or at least locate, your keel materials before you loft.

To get started lofting, you'll need a roll of that heavy builder's paper called "Red Rosin" (available in 3- by 100-foot rolls for about $13 in any good lumberyard); the longest 1×2 clear (no knots) batten (fir and redwood are available in lengths up to 24 feet) you can find; a

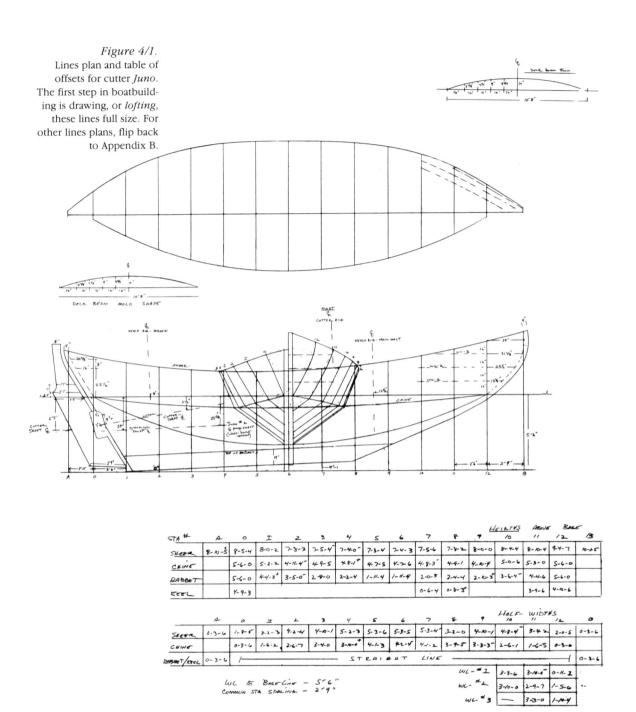

Figure 4/1.
Lines plan and table of offsets for cutter *Juno*. The first step in boatbuild- ing is drawing, or *lofting*, these lines full size. For other lines plans, flip back to Appendix B.

STA #	A	0	I	2	3	4	5	6	7	8	9	HEIGHTS 10	ABOVE 11	BASE 12	13
SHEER	8-10-3	8-5-4	8-0-2	7-8-3	7-5-4	7-4-0	7-3-4	7-4-3	7-5-6	7-8-2	8-0-0	8-4-4	8-10-4	9-4-7	10-4-5
CHINE		5-6-0	5-2-2	4-11-4	4-9-5	4-8-1	4-7-5	4-7-6	4-8-3	4-9-1	4-10-4	5-0-6	5-3-0	5-6-0	
RABBET		5-6-0	4-4-3	3-5-0	2-8-0	2-2-4	1-11-4	1-11-4	2-0-3	2-4-4	2-11-5	3-6-4	4-4-6	5-6-0	
KEEL		4-9-3						0-6-4	0-8-3				3-9-6	4-10-6	

	A	0	I	2	3	4	5	6	7	8	9	HALF- WIDTHS 10	11	12	13
SHEER	0-3-6	1-8-5	3-2-3	4-2-4	4-10-1	5-2-3	5-3-6	5-3-5	5-3-4	5-2-0	4-10-1	4-3-4	3-4-2	2-0-5	0-3-6
CHINE		0-3-6	1-6-2	2-6-7	3-4-0	3-10-0	4-1-3	4-2-4	4-1-2	3-9-5	3-3-3	2-6-1	1-6-5	0-3-6	
RABBET/KEEL	0-3-6				STRAIGHT LINE										0-3-6

WL TO BASELINE — 5'6"
COMMON STA SPACING — 2'9"

	WL #1	3-3-6	3-10-0	0-11-2
	WL #2	3-10-0	2-9-7	1-5-6
	WL #3	—	3-3-0	1-11-4

thin batten, say ¹/8 by ³/8 inch, about 12 feet long; a pound of #8 fin- ish nails; and a hammer, a 50-foot chalk line, a 50-foot tape measure, a regular tape measure, an 8-foot straightedge made by ripping a 6-inch wide strip from a sheet of ¹/4-inch plywood (the factory-cut edge of which is reliably straight), some pencils, a scale rule to take any measurements off the plans that the designer forgot to give you, and a roll of masking tape. You'll also need the remainder of the sheet of plywood that you made your straightedge from, ripped into 3-inch wide strips, a bottle of Elmer's carpenter glue, and a bunch of 5/8-inch carpet tacks.

You need a flat wood floor several feet longer than your boat, and as wide as the distance that the bow stands off the baseline. You can loft a boat in sections in a space a little more than half the boat's length, but I wouldn't do it that way—it's too easy to screw up.

Big wooden floors aren't all that hard to find. I've lofted boats in warehouses, school art departments, an abandoned army barracks, even the subfloor of a new house being built in the neighborhood. If you simply can't find a floor, lay sheets of 1/2-inch plywood down on a parking lot, hook them together with fence staples, and loft there. You can use the plywood for the walls of your shop, so it won't be a total waste.

HOW TO LOFT

Most builder's paper is 3 feet wide. Unroll several pieces, the length of your boat plus a few feet, and tape the edges together with 2-inch wide masking tape. The paper must be as wide as the distance from the baseline to the bow, or the half-width of the hull, whichever is greater. Stretch the paper out tightly by nailing several of your 3-inch wide plywood strips down each end. Pound a nail at each end of the paper, a few inches up from the bottom, and snap a chalk line. This is your *baseline*. Nail battens along the entire length of the baseline. This gives you something to hook your tape measure to, making it quicker and easier to mark out the dimensions.

The *lines plan* shows your boat's station spacing. Starting at one end of the baseline, mark off where each station goes, and pound a nail at each point. When you've got all the stations marked, erect a *perpendicular* at each end.

Here's how. We know from some dead Greek that $A^2 + B^2 = C^2$. Let A equal 6 feet, and B equal 8 feet. Mark a spot 6 feet down the baseline from where you want to erect the first perpendicular (station line); this is point A. Measure 8 feet straight up from the station (as best you can), and make a mark; this is B. If the line is vertical, it (C) will measure exactly 10 feet from point A to point B. If it isn't, adjust B until your C is 10 feet on the nose.

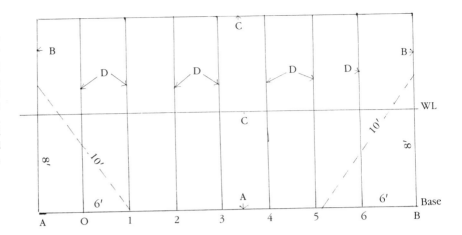

Do this same business at the station point at the opposite end of the boat. Extend both of these lines, the same amount, up to the end of the paper. Drive a nail in each one, and snap another chalk line; this will be exactly parallel to the baseline. Measure up from the baseline to the *waterline* (its distance above the baseline is given on the lines plan), snap it in, then pencil it in with your straightedge. Now you have three lines exactly parallel.

You've already marked the location of each station on the baseline. Do this again on the line at the top of the lofting, drive a nail at each point, snap in your station lines, and pencil them in with your straightedge. When you finish, you'll have a big grid that looks like Figure 4-1, except you'll have more station lines.

Now turn to your *table of offsets*, where you'll find all the dimensions of the boat. It's divided into two sections: *heights above baseline* and *half-widths*. Sometimes you'll see heights tables called "Heights Above and Below Waterline." It all depends on the designer's style. All measurements are given in feet, inches, and eighth inches. A plus or minus sign means plus or minus 1/16 inch. For example, 9-3-7+ reads as 9 feet 3 inches and 7/8 inch, plus 1/16 inch.

Although it really doesn't make any difference, it's normal to start drawing the *profile view* first. So turn to the *heights* part of the offset table and look at the first station. Hook your tape over the strip of 1/4-inch plywood nailed along the baseline, run it out the station, and mark down the measurement. Some people first mark the whole sheer, then the whole chine, then the whole rabbet, and so on. Personally, I mark all the measurements for the heights at each station; you're less likely to make a dumb error that way. Mark a cross at each measurement, circle it, and label it sheer, chine, rabbet, keel, or whatever it is.

Once you've marked all the points, you can start drawing in the hull lines. Start with the sheer and pound a nail at each point marked "sheer" on the stations. Bend your long batten around these nails,

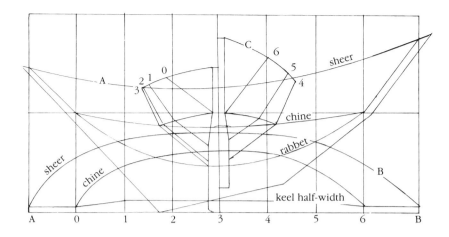

Figure 4/3.
Draw the boat full size over the grid. First draw the profile (A); then the half-width view (B). Correct the offset table from the lofting, and draw the body plan (C) using the corrected offsets.

using more nails to hold it tight against the station nails, then lie down on your stomach and eyeball the curve.

This is called *fairing*, and it's the main purpose for lofting. The designer drew the boat at small scale and transferred the measurements to the table of offsets with a scale ruler. After a while his eyes likely started to blur. Maybe he even measured to the wrong point—happens all the time! If you build the boat without making sure the offsets show a fair curve, you're apt to have a lot of trouble wrapping the planking around the hull.

The process of fairing is really quite simple. With your eye down at batten level it's easy to see if the batten is flowing smoothly. If you see a hump or dip anywhere, pull out the nail that's holding the batten out of line, and let it spring out where it wants to go. Drive a nail to hold it at this new point, and lie down and sight it again. You'll quickly get the hang of it.

Once the batten is set to a fair curve, pencil in the line. The batten rarely will be long enough to do the whole line, so stop drawing two stations from the end of the batten. Slide the batten forward, leaving two stations of penciled line as an overlap, fair this new part, and draw it in. On and on.

The lines plan will have measurements needed to draw the stem's curve. If there aren't enough measurements given to draw it accurately, take some more with your scale rule. Draw in this curve with your thin batten, just the way you drew the sheer, only on a smaller scale.

After you've drawn the whole profile, which is the sheer, chine, rabbet, and keel, you draw the *half-widths*, which is the deck view of the sheer, the chine, and the width of the keel. These are drawn just the same as the profile, using the baseline as the centerline.

Sometimes, when there's a lot of curve to a stem, the last few stations at the ends will be curved, which means the frames in this area will also be curved. *Waterlines*, given in the table of offsets, will show

how wide the station is at various points, normally 12 inches apart. These are handled just like the other half-width lines. This sounds trickier than it actually is. Remember, all you're doing is drawing the lines plan full size, so if you get confused just look at the plan and you'll see what you have to do. Nothing to it.

When you finish drawing in all the lines, look over the drawing. If any places have different measurements than the ones given in the offsets, write your corrected measurement in the table. You've just faired your lines.

The last part to draw is the *body plan*. Frankly, this is more tradition than necessity. Unlike you, a real boatyard will have a permanent loft floor where the lofting can be left out for reference as the boat is built; you'll be working on a roll of paper kept rolled up in the corner. I don't bother drawing in the body plan on the lofting since you have to do it on your frame assembly table anyway. However, it doesn't hurt anything if you do it, and it's traditional, so why not.

All the dimensions you'll need for the body plan are in your now-corrected offset table. Each point is given as being so high off the baseline and so far off the centerline. It's normal to draw the body plan as shown in Figure 4-3, using the midsection station as the body plan's centerline, with the forward stations on the same side of the centerline as the bow.

So, to find the sheer at station #1, look at the offset table. It says the sheer at #1 is such and such high off the baseline. Measure up from the baseline whatever distance the offset table says, and make a mark. Do the same thing two or three stations away, and connect the marks with a chalk line.

The offset table tells you that the sheer at station #1 is such and such wide. Measure along your line from the centerline (the midship station) that distance, and make a mark. That's it. Do the same thing for the chine, the rabbet, and any waterlines, connect the dots, and you have the station drawn. On curved frames, you'll draw in waterlines at whatever spacing the plans show, and mark the width of the station at each of them. Use the thin batten if you need a sharper bend.

Most designs have a station located where each main frame will be, so when you've drawn in the station you're actually drawing the frame at that position. If you want to have frames closer together than the stations show, draw in new stations on the profile and half-width view at whatever spacing you want, and measure off their dimensions so you can make frames later on. For the type of boats we're talking about, 24-inch spacing is fine, because later on we'll be installing intermediate frames between the station frames.

Draw in the shaft angle line, and the rudder if you feel like it, and you're done. Your lofting should now look like Figure 4-3, but probably with more stations.

Congratulations! You've finished the lofting and have actually progressed from talking about building a boat to starting it! You deserve a drink!

KEELS AND BALLAST

KEEL PATTERNS

OK. You've located your keel timbers and lofted the boat; it's a simple matter to make patterns for the whole keel assembly. You don't have to do this, of course, but it's foolish not to. These patterns allow you to saw out and assemble the backbone accurately with very little hassle. I can't imagine not doing it.

Some building books suggest other ways of marking out the keel pieces. One method commonly suggested is to lay the timber carefully down on tacks laid out along the lines of the lofting. Well, the 28 feet of 8- by 16-inch pressure-treated fir that makes up the main keel timber in my current boat probably weighs well over a thousand pounds. I can just imagine slinging it over my shoulder and "setting it down carefully on a row of tacks." Believe me, patterns are the way to go.

Some designers with no building experience (yes, there are a few) draw absolutely impossible construction plans, and the strangest part is usually the keel and stem assembly. When you're building a backbone, the fewer pieces and the less fitting the better; if your plans show an unusually creative assembly, you might consider doing it a simpler way. As long as you use basic common sense you'll be safe, and probably better off. Throwing out the construction plan and just building the boat is actually common practice in professional wood boatyards.

You might consider building a 3/4-inch-to-the-foot scale model of the boat, building each part in miniature before you do it on the real boat. This way you can play around with things and see what goes where and how you'll get it there. Three-quarter-inch scale is the easiest to translate into real life; 1 scale inch equals 1/16 real inch. That's easy to remember, and if you use a scale rule, you won't even have to remember that much. Hobby shops sell balsa wood in most of the thicknesses you'll need, and a balsa stripper will make whatever odd sizes that aren't available.

It's easy to draw in the shape of the keel timbers on the lofting. Just draw what you see, but be exact. Remember, you already have, or at least have located, your timbers, so you know what the actual

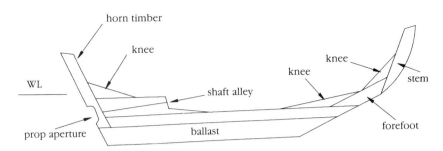

horn timber

knee

knee

knee

stem

WL

shaft alley

forefoot

prop aperture

ballast

dimensions are. If your timbers are 11³/16 inches high, then draw your lines 11³/16 inches apart. If you've changed the plans, spend some time thinking about the best way to join the pieces. Long, overlapping joints are good things. Don't taper anything out to a paper-thin edge. As I'll be saying repeatedly, just use basic common sense. Someday you might hit a rock all standing and you don't want the keel to break in half.

Make the keel patterns from 3-inch wide strips of ¼-inch plywood. Join two strips end to end by butting them together, then gluing and nailing (use carpet tacks) an 8-inch butt block over the joint.

Start with the main keel timber, just as if you were making the keel. Start building the pattern by running the plywood strips along the bottom of the keel timber (on top of the ballast if the design has a ballast keel). Run another strip along the top of the timber. Tack and glue a shorter piece of plywood at each station, extending them a bit above the timber, to connect the upper and lower pattern strip. In places where there are numerous timbers stacked up, extend these station-line strips high enough to cover the whole keel section. Mark on these strips 1) the station number, 2) which side of the strip is the station line, and 3) the rabbet line.

Now, lay down a strip along the top of the next timber that sits on top of the main timber. Repeat this until you have a pattern for the whole deadwood assembly. Figure 5-2A shows the deadwood pattern on a 50-foot hull lofting.

As you make this pattern, think about how you'll handle it. I make them in 8- to 10-foot sections, which is about as long as one guy can easily handle. Otherwise they flop around and are in danger of breaking. Nail the pattern securely to the lofting as you go, so that all the following parts will fit accurately against it. An accurate job here will really make things easier for you on down the line.

Figure 5-2B shows the forward edge of the main keel timber, the forefoot, and the forefoot knee. All three are separate patterns, but are butted together and nailed down on the floor.

Figure 5-2C shows the forefoot as it merges into the stem, the actual stem, and the stem knee. Note that here, because the stem was developing quite a curve, I nailed closely spaced ''pointers'' which

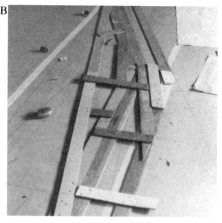

B

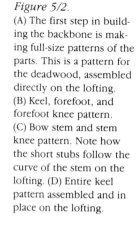

A

C

D

Figure 5/2.
(A) The first step in building the backbone is making full-size patterns of the parts. This is a pattern for the deadwood, assembled directly on the lofting. (B) Keel, forefoot, and forefoot knee pattern. (C) Bow stem and stem knee pattern. Note how the short stubs follow the curve of the stem on the lofting. (D) Entire keel pattern assembled and in place on the lofting.

show the outline of the timber, rather than sawing out curved pieces. This works just as well and takes less time.

Finally, Figure 5-2D shows the whole keel pattern, nailed down on the lofting. By taking the time to make good patterns of *each piece of wood in the keel*—only about 6 hours—I was able to saw out and assemble the keel of this 50 footer quickly and accurately in just a few days.

KEEL CONSTRUCTION

The lofting and patternmaking was pretty basic stuff, requiring little more than simply measuring and drawing lines. *Now*, you have to get in the habit of thinking ahead a bit.

For instance, now that you're starting the keel, give some thought to how you'll move the finished boat. Will it be trucked? Call around and see what sort of trailer rig is available in your area, and what sort of cradle they find the easiest to deal with. Some compan-

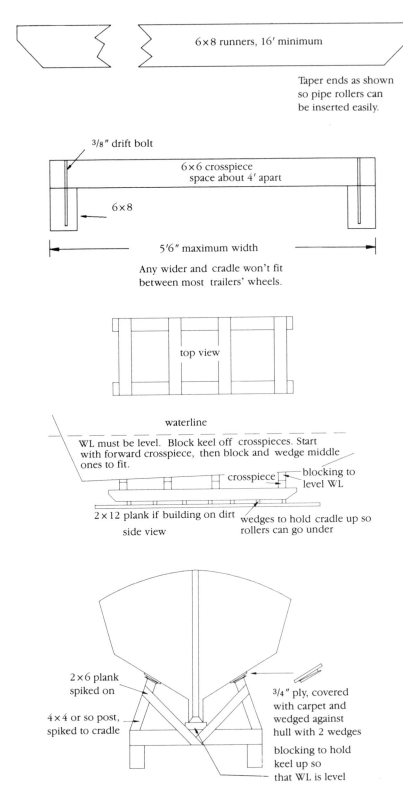

Figure 5/3.
You'll need a cradle to support your boat during construction and during the trip to the water for launching. Make it sturdy.

6×8 runners, 16' minimum

Taper ends as shown so pipe rollers can be inserted easily.

3/8" drift bolt

6×6 crosspiece
space about 4' apart

6×8

5'6" maximum width

Any wider and cradle won't fit between most trailers' wheels.

top view

waterline

WL must be level. Block keel off crosspieces. Start with forward crosspiece, then block and wedge middle ones to fit.

crosspiece

blocking to level WL

2×12 plank if building on dirt

side view

wedges to hold cradle up so rollers can go under

2×6 plank spiked on

4×4 or so post, spiked to cradle

3/4" ply, covered with carpet and wedged against hull with 2 wedges

blocking to hold keel up so that WL is level

ies, such as Evergreen Boat Transport in Seattle, have trailers that look like big pickle forks that can load a boat quickly without a cradle. Most companies, however, use low, flatbed trailers, and you'll need a cradle to support the boat while it's jacked, rolled, winched, and cursed up onto the trailer.

Details for making a typical cradle are in Figure 5-3. It should be about 5 1/2 feet wide, which will fit the normal trailer width of about 6 feet between the wheels. The first cradle I made was 2 feet wider than the trailer's width. Think ahead! Make it heavy; use big timbers or log runners, as long as possible; use lots of heavy crosspieces; drift-bolt the whole thing together.

SOLID TIMBER KEELS

Although lots of boats are built with laminated stems and keels, I prefer to use solid timbers. It's simpler, usually cheaper, more fun to shape, and looks more substantial.

Put the main keel timber on the cradle and tack the main keel timber pattern to it. Stack up more pieces of wood until the pattern is covered, clamp or toenail everything together so it can't slip, then draw each station line on the wood.

Most boats are designed with keels that have some rake to them, so put a jack under the front of the main timber and raise it up until the station lines are plumb. This makes it easier to transfer points to the other side. Mark the location of the rabbet and the top of the keel from the pattern onto the keel. Remove the pattern, transfer the station marks across the top of the timbers with a square, then down the other side with a level. Measure the distance down from the top of the keel on the first side to the rabbet and keel-top marks, then transfer the points to the other side of the keel. Drive a nail at each point, bend a batten around the points, and draw in your rabbet (and keel top if you're shaping it, too).

Figure 5/4.
A 28-foot long, 8- x 16-inch pressure-treated timber, bought from a salvage yard for $75, on its way towards a new life as the main keel timber of a 50-foot boat. Essential moving equipment for the typically large backbone pieces includes two 55-gallon drums, which allow one person to move really heavy timbers, and the indispensable $400 beater van.

Keels and Ballast

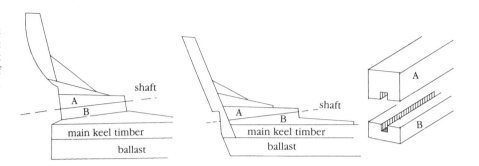

Figure 5/5.
Details of built-up shaft log construction. Saw slot 1/2-inch larger than shaft diameter. Round it off inside if you feel like it.

Naturally, each boat has a different keel construction layout, and you'll rarely be able to just stack up all the timbers without doing some shaping as you go. For instance, I always draw the prop shaft to run between two timbers. It's easier to rabbet out a tunnel in two opposing timber faces with a Skilsaw (Figure 5-5) than it is to drill a long, straight hole and have it come out where you want it. And since the shaft line is rarely level, it means that the lower timber has to have its top sawed to whatever angle the shaft runs. Of course, that means that the deadwood will all slope downhill, so you'll have to shape the rest of the timbers as well.

Cutting down heavy timbers to size isn't all that difficult. Just draw a line on both sides of the timber, run a Skilsaw down each line, saw down to the lines across the top at 4-inch intervals with a chain saw, then whack off the wood (interesting novelty, eh?) with an axe or an adze. When you're whacking off the wood, always start on the uphill side and chop down across the grain. If you start low and chop up against the grain, you'll split the wood past your line. Roughly smooth the top with a power plane, then finish it up with a long hand plane. Try to get the surface as flat, straight, and square as possible. It doesn't have to be perfect, because it'll be bolted together with lots of tar in the joint.

Figure 5/6.
Keel being assembled. The forefoot is propped up temporarily just to see what it'll look like.

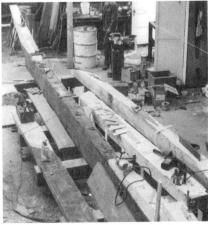

Buehler's Backyard Boatbuilding

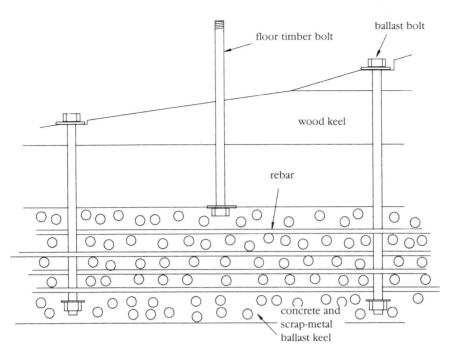

floor timber bolt

ballast bolt

wood keel

rebar

concrete and
scrap-metal
ballast keel

Boats with low freeboard can have a lower cabin floor if you shape the top of the keel to run parallel with the rabbet. In large boats with a lot of freeboard or a high cabin it doesn't matter. Either way, keep the top of the keel a minimum of 3 inches above the rabbet; 4 inches is better, especially if you're using heavy planking and long screws.

After you have all the timbers shaped, stack them back together, reposition the pattern so you know everything is right, and lay out all the bolts and drifts that hold the keel together. The construction plan likely shows the location of many of them, but regardless, let common sense lead the way. You can draw the location of each bolt and drift right on the wood with a brightly colored marking pen.

It's best to use through-bolts wherever possible, but the stern areas of larger boats may have deadwood stacked up 5 feet or more; use drift bolts here that penetrate the keel at least 18 inches. The ballast bolts, which generally are spaced on 24-inch centers, will go clear through the keel, and a couple of the bolts in the deadwood will go clear through.

You'll likely need lots of drift-bolts in the deadwood. These are just big nails, made from 1/2-inch or so rod. Their holes are drilled 1/16 inch undersize the whole length, and then reamed out to the rod's diameter for about half the length. Place the drifts on different angles throughout the deadwood, and the thing will never come apart. Here again, look around to see what's available for drift stock before doing any drilling. It would be too bad to drill a bunch of 1-inch holes only to find you can't get 1-inch rod.

Keels and Ballast

53

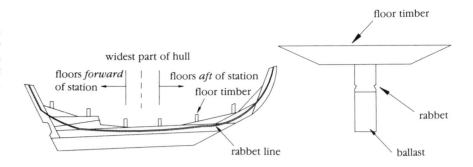

The floor timber bolts must be long enough to go through the keel and through the floor, with a nut on each end. If the cabin sole (floor) sits atop the floor timber, the floor is notched a bit so the nut stays below the top.

Ballast bolts are made long enough to go through the wood keel and down to about 1 inch or so from the bottom of the ballast, with room for a nut on each end. If you want to weld a steel box around the ballast (see below), then make the bolts exactly long enough to hit the bottom of the ballast, although an inch either way won't make the boat float upside down.

Some builders run ballast bolts right up through the floor timbers. I don't, because it seems to me that it's stronger to use separate bolts for the floors: 5/8-inch bolts for 4-by floors, 1/2-inch bolts for 3-by, and 3/8-inch bolts for 2-by floors. I use 3-by floors on boats to 30 feet, and 4-by floors on larger ones.

There'll be a floor timber at each station to hold the frame to the keel. The station line marks the *widest* part of the frame. On a normally shaped boat, all frames aft of about the middle are *aft* of the station and the floors are *forward* of the station. All frames forward of the amidships frame are *forward* of the station, and the floors are *aft* of the station. The exact station where the switch occurs depends on where the boat starts getting narrower. Just remember that the station line marks the *widest* face of the frame. If your boat was pyramid-shaped, like an SK drag boat, then all the floors would be aft of the stations, and all the frames forward. If you screw up and put the floors on the wrong side of the stations, your hull will have a hollow or bulge at that point, and you'll have to shim or cut down the frame. Think ahead.

When laying out the floor bolts, first figure out on which side of the station the floor goes, then mark a point half the thickness of the floor from the station.

Once all the bolts are made, hold them against the keel and mark which goes where with a symbol next to the hole and on the bolt. When drilling holes, try not to put one through the shaft alley, and don't put one right in line with a place where the rabbet crosses a joint between two timbers. You'll be drilling a hole at these points through the rabbet, clear through the keel, to install a round dowel, called a *stopwater*, to make sure the joint won't leak, and you don't want a bolt in the way. To help you drill holes where you want them, nail a guide board along the keel. The board should stick up in the air a foot or so at the same angle as the proposed hole. Sight down the board as you drill, and as long as you hold the drill parallel to the board you'll be alright. If you come out of the side of the keel accidently, just drive a wood dowel in the hole and try it again.

After you have your holes drilled, unclamp the timbers and spread a thick layer of bedding compound on each meeting face. Stack them back together, and with a stick or something ream some tar down the bolt holes. Drive the bolts through, and wrap a bit of cotton dunked in tar beneath each washer. This will keep the boat from leaking through the bolt holes before the keel swells up.

The floor timber bolts are driven from the top down until they come through the bottom. The ballast bolts are driven from the bottom up until they come through the top. If you rub a good coating of Ivory soap on the bolts they'll drive much easier.

You may find that the deadwood timbers don't want to close tightly together. You can fix this by cutting a piece of pipe to fill the distance between the keel and the end of a ballast bolt or floor timber bolt, and then cinching hard on the nuts. On practically all designs you'll have a much easier time if you cast the ballast before you bolt on the horn timber and the forefoot and stem timbers.

LAMINATED KEELS

Some boats might have unusually long or wide keels, and it can be hard to find solid timbers large enough to do the job. Before you give up and think about lamination, give a good look around. Recently I've seen 46-foot 14 by 16s and 60-foot 12 by 12s for sale from building wreckers here in Seattle, so I know big stuff is out there. Another idea is simply to buy a tree—preferably seasoned—and square it up with a chain saw. I once saw a very respected yacht-building firm do that when they needed a big, wide keel for a 60-foot Herreshoff design. You can make a damned hefty keel in this fashion.

But the laminated keel is quite common these days, and although it's often more expensive, and always more time consuming and bothersome than the solid timber keel, it might just be the only way you can find to do it. The only problem with it is that you're completely dependent on the glue, and I'm one of those people who trusts glue only when there's a bolt through it. Still, lamination does give you real freedom in making huge blocks of wood. For instance, if you want to build a keel that's 23 inches wide, you'll almost certainly need to laminate it.

I've worked with laminated keels twice in professional shops; once on a 42-foot ketch, and once on a 125-foot schooner. Even though these boats were so different in size, both keels were built up from wood less than 2 inches thick. This made me think that perhaps 2 inches is as thick as you can safely go without running the risk of the wood swelling and breaking the glue bond after it gets wet. This also works out well for you, because "2-by" is a standard lumber dimension, readily available anywhere.

I know that the epoxy people claim that you can seal out moisture by coating the timbers with glass cloth and epoxy, and I've used it myself on decks, but underwater things are different. I'd always be afraid that someday things would start to move, breaking the glue bond and causing all sorts of hassles. My fears are probably groundless, but just the same I'd worry about it, so I'd stick to using thin stuff in laminations.

Let's say we want to laminate that 23-inch-thick keel. First you need a stable platform that is perfectly straight, such as a line of sawhorses about 4 feet apart. Your building cradle will also work, and you can extend it out on each end with low horses.

Obviously, the glue you'll use in laminating is very important, so use a good one. For years all I'd trust was resorcinol, but I've slowly come about and now I like epoxies because they're so easy to use. Where resorcinol demands perfectly joined seams, the epoxies actually work better if there's a bit of a gap and hold well on end-grain connections. Epoxy really is magic.

Start off by gluing two 2 × 12s together edge to edge. If the keel is longer than your planks, just butt two more planks to them until you reach your length. Theoretically this butt joint is a weak connection, but it doesn't matter because you'll have several more layers on top, and the joints will be staggered.

The next day, after the glue has set, glue three 2 × 8s on top of the first layer. The day after use two 2 × 10s and a 2 × 4, and on and on. Try to overlap all joints by at least two layers before repeating a

Figure 5/9.
The laminated keel. Individual "timbers" are made by gluing up 2-by stock into finished blocks similar to solid timbers (such as 12 × 12s). These pieces are shaped, then glued and bolted together.

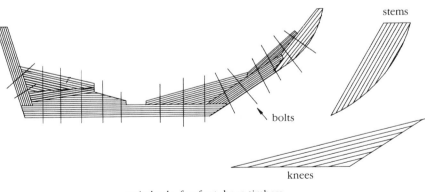

stems

bolts

knees

main keels, forefoot, horn timbers

sequence, and stagger all butts. Use a clamp every 16 inches or so to hold the edges together, and use staging nails driven through 3-inch square pads of 1/4-inch plywood to hold the layers down. When you pull the pads for gluing the next layer, the glue will fill the nail holes. There's no need at all to scarf the butts since you have multiple layers overlapping everything.

Another example of lamination is where you need a 12 × 12 keel but all you can find are 4 × 12s. Three of these stacked up will make one big timber, but it's a toss-up whether or not you should glue them. You see, all wood swells when it gets wet, and the bigger the piece the more it swells. As I mentioned before, I'd be very worried that 4-inch stock could swell and break the glue bond, so instead I'd bed them in a thick layer of tar and rely on mechanical fasteners like through-bolts. Now, I have seen people glue heavy pieces like this, but I've never seen a pro do it, so it's up to you. I wouldn't.

If your 4 × 12s are too short you should join two pieces end for end with scarfed and glued butts. The scarf should have at least a 4 to 1 angle, so a 4-by plank would have a 16-inch long scarf; a 2-by plank an 8-inch scarf, etc.

The easy way to scarf is to stand the two planks on edge overlapping each other, stretch a string to make sure they're straight, and clamp them down. Saw a scarf where they overlap, and bond the two together with epoxy.

If you're going to do much of this scarfing you might make a scarfing jig. This is an aluminum tray without a front or back, with the sides sloped to whatever angle you want to scarf. The jig is positioned under the end of a plank, and you whack away with an adze or something until you've carved a face parallel to the tray sides. The easiest tool to use here is a power plane with attached arms that ride on the edges of the tray. With the arms holding it at the same angle as the tray, the plane automatically shapes the face perfectly.

STEEL KEELS

A few years ago I saw a homebuilt boat with a keel made up of a steel box with a flange to which the planking was bolted. The builder had done only the keel this way, and attached a wood stem and sternpost to it (Figure 5-10). This looked pretty slick. For that matter, I don't see why you couldn't build the entire backbone of steel. I'd make it box-sectioned so it resembled a wood keel.

I read about another boat built by a junkyard owner in Brooklyn. From the waterline down the boat was steel, with wood topsides, deck, and house. It sounded interesting. Many large yachts have been built with steel frames and wood planking.

One problem with a steel keel would be fastening the frames to the keel. Rather than simply making steel floor timbers, I think I would weld a piece of heavy, flat bar across the keel where each floor

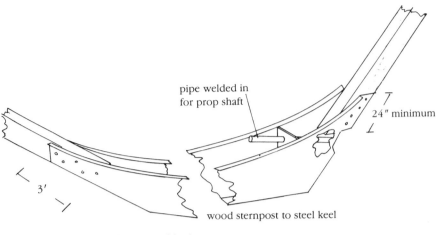

Figure 5/10.
An alternative to the traditional all-wood back-bone structure is a hollow steel box keel filled with concrete and scrap metal. Wood stem and sternposts are attached with bolts.

pipe welded in for prop shaft

24″ minimum

3′

wood sternpost to steel keel

wood forefoot to steel keel

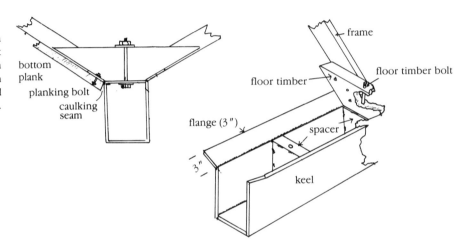

Figure 5/11.
Steel keel details. Put in spacers on 3- to 4-foot centers. Fill box with scrap and concrete even with top edge, then weld on cap.

bottom plank

planking bolt

caulking seam

frame

floor timber

floor timber bolt

flange (3″)

spacer

3″

keel

goes, and then bolt a wood floor to the steel. Of course, it could be done with steel floors, too, except that wood-to-steel butts generally make the wood rot eventually. However, coating the steel with epoxy and bedding the frame in lots of tar might avoid that.

Another advantage of wood floor timbers over steel is that floor timbers generally end up getting notched here and there for stringers and whatnot, and it's simpler to shape wood than steel. I suppose if you did a really good lofting job, you could plan out all this in advance and notch the metal floors before putting them up, but it's the rare home builder who is that organized (or knows enough about what he's doing).

Another problem would be attaching the planking. You'd need a flange that followed the correct bevel, but that wouldn't be so hard to do. If you installed the frames first, you could clamp the flat bar flange to the frames, which would give it the correct angle, then weld it to the keel.

Fastening the planking to the keel flange would be tedious. You'd have to drill and bolt the flange for its whole length, making sure to use bolts that have just a bit of thread on the end, rather than the "all-thread" kind. The all-thread bolts leak when used underwater, and are only good for deck and interior work.

Giving the flange a good coat of epoxy, and bedding the planks well in tar, should keep rust from starting up. If you were planking with plywood, you'd install the first layers by fastening them just to the stringers and frames, and then, after the final layer was on, bolting through the whole works into the flange.

BALLAST KEELS

If you're building a sailboat you'll need ballast of some kind. The theory behind ballast is that the lower you get it the more efficiently it holds you rightside up. But, as with all other aspects of design, there are other things to consider.

Ballast can be all external, all internal, or some combination of the two. Boats with all their ballast outside stand up to the wind better than those with only inside ballast, but the low center of gravity can give the hull a "jerky" roll, and it locks you into carrying all of the weight of the ballast all of the time. If you need to lighten ship in an emergency or to carry more cargo, you're out of luck.

Plenty of boats, both shallow and deep, used to be built with all inside ballast, although you don't see it so often these days. Yet it's the simplest and probably the cheapest way to go. All inside ballast is the least efficient in holding the boat up into the wind, and it takes up a lot of interior storage room, especially on deep hulls. On the plus side, the higher center of gravity dampens the roll, making the boats much more comfortable to sail than those with all outside ballast.

A good compromise seems to be to install at least half the ballast outside, and the remainder inside. This gives you a bit more initial stability than all inside ballast, and a bit higher center of gravity than all outside ballast, which makes for a more comfortable motion at sea.

It also gives you reserve buoyancy. I read about a sailboat that ran aground off Greenland, in an area with little tide. The crew were able to refloat the boat only because it had a good deal of inside ballast, which they were able to throw over the side, raising the boat and allowing it to float off. They replaced the lost ballast with beach stones, and were able to sail back to England. In the same situation, a boat with all outside ballast would have been lost.

Casting a ballast keel

Perhaps the most intimidating part of building a boat is casting an iron or lead keel. Lead keels can be worked at home, but it's a pricey proposition. Not only is the lead itself expensive, but to avoid electrolysis you must use bronze bolts and planking screws, which are at least three times as expensive as galvanized fastenings.

Cast iron keels don't come cheap either. Not only do they have to be cast by a foundry, but the material is too hard to be drilled so you have to make a form with all the bolt holes lined out to match the ones in the wood keel. I think this much precision planning would scare me enough not to start.

Fortunately there's an alternative: a keel cast from concrete and scrap metal. It's simple to do, cheap, and as many of the old bridges show, concrete holds up well in salt water. I've run over rocks with several concrete keels without hurting them, so it seems to be strong enough. The boat's resale value will be lower than one with more conventionally approved ballast, but so will the building costs. For many of us, that's more important.

Concrete and metal scrap isn't as dense as solid metal, and you'll be doing well to achieve a density of 250 pounds per cubic foot, compared to 400 for iron and 700 for lead. This means you'll likely be supplementing your concrete ballast keel with inside ballast.

To get started, you need to build a form for the concrete, just as if you were making a sidewalk. Turn the keel assembly on its side on the cradle and drive the ballast bolts through the holes. Block up under the keel. You'll need a sheet of 1/2-inch plywood for the bottom of the form (the side of the keel). Slide it up under the keel so that it overlaps the wood keel by 2 inches. Block up the plywood securely so it doesn't sag under the weight of the concrete.

Make the end of the form (the keel's bottom) by nailing a 2-by-whatever-the-thickness-of-the-keel along the outer edges of the plywood. The exact shape is shown on the lines plan. The front of the keel often is shown as a sweeping line on the plans, but it's a lot simpler if you make it a straight line. Regardless, the exact shape is easily read from the plans. Nail a 2×4 from the keel to the edge of the form every 6 feet or so to keep the ends square. If you want a nice round edge to the finished casting you can nail a triangular strip along the outer edges of the form, but I never bother.

You'll want to reinforce the keel with plenty of rebar, but how you handle it depends on the kind of scrap metal you intend to add to the keel. There's all sorts of steel out there, if you look around. Railroad spikes, bridge rivets, horseshoes, boiler punchings, and so on. Some of the best scraps are the "mill ends" you can get at a steel mill, if you can find a steel mill in America any more. Any big city will have a scrap dealer listed in the Yellow Pages, so call around.

What you use depends on how much room you have and how much you'll need. A little boat might need the weight as concentrated as possible, so you'd want chunks of steel. In a worst-case scenario you might need lead, but try to avoid that. It's expensive, and if water gets to it you might have problems with electrolysis, unless you first paint the lead with epoxy to seal it.

A

B

C

D

E

F

Figure 5/12.
(A) Details of ballast keel casting. When using big pieces of steel in the casting, hang rebar from bolts about 3/4-inch above bottom of form. Put in the second layer as you do the pour. Note crossbraces between bottom of keel form and wood keel. (B) When using little pieces of steel (boiler punchings or the like) in the casting, wire rebar directly to the ballast bolts. Note the big washer on the bolt. (C) Old machine parts used for added weight in the keel casting. Note rebar tied to ballast bolts. (D) Finished concrete ballast pour. (E) I never could pass wet cement without signing my name. (F) After casting cures for two weeks, stand it up and bolt on the frames. All floor timber and ballast bolts are installed in the wood keel *before* the ballast is cast.

A big boat will have the room to put in whatever you can find. Rebar makes great ballast, but it's expensive. If you live near a city, you might go talk to a foreman at a skyscraper construction site. Occasionally the steel in these projects gets really overbought, and

Keels and Ballast

there will be piles of leftovers to get rid of without tipping off the investors. A little cash to the right guy and maybe it's yours.

If you can find something small, like boiler punchings or bridge rivets or railroad spikes, you can weave the rebar around the ballast bolts. The easiest rebar to work is 3/8 or 1/2 inch. An 18-inch-deep ballast casting will contain, say, 8 pieces of rebar.

If you find a good source of heavy rebar, 1-inch or bigger, you could use lots of that to supply added weight. You'd pour an inch of concrete, lay in a bunch of bar, cover it with concrete, lay in more bar, and so on. I'd wire a few pieces to the bolts, but then pack in the rest loose. The concrete will hold things together.

If you're dealing with larger chunks of steel, hang the first layer of rebar from the ballast bolts with heavy wire. The bar should be about 1 inch from the bottom of the form. Pour enough concrete to cover the bar, lay in the scrap metal, cover that with concrete, lay more rebar on top, then fill up the remainder of the room with concrete.

Alternatively, pour an inch of concrete, lay in enough steel scrap to come flush with the tops of the ballast bolts, lay rebar on that and wire it to the bolts, cover the whole business with concrete, lay in more scrap until you're close to the top of the form, then cover everything with concrete.

The preferred concrete mix is open to debate. I've cast three keels using 2 parts sand to 1 part cement, with just a bit of water. All

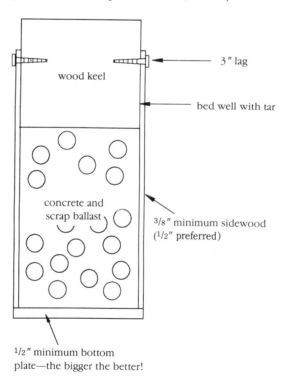

Figure 5/13.
Another way of adding weight to a ballast keel. Heavy steel plates are lagged to hull after completion. Start by sliding plates below keel between blocks, then reblock hull to hold plates tightly against ballast. Weld them together, then attach sides and weld them to bottom. Note that bottom overlaps ballast enough to catch side pieces.

3" lag

wood keel

bed well with tar

concrete and scrap ballast

3/8" minimum sidewood (1/2" preferred)

1/2" minimum bottom plate—the bigger the better!

had small bits of steel, like bolts and stuff, mixed in. Two of them went on the rocks and remained undamaged, so they seemed pretty strong.

However, the owner of a cement joint told me that good concrete needs gravel in addition to sand and cement, so for my last keel I used 4 parts sand, one part pea gravel, and one part cement. I haven't hit anything with it yet, but I trucked the 20,000-pound hull for 50 miles on a trailer that supported it at only two 4-inch wide spots along the ballast. Nothing broke, so it seems strong enough. I still don't know what mix is best!

Whether to mix it dry or wet is another open question, and experts will tell you to do it both ways. I like it mixed just a bit runny so I know it will flow around all the metal in the casting.

To make the casting job easy, I've found that you'll need a rented cement mixer, a wheelbarrow, and about three willing workers. I always do the mixing myself, just to be sure it's done the way I want it. The other two people spread the stuff and poke it with a stick to make sure that it's really flowing everywhere. Like other concrete work, the whole casting must be done in one pour.

When you finish, cover your new ballast keel with old carpet or rags and keep it damp for a few days. Let the casting sit on its side for a couple of weeks before righting it. You can make the frames while it cures.

Welded steel ballast keel

The method just described is the easiest and cheapest way to cast a ballast keel, but it isn't the most efficient at producing weight for its size. It is the simplest system, and a lot better than nothing, but a better way would be to use a steel box keel, shown in Figure 5-14.

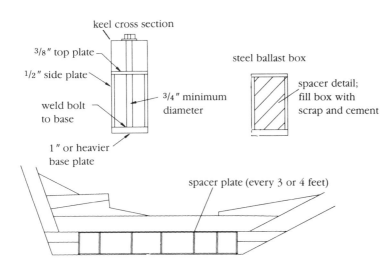

keel cross section

³⁄₈″ top plate

¹⁄₂″ side plate

weld bolt to base

³⁄₄″ minimum diameter

1″ or heavier base plate

steel ballast box

spacer detail; fill box with scrap and cement

spacer plate (every 3 or 4 feet)

Figure 5/14.
The steel ballast box produces a more efficient ratio of weight to size.

Keels and Ballast

Here again, start off with the wood keel lying on its side, but before you drive the ballast bolts, lay a cardboard or plywood pattern along the bottom of the wood keel and mark the locations of all the ballast bolts. Lay this pattern on a piece of steel the same width as the wood keel, and burn out the holes. Again, the shape of the keel is shown on the lines plan.

You'll probably need to do some cutting or shearing to get this plate to the exact width required. I'd be tempted to buy a wider plate to the next full inch, and later glue and nail a tapered wood strip along the overlap to "fair" the extra width to the wood keel. That would probably be cheaper than having the plate cut to width.

Slide the lower keel side in place, and tack weld it to the piece along the keel. Weld on a few steel spacers, the same dimension as the inside of the keel's cross section, about 3 or 4 feet apart. These will reinforce the keel box and serve as a level gauge so you'll know how much concrete and scrap you can add to the box and still fit the top on. Stand up the bottom of the keel and weld it to the side and to the spacers.

You can't bed the top of the keel box against the keel with tar, which is flammable and could easily start a fire during welding, but the metal-to-wood joint could prove an annoying source of rot, so you'll need to do a little extra work here. Drive the ballast bolts, which should be 2 or 3 inches longer than the depth of the keel, down through the wood keel and through a piece of oversize pipe. Weld the pipe to the top and bottom plates; the bolts should be free inside the pipe.

Slide the ballast box a few inches away from the keel, paint the inside of the box with phosphorus (buy it at an autobody shop; Phospho is a popular brand) to glaze the steel, then paint it with epoxy to protect it. When the epoxy cures, fill the box with as much scrap steel as you can, with a bit of runny cement to hold the scrap together. Lay down the top piece of steel and weld it to the keel top, alongside the keel, and to the bottom. After it cools, slop lots of tar on the wood keel's bottom and lever the keel box in place. Cinch up the keel bolts with nuts, then burn them off flush with the bottom and weld them in place.

FRAMING UP

About this point in a boatbuilding project I stop and say to myself: "Yumping Yesus. Vat have I got myself intew now?" Money's flowing out at an alarming rate; all but the most unusual Main Squeeze is beginning to bitch at all the time you're putting into this . . . *Thing.*

But there's something about this big phallus of a keel laying there—chunks of wood shaped and bolted together by *you*, of all people. Admit it! It's pretty goddam neat, ain't it? By golly, *this* is a *keel*, mon! This is a keel that can cleave rocks; the waves will part before it and the dolphins will guide it as you steer it bare headed under full sail, over a whale, in a full gale . . . . OK. Put down the jug; it's time to get back to work.

SINGLE-CHINE FRAME CONSTRUCTION

Chine boats have simple frames—just straight lines joined together at the corners, or *chine*, by plywood *gussets*. This makes them very simple to assemble from commonly available materials—even salvaged wood (a few nail holes won't hurt). We've already discussed materials. As you've certainly heard, there are ideal woods for boatbuilding. If you live in a place where you can get them, use them. If you don't, use what you can find. A good source of information is a local workboat repair yard.

Although hardwood is ideal for frames and keels because it holds fastenings so well, many softwoods, like fir, yellow pine, and so on, are commonly used *both* in yachts and workboats. Softwood works fine for our chine hulls because the heavy framing holds fastenings well. Once again, don't use hemlock in your boat; it doesn't last. I use 2 × 4s for boats to 30 feet or so, and 2 × 6s for boats around 45 or 50 feet. I prefer using 3-by stuff on these bigger boats if I can find it, but 2-by will serve. Four-by would be nice, but it's just a bit thick to be sawed by the average backyard builder's tools.

These big frames have all sorts of advantages: They allow you to use normal-dimension, off-the-shelf wood from the lumberyard. I like to incorporate as much of this stuff into a boat as possible. I also like the psychological effect of big frames: They may take up room inside the cabin, but I dare anybody to get into a storm and complain about that. And big frames leave you plenty of wood to fasten the chine to after you saw out the chine notch, without the bother of having to piece in a "filler" at the chine.

The plywood gussets hold the side and bottom frames together at the chine. These gussets are placed on each side of the frame, glued, and through-bolted with 5/16-inch bolts. On smaller boats, under say 26 feet, you can use screws to fasten the gussets, but this isn't as strong. I use 1/2-inch plywood gussets in little boats, 3/4 inch in boats to maybe 33 feet, and 1 inch on big boats. House "underlay" plywood is good stuff here. Big boats can also use 1/4-inch steel gussets, but steel against wood tends to rot, and the steel is harder to shape. I suppose aluminum would work, and it's a lot easier to shape than steel, come to think about it. If you're using metal for gussets, lay a piece of tarpaper between it and the wood.

The chines will be made of standard-dimension lumber as well. I always use two or more layers of 1-by, which comes to you finished 3/4-inch thick. A boat up to about 30 feet will have a chine made from two pieces of 1-by. Between 30 and 34 feet you can go either way, depending on how tough you want to make her. Over 35 feet, use three pieces of 1-by. My current 50-footer has 3-by frames and 3-inch thick chines. I used four pieces of 1-by at the ends to make the curves easier to bend, and two pieces of 2-by in the middle, where bends are easier.

You'll need a big table made from 2 x 4s and 1/2-inch plywood on which to assemble the frames, a bit wider than your boat's maximum beam, and a bit higher than the tallest frame. To save your back, have the table about 3 feet off the ground. Paint the table white with some cheap latex house paint to make pencil marks more visible.

Figure 6/1. Frames drawn out on an assembly table. This example shows a boat with constant deadrise shape and a parallel keel, which makes the rabbet for all frames start at the same point. Make several frames, then paint the table white with latex paint and draw on some more.

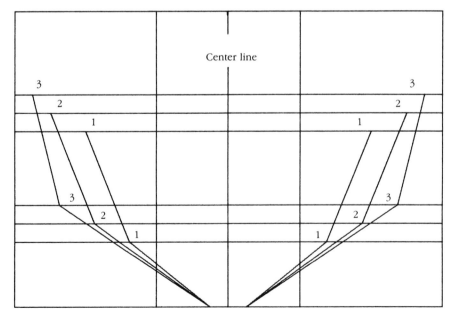

Lay a *baseline* along the bottom edge of the table, erect a *perpendicular* on each side, and a *centerline* down the middle (remember the dead Greek). Now you're ready to draw out the frames, just as you did when you drew in the stations on the lofting.

It doesn't matter which end you start with—bow or stern. You get the frames' dimensions from the *corrected table of offsets* you made after lofting, but you have a bit of math to do first. The offset table's *heights* are based on heights above the baseline on the profile view; you want to draw the frame without having to draw in the whole keel height.

The baseline on the table is "0" height; you'll make all your measurements up from there. Mark the width of the keel at whatever station you're doing on the baseline, each side of the centerline. If there's any confusion, remember the completed keel is right behind you, so go measure its actual width. Be *exact*! If the keel is 7¹/₂ inches wide, then make a mark *exactly* 3³/₄ inches each side of the centerline; this is the *rabbet* point.

Now we'll find the height of the chine. Let's say the offset table tells us that at the station we're doing, the chine is 5-0-4 (5 feet, 0 inches, and ⁴/₈ inch) off the baseline, and it tells us the rabbet is 2-1-5 off the baseline. Subtract the height of the rabbet from the height of the chine:

$$5\text{-}0\text{-}4$$
$$-\ \underline{2\text{-}1\text{-}5}$$

Howdoya subtract 2-1-5 from 5-0-4? Subtract 1 foot from the feet digit and add it back in inches and eighths. Now you'll have 4 feet, 11 inches, and ¹²/₈ inch, from which you can easily subtract 2-1-5.

$$
\begin{array}{rrl}
5\text{-}0\text{-}4 & = & 4\text{-}11\text{-}12 \\
& - & \underline{2\text{ -}1\text{- }5} \\
& & 2\text{-}10\text{- }7
\end{array}
$$

Get it? Now we know that the chine is 2 feet 10⁷/₈ inches above the rabbet, so measure that distance up the perpendicular lines on each side of the table, make a mark, and connect these two points by snapping a chalk line across the table. Look in the offset table to see how wide the station is at the chine. Measure out from the centerline and make a mark to indicate the chine's width on each side. You got it!

Now for the sheer. The offset table says the sheer is 8-4-6 above the baseline at this station. First, subtract the rabbet's height from the sheer's height:

$$
\begin{array}{l}
8\text{-}4\text{-}6 \text{ (sheer height)} \\
\underline{-\,2\text{-}1\text{-}5 \text{ (rabbet height)}} \\
6\text{-}3\text{-}1
\end{array}
$$

Measure 6-3-1 *up* from the baseline at each perpendicular and snap a line across, just as you did with the chine. Find the station's width at the sheer in the half-widths part of the offset table, measure out from the centerline on each side and make a mark. Now you have a mark for the sheer, the chine, and the rabbet. Connect these marks with lines, and you've drawn the frame.

Every chine boat I design has a station at each frame, so the offset table will tell you all the frame dimensions. However, as I mentioned in Chapter 4, if you're building a design with stations spaced wider than your desired frame spacing, you can draw new stations in your lofting, take the measurements from them, and space the frames as closely as you want.

Almost all boat plans are drawn to the *outside* of the planking these days, so you'll need to subtract the thickness of the planking before assembling the frame. The easiest way to do this, after you've drawn the frame, is to rip eight 6-inch-long pieces of planking stock so that they're "square," and nail them along the inside edge of the lines, two for each side frame and two for each bottom frame. Butt your frame stock against these and you'll come out right.

The frame's side piece runs all the way down to the chine, and the bottom piece butts against the inside face of the side. Cut a piece of wood about a foot longer than you need for the side and lay it on the table against the blocks. Make a mark at each side where it crosses the line indicating the bottom frame, then saw the angle. Draw a line on the table down the side frame's inside face.

Now take off the side piece and lay your bottom frame piece in position. Mark the angle where it butts against the side frame, and mark the angle where it butts against the keel (the rabbet). Saw across these angles, and do the same thing for the other side of the frame. Nothing to it.

Now then. The frames must be beveled to match the angle of the planks as they wrap around the hull, and the bevel is different at each frame. It's common practice to bevel both the frame's inside and outside edges, but if you're not going to put ceiling in the boat there's no reason to do the inside, other than aesthetics. I never use ceiling in a boat, but I like the look of the beveled frames inside, so I always do it. Many people bevel the frames after they're erected, but I think it's much simpler to do it as you assemble them.

Now unroll your lofting and get out a bevel gauge. For the *side frames*, measure the angle on the *half-width* drawing at the sheer and at the chine at the station you're working on; use whichever angle is *least*. For the *bottom frames*, measure the angle on the *profile* drawing at the chine and the rabbet and use whichever angle is *least*.

A

B

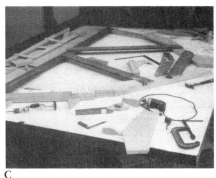

C

Figure 6/2.
(A) Frame pieces blocked into position on frame assembly table. (B) Gussets screwed down to hold things in position. (C) **X**-bracing installed to hold frame halves in position; now gussets are glued and bolted in place.

When you're planking you'll probably have to plane a bit off the frames to make the bevels perfect, but you can use a table saw now and get everything close enough. This will save you lots of labor; beveling a standing frame is a pain. When you're beveling the inside face of the side pieces, be sure to stop the bevel high enough up from the chine so that the bottom piece can butt square to the side piece.

Lay the beveled pieces on the table in position. Pay attention to which way the bevels are laying. The wide face must be down, which makes the frame lay with the beveled edge leaning *away* from the line on the table. This is obvious, because this makes the bottom edge of the frame touch the line (or planking sample). If you have it upside down, the bottom of the frame will be ''inboard'' of the line and the top will be overhanging. Nail blocks against the frame's inside faces to hold the pieces securely in position.

Make a cardboard pattern showing the shape of the frame at the chine. Draw your gussets on it, and saw them out. You'll have two per side, four per frame. How big should the gussets be? It doesn't matter. Make them so it looks like you could drive a car up the frame without breaking it at the gusset and you'll be OK. Note the photos showing frames under construction. You'll see the gussets are pretty hefty. The same pattern will probably work for several frames at a time. If frames start flowing on different angles than your pattern, make a new one.

Lay a gusset in position, on top of the frame at the chine (intersection of side and bottom) and screw it down tightly to the frame with four big screws, two into each piece of the frame. Run a pencil underneath to show where it covers the frame. Pencil in where you want to drill the holes for the bolts ($1/4$- or $5/16$-inch bolts). Remember, you'll be sawing out a notch for the chine, so don't put a bolt in the way.

Nail a 1×6 across the top of the frame with the *bottom* edge at the sheer. Nail another 1×6 across the bottom pieces about halfway between the chine and the rabbet. Nail two more 1×6s to make an **X** between the first two. This will hold the frame securely in position until it's bolted into the boat. Mark the centerline on the top piece; you'll need this later on.

Gently lift the frame up a bit and slip some blocks under it to hold it off the table. Position the bottom gussets underneath, and clamp them tightly to the frame. You want the clamps on both gussets to hold them while you drill. Remove the screws holding the top gussets and drill the bolt holes. Remove the clamps and top gussets, spread a good layer of glue (I use Weldwood Plastic Resin or Wilhold here; no need for epoxy) on the gusset and on the frame, then put the top gusset in place and start the bolts. Slip out the bottom gusset, spread glue on it, put it back in position, and drive the bolts through. Block up a side at a time, tighten down the nuts, and you have it. Write the station number on the top crosspiece, and mark which face is forward. It's too damned easy to erect a frame backwards, although if you've made sure to assemble the frames with the wide part down, you should work out OK. Label it just the same.

After the frame is all bolted together, rough out the chine notch. Measure the height of the chine piece up the side frame, usually about 2 inches. Measure the thickness of the chine at 90 degrees from this point. Draw a line from this point parallel to the outside of the frame. Flip the frame over and do the same thing on the other side.

Figure 6/3.
Frame assembled, ready to erect on keel. Note that bottom of crosspiece marks sheer. Plywood (or steel) gusset installed on both sides of frame at chine, bolted with 8 to 10 $1/4$- or $5/16$-inch bolts.

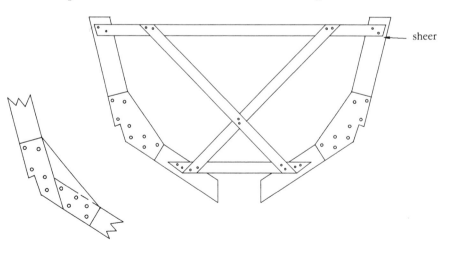

sheer

Connect the lines across the faces, and saw out the notch. I use a hand ripsaw here because it's easier to check the sawing angle, and you make mistakes a lot slower than with power tools. Since you've beveled the frames in advance this method will give you a chine notch that will be very close to correct.

Floor timbers

After you make a frame for a station, saw out the floor timbers, which hold the frames to the keel. Their widths were determined already; you have the bolts in the keel waiting for them.

The floors are easy to make. After you've assembled a frame, go over to the keel and measure the distance from the *rabbet line* to the top of the keel at the station you just made the frame for. Go back to the frame assembly table and draw in a line that same distance above the rabbet. This will be the bottom of the floor. Measure up from that line whatever height you're using for floor timbers, and draw in another line parallel to the first to represent the top of the floor. Again, these heights should already have been figured out because your bolts are already in place.

There are a few things to think about when making floor timbers. First, the name itself doesn't have anything to do with the boat's floor. As a matter of fact, a boat doesn't have a floor like a house. It has a *sole*. Sometimes the sole happens to lie on a floor, and if that's happening then you must notch the floor where the bolt comes out so the nut will be countersunk and not interfere with the floorboards. They're called floorboards, not soleboards, but are not to be confused with floors, which is what I'm talking about at the moment.

The other thing to think about is how close you want the floors to come to the planking. Some people make the floors completely overlap the frames, fitting them snug to the planking. This may be good on a boat with small bent frames, but the large frames we're using have plenty of meat to bolt against the floor, so I leave the floor about 1/2 inch short on each end.

I feel that if a joint doesn't have to be watertight, it's best to leave it well open for air circulation. Nothing starts rot faster than an almost-tight joint that doesn't quite fit. Cancer, or rot, as it's called in boats, is mainly caused by bad air circulation. Dirt gets in and stays moist, no air can get at it; and pretty soon—rot. True, fresh water doesn't help wood, but dead air space is what really gets it. So, I leave good gaps wherever I don't need perfect fits. Go ahead and fit the floors tightly if you want, but when you plank the bottom use lots of bedding compound between the floor and the planking.

Anyhow. You have the floor drawn on the assembly table. Figure out how shy (far away) you're making it from the outer edge of the frame. Make a cardboard pattern (or just transfer the measurements;

there ain't much to it), draw out the shape on whatever stock you're using for the floors, and saw it out.

Be sure to draw in its vertical centerline. If the floor is near the ends of the hull you might need to saw the sides on an angle similar to the frame's bevel. Don't worry too much about this now. Later on, when you're planking, it will be obvious if you need to trim some meat off, and a Skilsaw does it in a hurry.

After you've made a few frames and floor timbers, repaint the tabletop to get rid of all the pencil lines. Things are confusing enough without having to figure out which marks you want to use! Keep going until you've made all the frames and floor timbers.

Setting up the keel

After the concrete casting has had about two weeks to cure, stand the keel up on its base. You can do this with one big railroad jack and some chain (as the photo shows), or a lot of people, beer, wedges, small jacks, and swearing. Once it's standing upright, jack up the front of the keel so that it's sitting at the same angle shown on the lines plan, which will make the waterline level. Wedge it left or right until it's sitting exactly vertical. If you set the keel up right in the first place, you'll have a fair chance of building the hull more or less symmetrically and having all the bulkheads, deck houses, and cabinetry come out plumb.

If you're building inside a shop, now is a good time to stretch a centerline string from one end of the shop to the other, high enough up in the air that you can erect the frames and stem under it. This is easy if you have a person on each end of the string to shift it, and two plumb-bobs with a person to watch each one. Move the string back and forth until the plumb-bobs hang over the center of the keel on each end. If the keel timber is a bit warped, which happened to me once, ignore it. Although the overhead string is simpler, if you don't have walls to fasten it to, you can wait until you have the stems and/or transom clamped up, stretch a string between them, and shift them around until the plumb-bob says everything is more or less straight.

Once the main part of the keel is in place, you can bolt on the forefoot and horn timber. I left off the stem and sternpost until the frames were up once, and I don't know if I'd do it again because it's fun to look at the entire keel standing there. It doesn't matter, though. A complete description of raising the stems is given later on in this chapter, after the frame section is completed.

To position the forefoot and horn timber, leave the main keel pattern nailed to the keel, and clamp the new keel pieces—the rest of the deadwood and the stems—in place. After they're clamped up, put their patterns on as well, lined up carefully to fit against the joining pattern, to be sure everything is going together as the lofting said it

Figure 6/4.
One big railroad jack and some chain is the easiest way to stand up the keel. It *can* be done with sufficient auto jacks, wedges, swearing, and beer. Be sure to block up the keel on the same slope as shown on the lines plan.

Figure 6/5.
Hoist made from 2 × 6s to lift heavy keel pieces.

should. About now you'll be appreciating the few hours you spent making those patterns. They really make things easier.

You may have some hefty chunks of wood to hoist around when putting together the backbone. You can handle them easily with a homemade hoist, as shown in Figure 6-5. Clamp together two 2 × 6s into a big **V**, lean it a bit, hold it up with a rope run from a floor timber bolt, and hang a come-a-long from the clamp. One guy can lift very heavy things with this system.

Keel rabbet

Assuming you've been doing stuff in the order I've been describing it, you should already have the keel rabbet marked out on the keel. If

Framing Up

Figure 6/6.
Plank drawn on
station with least
deadrise to give
you the angles for
cutting the rabbet
lines.

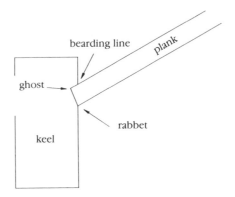

you don't, then put the pattern back on and mark where the rabbet goes.

Unroll the lofting and find the station that looks like it hits the keel at the "flattest" angle. Draw a plank, the thickness you'll be using, at this station; show it entering the rabbet (see Figure 6-6). Remember that the rabbet line shows the *outside* face of the plank.

Measure the vertical distance from the rabbet to the top, or inside edge of the plank on your lofting. Turn to the keel, and at each station put a mark this distance above the rabbet. Drive a nail at each mark, bend a batten around, and draw a line parallel to the rabbet. This is the *bearding line*.

Set a Skilsaw to the angle of the "flattest" station, and set the blade depth to whatever depth the drawing shows the plank sticking into the keel. Run the saw down the bearding line. Reset the angle and the depth according to what the drawing shows is required to go from the rabbet to the inside of the bearding line (it's called the *ghost line*) and saw that.

You now have a rabbet ready for planking. If there is much variation in the deadrise between the stations you might have to trim the rabbet a bit as you plank. Frankly, although it isn't traditional, it's usually simpler to plane a bit off the end of the plank, but that's up to you.

If you're building a design that has a marked change in deadrise—for instance, flat at the stern and very deep at the bow— you might be better off to figure the angle of the rabbet at each station and cut it by hand with a chisel. That pleases the purists, but it takes too long for me, and I use the Skilsaw as much as possible.

Floor timber erection

As mentioned before, it's important that the bottom of the keel be blocked up on whatever angle is needed to make the waterline level.

Take a floor to its station, hold it in place, and check the bolt for plumb with a level. If it isn't, bang on it with a big hammer or put a

Figure 6/7.
Straightedge clamped to
wood serves as a guide for
drilling straight holes.

pipe on it and bend it until it stands vertical. If you're using the hammer, put a nut on the threads first so you don't mess them up.

Now, put your bevel measure against the bolt and measure the angle of the top of the keel to the bolt. Plane (or easier, use the table saw) the base of the floor to that angle so it can stand vertically. Stand the floor in front of its location as close to the bolt as you can, and draw a line on it where the bolt goes. Flip the floor upside down, and drill the hole for the bolt exactly in the middle. When you start on the bottom like this, you *know* the bolt will enter the floor where it needs to, which is the important thing. It won't really matter if the bolt doesn't come out exactly right on top because it will bend some if it needs to.

You'll need a strong drill motor for this, and a good bit. You can drill a very straight hole, at the exact angle you want, if you clamp a stick a few feet long to the floor along the line you want to drill. Sight down between the long bit and the guide stick, and you'll be able to guide the bit very close to where you want it. If you don't come out exactly in the middle of the floor's top the world won't end, but you do want the hole to be exactly in the middle on the bottom, which is why you start drilling there.

Stand the floor on the keel against its bolt. Be sure that the bottom sits flat on the keel, that the centerline matches the middle of the keel, and that the bolt is long enough. If it isn't, notch the floor. If the sole is supposed to sit on the floor and the bolt is too long, then saw off the bolt, rethread it a bit, and notch the floor. If you need to rethread a bolt, hook a pair of Vise-Grips to it to keep it from spinning in its hole.

If you don't have outside ballast in place, or if you're going to be using drift bolts, such as in some areas of the stern, then you won't have a bolt in place and things will be a bit simpler. Just drill the floor,

Framing Up

make a drift, stand the floor in position, drill through it into the keel an inch or two to be sure you start the hole exactly right, remove the floor, and finish drilling the hole.

Slop lots of preservative on the floor's end grain. Put it on "wet on wet" until the wood won't absorb any more, then pour some down the bolt hole. Spread a nice bit of tar on top of the keel where the floor sits, bang it down over the bolt, square it up to the keel with a framing square, and you're set. Don't cinch it down really tight: You might have to shift it a bit once the frames are up and being aligned. If you're using two drifts instead of bolts, put in only one for now.

ERECTING THE FRAMEWORK

Once the floors are in position you can stand up the frames. Now, you have the choice of throwing them up as quickly as possible—they do look good standing there—or you can start planning ahead. This doesn't deliver the instant gratification we have come to expect in our society, but it saves a lot of hassle down the line.

With just a keel and some floor timbers—the whole business being just a few feet off the shop floor—getting big stuff in place, like an engine or big tanks, is no real problem. If you put up the frames, though, getting anything big inside the boat becomes a much bigger deal. You'll have to hire a boom truck, build some sort of Rube Goldberg ramp, hang a winch from an overhead beam, or some combination of the three. I've done it both ways, and I can say from experience that it's easier to plan ahead. In fact, that's a basic rule of boatbuilding: "Think ahead, stupid!"

Assuming you're going to plan ahead, the first frame you'll put up is the one located just forward of the engine. Remember, the station lines on the keel mark the *widest* point of the frame at that station. Be sure first of all that you put the frame on the correct side of the floor timber, and second, that the frame is facing the right direction. Both mistakes are easy to make and happen at least once in each boat, resulting either in a hollow you'll need to shim out or a bulge you'll have to plane down when planking. Think ahead.

Position the frame and clamp it in place so that the bottom tips are even with the *bearding line*, and a plumb-bob hung off the center of the sheer crosspiece hits the center of the keel. Put a level on the crosspiece after the 'bob is pointing at the center of the keel. The top should be level, the 'bob should be pointing at the middle of the keel, and the bottom tips of the frame should be even with the bearding line. If all three of these things aren't happening, split the differences.

I don't know which one of the three is the most important. If you assembled the frame correctly, the crosspiece will *have* to be level if the plumb-bob is pointing at the middle of the keel, assuming the keel is vertical. If you have to cant the frame a bit, making one frame tip a bit (maybe $1/2$ inch or so) above or below the bearding line, don't worry about it. You can smooth things up later. I don't think there ever was a boat built that was perfectly symmetrical anyway, although of course one should always shoot for that. Again, the keel itself must be sitting vertical. When you have the frame aligned to your satisfaction, fasten it to the floor, using at least three bolts per side.

As you erect the frames, sight down both sides of the hull. The frames should be flowing at the same angle on each side. If they don't, you'll quickly spot the wrong one. When this happens, it means you've assembled half of a frame to the wrong line, and you'll probably have to make a new one. This seems to happen at least once per boat as well; I think it's a natural law.

Engine beds

Again, I suggest you install the engine before you frame up the whole hull. The problem with this is that you have to buy the engine now, of course, and if you wait, you'll probably find a better deal. Be that as it may, after you erect the frames in the way of the engine, you have to design some sort of *engine bed*.

Figure 6/8.
(A) When you plan ahead for an engine installation it's easy. (B) When you don't, it's a pain.

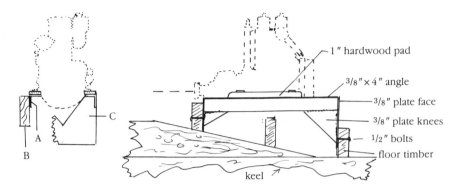

Figure 6/9.
Engine mount details. Engine mount can be a 3/8-×4-inch angle flange (A) bolted to a heavy timber (B) which is in turn bolted to the frames and floor timbers. A better system uses an all-steel mount (C), bolted in between floor timbers. Note wood pad between steel and engine. Width of mount depends on the engine used.

The most common mount probably is wood timbers, but I like steel much better. It's neater, takes up less space, and makes it easy to through-bolt the engine to the beds, instead of lag-bolting it, as you often must do with wood.

The first step in engine-bed design is determining the *shaft angle*. Nail a stick across the outside opening of the shaft log, right across the center of the hole. Notch it a hair, tie a string to it, shove the string through the shaft log with a rod, and extend it past where the engine will sit. Fasten the end of the string to a board, hold it against a floor timber, and adjust it until the string runs exactly out the center of the shaft log opening inside the boat. That's your shaft angle.

All engine manufacturers provide schematic drawings showing the dimensions of their engines, so if you're using a new motor, it's simple to see what sort of mount you'll need. If you're using an old, off-brand engine for which you can't get manufacturer's specs, you'll have to take them off yourself. To do this, prop the engine up on some timbers that are longer than the engine, so that its mounting pads are supported on a level plane. This will show you how far apart the engine mount's bearers must be. Lay a straightedge across the bearers and measure up from it to the center of the engine's shaft coupling. This will tell you how low or high the mount must be in relation to the shaft line. Make the mount 3/4 inch to 1 inch lower to leave room for hardwood pads between the engine and the mount, and for shimming the engine to its exact position.

Now that you know the relationship between the shaft line and the engine, go back and figure where this position is on the boat. Be sure there will be enough room below the engine for the oil pan and whatnot to clear. In fact, try to leave enough room to change the oil easily.

If you're going to use wood mounts, you can simply through-bolt two heavy bearers, such as 4×6s or 4×8s, directly to the frames, and either through- or lag-bolt the engine directly to that. Some people bolt steel angle irons to the bearers, then bolt the engine to the steel. For heavy engines, you can add two or three steel angle braces from the bearers to the floor timbers.

A

B

Figure 6/10.
(A) Steel engine mount installed. Note that the engine sits on a wood pad; the mount is bolted to the floor timber; front of mount is "veed" to provide good access to engine. (B) Stern section of hull framed up and engine installed before proceeding further forward. Note X-bracing is removed after the frame is bolted to the floors. Leave the sheer crosspiece in place until you're ready to install deck beams.

The best mounts are all steel. If you aren't a welder yourself, the best way to make an all-steel mount is to make a pattern of the whole deal from 3/8-inch plywood, and take it to a welder. Use glue and screws and do a good job. You won't have to make imitation angle iron top pieces. Just use wide pieces of plywood for each side; these should hold the front and back in the correct position. You can draw the knees and the angle on these side pieces. You may have to notch the steel angles if a starter or oil filter or something on the engine is in the way. Mark all of this on the pattern.

There's no need for a solid flat plate across the front and back of the mount. In fact, the back plate probably will have to be cut out for the gearbox and shaft. Cut a wedge out of the front, too, to make the engine more accessible.

I made a pattern like this for my last boat and gave it to Darold Brekke in Seattle. We dropped the mount he made into position to test the fit. It fit so well we couldn't lift it out again, so we just bolted her in.

Up with the frames

Anyhow, after the engine is in place, you can put up the rest of the frames. As I said earlier, this is exciting stuff, especially after you get half of them up and each new one starts getting smaller. You stand in front of the thing and sight down it and it just looks pretty neat—like a dinosaur skeleton. In fact, I've known a few cases where the final frames take several days to get up. After each new one, the people would lay around and drink wine and just stare at the boat.

If there's much curve to the bow, the end frames won't be just straight lines, they'll have some shape to them. Rather than bothering to build curved frames, I just leave out as many frames as it takes (within reason of course; I left out about 7 feet of frames on my current boat) to get back to straight-sided frames. After the sides are about three quarters planked, I laminate in the missing frames using thin stuff. This allows the planking to take its "natural" curve, and works fine. You can do the same thing if you're planking with plywood. In this case, the longitudinal stringers will flow in a natural curve.

This kind of system is pretty hard for a lot of White Western Civilization types to accept. Many of them can't stand to see a natural thing, and must plot and predetermine how *everything* comes out before they'll attempt it. I suppose this singlemindedness helped them conquer the world, but take my advice: Try to break from it a little. It saves a lot of bother.

This leads up to a whole different system of framing, which I watched some guys do on a 60-foot fishboat down in Mexico. After the keel, stems, and transom were up, the builder installed three frames: one in the middle, and one on each side of the middle, about halfway between the ends and the midsection. This gave him the boat's basic shape.

Next he wrapped long, heavy battens, like a spliced 2 x 6, clear around the boat at the sheer and at the chine. This outlined the hull. Then he went in and assembled the frames right inside the boat! The heavy battens served as guides, and it was a simple matter to lay a piece inside, scribe it to whatever angle was needed, and cut it. All floor timbers were then drift-bolted to the keel after the frames were in.

This was slick, but I've never been able to bring myself to try it. My German blood rebels at allowing curves to develop so casually. I do allow them to flow in as I described with the forward sections and curved stems, but to do the whole boat this way sounds too easy. There's got to be a catch!

Stems and transom

You can put up the stem or transom before or after you put up the frames; it really doesn't matter. It's an easy job to saw out the stem, or

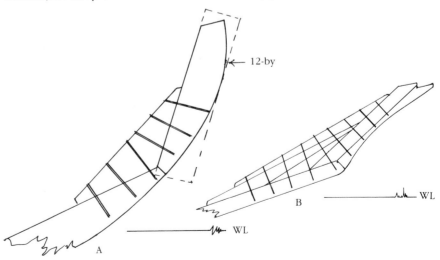

Figure 6/11.
Typical bow stems.
(A) Small boat stem and knee assembly made up from 12-by material.
(B) Large boat stem assembly made up from 12-by pieces. Note the big knees and long overlaps. A stem like this can really bash things!

Buehler's Backyard Boatbuilding

stems if you're doing a double-ender. Just take the shape from the patterns you made after you lofted.

Just remember, you want that stem connection solid enough so you can hit something all standing and survive, so be sure you have good knees backing it up. Lay the patterns on whatever chunks of wood you're using, and saw the pieces out. As mentioned earlier, it's easier to make patterns for curves using closely spaced pointers rather than actually shaping the pattern to the curves. Make a mark at each pointer, drive a nail at each point, bend a batten around the nails, and draw the line (see Figure 6-12).

A

B

C

Figure 6/12.
(A) Scribing the stem curve with a batten. Find the shape from the pattern you (hopefully) made from the lofting. (B) Rough-carving the stem rabbet with chisel and mallet. (C) Finished stem in position!

The stem and knees are held together with lots of through-bolts, and it can be, or rather used to be, really awkward to clamp things together well enough to drill the holes, especially with a rounded stem. You have to saw out the pieces, stand them together, and try to make good fits—dusting them with chalk to show up the high and low spots, paring them down, and trying again.

All this has changed with epoxy glue. You still want to fit the pieces pretty well, but today there's no need to be really compulsive. Fit the pieces fairly well, mix up some 2-to-1 epoxy, stir in some fine sawdust from under the table saw, and mix it till it looks like wet bread dough. Paint the meeting faces with straight epoxy, then smear on your sawdust mix. Stand the pieces together, and toe-nail them with two or three nails to keep them from slipping. Keep things straight with a plumb-bob dangled over each end, and shift things around until the assembly is straight. Then, with a wide putty knife, force more of the mix into any gaps in the joint that aren't oozing epoxy.

That's all there is to it. Give the pieces a day or two to dry, and you're ready to drill the bolt holes. Real epoxy fans say that you don't need any bolts, but I feel better knowing there's a bit of iron behind the glue!

The drawing shows typical bolting patterns. Just use common sense. You don't want so many bolts that the wood is weakened, but you do want enough to really hold things together. Countersink the outer end of the bolts an inch or so. These holes can be filled with a wood plug, which is traditional, or with an epoxy/sawdust mix, which is easier.

It's far easier to rough in the rabbet before you stand up the stems. As with the keel, the correct angle for the stem rabbet comes from the lofting, but this time it's a bit trickier; there's often a marked difference in the angle at which the planks hit the stem between the sheer and the waterline. Recently I cheerfully carved the whole rabbet to the angle of the sheer plank, and later had to epoxy in a filler piece so the rabbet could be recarved to the correct angle farther down.

Chances are the rabbet runs parallel to the stem's face, so set a try-square against the stem, extend it the distance of the rabbet from the face, put a pencil against the end of the try-square rule, and run the square along the face, drawing in the rabbet. To find the angle at which the sheer plank hits the stem on the lofting, draw a plank hitting the stem on the half-width lofting, and take the measurements for the bearding line and the ghost, just as you did for the keel; do the same thing at the chine.

Now, I suggest you just carve (use a chisel and mallet) about a foot of the rabbet at these points. This will get you started planking; you can easily see how the planks are running as you plank, and can continue carving the rabbet as you go. Pros will figure the angle for the whole thing right off the lofting by drawing in waterlines at 8- or

12-inch intervals, continuing the line to the stem to find the angle there. That's well and good, maybe even better, but you can accomplish the same thing by carving as you plank.

The stem assembly on larger boats will be made from massive chunks of wood, most easily handled using the A-frame described earlier. Once you hoist them up, drop a plumb-bob down from your overhead string to get things straight, then clamp the assembly tightly to the keel. With luck it will fit well; if it doesn't you'll have to fit it.

The easiest way to do this is to run a handsaw along the joint. Start the saw and run it in until it's about 1/3 the way through. Nail or clamp boards on both sides of the keel and stem behind the saw to keep the clamping pressure from teetering or lowering the assembly as you saw. Go in another 1/3, and nail on more supports. Repeat this business until you get a good enough fit, then fasten her down.

If the assembly is all above the waterline you can use thickened epoxy in the joint as described earlier. If it's below water, I worry about the swelling wood and the glue doing something weird, so I just use a thick layer of tar. Either way, bolt things together and you've got it.

If you aren't building a double-ender, you'll have to deal with a transom. Transoms are handled in pretty much the same way as the stems, except you're fastening on a square end. The first step is to erect a *horn timber*, which supports the transom and covers the end grain of the keel pieces. It's also possible to continue the keel pieces clear to the boat's end, attach the transom with a big knee, and protect the end grain with epoxy. Whichever, this is something you should have decided long ago while making the keel patterns.

Back when I talked about making the keel patterns I mentioned that, if the designer was unusually "creative," you might want to change the way he specified the assembly. Well, here is the sort of place where you might think about changing the designer's construction plan. Some of the old guys, who were also ace carpenters, drew

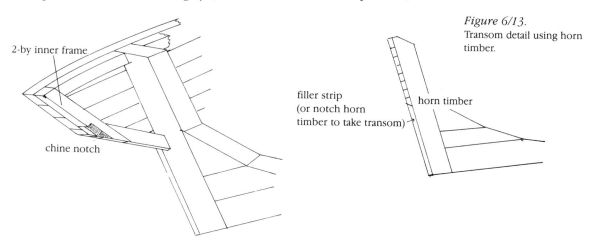

Figure 6/13.
Transom detail using horn timber.

2-by inner frame

chine notch

filler strip
(or notch horn
timber to take transom)

horn timber

sternpost assemblies with zigzagging, interlocking joints that today require a Zen master to assemble. Some young designers who've never seen a chisel draw the same sort of thing, too. The fact is that the simpler way likely will serve.

It's a straightforward job to find the transom's shape from the lofting. The *profile* view gives you the lengths—the distance from the rabbet to the chine and from the chine to the sheer. The *half-width* drawing shows you the transom's width at the chine and the sheer. With these dimensions you can draw out the transom full size on your frame table, just as you did the frames.

The simplest transom is just a sheet of plywood, several sheets if it's a big boat. A planked one is fairly easy, too: just screw the planks to the horn timber. Some people use both—a sheet of plywood topped with a layer of planks. Mahogany is the traditional transom wood, and it does look nice with a natural finish, but then so does fir.

Whichever way you go, you'll need some sort of backing—2 × 4s or 2 × 6s—around the transom's edges to support the ends of the planks and chines and receive the fastenings. On some boats, the transom planks overlap the side planks; on others, the side planks overlap the transom planks. I prefer the latter: it seems easier to have the side planks just run out past the transom and saw them off later.

Some people cover the corner of the planking at the transom with a metal angle to further protect the end grain. Because the metal angle is likely to trap water, I'd probably paint the end grain with epoxy to seal it. Actually, since the epoxy will protect the ends of the planks pretty well, you probably don't need the metal at all.

Rounded transoms look sharp but are a real pain in the ass to build. The old-time way is to glue and dowel up some thick wood, then adze away (power plane today) until it's the shape you want. The common modern way is to make a curved form and laminate several layers of wood over it. Frankly I don't see much point to all the bother. Rounded transoms and the like may look beautiful on the designer's drawings and show what a hot-shot draftsman he is, but they add little to the boat compared with how hard they are to build.

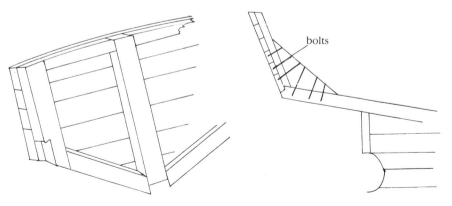

Figure 6/14. Alternative transom construction. Bolt transom to knee and sternpost just as you did the bow stem.

bolts

I would probably make the transom flat to save the extra work, but that's up to you.

Squaring up the frames

Now that you have the boat's basic skeleton erected, you can square up the frames. Starting at the midsection, measure from each sheer mark to the centerline of the keel, about 10 or 12 feet away, then shift the frame until the distance is the same. If it won't twist, loosen the nut holding the floor timber down. Now measure from your just-squared midsection frame to the next frame forward, and shift it until it's in line and all the measurements are equal.

Lay some 1×6s down each side of the sheer crosspieces, and as you square one frame, nail the 1×6 to the crosspiece on each side. This will hold the frame "square" while you plank. Keep going until you've done all the frames. Nail and brace everything well; there'll be a lot of pressure exerted during planking. Run some bracing from the frames down to the floor to keep the whole works straight. When you're through, go back and tighten down the nuts on the floor timber bolts.

Installing the chine piece

You *could* start planking now, but I like to go ahead and finish off the entire framework first. That way I can start planking and keep at it until I have a hull, without feeling that I'm going backwards every time I have to stop planking and redirect my thought processes towards a different problem. I don't know about you, but the older I get the less I like rapid changes. I like to psyche myself up for one problem at a time. Otherwise, I just tend to pour another drink and put it off for a bit.

Anyway, now that the frames are all squared up, it's time to install the chine. There are several ways to do this, the traditional way being to steam a heavy piece of oak around the hull. That's too much bother. It's far easier, and probably stronger, to laminate a chine from several layers of thin stock, which is why I went on earlier about cutting the chine notch to take several thicknesses of 1-by material.

Measure the inside height of the chine notch at any frame, since the notches are all the same, to see how wide a board you'll need for the first piece. For instance, a typical 35-footer might need a 1×8, a 1×6, and one piece of 1×4. The pieces don't need to run full-length because you'll be overlapping the butts.

It's important that you position the first piece of the laminated chine far enough back from the stem rabbet so that the following layers form a smooth, straight run along the outer face of the chine into the stem rabbet. If they don't, the planking won't hit the rabbet. If

Figure 6/15. (A) First chine piece pattern laid out on a wide board. (B) Sawing out the chine piece with a Skilsaw. (C) After glue dries on succeeding chine layers, remove screws and fill holes with glued wood slivers.

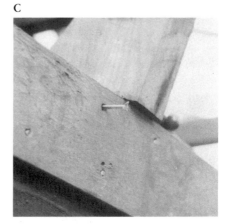

you're too far outboard you can plane it down, but if you're too far inboard, you'll have to glue on another 5- or 6-foot piece and plane it down to make a smooth run. Of course, you can re-cut the stem rabbet, but that looks pretty shoddy since the last side plank will be on a different plane than the ones above it.

The end of the chine is beveled to fit as well as possible, and then simply screwed to the stem. Screw the first layer in good, and after the other layers are glued on, put big screws through the entire end into the stem.

Finding the position of the chine's first layer is easy enough. Take a 6- or 8-foot piece of whatever you're using for the first layer and hold it in the chine notches. Scribe the end and rough cut it so that it hits the stem more or less where the plans say it should hit. This is usually pretty obvious, because the bottom rabbet and the stem rabbet intersect at the chine, and there will be a definite "corner" at the spot. If there's a problem seeing this spot, unroll the lofting and measure how far forward this spot is from the station just aft of it.

If you're making a three-layer chine, nail two more 6-inch pieces onto the first piece. Cut these roughly to the correct angle to hit the stem also. Now, simply hold this whole thing in the chine notch and against the stem, and move it around until the outer layer is a smooth run into the rabbet. Make a mark where the first layer hits the stem, and you've got it.

The simplest way to make the chine piece is just to wrap a wide board around the notches, and resaw whatever notches need to be higher to get the board to fit. Then whack off the bottom edge flush with the bottom of the frames. This works fine, but although it sounds simple it's actually more work than doing it the "proper" way. It also results in an asymmetrical, rather sloppy look inside the boat, since the chine will be bigger in some places than in others. And you know how asymmetry bugs some people.

I finally tried doing it the "professional" way, and I think it's the best: it looks neater, and it's actually easier than resawing the frame notches. This way you find the chine's shape by a process called *spiling*. You'll need to do some of this when planking, so you might as well learn it now.

Rip a sheet of 1/4-inch plywood into 3-inch wide strips, and tack them into the chine notches. You want this pattern to start at the stem and extend back a fair distance, say 16 feet. You want to use pieces as long as you can because it's easier to wrap a long piece around the hull than a short one. However, don't make one real long and the second half short!

If you're building a smaller, double-ended boat, make the pattern butt about in the middle so you'll be able to use long pieces for the chine on each end. It doesn't matter with a transom boat, because you won't be bending the chine pieces so much at the stern.

Overlap the butts between strips and nail them securely. Be careful not to work any edge-set into these strips; just let them lay as they want. If one 8-foot piece won't hit all the notches in its path without edge-set, saw it off and nail on another running at whatever angle you need to hit the notch. You have to hit all the notches.

Now, put a horizontal mark on the pattern at about the middle of a notch. Measure up from this mark to the top of the notch, and write that above the mark; measure down to the bottom of the notch and write that distance below the mark. Do this at every notch.

Remove the pattern and lay it on whatever board you're using for the first piece of the chine. This plank will have to be fairly wide, probably a 10- or 12-by. Tack the pattern down, then make marks above and below the center-of-notch mark to the dimensions written on the pattern. Remove the pattern, start an 8d finish nail at each mark, bend a batten around the nails, draw the line, and saw it out. It should fit pretty well. Now paint the chine notches well with preservative, slop on some tar, and install the first piece. Screw it just well enough to hold in position, because, as mentioned earlier, once all the layers are on you'll go back and put heavy screws through the whole works. Remember about positioning this first piece back from the rabbet!

If your boat has wide frames, or if it's a longish hull that has a "flat" area amidships, you can just trim this first piece to end in the middle of a frame and butt the next piece right to it. The proper way is to end it halfway between two frames, allowing the second layer to hold the butts of the first layer in a smooth curve. But butting on frames works OK, and it's easier.

Once you have the first piece of the first layer on, make another pattern, saw out another piece, and finish the first layer of the chine. Simply repeat the process for each succeeding layer, using the patterns you've already made. These following layers won't have to be as wide as the first one, because the V-bottom frames make the chine skinnier on the outside than they are on the inside. If you want to know exactly how wide this next piece has to be at each frame, run a handsaw down through the first piece at each frame, until the teeth lie flat along the bottom frame face. Make this second piece just a hair wider than you need. It's easier to trim the chine in place than to try to figure out the exact size.

Now glue on the second piece. This is one of those places where plastic resin glue works fine. I think it's preferable to epoxy in this situation because it has a lot more working time (except for the slow-kick, 1-to-1 mixes), it's considerably cheaper, it's less messy, and it will hold quite well, backstopped as it is by all the plank fastenings.

To clamp this chine properly you'd need about 500 clamps, so I'd use #12 wood screws instead. There's a lot of screwing to do here. Although a brace and bits makes a fine driver, a 3/8-inch, variable-speed reversing drill motor is far faster and a lot less work. Stainless screws work well for this job because they're strong enough to take repeated inserting and withdrawing with a power driver.

After the glue dries, remove the screws and fill the holes with glued slivers of wood. You don't want to leave fastenings in the chine because you'll be fastening the planks here, and you'll almost certainly hit one with your drill. Repeat this process until your chine piece is the required thickness.

Using 1-by material to laminate the chine is a good way to go because the 3/4-inch stock is easy to bend, especially in longer lengths. With bigger boats where the curves amidships are more gradual, there are shortcuts you can take. Recently I made a 44-foot-long chine piece using two layers of 1-by at the stern, butting that against a long piece of 2-by, which was easy to bend in the middle area, then two more pieces of 1-by at the bow. I added two more layers of 1-by in the stern area, which overlapped the first two by 6 or 8 feet, then another single layer of 2-by from there, which overlapped the forward joint. Then I finished off the front with two more 1-bys. I ended up with a 3-inch-thick chine, but with less time-consuming laminating to do.

After you get all the layers on, screw your completed chine with big screws into each frame and on the ends, countersinking these screws a bit so they won't get in the way when you plane down the face. Notice I didn't say *if* you plane down the face; nobody gets the chine exactly right, and it's almost certain you'll have to trim the face a bit.

When assembling the chine, you might find that one frame is a bit narrow at the chine, or that a notch is cut too deep, and the chine piece won't touch the frame. The proper response is to remove the frame and put in a new one the correct size. The easiest way is simply to shim out the notch, and if necessary, the bottom face of the frame.

Now it's time to shape the bottom of the chines. Go back again and run the handsaw through the bottom of the chine at each frame

A

B

C

Figure 6/16.
(A) Find angle to trim bottom by running hand-saw through chine at each frame until saw teeth lie flush with frame face. (B) Lay batten along top of saw cuts and draw a line. Now all you have to do is whack out the wood below the line, staying flush with the bottom frame faces. (C) Sometimes you have to trim the face, too. Again, use a saw to get the exact depth.

Framing Up

until the saw lays flat against the face of each bottom frame (see Figure 6-16). This gives you a guide to whack toward on fairly close spacings; all you have to do is chop out the wood between the saw lines.

Take a long, flexible batten, like a 1 × 2, nail it to the face of the chine so that it connects the tops of all the saw cuts, and draw a line connecting these points. If you assembled each frame correctly, this will be a smooth, fair curve, but it's fairly common to have one frame or another a little off, say 3/8 inch or so. Don't worry about it! Just adjust the batten to "split the difference," as they say, then draw the line. You want the chine to flow in as smooth a curve as you can.

Now, you have a pencil line on the side of the chine indicating the actual intersection of the bottom and side, or chine, of the hull, and you have the saw cuts at each frame to guide you in cutting off the excess wood to shape the bottom. The best way to shape it is to rough it in with an adze, then finish up with a power plane followed by a hand "smoothing" plane. This is hard, physical work, but it feels quite traditional and is kind of fun.

Finally, you should finish up the top of the chine by running a Skilsaw along it to saw the top so it slopes downhill a bit, away from the planking-to-come. Alternatively, cut a little notch beside each frame, front and back, to allow any water to run off the top of the chine. You can also pour melted pitch along the top of the chine after the hull is planked. It's little things like this that make the difference in whether or not you have a long-lived hull.

Finishing the frame

There's just a few more things to do before you can start planking, and the illustrations in Figure 6-17 show them fairly well. In fact, to quote President Lincoln at Gettysburg, they do "far more than our poor power to add or detract . . . . " Just the same, here's a few comments.

Every joint located between two keel timbers and crossed by the rabbet line is a potential source of leaks, unless you block the path with a *stopwater*. A stopwater is simply a 3/4- or 1-inch-round piece of softwood, run through the keel in the middle of the rabbet line at each keel joint. The best way to make the dowel is to have a machine shop drill the correct size hole in a 6-inch-square piece of 1/4-inch steel plate. (You can make a dowel sizer from a piece of hardwood like oak, or even heavy plywood, but steel works better.) Rip a piece of wood on the table saw about 1/8-inch bigger than you need and plane it roughly round with a block plane. Now drive it through the metal plate, which automatically sizes the dowel.

Paint the dowel with preservative before driving it. This lubricates it and makes it go in easier. Drive it through, and trim it flush

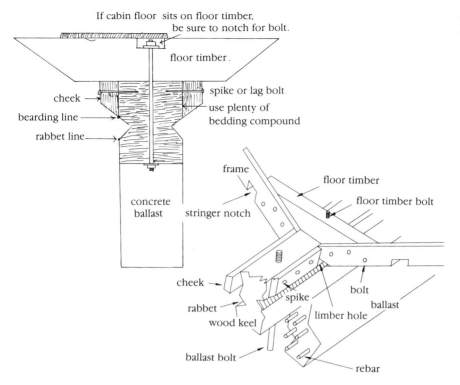

with the rabbet on each side. Stopwaters are necessary at all underwater keel seams, and won't hurt anything above water.

Install *cheek pieces* made from 2-by stock along both sides of the keel rabbet. These back up the rabbet and make a good wide base for the bottom planking butts to rest against. For some reason, "cheeks" seem to be unique to chine hulls, but I can't see how they'd hurt in a round-bilge hull. Use plywood patterns to get the shape and the curve of the bottom (parallel to the rabbet). Cut them to fit tightly between the bottom frames, and bevel the bottom so that it slopes the same as the angle of the bottom frames hitting the keel, which is supposed to be the same as the rabbet. Mount them flush with the bearding line, so they end up being a continuation of the rabbet. Fasten them with long spikes or lags, with plenty of tar or other bedding compound behind them.

These cheeks needn't be flush with the top of the keel, but they should be at least several inches high. I make them all from, say, 2×6, and let the tops lay as they will, unless they stick up higher than the keel. In this case I trim them flush.

Next you'll need to install several *bilge stringers* to support the bottom planks. These run more or less parallel to the keel and should be spaced about 12 to 18 inches apart at the widest place, which will be the midsection area. Toward the ends they'll run pretty close together.

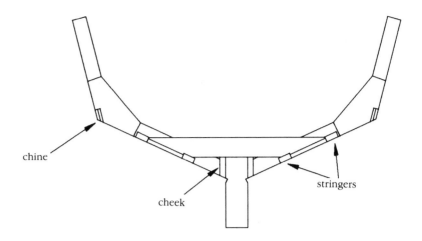

Figure 6/18.
Install bilge stringers
notched into frames to
support bottom planking.

chine

cheek

stringers

I use 2×4 stringers in any boat with 2×4 or larger frames. In short boats I make the stringer from one 2×4, and in longer boats I laminate it up from two pieces of 1×4 with overlapped butts. If you want thicker stringers, I think it's best to do it by gluing up layers between each frame on the inboard face of the installed stringer. This would spare you from having to notch the frame too much. You can also thicken up the chine this way if you feel like it.

Figure out how many stringers you're going to install, and split the distance between the keel and the chine, spacing them closely enough so you think they'll support the bottom planks when you're bashing around Cape Stiff or something. Take a long 1×4 and screw it lightly to the frames where you want to install the first stringer. Set a Skilsaw to whatever depth the notch needs to be plus the thickness of the 1×4 batten screwed to the frames. Now, using the batten as a guide, run the saw right along the batten and it will automatically cut the notches in the frames to the correct depths and angles. In places where the batten runs through a floor timber or a plywood chine piece, it's usually easier to move the batten once or twice and get several cuts. Of course you can also make these extra cuts with a handsaw, but the batten is easier.

It's easy to whack out the wood between the cuts with a chisel. After you chop out the notches, trial fit a short piece of stringer stock in each notch. If the notch looks too deep, shim it up a bit. If it's not quite deep enough don't worry about it. You're going to have to fair everything up later anyhow. It's actually better if the notch is a bit wider than the stringer; saves the bother of cutting waterways, you see.

After the notches are right, install the stringer. If it's one solid piece, just glue and screw it in. If it's laminated, glue and screw the first layer to the frames, then glue and screw the second layer. After the glue dries, pull the screws and fill the holes with slivers of wood glued in, just as you did with the chines.

Figure 6/19.
Cheeks spiked to keel to support garboard plank; frames notched to receive bilge stringers. Disregard the side planking. Yours shouldn't be on yet.

On boats with wide frames, you can avoid the hassle of laminating by just using 2 × 4s, and butting joints on a frame. This is poor construction, but if you have two or more stringers and the butts are staggered around, it works OK. These stringers don't have to hit the keel or the chine. Just saw them off flush with the last frame they cross before they'd hit.

After all the stringers are installed, fair up the bottom for the planking. You want it to be a straight shot from the rabbet, across the cheeks, over each stringer, to the chine. So take a straightedge and lay it on the stringers, sloping backwards about 20 degrees from square off the keel. Slide it around. It isn't hitting the chine or the keel everywhere, is it? So get out a power plane and start in on whichever stringer is high. This isn't very difficult and won't take too long. If shaping the chine wasn't enough impetus to get you to buy a power plane, you really should consider it now. They're pretty handy.

Plywood boats will handle the stringers a little differently. Since you'll be using several layers of plywood all glued together, I don't think you need such heavy stringers. I'd just use a single layer of 1 × 4 and butt them on the frames, although I'd stagger the butts well.

Plywood hulls will also need stringers running clear up the topsides. Space them a bit more closely, say 12 inches apart. Finally, install a stringer along the sheer. This one is a bit tricky because the top won't be square. Install it square, but let it run about 3/4 inch higher than the sheer mark so there'll be enough wood to cut or plane it down flush with the deck beams after the plywood side planking is on. You'll nail the deck into this sheer stringer.

After you do one side, stick a straightedge across the hull at each frame and put a level on it. Mark on the opposite side where the level says you're level. It's often hard to get the sheer exactly where it's supposed to be, and if you do one side as well as you can then level across to the other side, you'll get the hull pretty much symmetrical.

PLANKING

A FEW THOUGHTS ON PLYWOOD PLANKING

Before you go any further, give some thought to planking the hull with plywood. For some reason, plywood has fallen from favor as a planking material. Lots of little skiffs are made from it, but it's rare to see a large, heavy-displacement plywood boat here in North America. Big or little, the plywood boat suffers from a second-class image, which is silly, because plywood is just about the strongest material for the weight you can get. It's one of the easiest materials to work and is readily available everywhere.

When plywood first came out it was billed as a miracle material that would revolutionize the construction industry. It sure made a hit in house building, and it's pretty hard to imagine building any sort of structure without using the stuff. But boats are different. Never mind that plywood, for its weight, is stronger than steel, far stronger than fiberglass, and has all the flexing powers of wood. Never mind that, like wood, plywood doesn't suffer from condensation, so that it doesn't need added insulation to keep your interior dry. Never mind how quick and simple plywood is to work with. People in the States just don't like it, and if you build a large plywood boat you can expect a lower resale value than for any other material except ferrocement. Yet in Europe, plywood boats are quite popular, and several are even made by production shops.

Perhaps plywood's bad rap is a carryover from the early 1960s, when some really shoddy plywood was around. There was a story making the rounds of the Oregon mill town where I grew up that some plywood was being made with animal blood and wheat for glue. It looked just like exterior glue, but it would come apart when the plywood got damp. The story was that some of our plywood was going to China, which wasn't our friend at the time, and our guv-'ment wanted to mess up their construction industry. Even though this stuff was intended for the export market, apparently a lot found its way into American lumberyards, too. Even today I've had an occasional piece of ACX plywood come apart just from the dampness in the air, which makes it really worthless stuff for a boat *or* a house.

I try to buy plywood stamped by an Oregon mill. I've never had problems with plywood made there. I've also heard that Lauan plywood from the Orient is pretty good stuff. Regardless of where it's made, before you buy it, look at the edges. If you see a lot of big voids, don't take it.

Like everything else, plywood has a few disadvantages: It's boring to work and hard to repair. Compared with traditional planking, it doesn't look as neat, has a lower resale value, and it just isn't as ''nice.''

On the other hand, plywood is quick and requires very little skill to work, it doesn't need caulking, it's super strong, it will never leak, and when covered with glass cloth and epoxy resin it will never be eaten by teredo worms. In many areas of the country, it might be the only thing you can get, and it probably will be cheaper than planking-quality wood.

There may even be a solution to poor resale value. Plywood is made from several layers of wood glued together, with the grains running at 90 degree angles to one another. Cold-molded construction, which is just multiple layers of wood glued together at about 90-degree angles, is all the rage these days in wooden boatbuilding. Perhaps if you say your boat is ''cold molded,'' and not mention plywood, it will actually be worth more! Just a thought.

As I mentioned in Chapter 3, there's all sorts of ways to go with plywood planking—from the first-class, all-marine plywood approach to using lumberyard AC, with any number of variations in between. Let your pocketbook be your guide. If you're on a real budget, or if you live on a ranch in Nebraska and can't get anything else, don't hesitate to use AC exterior if your choice is between just using that and not having a boat. If you need a memory refresher to help you decide, turn back to Chapter 3.

Anyway, practically any chine hull, and some round-bottom hulls, can use plywood planking. You'll read that the hull must be ''conically developed'' to take plywood, but that isn't necessarily true. It's really surprising how much you can bend plywood if you don't know it can't be bent.

Using the multiple layers of plywood I recommend you'll find it pretty easy to bend the material to fit the boat's shape. Two $3/8$-inch sheets will bend around a hull a lot easier than one $3/4$-inch sheet, and be simpler to handle because each sheet is lighter weight. If a full sheet just won't bend into the bow or stern, you can practically always make it go by ripping it into 6-inch-wide strips and running it on a diagonal, then going back and running another layer over it diagonally in the other direction (see Figure 7-1).

This is cold-molded planking (more on this later), which as I said is quite popular these days, although usually with solid wood instead of plywood. It's been around since the late 1800s, when it was known as ''Ashcroft'' planking, used originally on British lifeboats. They didn't have epoxy glues back then, but it still seemed to work! This is just another reminder that there's very little new under the sun, either in building or design ideas, although the names and methods may change over the years.

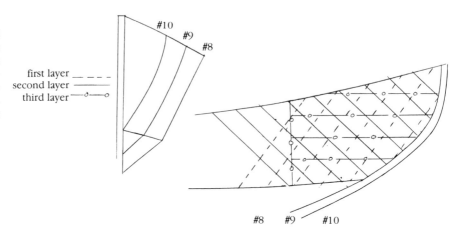

Figure 7/1.
Narrow strips of plywood placed diagonally can be used if bow or stern has a lot of curve to the sections. This method also allows hulls with compound curvature to be planked with plywood.

first layer _ _ _ _
second layer ————
third layer —o—o

#10
#9
#8

#8   #9   #10

Getting started

I'd make a plywood hull the same thickness as a hull with regular planking. Theoretically you don't need to for strength, but you want the weight for puncture resistance and to maintain the basic idea of heftiness that I think appropriate for all offshore boats.

How thick can you make a plywood hull? As thick as you like! I saw a 65-footer with a plywood hull that was 2 inches thick—four layers of 1/2-inch plywood. The owner told me he rode out a hurricane in it; the hull stayed absolutely tight, and it made no creaking noises at all. Plywood is good stuff!

As we discussed in Chapter 6, the framework for a plywood boat requires numerous longitudinal stringers notched into the frames to which to nail the plywood: one at the sheer, several between the chine and sheer, and several between the rabbet and chine. There's no exact placement to follow: just "split the difference" so they curve more or less naturally without really having to force them into position (see Figure 7-2).

Figure 7-3 shows a boat planked with three layers of plywood. The dotted line is the first layer, the solid line is the second, and the long dashes with a circle between them is the third. At the bow the sides are higher than 4 feet, the standard width of plywood, so you make a butt on one of the longitudinals, then lap it well with the second layer. Figure 7-1 shows the bow pieced in with 6-inch-wide strips, which as I said will wrap around almost any curve. Many boats won't need this treatment, and before you bother doing it, try bending a full sheet in.

The thinnest stock I'd use to make up these multiple layers is 3/8 inch. It's quite flexible yet still stiff enough to bend "fair"; 1/4 inch is just a bit thin and can sag between the nailing surfaces. The shape of the hull will determine the thickness of plywood you can use. Since the fewer layers you use the less work it will be, I'd first try 1/2-inch ply. Start at the place on the hull that has the most curve and see if

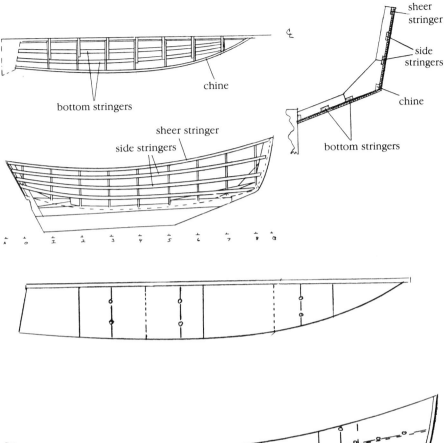

Figure 7/2.
Install longitudinal stringers to support the plywood planking. Try to let them run naturally; don't force them into position.

sheer stringer

side stringers

chine

bottom stringers

sheer stringer

side stringers

chine

bottom stringers

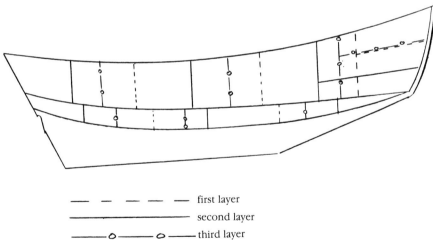

Figure 7/3.
Use two or more layers of thin plywood rather than one thick one. Stagger the butts.

— — — — — first layer
———————— second layer
———o———o——— third layer

you can get the plywood to bend on. If it won't bend on the sides, it might on the bottom.

The easiest way to fit the plywood is with patterns. As I've said numerous times before (and will again), the easiest way to fit *anything* is with patterns. Rip a sheet of 1/4-inch ply into 3-inch wide strips, and make a pattern for each piece you're putting on the hull. Again, use 3/4-inch carpet tacks to hold the pattern together.

Planking

97

When installing the first of the plywood planking pieces, glue and nail them well to the framework with ring nails. You can get galvanized ring nails for less money than bronze, although they're getting hard to find. Glue and nail the second layer well to the first layer. Use small screws at the end butts if they fall between stringers or a frame, and it doesn't look as if the end is lying tightly against the first layer.

I just might use epoxy glue for this plywood lamination. Regular powdered glue works fine on a deck lamination, but that has the assistance of the curved beams forcing the second layer to lay tightly to the first layer. On the hull, you generally won't have any curve to the frames—and not much per 8-foot panel—and it might be hard to get each layer to lay really tightly against the previous layer.

Since epoxy, the wood butcher's pal, prefers loose fits, it's just the ticket for plywood planking. The problem is the speed with which the stuff sets up, so I'd use one as slow to kick off as I could find. There's companies making a 1-to-1 mix that takes a good hour to kick, which gives you plenty of time to nail down a panel.

Although you don't have to be too compulsive, you should fit the pieces of planking together pretty well. If you have any really bad fits after you finish one layer, go back and fill them with a mixture of epoxy and sawdust. Space the butts of the second layer so they overlap the butts of the first layer as much as possible. Try to space the butts of a third layer to miss the others, and so on. After the third layer, butts can fall where they may.

On the final layer, I'd use nails long enough to go through all the previous layers and into the frame. Countersink the nails a hair if you care about a really smooth job, and fill in the dents over them with some kind of bondo.

Sheathing with cloth and epoxy

Now comes the worst part of the whole deal. You really should cover the plywood hull with a layer of glass cloth and epoxy resin, and this won't be any fun. Now, you don't *have* to, but I would, if for no other reason than fir plywood checks so badly, even when painted. (Mahogany-faced plywood doesn't seem to check at all.) The epoxy/glass coating also will keep worms and water from damaging the plywood. However, I've seen many boats made from MDO plywood that aren't epoxied, and they seem to last indefinitely. I have a 30-year-old lapstrake Chris-Craft Sea Skiff that appears to be planked with some sort of MDO, still looking good.

It wouldn't be so bad if you could just paint on a few coats of epoxy and call it good. Unfortunately, you have to use cloth, too. I've been told by the owner of an epoxy company that straight epoxy on plywood doesn't really last, and if he'll admit that, then it must be true.

Here's the one time when building the boat upside down would have been the thing to do, because hanging that cloth is going to be a first class pain in the tail. In fact, most of the cold-molded boats designed to be sheathed with epoxy and cloth are built upside down for that very reason. I still wouldn't do it, because it's more fun to see the boat go together rightside up, and other than hanging cloth, it's easier to build it that way.

I've never sheathed a large hull with cloth. But I think the way to do it is to staple the cloth right to the hull, at the corners, then paint on the resin. The cloth is just for protecting the plywood, and not for strength, so I'd just use a moderate weight, and I think that one layer is enough. I might wrap the chine with a second piece, overlapping both sides by maybe 12 inches.

When spreading resin, try using a tight "nap" roller, which is easier to use than a brush. If you use bronze or stainless staples you can leave them in. Again, I'd use an epoxy slow to kick off; I'm sure there's going to be all sorts of problems with the cloth trying to stretch or sag or something, and you'll need plenty of time to work it into position before the stickum sticks.

And use epoxy, not polyester ("traditional" fiberglass) resin. Fiberglass resin certainly has its place, but not on wood. There's about 2,000 old plywood trimarans hauled out around the country with their fiberglass skins falling off that prove this point. Polyester resin just doesn't stick to wood.

I know some people claim they can make it stick. One idea I've heard is to mix up a batch with hardly any hardener, paint the hull with that, and after that dries use the normal polyester mix. That might work. I tried it on a skiff that held together fine for six years before it got crushed on the rocks, but I wouldn't risk it on a large boat. Enough epoxy to coat a hull doesn't cost all that much, and it almost always (I *have* seen failures) sticks well.

I've used a fast-setting epoxy to fix a leak in my truck's gas tank, *while it was leaking gas*, and it stuck! The stuff may cost more than polyester, but by God she do stick good. Coating the hull with cloth and resin is such an unpleasant job—whether you use polyester or epoxy—that I know you won't want to do it twice.

Once you have the stuff on the hull, you'll be faced with the really unpleasant task of sanding it smooth. How good a job you do on this is up to you. The one small boat I covered I never did sand because I didn't want to breathe all the dust. But if you want a smooth job you'll have to sand it. Most people use pieces of Styrofoam about 1 foot long as sanding blocks. The long pad keeps you from digging holes, and the Styrofoam is flexible enough to follow the hull's shape.

Another approach to smoothing the hull is to forget about most of the sanding and skim over the hull's surface with epoxy fillers. You can make this stuff yourself from epoxy thickened with talc, or use one of the various proprietary fillers available to do the job. Basically you smear the stuff over the hull and squeegee it smooth with a windshield wiper blade or the like. It's a bit like plastering a wall. If you do a good job, you'll have very little sanding to do.

Finally, although it's the "done" thing, I wouldn't coat the inside of the hull with epoxy. Plywood may be processed, like American cheese, but it's still wood, and it needs to breathe. I'd worry about moisture finding its way inside the wood and being trapped if you coated the inside with epoxy. Instead, I'd treat the inside with normal wood preservatives, just like a planked hull.

As I said before, plywood has revolutionized the house construction industry, and it's standard procedure for decks and interiors of many modern boats. Its strength, availability, and workability make it sort of a "natural steel" hull material, but more suitable for the typical backyard builder. Plywood makes an excellent boat; if the resale value suffers from snobbish and uninformed prejudice, who gives a hoot!

A FEW THOUGHTS ON PLANKING

Up until now, what you've been doing isn't much different from what you'd be doing if you were building a sawn-frame, round-bottom hull. But now, with the planking, the two hull types show their true colors as far as expense and ease of building go.

What kind of wood should you plank with? I covered some of this in Chapter 3, but the subject is so complex it may be useful to revisit it.

All different kinds of wood are used for planking, with the main criterion in most commercial and many pleasure boats being what was available locally. It really doesn't make sense to pay a lot extra for wood that isn't commonly available where you live, which usually means wood that doesn't grow in the area. It's true that specific uses might demand specific woods. For instance, if you want to cruise to the Arctic it wouldn't hurt to use oak planking. In some special situations requiring high strength to weight, the designer might suggest very specific woods of known strength. But like wines and musicians, imported wood has more glamour, and many designers won't specify a wood that doesn't grow at least 2,000 miles from their office, even if the native woods growing right in their neighborhood are considered desirable boatbuilding wood in other areas.

If your plans call for a specific variety of wood, there's no reason you can't use something else. Just use basic common sense. Say the plans call for 3/4-inch fir and all you can get is red cedar. Well, use that, but since it isn't as strong, you might want to go a little thicker, say to 1 inch. Also, red cedar swells and shrinks quite a bit, so you'd want to use good dry stock, and keep the topside widths down to around 3 inches.

It's true that boats built of local woods live longest in the climate zone in which the wood grew. For example, the softwood trading schooners built in the States back in the 1800s didn't live long in the tropics. Again, as I've been saying frequently and will continue to do so, liberal use of preservatives and good ventilation will do a lot toward solving that problem.

The planking will generally be the best wood in the boat. The standard planking wood is *vertical grain,* and will be clear or have small, tightly spaced knots. This stuff is nice because it swells and shrinks more across its thickness than it does across its width. If the wood is nice and dry when you use it, the boat will stay pretty tight above the water. This can be important!

I read about a boat that sailed to some tropic Island and anchored. Being in smooth water like this, the sides didn't get wet, and the planks started drying out and shrinking. The owner didn't notice, being from the Northwest where nothing *ever* dries out, and a month later, fat, dumb, and happy, he up-anchored and headed out. After an hour or so he noticed the boat was feeling a little "funny," and when he looked inside, he saw water over the floorboards, and more pouring in through the gaps between the planks. Well, he didn't have an engine, and the anchorage was straight into the trade-winds, so he had no choice but to keep going to the next Island. He barely made it afloat.

I wouldn't use anything wider than 4 inches for topside planking: The narrower it is the less it will swell and shrink. I'd also suggest you try to find vertical grain, or VG as it's called, at least for the topsides. It costs more, but not only is it more stable, it also takes a smoother paint job.

I came across such a good deal on clear, flat-grain 2×6s while building the boat I'm working on now that I put the last paragraph out of my mind and used it. The boat hasn't been launched yet, but it's been interesting watching the planking while the boat sits in my shop. In the summer, the seams loosen; in the winter they swell tight. Now, VG will do that too, but these wide, flat-grain planks are doing it a bit more than I care to see!

This was startling behavior, so I waited until the height of summer and caulked the thing really tightly with oakum spun almost into a rope. I'm hoping this will fix the problem; the planks haven't shown any light between them since last summer.

If I had ripped the 2×6s down to, say, 2×4, I don't think I would have had nearly as much of a problem. As it is now, if I ever go south with it I can see myself rigging up a garden-hose sprayer on deck and running seawater down the topsides for a day before leaving an anchorage, just to swell up the sides. If that happens, I think I'll just replank it—or nail 1/4-inch plywood to it and epoxy sheathe it. Perhaps, dear reader, I should have called this treatise "Boatbuilding in Hind-Sight," or maybe, "How I Wished I Done It." Oh well.

Although VG wood is undeniably preferable for planking topsides, flat-grain wood is perfectly acceptable below the waterline, where it will stay swelled up, and you really don't care how smooth the finish is. And it will work on the topsides, as long as it's good and dry and in narrow widths. Just be aware that the grain will mean you can't put on as smooth a paint job as you could on a hull planked with VG. On the positive side, flat-grain wood has better abrasion resistance than VG, and costs 25 to 50 percent less.

The planking wood must be good and dry before it's used. Now the best is air-dried, but that can be quite hard to find. Actually, if you buy green planking wood right when you start the boat, "sticker" it, and keep it covered, it might be dry enough to use by the time you're ready for it. Figure at least a year to dry it out. However, the simplest solution, although not the least expensive, is to buy kiln-dried wood, or KD, as the lumberyards call it.

A lot of people don't like KD, because they say that the kiln destroys the cells of the wood, making them less resistant to rot, and the board less flexible. This may be, but sometimes KD is all you can get, and I've used plenty of it. Remember, rot is caused by fresh water and a lack of ventilation. If you make sure there are no dead air spaces in the boat, and use plenty of preservatives, I don't think you need worry about KD planking. And if it's all you can get, well, it's a hell of a lot better than nothing.

For reasons of economy I like to stick with normal dimension stock, which means either $^3/4$ inch (1-by) or $1^1/2$ inch (2-by). The problem is that $^3/4$ inch is really a bit light for any boat over 28 feet or so, and $1^1/2$ inch might be hard to bend around a small boat with full ends. Variables enter in, of course. You can get by with $^3/4$-inch fir planking in lighter-displacement boats over 30 feet, especially if you back it up with closely spaced intermediate frames between the main frames (more on this later).

If you're building a larger boat and want planking thicker than $^3/4$ inch, the thing to do is buy one planking-grade 2×4, as long as you can get—often 18 to 20 feet. (Consider the type and species, too. Air-dried fir will bend easier than KD fir, and air-dried cedar will bend easier than that. On and on.) Find the part of the boat with the sharpest curve, which on a double-ender usually is the stern at the sheer, clamp it to the stern stem, and see if you can bend it around the hull. Clamp it to the frames and wait a day to see if it will crack. If you can get it around without breaking it you've got it made, and you can use 2×4s for the whole topsides. If it won't go, you have the choice of building a steamer and steaming the ends, which is a pain in the ass, or having the lumber planed down.

Assuming, like me, you'll opt for the easy way out, take the 2×4, or a new one if you broke the last one, to a cabinet shop or milling joint and have it planed down to $1^1/4$ inch. That should go on OK. If it doesn't, rather than plane off any more, check with the lumberyard to see how much "$^5/4$" wood costs. It might be cheaper to buy this stuff, which is commonly used for stair treads, than to pay for the 2-by and the milling charge. You might consider buying your own thickness planer, too. This is a handy tool to have, and I see what looks to be good-quality small ones on the market these days for around $700; under $400 for the smallest ones. Take care of it, and you could probably sell it for only a small loss when you're done.

On your search for suitable planking wood, I'd stay away from the big lumberyards at first; call around to small mills and see what they can do for you. As they say, let your fingers do the walking through the Yellow Pages! But don't buy anything until you check the prices at the big lumberyards: sometimes they have deals. Also, many lumberyards will let you go through the stacks and take what you want, as long as you restack things neatly. Sometimes some good stuff ends up in the construction-grade pile. For instance, after Mount St. Helens blew up, a lot of old-growth fir was knocked down in the blast. After the lava cooled, Packwood Lumber went up and got it, and for several years some Seattle lumberyards had really beautiful construction-grade fir, much of it almost clear VG. Don't be hasty buying your planking. You should be thinking about it well before you need it; thoroughly research your area before buying from anybody.

How much will you need? Well, for the topsides, measure the length around the sheer; measure the length of the longest side frame up near the bow. If the distance around the sheer is, say, 40 feet, and the length of a side frame near the bow is, say, 4 feet, and a 2×4 is $3^1/2$ inches wide, then you'll need 4 feet divided by $3^1/2$ inches times 40 feet, times two for both sides, which comes to 1097 linear feet. This will be pretty close.

In January, 1990, top-grade green VG fir was available for $2.20 a board foot at a mill near me (one linear foot of 2×4 equals .66 board foot). So, buying the best grade would have cost $1592.84. That's probably at least five times as expensive as the cheapest way, using culled construction-grade, but if you can afford to go first class, do it. If you can't, then see how much top-grade flat-sawn lumber costs, and use it. But remember what I've learned from bitter experience on my last boat: It's better to pay a few hundred bucks more for good stuff, at least on the topsides. You'll save a lot of hassle.

HOW TO PLANK A CHINE HULL

Before you can get started planking, you'll have to figure out some sort of staging to get you high enough off the ground so your waist is even with the sheer. I've done it all sorts of ways, and come close enough to breaking my neck often enough that I take the trouble to do it properly nowadays.

I build six or eight tall sawhorses, about 8 feet high, 3 or 4 feet wide, with legs about 7 feet apart on the ground. To keep the horse

Figure 7/4.
Before you get started planking, make six or eight staging horses. These should be tall enough to bring the sheer waist high. Use 2 × 4s for frame and steps, with 1/2-inch plywood gussets at the top. X-brace one side if the horse sways much.

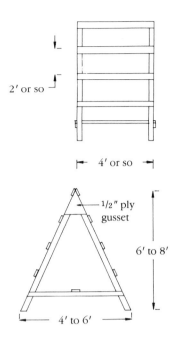

2' or so

4' or so

1/2" ply gusset

6' to 8'

4' to 6'

from swaying, I nail 2 × 4 crosspieces up one side at 2-foot intervals to serve as steps, and nail a 2-foot-wide piece of plywood across the top on the opposite side. I walk on 2 × 10 or 2 × 12 planks about 16 feet long, with a 2 × 4 nailed crossways on the end of every other one so the plank can't walk off the crosspiece of the horse (this happened to me once). Lay these planks down, then connect them with planks laying on top of them, and edge-nail them to the lower one with 16d "duplex" staging nails.

There's all sorts of ways to plank a boat, but planking chine hulls can be the simplest, and this is the simplest way to plank chine hulls. Here's what Sam Rabl called "Planking a la Maryland," with variations on the theme by me.

You start planking at the sheer and work down. First, take a long 1 × 2 batten, fasten it to the sheer mark at one end, and wrap it around the hull, lining it up with the sheer marks at each station. Sight down the batten and make sure the curve is fair. If it isn't, adjust it until it is.

Now take a straightedge long enough to go right across the hull, place one end on the sheer batten, and hold the other end at the sheer mark at the same station on the other side of the boat. It should be level right across. Assuming the frame has been erected "square" to the floor, make a new sheer mark if it isn't level across. Do this for all the rest of the frames. If you find a series of frames all need to be adjusted the same amount, it means the hull probably is leaning. Things should be pretty straight, though. You had to plumb-bob the frames to erect them, and should have caught any lean then. It never hurts to doublecheck.

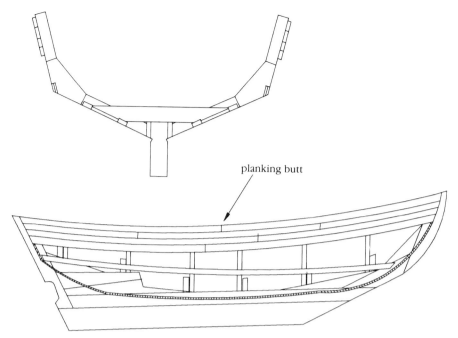

Figure 7/5.
Start planking at the sheer and work down to the chine. Stagger the planking butts well. Note that there's more space to plank forward than aft; you'll have to fill in the space with stealers.

planking butt

You'll want a minimum of eight **C**-clamps, with a throat at least 2 inches larger than the combined thickness of the frame and planking, and at least three sliding bar or pipe clamps, with bars long enough to span the side from sheer to chine. It wouldn't hurt to have a 12- to 18-inch-deep, 2-foot sliding bar clamp for holding the end of a plank in the stem rabbet. I bought one at Hardwick's Hardware in Seattle for $45, and it was worth it!

Get the longest plank you can find, fasten one end to either end of the boat, then wrap it around the hull, clamping it to the sheer marks at each station. A second person is a big help here, although I've hung a lot of long planks alone by using a rope tied to the ceiling to hold up one end. I paint the frame's faces, and the back of the plank, with preservative before installing it. Some people bed each one with tar or Dolphinite, too, but that's a lot of hassle. It can't hurt if you want to bother with it.

As mentioned before, keep the topside strakes narrow; 3½ inches wide is plenty. I really suggest you use VG grade here, but if using flat grain, pay attention to the "annual ring" grain pattern at the end. You want to position the plank against the hull so that the rings of the end grain are curving towards the frame, rather than away. The plank is likely to cup a bit, and this will make the outer edges get tighter rather than open.

Assuming you have a helper, have him wrap the plank around the hull while you holler "Up!" or "Down!" until the plank is aligned with the sheer marks. Clamp it at each frame as it lines up. You can use screws or nails to hold on the planking; I prefer screws. I use

Figure 7/6. Long planks can be awkward to deal with when working alone. Use your imagination! Rope tied to a rafter or a 2 × 4 clamped to a frame will support a plank end while you work it in place. Always start planking at the end of the boat and work toward the middle. Use as long a plank as you can find. It's surprising how much you can bend even a 2 × 6 without steaming if it's long enough. In this photo I've hooked a "come-along" to a frame on the opposite side of the hull to pull in a plank that didn't want to go. It went! When you're doing this stuff, try to stand in a spot past the end of the plank; if she breaks and you're in the way, you'll be knocked flat.

fairly heavy ones—#12 on 3/4-inch planks, and #16 on 1 1/2-inch planks—twice as long as the planks are thick. Use three at the plank's ends and two, staggered, in each frame.

If you have a heavy-duty 3/8-inch variable-speed drill motor rigged with a screwdriver bit, and another one rigged with a Fuller countersink bit, you can drill the hole for the screw and a wood bung in one operation, and whip in the screw with a second. Rub Ivory soap on the screws before driving them, and they'll go in much easier. And try not to scratch the galvanizing! Hold the driver square to the hole, and lean on it as you drive the screw. Don't fasten down the last 6 feet of this first plank for now.

Now, if your boat is short enough to wrap two planks around the sheer with plenty of overlap, take a second long plank, fasten one end to the opposite end of the hull, *one plank width down* from the sheer, and wrap it around, clamping it at each frame as you go. This plank needs to run underneath the first plank at least 5 feet—the more, the better. This will force the first plank's outer end to carry a fair curve, avoiding a "hard spot" at the butt. On longer boats, where this second plank can't overlap the first one sufficiently, center the second plank under the end of the first one.

You'll need to put a *caulking seam* on the top edge of this second, and all succeeding, planks. The caulking seam starts at 1/3 to 1/2 the plank's thickness from the outer face, and tapers to about 1/8- to 3/16-inch wide at the plank's face (see Figure 7-7). You also want a caulking seam on the end of a plank where it butts against a stem or a transom, and one in one plank only at the butt joints between planks.

You'll need to mark the seam with a pencil line. Hold the pencil with your thumb and forefinger, and let the forefinger's knuckle ride on the board at the correct distance in from the plank's face. This way you'll be able to put a straight line down the plank with little fuss. A power plane makes short work of trimming the top seam. Use a block plane or a disk sander (the fastest and easiest way to remove a

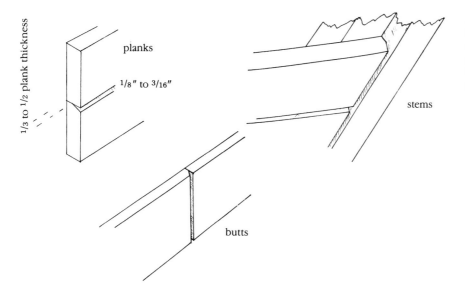

lot of wood) for the end-of-plank seams; a power plane will tear up the end grain too much.

Put sliding bar clamps on the two planks where they overlap, and pull up the second plank tightly against the first. (Use 3-inch square pads made from 1/4-inch plywood to protect the planks from being crushed by the clamps.) Fasten this second plank *only* where it overlaps the first one, leaving the rest of it clamped lightly to the frame. Now, go back and finish fastening the sheer plank. If it's a bit high or low, you can adjust the plank below—which is why you waited to fasten it.

Before you put on the next strake, decide where you want the planks to butt together. The butt joints should never fall on a frame face, although cheaper production builders often do it that way. Instead, cut off the first plank so that its end falls 1/4 the distance between two frames. You'll be installing intermediate frames later, so be sure you are 1/4 the distance between frames, *not* half.

Butt blocks (see Figure 7-8) should be *at least* as thick as the planking. I use 2-by blocks on all planking up to 2-by. The block

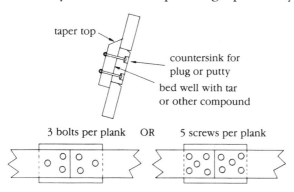

Figure 7/8.
Butt block details. Butt blocks are wider than the planks they're joining. Use 6-inch blocks with 4-inch planks. Make blocks narrower than the space between frames and taper the top to drain off moisture. Try to get two full planks between any butts in the same line of plank.

Planking

107

Figure 7/9.
Try to space butt blocks as far apart as possible, without wasting material of course. Remember to space butts 1/4 the distance between frames to leave room for the intermediate frames, which will be installed later.

should be wider than the plank so that its face bears on the plank above and below it, too. If your planking is 4 inches wide, make the butt blocks from 6-inch-wide stock. The butt block should have a 3/8-inch gap between it and any frame, including the intermediate frames to be installed later (think ahead). Trim off the butt block's top at a 45-degree angle to keep water from accumulating there. If the block is in a part of the hull with much curve, you'll have to shape its back to match the curve of the planking. Again, a disk sander does jobs like this in a hurry. Install the butt block with lots of bedding compound behind it, and fasten each plank to it either with five screws, or with three bolts. (You'll only need bolts on really heavy-duty construction.)

As you plank the hull down to the chine, try to space the butts as far apart as possible. Of course, for ease of bending you want to keep the butts in the "flatter" part of the hull amidships. If you can avoid it, don't put a butt in line with another butt unless there are two solid planks between them. The boat won't break in half if you do, of course, but that's an old rule it doesn't hurt to follow. Finally, the butt blocks in the sheer strake should be positioned just a bit low, like 1/2 inch, so the deck will fit over it.

After you've got the first two strakes on one side, do the other side. You've already leveled the sheer from side to side with the fairing batten, but if the actual sheer plank missed the marks, then level across again by putting a straightedge and a level on the plank and marking the sheer on the opposite side. Standard boatbuilding practice is to plank both sides more or less at the same time to keep the weights and the stresses on the framework balanced. I hang two or three planks on each side, then move to the other side, and it works fine.

This is the very simplest way to plank, and it's amazing the amount of edge-set you can work into a long plank to force it to conform to the hull's shape, especially when there's a lot of flare to the sides. However, if you're building a hull with so much sheer that you simply can't edge-set the sheer plank sufficiently to have it lay fair, then you'll have to spile it (refer back to Chapter 6, where we found the chine's shape by spiling).

Wrap the first plank around the boat, at least 3 inches below the sheer, edge-setting it as much as you can so that it follows the sheer line. Now, measure the distance from the top of the plank to the sheer at each station. Lay out the station spacing and these dimensions on a wide plank, drive a nail at the station marks, bend a batten around them and mark the line, then saw the top to the curve. This should fit fine.

If you're one of those folks who believe edge-set is bad building practice, I suggest you read *Boatbuilding*, by Howard Chapelle (W.W. Norton, 1941 and 1969) or Bud McIntosh's *How to Build a Wooden Boat* (WoodenBoat Publications, 1987). These books will show you the time-honored (time-consuming) way to lay out planking. You see, some people say edge-set makes the hull develop "hog." Now this might be a possibility in a lightweight, bent-frame boat, but with the heavy-chine boats we're talking about here, it will be a cold day in hell before the massive keel and concrete ballast bend from the pressure of a few edge-set 2 × 4s.

Some of you might have noticed that I didn't mention shaping the top of the sheer plank to match the deck. You're right! It's far easier to align a square-edge plank with the sheer marks. After the deck beams are fitted, plane the top of the plank to match. The deck will end up being 1/4 to 1/2 inch lower than the plan, but so what? It's far easier this way.

Intermediate frames

After you plank about halfway down the sides it's time to install the *intermediate frames*. These serve several functions: They stiffen up the planks, provide additional support for deck beams, and help in building the interior furnishings.

Normally these intermediate frames are installed halfway between the main frames, although there's no reason you can't space them more closely. It all depends on the size of the boat, its intended use, and the spacing of the main frames. I always space the main frames closely enough so that I only have to install one intermediate between each pair of main frames. I end up with frames on 12 to 16 inch centers.

Intermediate frames generally are made the same size as the main frame, although they don't need to be. It's normal to bevel their edges to follow the planking lines, with the frames laying square to the centerline, just like the main frames. Although this is a bit of a has-

Figure 7/10.
Side planks look a bit
ragged before intermediate
frames are installed.

sle, it's quickly done on a table saw, makes a better-looking frame, and makes it easier to attach deck beams and bulkheads.

Intermediate frames are pretty simple to make. First, mark on the sheer and the chine the location of each frame's forward edge, on both sides of the hull. Now, working on one pair of intermediates at a time, put a straightedge across the hull between the marks of opposing frames, and measure the angle with a bevel gauge. Measure the frame's length, allowing several inches overlap at the chine (see Figure 7-11), and cut them roughly to length. Set your table saw to the angle you took off with the bevel gauge, and bevel both the front and back of the frame.

Set the frame in place, lined up with the marks, scribe around the chine's shape onto the frame, and saw out the notch. Stand the frame back up, mark its length, and saw off the top to run 1/2 inch or so below and level with the sheer. You want to leave some air space between the frame head and the deck.

Put lots of bedding compound on the notch, stand the frame back up, and clamp it at the sheer and chine. Run a pencil line down the outside planking indicating the center of the frame, and fasten it in with the same fastenings you used for the main frames. Fasten the bottom of the frame through the chine with a bolt. I put the bar clamps on the planks before fastening in the intermediate frames just to ensure everything is pulled in tight. When fastening, always put the first screw in the *bottom* of the plank. In fact, I do this on all planking. That helps pull it into the frame.

This is a pretty simple process, and it goes quickly. However, if the ends of the boat have much curve you'll have to laminate in the intermediate frames. This is time consuming, but not all that difficult.

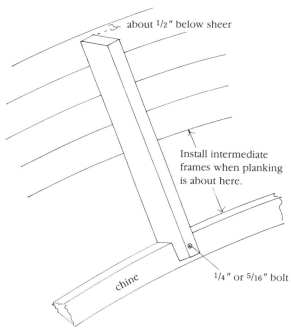

about 1/2" below sheer

Install intermediate
frames when planking
is about here.

chine

1/4" or 5/16" bolt

If the curve is gradual you can make the lamination using 1-inch pieces. The more the curve you have to deal with, the thinner you'll have to make the layers, of course. Recently I had to use 1/4-inch strips on a boat.

Lay out the location for these frames as you did before. Rip a piece of frame stock on the table saw and try it. If it doesn't bend in easily, rip it thinner. Once you get one that will take the curve, bend it into position and draw a pencil line on the planking on each side of the frame. Now, drill pilot holes through the planking and mark on the inside of the plank, next to the frame, where the holes are. When drilling the pilot hole, *think*. (Think ahead, Stupid! number 76.) On the forward side, lean the drill so the holes angle forward; on the back, lean the drill so the holes angle aft. That way the staggered screws won't miss the frame.

Nail the first strip to the hull with small nails, and spread glue (powder glue is fine; no need for epoxy) on its inboard face. Now spread glue on a second strip, and nail it to the first. Continue doing this until the frame is as thick as you want it. I don't make them as deep as the other frames—just big enough to fasten a deck beam to, say 2½ or 3 inches. When nailing, be sure that you *don't* put a nail near the mark you made on the planking where the screws will go.

Attaching this laminated frame to the chine can be handled several ways. The simplest is to bolt a ''sister,'' which is what they call a frame installed beside an existing frame, to the inside of the chine, next to the laminated frame. This sister piece should extend maybe 6 inches above the chine, with its top sawn off on a downhill slope so it looks neat. Bolt the laminated frame to the sister. Be sure to bed the joint well!

Planking

111

If the boat has a lot of overhang and you're laminating in curved frames that extend up the stem past the keel, you can drift-bolt in some extra floor timbers made from, say, 2 × 8s, and bolt the frames to them.

In places with a great deal of curve, it's simplest to laminate the pieces square to the planks, rather than trying to make them square to the keel. If deck beams, floor timbers, or something else needs to be fastened to them, you can fill the gap with a wedge-shaped shim. I know it sounds sloppy, but it works fine. If the curve isn't too great, you could cut the first piece on whatever bevel you need to make it square to the keel, assuming you want a "neater" job.

After the laminated frame is in place, clamp it tightly at the sheer and at the last plank you've hung on the hull, and screw it down good. If the hull sides have lots of curve, the planking probably resembles a staircase. This is where a deep-throat clamp is really nice: You can pull in the planks really tightly. Do the best you can; to pull the plank in even more, be sure to put the first screw in the *bottom* of the plank. Don't worry if you can't get the planks perfectly tight to the frame. It doesn't matter. The hull will be smoothed up later when you plane it off.

Planking to the chine

As your planks approach the chine, if the boat has any sheer at all there will be more space to cover on the ends than there is in the middle. The simplest way to deal with this is to use long *stealers*—wedge-shaped planks added to ends of plank runs to help them run parallel with the chine.

Let's say you're planking with 4-by (3½-inch) stock. Take a long 6-inch plank, and cut it into a wedge 6 inches wide at the stem and 3½ inches wide at the end. Put this stealer on the hull, put a 3½-inch plank in the middle, then another tapered one at the end if needed.

If you start doing this soon enough, you can even out the distances easily. But if you wait until you're near the chine you'll need more taper. To fill in the distance more rapidly, start with a plank 6 inches wide and taper it down to half the thickness of the middle plank. Now cut a section from the middle plank, half the plank's width and several frame spacings long, and fasten it on so that the long tip butts against the tapered plank. Now run another tapered plank down to fill the notched-out area in the middle plank (see Figure 7-12). Install enough stealers until the distance from the last plank to the chine is small enough to be covered by one plank. This last plank likely will be a shape that won't edge-set into place, so you'll have to spile it out of a wide plank.

Before you actually finish planking the side, you'll have to decide just how you're going to handle the chine connection. Figure 7-13

Figure 7/12.
Using stealers to gain
height at the boat's ends.
The bottom row of plank-
ing overhangs the chine
for now; it will be mitered
to meet the bottom plank-
ing after all the chine
planking is installed. Note
how the planking fasteners
are staggered. If they were
all in a line, they might
split the frames.

shows three different ways of doing it: mitered, bottom overlapped,
and side overlapped.

Never have the side overlap the bottom! The resulting joint is
under constant pressure from passing water and is impossible to keep
tight. I know: I did it this way on one boat and never could keep it
from leaking.

Shallow **V**-bottoms can get by with the bottom planks overlapping the sides. This is a simple, very common method that only
involves shaping the last side plank so that it continues the angle of
the chine. The bottom planks are easiest to fasten on with this
method, because you can let them run past the chine and saw them
off later. It won't work on a deep-**V** hull, however, unless the chine
piece is really wide, and it leaves the end-grain of the bottom planks
exposed. Some boats that are pretty flat in the middle but **V** sharply at
the bow switch from overlap to miter as the bottom planks approach
the bow.

A *mitered* chine joint is probably the best. Although it looks
tricky there isn't much to it, and I think I'd do it on any chine hull.
Just be sure to install the last side piece a bit wider than needed so
that it overlaps the chine by 3/4 inch to 1 inch. Clamp the middle

Figure 7/13.
Chine planking detail.

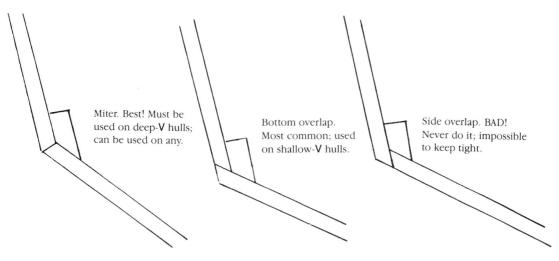

Miter. Best! Must be
used on deep-**V** hulls;
can be used on any.

Bottom overlap.
Most common; used
on shallow-**V** hulls.

Side overlap. BAD!
Never do it; impossible
to keep tight.

Planking

plank in position on the hull first, and draw a line on the end showing how much taper is needed to make a square-faced bottom plank butt tightly against it. Run a pencil down the chine to put a line on the inside of the plank showing where the chine lies. The line at the end shows the angle, and the line on the back shows how wide the plank needs to be. Unclamp it and rough-saw it out with a Skilsaw. Leave it a good 1/4 inch wide. After it's installed you can finish trimming it up with a rabbet plane. It's far easier to do this accurately *after* the plank is installed; things seldom line up exactly right on the second pass—at least for me.

Regardless of which system you use, be sure to put lots of bedding compound against the chine before fastening on the last plank—and, as Figure 7-12 shows, use lots of fasteners in this last piece.

BOTTOM PLANKING

As I've mentioned, the cross-planked bottom is a snap to do. You'll race through it and have a completed hull in no time at all. I see no reason to waste all the extra time and materials you'd need to plank a chine hull's bottom fore-and-aft. I know cross-planking might look odd to you, but believe me, it's worked for generations down South. It's strong, simple, and easy to repair; it's easy to figure out what materials you'll need almost to the inch; and it can be installed with minimal waste.

If you've been doing things in the order I've been writing about them, you'll have the cheeks and bilge stringers already installed. If you haven't done this, you'll need to do it before you can start planking (refer back to Chapter 6). Again, the planks need to lie flat between the chine, all the stringers, and the rabbet. If you didn't fair things up earlier, then do it now.

I'd suggest using 2 × 6 bottom planking for most boats, and 1 × 6s for smaller boats, say under 28 feet, unless they're heavy displacement, of course. If you use material wider than this the planks might swell up after launching and pop off. This would be a drag, so stick to 6-inch-wide planks.

Cut a piece of plank stock to roughly equal the distance from the chine to the keel at the middle of the boat, and hold it in position angled back from the keel, shifting it about until it seems to lie flat on all the stringers and the chine, and hits the rabbet.

There's no set rule governing the angle the planks have to take in relation to the keel. Most boats average 15 to 20 degrees; less angle than that often requires the planks to be twisted somewhere in the run; more than that just doesn't look right—at least to me. However, I've seen planks laying almost square to the keel, and I've seen them angled back as much as 45 degrees, so do what you please. Myself, I like 15 degrees or so.

Saw the bottom of this test plank to the angle required to hit the rabbet. Slip it into the rabbet, then saw the top at the angle required to hit the chine. Clamp this board in position, then cut a 6-inch piece of the same material. Lay it alongside the first piece at the chine and make a mark; do the same at the rabbet. Continue down the whole hull and mark where each plank will lie. Go back and measure the lengths of each plank from chine to rabbet, and write the length above each position on the chine plank. Put a heavy mark on the hull to show where, say a 16-foot plank, or a 14-, or a 12-footer—some common lumberyard length—will work. After you've measured the whole bottom, go back, total up all the lengths, and make a materials list. If you spend a little time at this you'll be able to buy just the material you actually need, with hardly any waste.

Now you're ready to go to it. Starting around the middle of the hull, fit the first piece, as always, using a pattern made from 1/4 inch plywood ripped into 3-inch strips. Use a short piece at the chine and one at the rabbet, and two overlapping long pieces clamped together to get the length. This first section is the only one that requires much thought. After you get it fitted the rest are very easy.

After fitting the first piece, clamp it in position. Lay a bevel square against the chine and the first plank and measure the angle. Take off the first piece, and lay it alongside a new piece of planking stock. The meeting side gives the plank length required, the bevel square gives the angle at the chine, and the lower half of the original plywood pattern gives the angle of the bottom. Nothing to it. After you get it marked, saw out the next plank with a Skilsaw.

After you've used the first piece to get the size of the next piece, put a caulking seam on the meeting edge, the chine, and the rabbet, and screw the first plank on. Use *lots* of bedding compound at the rabbet and the chine. I bed the stringers, too, and especially the end grain of any plywood gussets I cross. Bed everything! It can't hurt. Roofing tar works well here—it's cheap and long-lived—just messy.

Fasten the plank at the chine, rabbet, and stringers (you won't need to fasten it to a frame). On bigger boats with 2-by planks, the screws used at the chine and rabbet will be too long for the stringers, so you'll need shorter ones. I fasten the ends of 2-by planks with 3-inch #16 screws, and use 2 1/2-inch screws at the stringers, counter-sinking the screws for a wood bung just like the topsides. Of course there's no reason you can't fill the holes with a mix of cement and water; it's both simpler and quicker.

After this first plank is on, refit the second one to be sure it still fits, then repeat the process for the next plank, using each new plank to gauge the size for its neighbor, putting on the caulking seams, and installing the plank. On and on.

The angle you chose for the first plank at the rabbet will remain constant throughout the hull, but you'll notice that every five or six planks this angle you sawed on the bottom edge will be off and the

Figure 7/14.
(A) Adding final screws to chine plank after miter has been shaped and bottom planking is all on. It's easier this way. (B) Bottom planking going on. Planks are fastened at the chine, rabbet, and stringers. (C) Bottom planking finished. The planks were tapered to keep the angle the same at the rabbet.

plank won't fit the rabbet properly. Don't change this bottom angle. Instead, saw the next plank to the predetermined rabbet angle, but leave it several inches longer than it needs to be to fit. Clamp this plank to the stringers, as close to its position as you can, but at the angle required to get the bottom to fit into the rabbet.

Now measure this plank's distance from the adjacent plank. Say it's 2 inches at one end. Measure at the chine $2^1/8$ inch from the plank already installed and make a mark. Do the same thing at the other end. Remove the plank, draw a line to the marks with a straightedge, and saw the plank to this line. Hold it in position and mark its length, and saw it to fit at the chine. This trapezoidal plank will get the bottom angle back where it's supposed to be.

As I said, this will likely need to be done every five or six planks. If you don't do it, pretty soon you'll have the planks leaning way back, which isn't good. I think a 15 to 20 degree angle is the strongest.

Figure 7/15.
Plugging the fastener holes with wood bungs is a nice, restful job you can do while recuperating from more taxing tasks. Paint the screw hole with thick primer and drive in the bung. Make sure its grain is aligned with that of the planking.

Accurate fits are important, of course, but you have a little slack. Because of the big chine, the deep rabbet and cheeks, and the fact that you're really putting the tar to it, if you saw a plank 1/4 inch or 3/8 inch or maybe even 1/2 inch too short it will still work fine.

I always plank both sides of the hull at the same time to keep the weights and strains on the framework even. I don't know if it really matters, but about every 10 or 15 planks I switch to the other side.

Another thing to consider as you plank along are *waterways* in the frames to prevent water from being trapped in the unlikely possibility that your boat leaks. So, before planking over a place where a frame hits the keel, chop off the tip of the frame to make an opening to pass water. Granted, the odds are you'll be filling her up with concrete ballast, which will plug these waterways. Regardless, it's good to have them, especially at the launching. They allow water to travel to the boat's lowest point, where you'll have a pump waiting.

As you approach the very ends you'll likely have a bit of twist developing in the planks. This can be handled easily by sawing the planks into triangles; the last plank might end up with its grain lying fore and aft. Another approach is to shape a thicker plank to fit, but using triangular planks is a lot simpler.

The very last plank at the stem is tricky to fit, but no big deal. Make a plywood pattern of the shape required. Remember this plywood pattern is of the *plank's inside* face, so figure the bevels from the inside out, rather than outside in when cutting the piece. You'll probably cut the first one wrong, but you'll catch on.

FINISHING THE HULL

Now that the hull is planked, it's tempting to get right at the deck and interior. However, it's more "organized" to finish off the hull by smoothing and caulking it. If you're not experienced at caulking, it's probably better to caulk now, before the deck is in place, so you can look inside to see if you're driving the caulking completely through the seam or splitting the plank—both are easy for inexperienced caulkers to do.

Smoothing the hull

The side planking in particular probably looks a bit rough; almost like a staircase near the ends. Well, believe it or not, the old *smoothing plane,* which is one size down from a jack plane, is still the simplest way to smooth off the hull. Funny. This is one of the few places where there still isn't an electric tool that does the job.

When you're planing, concentrate on the edges; the middle of the plank usually can be left alone. Take long swipes at the wood, as long as you can. This is good exercise, but not too bad, although of course it all depends on how compulsive you are about a smooth finish. Speaking of which, I've never bothered planing the underwater area; suit yourself.

Once you've planed the hull fairly smooth, finish things up with a soft pad on a disk sander. Makita has one that's pretty neat; it's variable speed, and weighs 1/3 less than the others. Use 50- or 60-grit paper, and keep the machine moving to avoid digging holes. You don't have to get the hull perfectly smooth now, since you'll be sanding it one final time to remove excess seam compound.

Caulking

Caulking is sometimes called ''corking'' here on the West Coast, and caulkers are called ''corkers.'' This probably dates back to the old days when there were many full-time caulkers caulking up big craft. These fellows developed huge arms, and after a few years of day-in and day-out monotony, swinging a hammer and listening to the CLING . . . CLING . . . CLING of the hammer hitting the caulking iron, they tended to go deaf and walk around a little glassy eyed. After a day of caulking, the fellow just wanted a drink. Townspeople would see one go by and say, ''Ain't he a corker!'' Although this old expression is rarely heard these days, it used to be fairly common—often in conjunction with ''by cracky.'' For instance: ''By cracky, Sven, the way Ola caulked up my boat was a real corker!''

Call it ''corking'' if you want to preserve a nice example of West Coast vernacular, but the word is c-a-u-l-k-i-n-g. Caulking.

Caulking both stiffens and leak-proofs a hull, and traditionally consists of hard-driven strands of cotton or oakum topped with an elastic seam compound. Now, there's some new seam compounds on

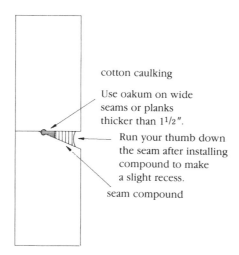

cotton caulking

Use oakum on wide seams or planks thicker than $1^{1}/_{2}''$.

Run your thumb down the seam after installing compound to make a slight recess.

seam compound

the market made from powerful chemicals which their Makers claim work so well you don't need cotton.

I used one of these once. The can said, "It swells! It shrinks! It's the Best Seam Compound you can Get!" Well, three months later it had separated from the seams all over the boat. It did stick real nice to the cotton caulking, though. It took a month with a razor blade to cut the stuff out of the hull and recaulk the boat.

Caulking material is either cotton or oakum—sometimes both. Either material can be bought at a good marine store, although good Norwegian oakum (the best) is getting hard to find. Where you use which is a question of individual style, although it seems pretty commonly agreed that cotton alone should be used on planking up to $1^{3}/_{8}$ inch or so thick, with oakum reserved for thicker planking. But then, some people say to put in a layer of cotton first, then a layer of oakum; other people say use a layer of oakum first, then a layer of cotton.

I don't know. I do know that my friend Dave Ullin, who is, among other things, a corker of a caulker (by cracky!), doesn't use both materials in the same seam, so I don't either. It doesn't seem to me that a seam less than 2 inches thick is gonna have *room* for all that stuff and still have the wood touch the plank above when the hull swells.

Anyway. Cotton and oakum come in *bales* consisting of long strands, sort of like really soft yarn. To prepare either material for caulking, you have to separate and spin it.

Sit down on a stool and put a clean box on each side of you, with the caulking material in the middle. Separate the strand in half, letting each strip fall into its box. Depending on what brand you get, you might have to separate it into 3 or 4 strips, as some of the stuff is pretty heavy. After you've separated it, roll it between your palms to tighten it up as you feed it into another box. (The finished strand

Figure 7/17. Making oakum caulking from several strands of marline spun together with an electric drill motor in reverse. The peculiar-looking round object is an old safe, which some members of the Diver's Institute of Seattle found in an abandoned building. They used $100 worth of acetylene to burn through it, and found a nickel.

should be about the size of your little finger.) I like to do this in front of my woodstove, with Getz and Gilberto on the machine, a corn-cob pipe, and some Cognac. It's quite relaxing, and you'll need to prepare your nerves for the coming CLING . . . CLING . . . of driving this stuff into the seams.

There's another way, although I won't know how it works until I launch my current boat. I thought of this when faced with filling the big seams resulting from planking the boat with wood that wasn't quite as dry as I thought. There were some *real* gaps to fill, so I thought oakum would work better than cotton.

Old-time marline is made of the same spun and tarred hemp as oakum, except it comes to you in a neat ball, sort of like string. It's available in different thicknesses, depending on brand, from 1/8 inch to 1/4 inch or so.

It seemed to me that a strand of this marline was just like a neat strand of separated and rolled oakum. So I unwound two rolls, tied one end to a fence, and hooked the other end to a hook chucked in an electric drill. Running the drill motor in reverse, I rolled the two strands together to make a solid rope, then I did another with three strands. Dave the corker caulker was there when I did the first one, and it met with his approval. The speed was really impressive, too. We found we could "spin" several strands together and caulk a 50-foot seam in less than 30 minutes for the whole operation! Those of you who are familiar with the traditional process of separating and rolling caulking material by hand will appreciate that figure. Also, it seemed this was an easier way to caulk because the strand was consistent in size, and so fed easily into the seam.

You'll need the right tools to do a proper job of caulking, too. Although I've seen people try to use a big chisel or putty knife as a caulking iron, don't you try it—it don't work. Buy some real caulking irons (you can find them at any good marine store), in two or three sizes. If the iron is too narrow at the tip you'll run the risk of splitting the plank; if it's too wide it won't push in the material far enough. The right one will be *right*, and it'll be readily apparent when you're using it.

A real caulking mallet is a beautiful tool to own, but not essential for caulking one boat. A heavy plastic mallet will work OK, as will a claw hammer, if your ears can stand the din it makes.

Buehler's Backyard Boatbuilding

Regardless of what material or tool you're using, to start caulking, put your box of material in front of you and gently insert a few inches of cotton or oakum (whichever you're using) in a seam with your caulking iron. Now, take the hammer or mallet and bang it in. That's caulking.

It's pretty hard to describe the process from here on, because it's entirely "feel," or "vibes," whichever word you prefer. The idea is to bang the stuff in to about the middle of the seam but no farther. Done right, this will squeeze the planks tightly together edge to edge, making the boat tight as a drum.

I suggest starting on the sheer strake, since it's the farthest from the water and your errors will cause the least harm. By the time you get this plank caulked, and maybe the one below it on both sides, you'll be getting the feel.

As the planks are probably not fitted together perfectly, every few inches you'll have a different-size gap to fill. Soooo, as you drive the stuff in you must "feel" how it goes. If it goes really easy that means you aren't putting in enough, so loop a little more material into the seam. If you can see lots of daylight between planks, double up or use big loops. If it goes really hard, thin down the strand. Keep in mind that if you caulk too loose the boat might leak, but if you caulk too tight a plank might buckle right off the hull when it swells! When it's right it feels, well, *right*! The iron bounces nicely, there's a good *tooonk* sort of sound—it's harder to describe than to do.

On a full-ended hull the planks are under a good deal of tension where they curve into the stem, and you can easily split one if you're not careful. If you do split out a plank it won't hurt anything. If it's near the sheer, fill the split with epoxy glue and nail it back down with ring nails. If it's near the waterline, do the same thing, but screw a 1×3 batten to the inside, too. If you hold the iron absolutely "square" to the seam the odds are good you won't hurt the wood.

If a seam is too tight to get the iron in, open the seam with a *seam reamer,* made from a big file. Take it to somebody who has a torch, heat the handle red hot, bend it about 45 degrees, and grind the tip sharp. This works great, as does an old-time router plane, if you happen to find one at a yard sale.

Caulk all topside seams, including the butts, the rabbet, and the chine. Be gentle caulking the chine and rabbet. You've got lots of bedding compound behind these areas so there's no need to really pound the caulking to her. You don't want the iron to lift a plank.

Traditionally, cross-planked chine hulls weren't caulked with cotton or oakum below the waterline. The seams were just filled with compound. When the boat gets old and starts to work, then it's caulked. One I built 12 years ago still doesn't leak, so that seems to show there's no need to caulk the bottom, unless you've got some big gaps. Since I screwed up on my current boat and used planking that wasn't as dry as it should have been, I had some wide seams to

Figure 7/18.
(A) Lightly push caulking into seams. This is a heavy strand of oakum being used to caulk a 50-footer. (B) Now drive her home. Note the poor grip of the non-pro. Also note the leather glove on the "iron hand." This helps cushion things when the non-pro misses the iron and flattens his hand. (C) When you come to the end of a strand . . . (D) . . . twist another one into it. This is oakum; cotton is far less bulky. (E) If a seam is too tight, ream it out with a scraper made from a bent file handle, sharpened on a grinder to a chisel shape. (F) When you're finished, "pay" the seams with compound. If using a traditional oil-base compound, first paint the caulking with flat white oil-base paint. Read the directions on the can!

A

B

C

D

E

F

fill in the underwater planks. I caulked them very loosely, mostly to keep the seam compound from going clear through.

Caulking isn't really very difficult. It's just hard to describe! The main thing to remember is that it's better to be light than heavy, so take it easy!

Paying the seams

Finally, once you caulk her up, you've got to *pay the seams*, which means fill them with putty. I mentioned my problem with the "wonder compound." Four other people I know had the same problem with it. Although some of these stickums on the market really sound great, they're all very expensive and don't always work.

The one-part, ready-to-use-in-a-toob compounds seem to cause the most trouble. They don't have a printed shelf life, and if the stuff sits around for a long time it seems possible the chemicals separate. Two-part compounds seem like a safer bet, because you can stir each chemical *before* mixing them together, then stir up the whole mess.

However, you will *never* have a problem with the old-time, oil-base seam compounds. They're cheap, and on a boat left in the water year around they'll last indefinitely. And as I mentioned back in Chapter 3, there's other, even cheaper things to use, too. Although I prefer putty on new construction, especially where there's no caulking in the seam, many commercial boats use a paste made of cement and water in the underwater seams.

I mentioned using tar mixed with cement in the seams, also. I don't know if there's an actual recipe to use. The woman who showed me how just dumped powdered cement into a half-full gallon can of roofing patch. She stirred it in, adding more until the mix was really thick. I've mixed plenty since, and I add enough cement to make the mixture hard to stir. Some people don't use any cement, but I think it's a good idea.

Again, if you do this, be sure you use *asphalt*-based roofing tar, not the petroleum-based ones, unless of course you don't mind painting the hull with a tar-based paint like carbon elastic. That (and epoxy paint, which I'm afraid is too brittle for a planked hull) is the only thing that the tar won't bleed through on a hot day.

You can seal the asphalt-based stuff with an aluminum trailer paint, then top that with regular oil-based paints, but it's definitely simpler just to buy good old Interlux seam compound, at least for the topsides. It's far less messy and not too expensive. When you buy it, put it on the shaker before you leave the store. This loosens it up and makes it much easier to spread. Finally, when you put the putty in the seam, work it in well with the putty knife, scrape the plank clean, then run your finger down the seam to indent it a bit. The planks will swell at the launching, and this might keep the putty from being pushed so far out from the seam that you'd have to go back and trim it off.

SIMPLE AND INEXPENSIVE "COMPOSITE" PLANKING

Recently I designed a 64-foot boat to be built in wood. When you get up to this size range, the planking in particular is pretty heavy, and it's difficult to handle alone. It's also difficult to find 2½-inch thick planks, and when you can they're expensive.

By good fortune I had been talking with Bob Pickett at Flounder Bay Boat Lumber, and remembered his description of "epoxy/strip" building. The idea here is that you put on an inner, strip-planked core, then cold-mold a layer or two of thinner, wider strips over it and coat the whole works with a layer of glass cloth and epoxy. Not only is it a very strong way to build, but the epoxy coating protects the hull from bug damage, a concern in the tropics.

Since my design used a single-chine hull, I didn't see any reason to actually "cold mold" a lot of thin layers. That method is too expensive: You have to mill the wood really thin, it's laborious to deal with all the little pieces, and you use epoxy by the drumful. Yet the basic idea is sound, and it *is* easier to deal with little pieces than big ones. After a bit of thought, here's what I came up with: a thick core of edge-nailed, edge-glued strips mechanically fastened to the frames, topped with two layers of plywood (see Figure 7-19).

You'll need a framework to start. Many cold-molded boats don't have frames, just relying on the glue to hold the hull skin together. That ain't for me. Some cold-molded racing sailboats might have frames every 4 feet or so, which is probably good enough since those boys subject their boats to tremendous strains, apparently oblivious to the forces at work.

Well, on a large boat I'd space frames on at least 3-foot centers; on the 64-footer I specified them on 2-foot centers. These are all main frames, with no intermediates, like the framing used with a plywood hull. In other words, the hull for this composite planking system is framed up just the same as you would a hull destined to be planked with plywood.

Since it isn't a good idea to glue heavy timbers together (because of possible expansion breaking the joint), the whole keel has to be laminated up, too, as you would if cold-molding a boat. I'd use 2-by stock regardless of hull size for these laminate components; on the 64-footer I specified 2 × 12s. I'd install a 2 × 4 sheer batten notched into the frames, running along the sheer, just as you would for a plywood hull. Although you probably wouldn't need to indent the planks into the keel with a rabbet, I'd do it anyway. However, I'd only do the inner planks of the laminate, allowing the outer layer of plywood just to butt square to the keel.

Start strip-planking the topsides first, but unlike traditional carvel planking, this time start at the chine, using a 2 × 4 for the first plank. Since the chine will be overlapped rather than mitered, you can

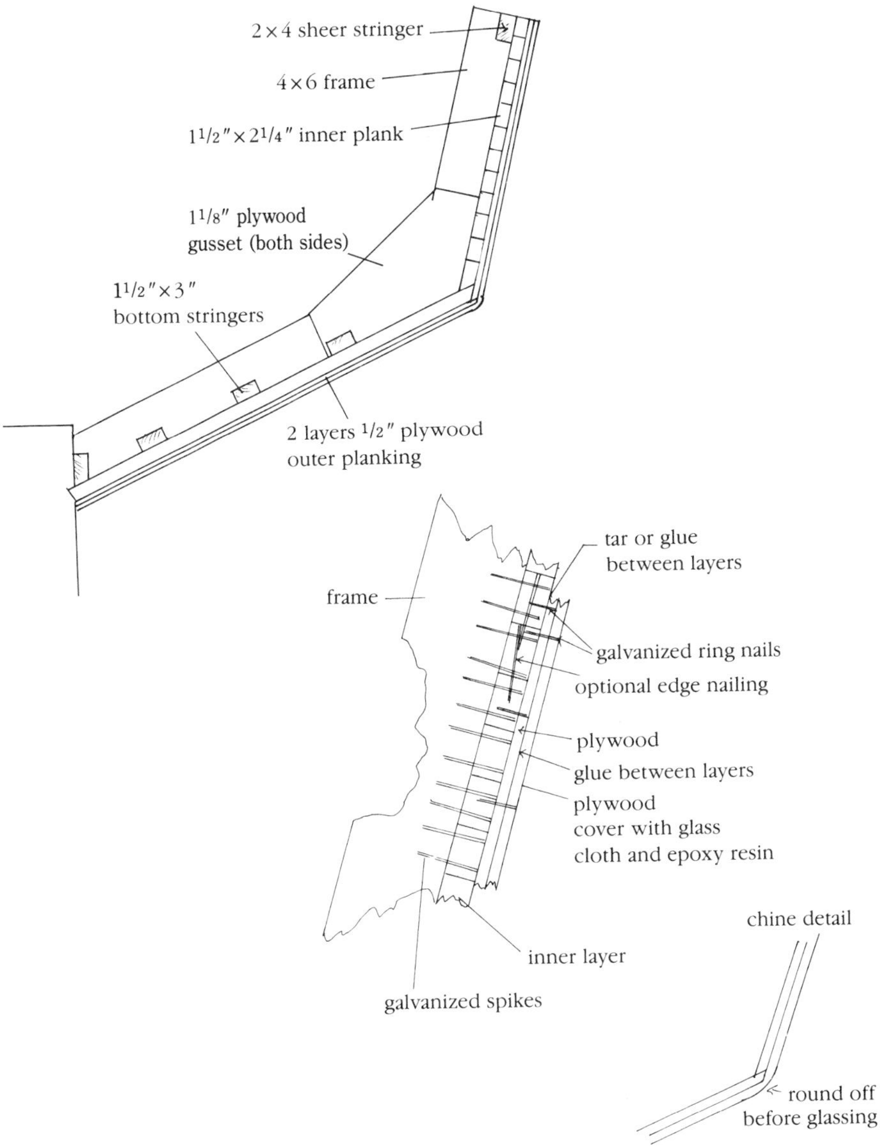

Figure 7/19.
A simple composite planking system. The dimensions shown are for larger hulls.

2×4 sheer stringer

4×6 frame

1½"×2¼" inner plank

1⅛" plywood gusset (both sides)

1½"×3" bottom stringers

2 layers ½" plywood outer planking

tar or glue between layers

frame

galvanized ring nails

optional edge nailing

plywood
glue between layers
plywood
cover with glass cloth and epoxy resin

inner layer

galvanized spikes

chine detail

round off before glassing

rough-saw the angle of the chine into the plank's bottom before nailing the piece up.

The rest of the planking will be 1½- by 2½-inch strips, made by ripping a 2×6 in half. These will be fastened to the frames and to the plank below with galvanized finish nails and glue. (Actually there's probably no need to edge-nail the planks together, but it can't hurt anything—sort of a belt-and-suspenders approach that may add measurably to your feeling of security some night hove to off Cape Horn.) If you're gluing the planking together then you'd better nail it too, so the seams are pulled together tightly. Drill pilot holes when edge nailing so you don't split the piece.

Planking

125

There's no need for butt blocks or caulking seams either, although I'd stop the strips on frames so I didn't see butts "standing proud" on the inside of the hull.

I wouldn't glue these strips to the frames; I'd rely on the fastenings. I don't care what the epoxy people say. If moisture does get into the wood, something's going to move. This is especially true on thicker stuff, like this ripped 2×6 planking.

Keep nailing on strips in this fashion until the sides are covered. As you approach the sheer, just let the strips run along the sheer stringer, and saw them off parallel to the sheer line. You may need a few wider fillers near the bow.

Now, cross plank the bottom with 2×6s, just like conventional planking. You could use edge-nailed strips here, too, but it may be more hassle than it's worth. Overlap the bottom pieces at the chine, and saw them off flush with the side.

Now you're ready to install the second layer. I'd use plywood, and on the 64-footer I specified two layers of $1/2$-inch.

You need some sort of goop between the plywood and the planked hull. You could use epoxy, but I don't think I would.

Have you ever tried to separate two boards stuck together with ATCO roofing patch? If not, spread some on a board, lay another on it, and try to separate them a week later. That stuff is sticky as hell, dirt cheap, and the petroleum oils in it act as a wood preservative. And even if it isn't ultimately as strong as epoxy, it doesn't really matter; unlike the epoxy boys, I "praise epoxy but pass the nails." We're *not* relying on glue, in other words. The outer layer is mechanically fastened. I just wouldn't feel comfortable further from shore than I could swim back to in a boat without mechanical fasteners.

We've talked about plywood grades before. I think if I was adding two layers I'd use MDO single overlay, with the overlay side against the planks (in the tar), so you'll have the plywood "bare to bare" when gluing them together. If I was using three or more layers, I'd use single-sided MDO, then one or more layers of T1-11 siding, then a final layer of single sided MDO.

I'd use $1/2$-inch ply only on larger boats. Two or three layers of $3/8$ inch or even $1/4$-inch ply would be a lot easier to deal with on most boats under 45 feet or so, although MDO doesn't come in $1/4$ inch. An alternative is Lauan plywood from the Philippines, which is fairly inexpensive and fairly decent stuff.

So, just as with plywood planking, make a pattern of $1/4$- by 3-inch strips (or tack up the first sheet and scribe around it). Mark on the hull where it will go, spread tar or glue on the area, and nail on the sheet with galvanized ring nails. Continue this until you've covered the whole hull.

If the hull shape has a lot of curve in the ends and the $1/2$-inch ply doesn't want to bend to it, stop the sheet back where the hull is still flat enough for it, then fill in the ends with two layers of $1/4$-inch ply.

Or, you could rip the 1/2-inch stuff into 1-foot-wide strips and install it diagonally.

After the whole hull is covered, glue on a second layer. I'd bet you could use roofing tar here, too, but I think I'd use glue—maybe even epoxy. If you use it, be sure to get one that kicks off slow. This might be a good place for Areolite glue, since it has a long pot life. If you've had to piece-in the ends, then have this second layer (and/or third and fourth at the end) overlap the first by a few feet.

After the whole hull is covered, round off the chine a bit with a disc sander to make it easier to wrap cloth around. Also, make a paste from epoxy and sawdust or some other filler and fill in where the plywood hits the keel to make a bit of a radius there, too. It might be easier to saw out a triangular strip that more or less fits the angle and nail it on.

As mentioned before when we were talking about plywood building, coating the hull with epoxy and cloth won't be fun. Again, since the cloth is there just to protect the plywood and not for strength, I'd think one layer of moderate weight would be enough, with maybe a second layer overlapping the chine. Just as with plywood planking, I'd staple the cloth lightly to the hull first, then put on the resin. I'd hire guys from the local mission to sand it smooth.

This type of planking could be done on any size hull of course, but the interesting thing about it is that it makes big boats feasible and affordable for backyard projects. Since the inner planks are protected by the outer layer, there's no need to use top grade planking stock. I'd use a good grade of construction fir. The prices are low!

Without figuring waste, here's how the costs broke down: The 64 footer is a very trim design and has roughly 1,130 square feet of hull area. Good fir 2×6 is available in the lumberyard near me for 29 cents a board foot, which works out to 58 cents a square foot of planking. That's $655 for the inner layer. It would take about 70 sheets of 1/2-inch plywood to cover the hull with two layers, which would cost maybe $1,000. Figuring a few hundred bucks for nails and tar, that's a pretty reasonable price for planking a 64-foot boat, less expensive than using plywood alone. Of course there'll be some waste, and the epoxy isn't cheap, but just the same, it's within the range of the "average" working guy. Plus, it's a system that a guy can do alone, without fancy tools, and it would make a bullet-proof, long-lived hull. There's no reason why it wouldn't work on most round-bottomed hulls, too, although you might need to rip the ply into 8- to 12-inch wide strips and put them on diagonally.

This same idea works on smaller boats too, of course. Smaller boats might use a layer of 3/4- by 2-inch strips, covered with two layers of 1/4- or 3/8-inch plywood. I'd use whatever combination it takes to make the completed skin the same thickness as single-layer planking would have been.

Recently I've learned about a few options that make both composite and straight plywood construction worth a closer look. A compulsive friend down the way is building a huge dome house, and he ordered all his plywood direct from a mill in southern Oregon. By buying in quantity, he was able to get a low price, but best of all, the mill ran a house construction grade (AC or AB, I forget which) for him that used a fir core. This gave him the same quality cored ply as marine or MDO, with more voids, of course, at a far lower price.

Also, I've been noticing advertisements in industrial supply catalogs for epoxies, frequently at prices as low as $1/5$ of the advertised prices in the yachting magazines. A friend called one of these places and asked why it's so cheap, and was told that the epoxy works fine, but it's "crude." They said it is very temperature-critical and can't be applied when the temperature is below 66 degrees, unlike the newer formulas which can be used down to freezing. For $10 a gallon, it might pay to rent some big heaters when coating a hull.

Anyway, this composite construction seems worth a try, and maybe I'll do it some day. The only big disadvantage I can see is that the finished hull will look rather boring. Like a 'glass hull, there'll be no caulking seams to look at, and I do like the look of a planked hull. But if you decide to try this system, let me know how it works.

DECKS

Well, you've built the hull and are probably pretty pleased with yourself, but you ain't finished yet. Now you've got to cover it with a deck. Decks are held up by a framework, consisting of *beams*, which run across the boat, and *carlins*, which run fore and aft and support the openings for hatches, cockpits, and the deckhouse. The deck plan should show the location and number of the framing members, but you have a few options to consider before you start building.

Will you have a normal deckhouse with side decks? If so you'll need to frame the opening for the house with carlins. Maybe you want a *raised-sheer* cabin? This is sort of a bastardized flush-deck idea, stronger than a conventional deckhouse, easier to build, and more spacious inside. It can look OK if you use long, sweeping coamings at each end and keep the sides fairly low (increase headroom with a high crowned roof). You'll need to add extensions to the frames (which you could have added when you were assembling the frames, although it's no big hassle to go back and add them now). If these house-framing extensions are vertical rather than following the flare of the sides, the whole thing will look better and be stronger to boot, since the hull rather than the house side will take the blow if you bash a dock or something.

Whichever way you decide to go, the first step is to figure out how many deck beams you need; the next step is to make them.

DECK BEAMS

A common mistake builders and designers often make is not putting enough curve, or *crown* as it's called, into the deck beams. The result, seen in every harbor around the world, is a boat with rotten ends or rot around the hatch coamings or cabin base, all because water couldn't run freely off deck.

Listen: Put a real crown in your beams, maybe 1 inch of rise for each foot of beam. A strong crown like this adds room inside the boat, makes the deck stronger, and looks great, not to mention that it lets water run off easily. This might be too much crown for the working deck area on a powerboat, but it's no problem on sailboats: The boat is leaning over anyhow, and the crown makes walking on the high side easier than walking on a flat deck.

Decks

On lighter-weight boats less than 9 feet wide, you can saw the beams right out of 2×12s or 3×12s. It's quick, but wasteful. If you have a powerful Skilsaw, bend a little more set into the teeth with pliers, set the blade so it just clears the stock, and you'll be able to saw the curved lines with no problem.

On bigger boats, or if you don't want to waste wood, you can laminate the beams. This is tedious work, but if you start doing it way back during the planking stage and do one every other day, you'll have them ready by the time the hull is ready to take them.

Laminated beams

How thick should these laminated deck beams be? Whatever looks right. But 3/4-inch-wide stock (1-by) is the easiest to get and the easiest to work with, so I prefer beams made from multiple layers of this, a minimum of 3 inches deep (four layers) on boats up to 35 feet or so. (You can use this size beam on larger boats if you space them closely.) You'll need at least five layers in the lamination to get the finished beam to hold the curve perfectly. Use fewer layers and the beams will straighten out a bit when you remove them from the mold. I've never worried about it, and I've never used five layers. Each beam springs back the same amount, so I saw a little more crown into the form than I expect the finished beam to end up with.

The beams on my current 50-footer are 2½ by 4½ inches (made from three layers of 1½-inch stock), spaced two feet apart. I didn't put in enough crown, which doesn't look too great, and cost me room inside the boat. The heavy pieces sprung out of shape and were a bitch to bend. Stick to 3/4-inch stock in laminations; you'll save a lot of hassle.

How wide? Well, if they're 1½ inches wide you can make them from 1×4s ripped in half. If they're bigger, rip a 1×6 or whatever you need. Your table saw will earn its way, if it hasn't already, during this deal. The stock should be at least 1/4-inch wider than you want the beams; you'll smooth them up after the glue sets.

How many beams do you need? Well, if the frames are a foot apart I put one large beam, say 2½ by 4½ inches, on every other

Figure 8/1. Deck beams being laminated over a form. Note the strong crown, the clamps made from 3/8-inch threaded rod and plywood caps, and the waxed paper between beam and form to keep the beam from sticking.

frame, assuming the decks will be plywood. If you're planking the deck (I wouldn't; it leaks, it's expensive, and it's hard to do right), put a beam on every frame. If the frames are farther apart, say 15 inches, put a smaller beam, say $1^1/2 \times 3$ inches, on every frame. If you're using these lighter beams, make the ones at each end of the cabin and each side of the mast twice as thick.

You'll need a form over which to laminate the beams (see Figure 8-1). I generally make one that handles one beam at a time, although it's possible to glue up wide stock and rip a bunch of beams at one pop. This is getting just a bit too efficient for the average backyard guy, and requires a big saw to cut out the beams. I never bother.

The form must be made from a plank wide enough to handle the whole deck crown. If you can't get one that wide, glue two together. If the beams are narrow, you can make the form from a 2-by, 3-by, 4-by, or whatever you can saw. You can also cut two 2-bys to the curve, stand them up parallel about 6 inches apart, connect them with 2×4 spacers that extend out several inches past each form, and nail a solid plank to the bottom. This is the slickest looking form. You can attach C-clamps to the crosspieces, and use the top ones as guides to hold the clamping bolts in place.

Regardless of how you do it (I do it without the crosspieces), the mold should be a few inches longer than the widest part of the boat.

Lay out the curve for the deck's crown on whatever plank you'll use for the form. (It might be simplest to use 2-by stock for this. If you want a wider mold, simply make another one or two and nail them to the first one.) Using the bottom of the plank as the baseline, draw a vertical line at the center and additional vertical lines spaced every 12 inches out from it. Drive a nail at the center to mark the crown's maximum height, then bend a batten around. Measure up the vertical lines while shifting the batten around until the batten measures the same on each side of the centerline. Drive nails to hold the batten, draw in the curve, and saw out the form.

Nail a piece of 2-by to the bottom, wide enough to stick out several inches from each side of the form (like an inverted T). Drill a $1/2$-inch hole an inch or so in from the edges every 6 inches on both sides of this bottom strip. Cut some $3/8$-inch threaded rod to fit each hole. This rod must equal the height of the mold, plus the thickness of the beam, plus a $3/4$-inch ply cap, plus a top nut, plus say 2 inches to make it easier to get the cap on while bending the stock, plus the thickness of the bottom piece, with enough left over for a nut below. When you put the rod into the lower holes, put a nut on each side of the base to hold the rod in position, with a big washer behind the lower nut.

You'll need some "holder-downer" caps, about 2 inches wide, for each pair of threaded rods. The best ones are made from $1/4$-inch steel, because there will be a lot of pressure on these top caps. Plywood works OK, but you'll have to replace them every once in a while.

Regular old Weldwood Plastic Resin glue or the equivalent works quite well for laminating deck beams. There's no need for epoxy here. Besides, epoxy sets up too fast, and is harder to work with.

Laminating the beams is really a pain—messy, too. You may want to wear some old coveralls or take a trip to Goodwill and load up on disposable clothes before you start.

After you get your strips ripped out, staple waxed paper to the mold to keep the glue from sticking the beam to the form. Spread glue on the pieces and lay them on the mold. Clamp one end down halfway or so, then do the same to the other side while you push, swear, and kick at the layers, trying to bend them down while keeping them halfway straight and even. The longer the clamps you use the better.

When you finally get the stock bent over the mold, put the caps on the hold-down bolts and cinch up the nuts really tight, banging the sides with a hammer to try to line up the layers. After everything is bent and clamped, go through and drive nails into the beam 6 inches apart to help hold the layers together. Can't hurt.

Finally, wrap the whole form and beam in sheet plastic, stick in an electric heater, and let the glue cook at 80 degrees all day. Now spend half an hour washing the glue off, and be glad it isn't epoxy you've got all over the place. Pour a stiff drink, sit down, and take it easy for a bit. When you take the beams off the form, you'll have to smooth up their outside faces. A jointer does this nicely, as does a power plane. A disc sander will work, too.

INSTALLING DECK BEAMS AND CARLINS

Compared with many things on a boat, deck beams are easy to install. Since a chine hull has such large, stout frames, you can avoid all the extra work of installing a clamp, shelf, or whatever to support their outboard ends, as you see in bent-frame boats, and just bolt the deck beams right to the frames. In areas such as a commercial boat's working deck, where heavy weights might be dropped, you can give the beams a little added support by bolting big knees (which incidentally look great) to them and to the frames. Deck beams don't have to fit perfectly; in fact, it's better if they don't. Leave a good 1/2 inch at their ends for air circulation.

To get started, you should still have a string running down the entire centerline of the boat. If you don't, put one there. Starting at whatever frame you want, remove the frame's crosspiece and saw off the top of the frame sticking up above the plank. I don't try to saw it perfectly flush with the deck; I like it an inch low to (at the risk of sounding repetitious) allow air circulation. Lay a deck beam across the hull and line up its center with the string. Scribe the beam ends to fit (you want the ends to be a little loose), and cut each side.

Clamp the beam in position. Now then, the top of the beam

should lay in a straight line with the *outer* edge of the side plank. As the sides almost always will have some flare to them, the inside edge of the plank will be too high and will have to be planed down. So, run a handsaw through this inside face until the teeth lie flat on top of the beam and just touch the outer edge of the plank. Bang the beam up or down with a hammer until it's positioned right. When you have it, fasten the beam to the frame with two 5/16-inch bolts.

If you're building a raised-sheer house, ideally your frames are already prepared, and all you need to do is bolt on the deck beams. However, there's no reason you can't decide now that you want to raise the sheer to make a house. As mentioned before, all you need to do is bolt some extensions beside the frames in the area you want to raise. Use material the same dimension as the frame, let the exten-

Figure 8/2.
Use a simple plywood pattern to find the length and end-cut angles of the carlins. Note that the carlins fit into angled notches in the beams. Also, note that the frames are cut off below the sheer. This is for air circulation.

sions overlap enough of the existing frames to look substantial, and make them stand vertical.

I'd erect all of them temporarily with clamps, wrap a batten around them, and sight down it to make sure all the frame extensions are standing fair. Adjust whichever ones aren't, then drill for the bolts, remove the pieces, spread glue on the joint, then stand them back up and bolt them in. Plank the sides, then install the deck beams as described earlier.

If you're going to be building a conventional deckhouse, then you've got to frame in the opening. Although it's simplest to run the cabin sides parallel with the keel, it looks better and gives a bit more room inside if the house walls are curved to run parallel with the deck line.

Think about the width of the side decks, too. The minimum width you can walk on is 9 inches, and 12 to 18 inches is more comfortable. I used 24-inch-wide side decks on my last boat, which has 11 feet of beam. Although this really robbed the interior of living space, it sure makes a nice, easy to walk on the side deck. I use the space below for shelves.

After some fiddling, I've ended up using a sort of "built up" carlin for house openings. I notch a 2-by into the beams (see Figure 8-2) where the house goes, then bend the carlin parallel (using sliding pipe clamps) with the side of the boat. Then I bolt the side deck beams to the frames, and notch them into the carlin, with a lag bolt running through the carlin into the end of the beam.

Remember that a house wall shouldn't be vertical, but should lean in a few degrees. Use a level to get a vertical line on the main beams you're notching to receive the carlins, then draw another line that tilts inboard a few degrees and cut the notch to suit. If you cut it wrong, Figure 8-3 will set you right.

Later on, after the deck is installed, I bolt a second 2-by carlin to the first, letting it stick up $1\frac{1}{2}$ or so inches above the deck. If the house wall is the type that is through-bolted to the carlin, this second

Figure 8/3.
If you cut the angle of the carlin butt wrong (God forbid), you can fix it by driving in a wedge and sawing it off. Nobody will guess; it's OK. Slop some preservative on the butt and wedge before driving it down.

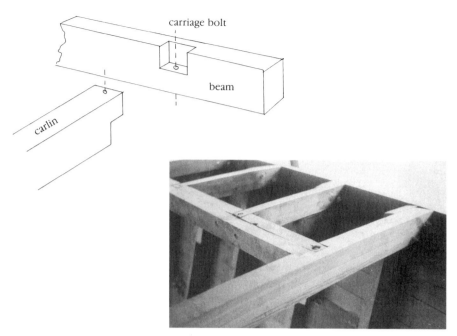

Figure 8/4.
Another common method of handling side deck beams and carlins, using a stepped, rather than an angled notch. The carlins on this large, heavily-constructed boat are doubled between the side deck beams with glued-on pieces. The inner carlin mentioned in the text will be bolted on here later.

piece of the carlin is bolted onto the first before the wall is erected. If I'm using plywood walls, I put in the second carlin after the house is up. On larger boats, I make the first carlin from 3-by stock or thicker. If you want to use 3-by but can't bend it, use two pieces of 2-by glued together.

Ideally, a carlin should have the same sheer cut into it as the sheer of the boat. If it's short, nobody will notice if it runs in a straight line. But if you're fussy and want it to follow the sheer, clamp the carlin stock to the side of the hull, next to where it will be going, then run a pencil along the top plank to transfer the curve. It might be easier to use a plywood pattern here (as always). Saw it out and try it on the hull.

Purists say that you should saw sheer into *any* carlin, regardless of its length, to avoid a "flat spot." That's up to you. It isn't much trouble to saw in the sheer, and doing it makes one feel rather "crafty" and adds to that boatbuilder's mystique, if you care about such things. Long ago I seem to remember I might have. But when I traded in my wire frames for contact lenses, and my wine and other relaxation things for Bourbon, I also started making straight carlins.

You can use straight side deck beams without anybody noticing either. Which reminds me. Efficient people make full-width deck beams in the way of the house. They install them full length, then saw them off where the house will go. This gives you a nicely curved side deck beam, and you can use the middle area of the beam near the ends of the boat, where shorter beams will fit. I can't think of any earthly reason *not* to do it this way, but for some reason I never have. Maybe you should try it.

Figure 8/5.
(A) Two-piece mast partner being installed. Note the heavy bar clamp holding things tightly together while the through-bolt is inserted and drawn up tight. (B) Simpler, one-piece mast partner suitable for a smaller boat (this is a 35-footer). Note that the through-bolts are counter-sunk into the deck beams.

A   B

Knees under the side deck beams add a nice final touch. Make them from 10- or 12-inch material the same thickness as the beams. I use the same wood I used for the frames. Draw the shape you want on a piece of plywood to make a pattern. These knees are rather decorative, so play around when making this pattern and make the face of the knee curved. Position the pattern on the material so that the wood's grain runs as far as possible up the knee (you want to avoid cross grain if you can). Clamp the knee in position tightly against the beam. Put two bolts through the frame and one down through the beam into the knee. The house walls help support the side decks, of course, but these knees can't hurt, and they look great, too.

You'll frame all the openings for the hatches, cockpits, and whatever, before you lay the deck. As you go along, think about where you might want to mount heavy-duty hardware, like stanchions or trolling poles or the like. Although I've never done it, I've always thought a good solid base for this stuff would be a piece of $1/4 \times 3$-inch plate, notched into the beam and through-bolted. A conventional backing plate works well below a plywood deck, but I like the idea of a *really* solid base for stuff, although I've never bothered doing it. If you do decide to bolt in some sort of backing plate, be sure that the bolts holding the beam to the frame aren't in the way. Most people just use 2×6s for backing plates, which are easier to handle than steel but more bulky.

Anyway, if you have a mast stepped through the deck you'll need to frame in the *mast partners*. Partners are just blocking with a hole, bolted to the deck beams. Use material as thick as the beams are deep, and make the partners in two pieces, with a hole about an inch larger in diameter than the mast (so you can drive in wedges to hold it tight). For instance, if you have a 10-inch-diameter mast, make the partners from two pieces of, say, 4 by 10. Cut a $5^{1}/_{2}$-inch half circle (or rectangle if your mast is so shaped) in each piece. Fit them together between two beams. You'll find the exact position on the lines plan, by the way. Glue the two halves together, and drill through them, bolting them to the beams with 3/8-inch threaded rod, with the nuts countersunk into each beam.

You'll have to frame in the cockpit, too, so you'll have to decide how big you want it. The following is a quote from my old Building Book, written soon after I had spent a year singlehanding, back in the days, as Dylan Thomas so nicely put it: "when I *was* a man you could *call* a Man . . . said the Old Gray . . . ."

The cockpit should (here's me from years back) "be a shallow foot well, short and narrow, watertight and self draining. Ideally it should be just big enough so you can crouch down into it. I remember when I was hove-to off Pt. Conception. There were ships all over the place, and I had to spend the night crouched down in the cockpit, trying to avoid spray and rain, ready to change tacks to avoid being run down. The cockpit should be just a little box for your feet while you sit on deck, just big enough to shelter you from the weather a bit . . . ."

By the way, to complete that story, I can now admit that I wasn't really being attacked by every ship in the world. In the morning when the weather cleared, I saw that I had been dodging Gawd-Damned *oil platforms*! I'd never seen one before. But at night, through the rain and wind, they looked like huge ships. I must admit I found it odd I never saw any running lights, and it confused me that most of what I was dodging never seemed to move. But then, *all* great navigators have their moments of confusion.

At any rate, we'll be getting into cockpits later on, but we're framing now, and you gotta decide what kind of cockpit you want, and frame it in. These days I think a cockpit should be a heated wheelhouse with a cassette tape player, a bar, and a coffee pot; failing that, it should be deep with comfortable seats. You may prefer something a little more Spartan. To each his own.

DECKING

Nothing compares with a planked deck for looks, but using plywood, like it or not, makes the most sense: It's quicker, simpler, and stronger; it will never leak, and when covered with some sort of coating, it is pretty much maintenance-free. The deck forms an important structural part of the boat. Two or three layers of plywood all glued and nailed together yields a deck that is one solid piece, bracing the hull in all directions.

The only time I might not use plywood decking would be on really heavy-duty workboat decks. My friend Dave's little log tug has laid decks worn down from years of spiked boots jumping around on it. I doubt that plywood, even if covered with miracle goo, would stand up to that kind of treatment for long.

It's common to see a light layer of planking laid on top of a plywood deck. Don't do it. The rot problems that will develop sooner or later can be really appalling. Regardless of how well the planks are bedded, you'll still get the odd leak. Even condensation from the metal fastening can let water into the plywood core. Rot develops inside the plywood, but you don't notice it because of the planking. So one day, 10 years or so down the line, you'll notice the deck feels a little spongy, it'll be too late to do a spot repair, and the whole deck will have to be ripped off and replaced.

I watched one guy lay a 3/16-inch-thick (or so) layer of teak over a plywood deck, gluing down the 2 1/2-inch-wide strips with epoxy. He used a few staples to hold the strips in place until the epoxy kicked, then pulled the staples and filled the holes with epoxy. Although it gave the boat the looks of a planked deck, it also looked like a lot of expense and trouble. Not only would I never do it, this guy said he wouldn't do it again, either.

Obviously the deck framing must be complete before you can lay the deck. Also, if you haven't already done it, plane down the top of the sheer strake so its bevel flows smoothly to meet the deck beams. Remember, you've got the saw line you made when fitting the beams to guide you.

If your boat has any sheer to it at all, you'll need to bevel the tops of the beams so that the plywood will lay flat. Hold a long 1 x 2 along the beams. Does it lie flat everywhere? If not, see how far off it is, put a pencil line on the high edge, and plane down the beam. Plane this bevel just as you probably did on a few of the frames to make their bevel right.

If you made laminated deck beams all on the same mold, as was described earlier, some of the deck beams might look a little out of line here and there, and you might see what appears to be a hollow area near the bow. I don't know why this happens, but don't worry about it: When you nail down the plywood everything will flow together, and the deck will come out looking pretty good.

On boats with heavy planking you can nail the plywood decking directly to the sheer strake. But if the hull's planking is less than 1 inch thick—which isn't much support for the edge of the crucial hull-to-deck joint—I'd widen the supporting base by adding a laminated rubrail.

Two layers of 3/4-inch-thick by 3- to 4-inch-wide wood will be thick enough for this rail. Glue and screw the first piece to the hull in line with the top of the plank. This first piece should be the width of the rubrail, *minus* the thickness of the deck. After it's on, plane the top to get it perfectly fair with the sheer strake. Later on, when the deck is finished, you can put on the second layer.

The last step before actually laying the plywood deck is soaking the tops of all the frames with wood preservative. I do this once a day for a week or so before I lay the deck. On my last boat I also painted the tops of the frames with epoxy on the theory that it might keep water out of the end grain of the frames. It sounded like a good idea at the time.

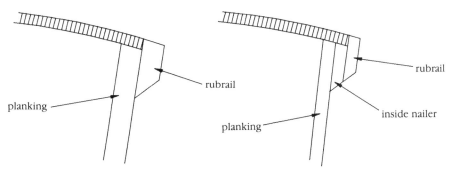

Figure 8/6.
Attaching the deck to the sheer. On large boats or those with thick planking, nail the plywood directly to the sheer strake. For smaller boats or those with thin planking, attach a nailer to the sheer, then overlap sheer and nailer with plywood. After covering the deck with fabric, attach an outer rubrail.

I've always used AC exterior plywood for the deck, but nowadays would use MDO single overlay for the first and last layers, and T1-11 plain (without the grooves) for any inner layers. This will cost only a little more, and probably will last a lot longer. The deck is fastened down with galvanized ring nails—1-inch nails for 3/8-inch plywood. You want to use plywood decking that's thick enough not to sag between the deck beams, but thin enough to bend. If your beams have a good crown, like 1-inch rise per foot of beam, use 3/8-inch ply. You probably shouldn't use 1/4-inch ply unless you have a deck with a lot of crown. Fairly flat decks can use thicker ply, like 1/2 or 5/8 inch.

How many layers should you use? Well, there are calculations and scantling charts that list the recommended sizes of all the parts of a boat, but I pay little attention to them, relying instead on my "gut" feelings. I'm no hero, and I never did like swimming. I make the deck thick enough so that I feel its strength is in balance with the rest of the boat, which, if you've been building as I've been describing, is pretty stout. This ends up to be something like two layers of 3/8-inch ply on boats up to about 30 feet; three layers of 3/8-inch on boats up to about 45 feet; and four layers on boats larger than that.

Think about how you'll lay out the first layer of plywood before you start banging nails; there's a lot going on here. The plywood will lie flatter with its long dimension running fore and aft. You'll need to stagger the butts around so you don't have a long, weak seam anywhere. Butt this first layer together pretty carefully, because the joints will be visible down below. Some people notch a 1 × 3 batten into the beams, parallel to the centerline, on 2-foot centers to give a solid edge for the plywood ends to land on. I don't know if it's necessary, and have built boats with and without this nailer. You don't have to be too compulsive about the fits, because you can fill any gaps with that fix-all, epoxy resin and sawdust.

If you used laminated beams you'll find that some of them aren't exactly straight, which makes it awkward to nail down the plywood without missing a beam. I tack a sheet down, scribe it to the side of the hull, then cut it a bit oversize. Then I glue and nail it down to the beam.

I see no need to use epoxy for the deck lamination. I use good old Weldwood or Wilhold or some other powder glue. I use lumberyard construction adhesive (comes in a tube, used for laying floors in house construction) on top of the sheer strake, rather than glue, because the plank will swell and shrink some, and I think the glue is too brittle to take it. After the plywood is down I go back and plane it off smooth.

When you put down the second layers (and following layers as the case may be) use lots of glue. Paint both faces. You must work fast so the glue doesn't set up before you've finished nailing. If you're doing this in warm weather work only in the early morning, mix the glue fairly runny, and you'll be alright.

Stagger the butts of the new layers to miss the previous layer's butts. After I've got the deck planked (plywooded doesn't sound right) I go back and drive long nails through the whole business into the deck beams. I also go back and paint the end grain of the plywood with epoxy to seal it.

You'll have to cover the plywood with some sort of protective coating. A lot of people still swear by (and sometimes at) traditional canvas covering. I personally don't like it because it always rots out eventually, and it's really a job to replace it. To do it properly, you have to remove all the hatches, bulwarks, and so forth. Instead I use a layer of fiberglass cloth, which will never rot.

The simplest, and I think the best coating, is Arabol, which will stick down just about any fabric—even burlap. Glass cloth is about the same price, however, wears better, and won't rot. Arabol, formerly made by Borden Chemical (now made by the National Starch Company), looks sort of like Elmer's glue, is water soluble until it sets up, and is used as a lagging compound for wrapping steam pipes and whatnot. You can buy it at many marine stores under various brand names such as Doc's Easy Deck, Thorpe's Easy Deck, or International Lagging Compound. (If you can't find it locally, try Thorpe Insulation, 24100 Broad Street, Carson, CA 90745.)

Covering the deck will go easiest with two people. Start at the cabin opening, and lay a piece of cloth right across the hull. (There's no need to tack it down.) Start in the middle of the cloth and spread a thick layer of Arabol with brushes (you might want to wear lightweight gloves; when Arabol hardens on your hands it looks like painted-on latex gloves and has to be peeled off like sunburn), working it in until the cloth is saturated and you have a smooth surface. In the beginning work the brush in only one direction or you'll wrinkle the fabric, although it's fairly easy to brush out the wrinkles. Let the cloth overlap the sheer by 2 inches and stick it down with more Arabol to protect the plywood's edge grain. Put on the next piece of cloth so it overlaps the first one by about 1 inch, and keep going this way until you're finished.

After the stuff dries, you can feather out the overlaps with sandpaper if you want. If you used the built-in rubrail I mentioned earlier for reinforcing the edges of thin-planked hulls, cut a 1-by to the same width as the rail on the hull, plus the thickness of the deck. Bevel the top so it's pretty close to the one on the boat, and glue and screw it on. You're done with the deck.

This Arabol and glass cloth combination is the simplest and cheapest way to handle the deck. It works fine and lasts indefinitely. For some reason I used epoxy resin instead of Arabol on my last boat. What a mess! It cost far more, required all sorts of sanding, and didn't stick in a few places. I'd never do it again unless I was covering a real working deck that would be getting heavy use. And don't use polyester resin. It doesn't stick well to plywood at all.

BOLT-ONS: RAILS, CHAINPLATES, POSTS, SPRITS, AND BULWARKS

CHAPTER 9

Now that the deck's on, it's tempting to build the house and move in, but you'll save a lot of hassle if you bolt on all the exterior hull stuff while the interior is still wide open and accessible. Remember: *Think ahead, Stupid*!

RUBRAILS

You have to have a *good* rubrail. Although the workboat folks know this, a surprising number of yachties don't, and they just hate to see me coming in my boat. When I raft up, my hull is protected by big, heavy rubrails and external chainplates, and I can rub right through fiberglass in no time. I also can rub against pilings and docks without hurting the hull.

The ideal rubrail is a thick piece of hardwood, with the bottom sawed at a 45-degree angle so there won't be a corner to catch and break if the hull is rolling against a dock or something. In practice, unless you're building a workboat and plan to be banging stuff frequently, a rubrail made from a fir 2×4 or 2×6 will work fine. If you're really going to bang into stuff, use oak, ironbark, or some other hard stuff. On my current boat I think I'm going to face the middle area of the rail with a piece of quarter-round steel, which will serve the purpose quite well.

You can install a solid rubrail, or laminate one up from 2 pieces (as we did for boats with 1-inch or thinner planking). Installing a solid rubrail is a two-person deal—at least. As with the planking, get as long a board as you can find, fasten it to the end of the boat first, then have your helper walk it in. Be sure to use lots of bedding compound

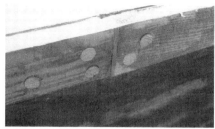

Figure 9/1.
If you cut the rubrail's pieces too short, you can fix it like this (Wood Butcher's Trick #63). I understand some people even use cedar shingles for house siding.

behind the rubrail. It probably won't fit perfectly tight to the hull all over. So it goes. As long as you have plenty of bedding compound behind it, it doesn't matter. Also, as mentioned before, it can't hurt to paint the end grain of the plywood deck with epoxy before you install the rail. You can fasten the rubrail with nails temporarily, then go back and screw it or bolt it—whatever—after it's on.

It's really a bitch getting this thing in place because there's nothing to clamp it to. I made a sort of hook by nailing a 4×4 block to a 12-inch piece of 2×4. Cut the face of the 4×4 to a 15- to 20-degree angle so it grabs the rail when it lays against the flared hull side, and hook a **C**-clamp to the 2×4. If you make two of these, you can hook one to one side of the boat, and use a come-a-long to pull on the other one, which is hooked to the rail. It sort of works; better than nothing anyway.

The easiest way to put on a rubrail is to laminate it in place using two layers of 3/4-inch material. The inner layer could be a softwood like fir or cedar, screwed to the hull, with an outer layer of ironbark or oak. Screw this on; then, if you think you'll be rubbing against stuff frequently, run bolts through the rail and frames. I've hung rubrails both ways, and will laminate them from now on. Bending a single heavy piece around a hull with nothing to clamp to is a bitch.

CHAINPLATES

Chainplates are the straps that hold the rigging wires that support the mast. I've never seen them poorly attached on workboats, but yachts often have systems that really look weak. Many yacht riggers not only attach the plates to interior bulkheads, of all things, but they also mount them as close to the centerline as they can. This is so the wires won't interfere with big overlapping headsails when pointing, allowing the sail to be sheeted in a bit closer than with a more traditional setup.

This is another example of cruisers and recreational boaters being detrimentally influenced by raceboat types. Yes, a narrow staying base will allow you to point higher when flying a huge sail in very light wind, but so what? You also get a system that isn't nearly as strong because the attachment point is inherently weak and prone to rot where the metal chainplates pass through the deck. It also doesn't

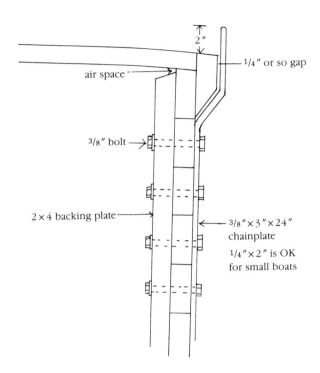

air space

2"

1/4" or so gap

3/8" bolt →

2 × 4 backing plate →

3/8" × 3" × 24" chainplate

1/4" × 2" is OK for small boats

offer the hull the intimidating and practical protection provided by heavy steel straps running down her side at her widest point. I tell ya, when some guy in a plastic boat comes up to raft against me, he thinks twice. My chainplates can rub through a dock, never mind a plastic boat!

Figure 9-2 shows what these things should look like—just a simple piece of flat steel bent to clear the rubrail, bolted through the hull into a backing plate. This is the simplest way to do it. Some people forge the ends, twisting the top 90 degrees for some reason. Nothing wrong with that, but why bother?

Whatever you do, don't put the chainplates behind the rubrail. Wherever a chainplate goes through a hull or rail you'll eventually get rot. Even if the joint is sealed perfectly, condensation from the metal will keep the wood wet, creating an ideal climate for rot spores. Perhaps that's why the old-time tree-nail-fastened (pronounced *trunnel*) hulls seem to last so long. No metal in them.

Your rigging plan should show the location of these things, but if not, take the sail plan, run a pencil line down each wire to the waterline, and measure the distance from the nearest station at the top and bottom of the chainplate. Transfer these measurements to the hull, draw in their shape, and you can figure out the dimensions for your chainplates. They should be long enough to stick up about 2 inches above the rubrail, running down the hull to just above the waterline. In practice I make them all the same length as the shortest one. I think that looks better on the hull, but it doesn't really matter.

On smaller boats, say under 30 feet, I use $1/4$- by 2-inch mild steel straps; on bigger boats I use $3/8$- by 3-inch straps. You'll have to have these things bent to shape by a metal shop; you can get them galvanized at the same place, usually. They can figure out the shape easily if you make a plywood pattern (you'll only need one) to fit against the hull, and notch it around the rubrail. The bend doesn't have to be perfect; the chainplate shouldn't actually touch the rubrail. Have them drill a big hole, say $3/4$ inch, at the top, within $3/4$ inch or so of the end, to attach the turnbuckles.

I once saw a boat built out in the sticks by a guy who had no access to metalworking shops or tools. His chainplates were really interesting. Rather than bending heavy steel to shape, he used multiple layers of thin (maybe $1/16$-inch) stainless he found in a scrap pile. He even laid it out so it tapered down to about two layers near the waterline. It worked fine, but looked like a hassle to do. Something to keep in mind, though, if you don't have access to a metal shop.

You can fasten the chainplate to the hull in various ways. Many people simply screw or bolt them through the frames. I don't care for that, generally, because the angle will be wrong in most places. It's no big deal, but it seems that if the angle of the dangle isn't the same as the wire, all the strain will fall on the chainplate's top fastening. If something bad happens, like one boat I know that had its mast hit by a seaplane, the shock might split the wood. Also, with the frames full of planking screws anyway, adding even more to take the chainplate fastenings (I try to put one fastening in each plank the plate crosses) seems like a lot of perforation for structural members to suffer.

To get around all this, I try to position the chainplates to miss the frames, and put a 2×4 backing plate behind the planks to catch the bolts. That way I can make the angle the same as the wire. If your plans don't show the chainplates laid out this way, then you might consider moving them around a bit. You won't hurt anything.

Some chainplates will cross the frames on a very sharp angle. This often can't be avoided, so you'll have to put backing blocks on each side of the frame being crossed. Another irritating thing is when you have a butt block in the way. Again, just use two backing blocks. Every time that happens to me I swear that *next* time I'll locate the chainplates before planking, and not put any butt blocks in their way—the old *Think ahead, stupid,* rule again. So far I've always forgotten.

After you make the chainplates, lay each one on deck near where it will go and label it. The bolt holes will probably be a bit different for each one, and you'll want to drill the holes and fit the correct chainplate in place without the hassle of smearing tar all over everything, then having to scrape it clean because you used the wrong plate.

Draw a line on the hull showing the centerline of the plate. Hold the plate in position and drill the top hole through the hull. Now, look inside the boat and be sure you've positioned the plate in a place where you can get a backing block behind it. If not, fill the hole with a glued plug, and try again. Once the top hole is correct, insert a bolt 1/2 inch or so into the hull to hold the plate, wiggle the plate around until you see the penciled centerline, then drill the lower hole.

Make your backing pieces and soak them well in preservative. The two holes through the hull show where the chainplates are going, so it's easy to fit these things. To install one, spread a thick layer of roofing tar on it and nail it to the hull with two nails, just to hold it still while you drill it and drive the bolts through. Like the frames, you don't want the backing plate to fit too tightly against the deck. A gap allows air to circulate, which (as you know by now) prevents rot.

Now, go back out and drill the top and bottom holes through the inside block. Put bedding compound on the chainplate and drive the bolts through the hull. Go inside, cinch up the nuts, then drill the rest of the holes and install the bolts. Like any other place where a bolt goes through the hull, do *not* use all-thread bolts—they leak. Just use normal bolts with an inch or so of thread on them (galvanized machine bolts, in this case, because the head will be against the steel chainplate).

If you have a chainplate that stands vertical and should lay right on a frame, it's quite tempting simply to lag it to a frame rather than screwing around with backing plates. When I do this, I through-bolt the top hole, lag the others, then install a few through-bolts crossways in the frame to prevent splitting, just in case an airplane or something hits the rig.

On really large boats you will need to bolt into something more solid than backing plates. I worked on one 125-footer where the hull was crisscrossed with 1/4- by 4-inch Monel straps, with big plates welded in where the chainplates go. This is pretty heavy-duty stuff. Even I, the *chicken of the sea* when it comes to cruising-boat scantlings, don't go that far. However, you can make a metal bracket out of, say 3/16- by 4-inch steel, with a lip on each end so you can bolt it to two frames. If you put two of these on each chainplate you should be able to knock down drawbridges before you damage the hull.

Finally, I think all cruising boats should have running backstays, even when there's also a standing backstay. You may never use them. Mine are left loose, tied off to the side rigging about 99 percent of the time. But say you're running in a strong wind, or you're hove to worrying you might capsize. You'll sit there thinking about that single standing backstay, and about all the strains on it, and you'll just want to go below and have a drink. In times like these it's quite reassuring to be able to walk forward, release the runners, and tighten them up. They might save the mast from going, and at the least they'll make you feel better.

I'll talk about rigging in Chapter 16, but you can install the chainplates for the runners now. All of my designs have them, but if your plans don't show them, I suggest you install them anyway. They should be positioned pretty far back, say 60 to 75 percent of the distance from the mast to the stern, and be pointed either at the masthead or, if you have two headsails, at the attachment point of the staysail. To find the location, draw them on the sail plan, then take off the measurements, just as you found the location for the main chainplates.

MOORING POSTS

Although a few cleats on deck are OK for making fast most lines, you'll want to install at least one serious place to tie a line. Normally this mooring, called a *samson post* (which should give you an idea of how strong it's supposed to be), will be in the bow. But if you have the room, it won't hurt to install one in the stern, too.

The samson post goes through the deck and is through-bolted to a deck beam and drift-bolted into the keel. Go inside the hull and figure out where you want it. Normally the bow post is placed on the centerline so that a bowsprit can butt against it, and so that it can be bolted into the keel.

Find the center of the deck and make a mark (if you're lucky you'll already have a pencil mark on the deck beam there). Hopefully

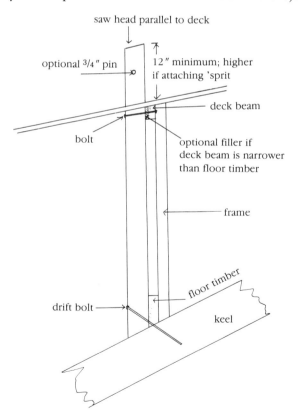

saw head parallel to deck

optional 3/4" pin

12" minimum; higher if attaching 'sprit

deck beam

bolt

optional filler if deck beam is narrower than floor timber

frame

floor timber

drift bolt

keel

Figure 9/3.
Samson post detail. Like its namesake, this thing should be *strong*.

the deck beam and the floor timber are on the same side of the frame. But if the deck beam is forward of the frame (the floor will be aft of the frame at the bow unless you've really screwed up), put blocking the same thickness as the floor timber against the beam so the mooring post can lay against both the beam and the floor and still stand vertical.

Draw a square on the underside of the deck about 1/2-inch or so larger than the mooring post. For instance, if you'll be using a 6×6, which you know is 5 1/2 by 5 1/2 inches, then draw a 6-inch square, with its forward face flush against the deck beam. Drill a hole through the deck at each corner. Go topside, draw lines to connect the holes, and saw it out. The reason you make the hole so much bigger than the post is because it's impossible for most of us to cut a hole that is just right. So, make the hole a lot bigger, then caulk it up.

I figure out the post's exact shape by using a piece of 1/4- by 3-inch plywood. Stick it down through the deck to the keel, clamp on another short piece that runs along the keel, and you got your pattern. The mooring post will stick up at least a foot off the deck, so add whatever height you want to the length of the pattern and saw out your post. Smear a lot of bedding on the bottom and on the deck beam, clamp the post in position, and bolt her home.

Cedar shingles are the simplest thing to use to caulk up the hole. I glue and drive in some shingles, spread some sort of bathtub caulk on top of that, and then lay a little glass cloth and Arabol or epoxy over that. Quarter-round molding nailed to the base of the post, with lots of goop underneath, looks good, too. If you're butting a 'sprit to the post, don't put the molding on the front.

Mooring posts in the stern often can't be on the centerline because stuff like hatches or cockpits get in the way. I still install them, but I make them smaller. I use 4×4s, position them close to the sheer, and bolt them to a deck beam. If you happen to have a bulkhead or cockpit floor support somewhere near the stern, you can position the post where you can also bolt it to one of them. Actually, a post bolted just to the deck beam will be plenty strong for normal use, even extraordinary use, but there's no such thing as *too strong,* and I want at least one thing on the boat that I can tie to and *know* it will not pull out.

BOWSPRITS

Bowsprits, or *'sprits*, are nice things. They're fun to sit on, greatly simplify anchor handling, allow you to carry more sail, and look great. A short 'sprit is handy on powerboats, too, but uncommon here in the States. We'll discuss rigging the 'sprit in Chapter 16, but this is a good time to bolt it down.

Although technically the 'sprit is just a pole bolted to the deck, give some thought to it. Lots of nice boats are ruined by awkward-

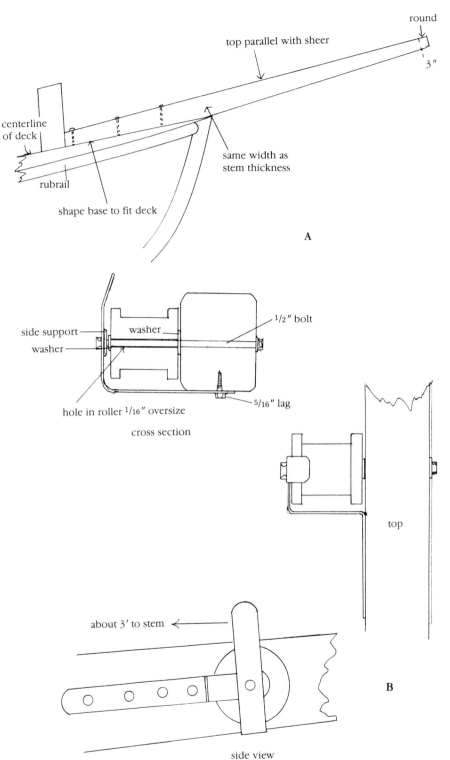

round

top parallel with sheer

3"

centerline
of deck

rubrail

shape base to fit deck

same width as
stem thickness

A

Figure 9/4.
(A) Bowsprit detail. Spend
some time on this; few
things can ruin a boat's
looks faster than a poorly
proportioned or oddly
angled 'sprit. (B) One of
the best things about a
'sprit is its ability to ease
the handling of ground
tackle. Here's an easily
fabricated anchor roller
you can make from 1/4 × 2-
inch steel and a rubber
boat-trailer roller. Mount it
about 3 feet forward of
the stem.

side support

washer

washer

hole in roller 1/16" oversize

cross section

1/2" bolt

5/16" lag

top

about 3' to stem

B

side view

looking 'sprits. The worst thing, to my eye anyway, is the British custom of running the 'sprit parallel to the waterline. It looks terrible!

I think the 'sprit looks best when it follows the sheer line. I also like a pole 'sprit. I think the wide, planked ones seen on some production boats are dangerous in heavy weather. If the bow is plunging down into solid water, a wide 'sprit may well leave you, sometimes taking part of the forward deck and maybe even the mast with it. A round or rectangular pole offers little resistance to the water, and is unlikely to be knocked off by a wave.

The stem fitting will be easier to fit, and things will look better, if the 'sprit is the same width as the stem. Assuming the stem is made from a 6-by, then the 'sprit will be, too. If the hull has a lot of sheer, you might need to use a 6×8 or a 6×10.

Some people worry that rot can start under the 'sprit if it lays on the deck, so they leave the whole thing propped up in the air a bit. I don't. I don't like the look, and I think that if you bed it well, there's little danger of rot starting, especially when the plywood deck is protected by cloth and Arabol.

If the plans don't give the 'sprit's dimensions, it's easy to eyeball it while making a pattern. The 'sprit will extend back to butt against the mooring post. So take a piece of $1/4$-inch ply—as long as the 'sprit and as wide as the material you're using—and tack it to the post.

Prop up the pattern right at the stem until it looks like it's following the sheer, then stand back and see how she lays. You'll need to stand back quite a way to see it right. I've had to saw more than one hole in shop walls to eyeball something properly. Scribe the angle at which the pattern butts against the mooring post and mark the place where the pattern is flush with the stem.

At the spot where you raised the pattern to make it look right, measure down to the deck. If it was, say, 3 inches, saw a tapered cut, starting at 0 at the point the 'sprit hits the stem, to 3 inches at the end where it butts against the post. Prop it up and stand back and eyeball it again to make sure it lays right.

The 'sprit will look even better if you taper the bottom and sides from the stem face to the outer end. A powerplane does this nicely. Although naturally it depends on the size of the boat, the outer end generally looks pretty nice tapered down to, say, $2\frac{1}{2}$ by $2\frac{1}{2}$ to 3 by 3 inches. It looks even better if you round the last 3 or 4 inches, which also makes it easier to attach the rigging fittings. Leave the top flat to make it easier to walk on. Regardless of the size of the boat, leave the 'sprit's outer end meaty enough so you can drive it through the side of anybody remotely your size who gets in your way.

Now you're ready to bolt the 'sprit through the deck, ideally through a deck beam or two. Go inside the boat and drill from the inside up through one deck beam underneath where the 'sprit will go. Go back out and lay the 'sprit in position. Clamp a block to the mooring post to hold the end down, and line the thing up so that it looks like it's running straight down the centerline. Have somebody stand on it while you go inside and run the drill bit up through the holes into the 'sprit just far enough to mark their positions. Remove the 'sprit and drill the holes the rest of the way through. Smear lots of tar on the bottom, maybe sit it on a piece of Irish Linen (what the workboat people call old-time tar paper) if you want, and bolt her home.

I like permanent 'sprits like the one just described. They're the strongest and the best looking. In England, reefing 'sprits were common, and in Holland the 'sprits are almost always mounted on big hinges so they can stand straight up in the air. Both of these features may be of value, especially if you're paying much for slip rent (which is figured by the foot, including bowsprits).

BULWARKS

All boats should have some sort of rail running around the edge of the deck. Even a 1 1/2-inch-square toerail gives you an edge to find when crawling around the deck at night. Perhaps the term *bulwark* is a bit grand for something like this, and maybe we should call it a *toerail*. A bulwark is something a man can lean against when spittin' his snoose to windward. A toerail is a thing to keep your jug from rolling off the deck. But what the hell, this is a liberal age. I call anything 3 inches high and up a bulwark—it has a good sound to it.

Personally, I think a 6-inch bulwark looks pretty good on most boats, and it's just low enough so you won't need special frames to support it; you can just bolt it through the deck. Lower ones can even be screwed or spiked down to the sheer strake.

It's no easy matter to bend these things to shape around the sheer, but it'll bend in a lot easier if you stop the rail 5 or 6 feet from the ends of the boat. It also looks rather sexy, especially on double-enders.

There's all sorts of ways to install these bulwarks. The strongest is the old fishboat system, where the rail is sawed out of wide timbers stacked up on deck. These rails were 4 to 6 inches thick, and a foot or so tall. Rugged it may be, but it takes a good-sized bandsaw to cut those timbers, and it wastes a lot of material.

Bulwark system 1

The simplest system, I think, is to bolt steel brackets to the deck every four feet, and bolt a plank for the bulwarks to these (see Figure 9-5). Some people like to space these brackets every two feet, but I suspect that's overkill.

The brackets are made from $3/16$-inch-thick 3- or 4-inch steel angle. Any metal fabricating shop with a shear can cut them up in just

Figure 9/5. System 1, steel bulwark supports made from 3/16- × 3-inch angle. The support on the left has a 3/4 I.D. × 2-inch pipe coupling welded on to support the stanchion post. Mount these on 4-foot centers; mount bulwark supports without pipe coupling in between.

a few minutes. Don't try to hacksaw them yourself; it isn't worth the effort.

I have a 3/4- by 2-inch pipe coupling welded to each bracket. You can screw in a length of pipe to make a strong, cheap, lifeline stanchion. Some people just weld the pipe to the bracket, but the problem with that is when (*not* if) you bend the stanchion against something, you'll have to remove the whole bracket to fix it. With the coupling, you just unscrew the pipe and replace it.

By the way, after you weld on the couplings, run a pipe threader down to fix any distortion caused by the heat. Then galvanize them, or at least paint them with a cold galvanizing paint (more on that later). You'll have to run the pipe tap down the couplings after you paint or galvanize them, too, because the threads will be clogged. If you paint the pipe stanchions with aluminum spray, from 20 feet away your 5 dollar stanchions will look like them 40 dollar stainless ones on the plastic boats. Personally, I like them painted black, trimmed with some fancy knot work. But more on that later, too.

The bracket will be located far enough inboard so that the wood bulwark, bolted to the outside, will be *inboard* of the rubrail. The brackets also must be far enough inboard so you can bolt them through the deck without hitting the sheer strake. The butt blocks on the sheer strake will probably get in the way.

It would be nice if you had thought about these brackets back when you started planking (Think ahead, Stupid), and had spaced them to avoid the butt blocks, but that's just a bit too organized for anything less than a production line. I get around this by placing the brackets inboard of the butts, too, unless I have very narrow side decks. So, if your planking and your butt blocks are both 1 1/2 inches thick, your brackets will be 3 inches inboard, plus the thickness of the rubrail, of course. Figure out how far in they must go, set a try square to that distance, and run a line clear around the deck.

If you are attaching stanchions to these brackets, you want a good-sized backing plate below the deck to spread the strain of somebody falling against the lifelines, unless your deck plywood is pretty thick. I think I'd use backing plates on any deck less than $1\frac{1}{4}$ inch thick.

I start in the middle of the hull and work out to the ends. To be sure I'm actually positioning the bracket between frames, I drill a hole from below to mark the center of the first bracket. Then, after this first one is bolted down, I measure *inside* the hull to be sure I can space them 4 feet apart. For instance, on my current boat, which has heavy framing, there's only $9\frac{1}{2}$ inches between the frames. Some of the frames aren't *exactly* where they should be (OK Jack; I bet yours ain't either), so my brackets aren't spaced uniformly. Nothing major: One might be 4 feet 2 inches from the next; it isn't noticeable. But if you don't measure inside to be sure you have enough room, and just happily drill holes on 4-foot centers, chances are you'll drill a hole into a frame top or something. Check inside first and you'll save yourself a lot of grief.

I thoroughly bolt down several brackets in the middle and one on each end. With the others I just drill one hole and drive the bolt down. Then I wrap a 1-by batten around the brackets, and clamp the *floating* ones to this 1-by to make sure the brackets are exactly in line. This fairing batten will show you if 4-foot centers are close enough for the bulwark to follow the deck line. If they don't, and maybe they won't on a fat, full-ended boat, install more brackets (you won't need pipe couplings on these) between the main ones. When you're satisfied, drill the rest of the holes, bed the brackets well with goop, and bolt 'em down good. I use a pattern of three $5/16$-inch bolts through the deck.

Wrap a 2×4 or 2×6 around the brackets, positioning it about $3/4$ inch above the deck to allow water to run off, and bolt it to the brackets. You can use thinner material, but a 2-by looks good. Unfortunately, it's also harder to bend in place. Cedar or some other soft wood will bend around the easiest, but fir will go with some strong-arm tactics.

To force the 2-by down to run parallel to the deck, I screw several L-shaped hooks made from pipe fittings down into the stanchion brackets after I've bent the 2-by around, then use wedges to force the 2-by down to where I want it. A fat friend standing on it will work, too.

You can either splice the butts or use butt blocks. If you want to be a little fancy you can glue a $3/4$-inch piece, 12 inches or so long, to the bottom of the bulwark piece at each end so that the rail actually sits on the deck at the ends. If you do this, run a bolt clear through the rail and deck to hold the ends down well. You can also simply end the bulwark at the last bracket. Either way, saw a bit of shape, like a Lazy S or something, into the end.

The next simplest system is to laminate the bulwark in place (see Figure 9-6). You can make a nice rail from 2×2s stacked four high. This rail is bolted to the deck, too, and so must be located inboard of the sheer strake, but this time it doesn't need to be inboard of the butt blocks. So, set the try square to the required distance, and run a pencil line around the deck, just as described in System 1.

It's important that the bulwark not extend outboard past the rubrail. If there is much crown to the deck, you might need to run the first 2×2 through a table saw to bevel its base a bit. Stand a level up on deck, measure the angle with a bevel square, and saw one side of the first piece to that angle.

Two people make the rest of the operation go much easier. Spread a thick layer of bedding compound on the deck; then, using as long a piece of 2×2 as you can get, bolt it down to the deck. You can drill it, install the bolt, then go back later and cinch up the nuts. Don't drill into any deck beams; don't drill where you'll have a water drain (*scupper*); and *don't* notch the piece for the water drain. Countersink the bolts just a hair. The remaining pieces are glued and nailed to the first one—just like strip-planking a boat. Again, there's no need for epoxy, but it can't hurt if you want to use it.

You'll need to figure out where you want scuppers. I make them about 2 feet long, about two feet apart. I start at about the middle of the boat, and run them fore and aft 6 to 8 feet each way, depending on the size and sheer of the boat, of course.

When you decide on the locations for your scuppers, staple some waxed paper to the top of the first piece at each location to keep the layers from sticking together there. Spread glue on the first piece and on a second piece, and nail her down with galvanized nails, drilling pilot holes before nailing to keep the 2×2 from splitting.

This waxed paper really simplifies things. After you finish adding all the layers, all you have to do is go back, drill a hole through the bulwark at each end of the paper, stick in a narrow saw (a keyhole saw works well), and trim the hole down to the deck (don't cut into the

Figure 9/6.
System 2, laminated bulwark. (1) Bed and bolt down the first layer. (2) Glue and nail the second layer; mark the nail locations on the side. (3) Glue and nail down a third (and a fourth if you like) piece, then bolt through to deck at about 16-inch centers. Note that the bulwark is set well back from the rail. See text for cutting out scuppers.

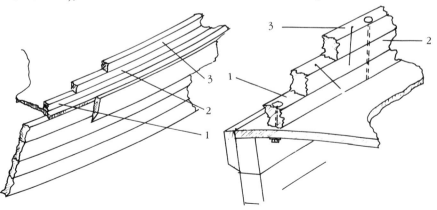

fabric). Pull out the piece, and there's the scupper. Saw these out fairly soon so that the bedding compound under the first piece doesn't have a chance to set up completely; it will be easier to clean off the deck. You can leave this area *bare* in the first place, but be sure to let the bedding compound overlap the *bare* area a bit so you'll have some under *all* of the first layer.

Be sure to mark the location of nails on the side of each strip as you go; you don't want to drive another one in the same spot as you add layers. You might find that you have trouble forcing a piece down tight. You can solve that with a nail set made from a 1/4-inch bolt. Just whack the sucker good and it should lay right down. Unfortunately, brute force solves many problems.

To change the subject a moment, this brute force business used to be called *Fort Mayne,* or *strong arm,* in France, and it meant the guy with the strong arm got his way. Over in England, King Arthur decided there was something wrong with rich folks dressing up in sheet metal and hacking up poor folks, so he tried a noble experiment. Standing up to accusations of being soft on commies, unpatriotic, naive, and all the other charges the corporate types have their front men put out every election year, Arthur tried to redirect Might for Right, and founded the Order of Chivalry and the Knights of the Round Table—kind of like today's Guardian Angels, although much hipper of course.

This was quite the deal; anybody who was anybody joined up, and for a good 30 years the poor folks were left more or less in peace. Well, human nature being what it is, the idea faded out, Arthur died in a rebellion led by his son, of all people, and today the world is as it is. So when you whack on that piece to set her down, imagine back to Arthur's day, and know that Arthur is likely watching with approval (he never really died) as you use Might for Right in getting that sucker to lay where it's supposed to go.

Bulwark system 3

If you want a *real* bulwark, a big high one you can lean back against, you'll have to install separate frames to support it. Extending the real frames up through the deck creates a prime spot for rot to get started, and it's difficult to repair the inevitable damage when the bulwark supports are part of the main structure.

The easiest way to fit these frames is to go inside the boat and, using a pattern of the frame stock, draw cutouts for the frames halfway between each pair of deck beams. Drill a hole through the deck at each corner of the square, then saw out the hole from the top. Since it's impossible to cut things perfectly, cut the hole a bit oversize. You can fill in any gaps later with super stickum or wedges made from cedar shingles, or both.

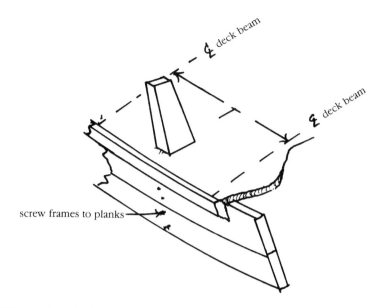

Figure 9/7.
System 3, real framed bulwarks. Install separate frames screwed to at least two planks halfway between deck beams. Bend a 3/4-inch plank around the frames, leaving a gap between the bulwark and the deck so water can run off.

deck beam

deck beam

screw frames to planks

The bulwark frames must extend several planks down into the hull. You'll have to notch the frames around any butt blocks in the way. Shape the frames so their tops are well inboard of the rubrail. Although some people loft these frames and cut each one on a slightly different angle, I'd make 'em all the same, myself. They'll look better and are less likely to be damaged if they're vertical, rather than squared off at the deck.

Draw a pencil line down each side against the planks to show where they lie, then drill pilot holes through the plank for the fasteners. Nail a crosspiece temporarily across the adjacent frames, then drive a wedge down between the crosspiece and the bulwark frame to hold it in place against the plank while you drill the holes. Bed the frames well, and screw them to the hull. Plank the sides with something—3/4-inch stock is enough—and leave a 1-inch gap above the deck to serve as a waterway.

Finally, any bulwark 6 inches high or more looks good with some sort of cap. Ideally this should be hardwood, because it's going to get wear from mooring lines and whatnot. You can also use soft wood, and screw down some 1-inch brass or stainless quarter-round in places where there's chafe.

The easiest way to cap the bulwark is to make a pattern from 1/4-inch plywood, then saw out the cap. Ideally, the middle should be hollowed out 1/2 inch or so to let it sit down on the rail. This isn't necessary if you have a framed bulwark, because the top of the frames are wide enough to make a secure base. Fasten the cap down with spikes or screws.

HATCHES AND HOUSES

HATCH FRAMES

A *hatch frame* is simply a set of watertight lips bordering a hole in the deck—the hatch opening. These lips keep the hatch from sliding around and water from leaking into the opening. Figure 10-1 shows two ways of building one.

The first version is probably the simplest, and it robs less space from the hole because the hatch sits directly on the deck, instead of atop a sill. Add a strip of hard rubber around the hatch's bottom edge, which should be curved to match the deck's crown, and it's fairly watertight. A refinement is to install a low sill piece around the frame, curved to match the deck and screwed into it, for the hatch to sit on. This sill should be bedded well to cut down leakage around the frame.

Whichever style you prefer, the hatch frame should extend at least 2 inches above the deck, or 2 inches above the sill if you're using one. Note the 2 × 2 cornerpieces shown on the hatch in Figure 10-1. You don't really need these on a low frame, but they can't hurt. You will need them if you're making a high hatch frame, like for a fish hold. I use them for most hatches. They're strong, and make fitting the corner joints easier.

I join the frame pieces with simple butt joints. Mitering or dovetailing looks slick, but it's difficult to get the fit right, especially when the frame isn't exactly square. Besides, the inside cornerpieces and the sill, which overlaps the frame butt, keep it from leaking.

A corner leak is a potential rot starter, so I really bed things well at every joint. Nowadays I also paint the intersection of the deck and hatch frame with epoxy or Arabol. Later on, if you see *any* dripping inside the boat around the hatch (or anywhere else), fix it. It will rot the deck out if you don't.

The second method is one I've used for a number of hatches. The advantage is that the actual base of the hatch is a straight line, so it doesn't have to be fitted to the deck crown. The disadvantage is that the frame takes up more of the hole, since it's twice as thick as the first method. I don't know which, if either, is better. I now use the first method, for whatever that's worth.

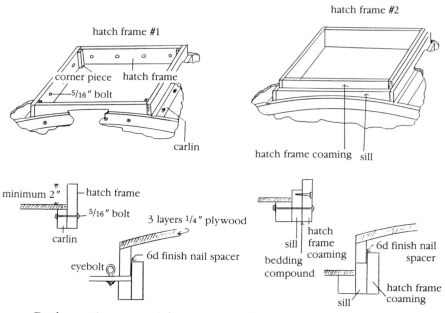

Figure 10/1. Two methods of constructing lift-hatch frames. Use 2-by stock. Bed everything well. Make the hatch cover from three layers of plywood laminated over a form, or use heavy Plexiglas, which bends fairly easily if you soften it with a hair dryer.

Both versions use 2-by material for the frame, except on the smallest boats. Why not? You want the frame to be strong, you know. Make the hatch top's frame from the same 2-by material as the sill. If you're building a big, heavy hatch, like for a fish hold, use 3-by material.

After building one that wouldn't fit over the frame, I learned that the actual hatch cover should be assembled *on the frame*, with a couple of 6d finish nails for spacers between each piece and the frame. That guarantees that the hatch will be loose enough to be easily removable.

The hatch will look far better if its top is curved, but this means you can't bend heavy plywood over it. Instead, laminate the top using three layers of 1/4-inch plywood, then cover the whole thing with glass cloth and Arabol, just as you did the deck. Plexiglas makes a good cover, too, but make it heavy enough that it can be stomped on without breaking.

Plexiglas can be quite slippery to step on, so attach some sort of wood strips running fore and aft on, say, 6-inch centers, so you don't break your neck some night.

I never use hinges on deck hatches, because they always seem to get in the way. I prefer to have the hatch completely free so I can remove it. I install a 5/16-inch eyebolt on two sides of the hatch cover, or all four if it's a big one, so I can lash it down tightly when in open water. I don't mean to go on about this ''Man Against the Sea'' stuff, *but*, if you're going to venture out into open water farther than you care to swim back, you want all parts of the boat *stout*. You'd feel pretty stupid, before you got drownded, if your boat was knocked down, the hatch was washed off, and you sank. A heavy hatch, secured down by rope woven through eyebolts, is safe from most any attack this side of a chain saw.

DECKHOUSES

Although there's several ways to build a deckhouse, the idea to always keep in mind is that she must be strong—*real* strong, if you're going out in open water. In really bad weather, the house is often the most vulnerable part of the boat. If you lose it, you'll have one helluva hole.

Miles Smeeton's *Once Is Enough* (Ashford Press, 1959) contains an interesting account of a yacht that was pitchpoled and lost the house while trying to round Cape Horn. They managed to avoid sinking and got into Chile, where they built a really heavy house, then tried again. Well, they were pitchpoled again, and the house, which was through-bolted down, was just moved several inches sideways. Although this made a nasty hole in the deck, too, at least it was small enough to plug up with blankets and whatnot, and they finally made it around the Horn.

Conditions like this are unusual at sea—at least in the parts of the world cruised by folks a little less adventurous than the Smeetons—but it does show that if you're planning on going out in open water you want the house as stout as you can make it.

Your best defense is to keep the house as low as possible. Add-on wheelhouses should be small, with watertight floors and heavy bulkheads on each side. Two schools of thought exist on wheelhouse windows. Some people like them made from nearly bulletproof Lexan. Some prefer weak windows that would break away, easing the strain on the house itself in the event of capsize. The jury is still out.

When figuring how high to make the sides, keep in mind that the more crown you put into the roof, the lower you can make the walls. Also, about the only place you need full headroom is over the floor, where you'll be standing and walking back and forth. You could have a cabin roof crowned, say, 12 inches on the centerline, and lower the side walls 12 inches without losing usable headroom.

Plank-on-edge house

The most common way to build a low house is to through-bolt a plank on edge into the deck framework. Usually you'll need two planks on edge, and maybe three on the ends. I've built several houses like this and I like them. It's probably the strongest way to go, especially if there are no bulkheads inside the cabin area. The problems? It's hard to find nice, wide, dry planks; drilling a long hole through a $1^{1}/4$- or $1^{1}/2$-inch-wide board can be tricky (I wouldn't try drilling planks thinner than $1^{1}/4$ inches); and the swelling and shrink-

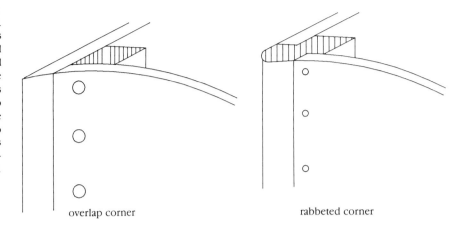

Figure 10/2.
Deckhouse corner posts. The overlapped corner is the easiest. Nobody will guess as long as you round off the corner a bit. The rabbeted corner post is traditional but difficult to fit well. You can get the same look by leaving a gap between the house sides and putting in a quarter-round molding.

overlap corner   rabbeted corner

ing of the planks can cause the butt to open up (although this can be fixed with a little caulking, and an epoxy coating might eliminate the movement).

The wide sides are assembled around stout cornerposts. The slickest ones are rabbeted to receive the side planks, but a simple butt joint over the cornerpost works just as well and is much easier to do. Once the hull is painted nobody will ever know.

If you're using simple overlap-style cornerposts, you'll install them after you have the walls up. Screw the walls together where they butt to hold them until the post is installed. Simply bolt the post to the carlin and deck beam, then screw the house sides into it. Use lots of glue, too.

If you're going to rabbet the corners, stand the posts up before you erect the walls. I use a plywood guide stood on deck (see Figure 10-3) to give me the angle I want for the cornerposts. The side walls should slant inboard a few degrees. If you make them vertical they'll look like they're leaning out, *but* if they lean too far in, rain will come in when you open a window. Some people, including many production-boat designers, slant the back wall forward and lean the front wall aft. I suppose this looks rakish, but it also lets in water when the hatch and front windows are opened. I keep my end walls vertical.

Some people also put a rabbeted sill on deck for the house to sit in. It can't hurt anything, but it seems like a lot of extra hassle to me. Instead, I install another carlin inside the cabin after the posts are up (see Figure 10-4). This gives a good lip to bed the bottom of the house against, provides a place to run in some extra fastenings, and finishes off the inside, hiding the decking and the base of the house wall. This extra carlin should stick up about $1^{1/2}$ to 2 inches above deck level; slope its top 30 degrees or so for looks and drainage. Put lots of bedding compound behind it, and bolt it to the original carlin and deck beams with $5/16$-inch bolts.

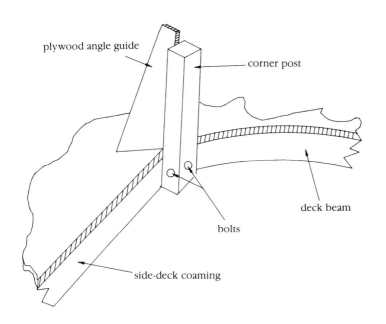

Figure 10/3.
Find the angle of deck-house corner posts with a plywood pattern. Cut its bottom to make the house side's face lean inboard a little.

plywood angle guide

corner post

deck beam

bolts

side-deck coaming

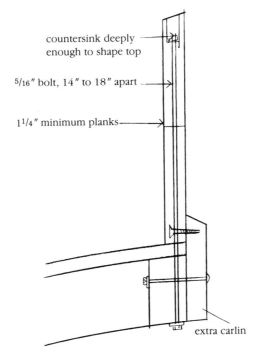

Figure 10/4.
Plank-on-edge house wall, through-bolted into the carlin. Bed everything well.

countersink deeply enough to shape top

5/16" bolt, 14" to 18" apart

1 1/4" minimum planks

extra carlin

As mentioned earlier, the cabin sides often will have to be made up from two planks. I think I'd use planks no wider than 8 inches, just to keep swelling down. Take the first one, clamp it in place, and scribe the bottom so it fits the deck.

The simplest way to clamp the sides in position is to make a form. Take a few long 2 × 4s, nail one end to a bottom frame, clamp them to the carlin, and nail a crosspiece to the top to keep them from moving. You'll need to notch these 2 × 4s to clear the inner carlin. Be sure to erect them on whatever angle you want the house walls to be. A form like this every 3 or 4 feet will make it much easier to attach the walls, especially if there is much curve to the sides, such as when the carlin and house sides are parallel to the side of the hull.

Once you get the first side piece fitted to the deck, remove it, put lots of bedding compound on the deck where it sits, put glue on the cornerposts, pull it down tightly against the deck with sliding bar clamps, and screw it to the inner carlin and at the corners. Don't worry about trying to make the first piece on each side the same height. You can saw the second pieces to match.

Fit a plank to the deck at the front and back of the house opening. After it's cut to fit the deck crown, clamp several more to it until you have a finished board wide enough to make the ends. Draw a curve on the top board, just as you did for the deck beam mold. Saw the pieces to the curve, then attach the first piece to the deck just like the side piece.

Now then, here comes the fun part: through-bolting the cabin walls to the deck and carlin. Even though 1/4-inch rod will be strong enough, I'd use 5/16-inch rod for this: A 5/16-inch drill bit will track straighter than a 1/4-inch one over a long distance.

Clamp the second piece onto the first on both sides, using bar clamps to hold them down tight. Level across and see if these boards are even. Odds are they aren't, so mark which one (or both) need to be trimmed, and do it. Draw on any window cut-outs, then draw a line where you want the bolts: 14 to 18 inches or so apart is fine. Look inside and make sure you aren't planning to run a bolt through one already in the carlin.

Take off the second piece, flip it over, and start drilling the hole on its *bottom*. (You might want to practice drilling these long holes on a wide board first.) This way, at least you know the hole will be in the center of the wall in the middle, which means your chances of making it clear through the board without coming out the side are a good 50 percent greater. Before drilling, clamp a straightedge several feet long to the board, and sight along that to keep the drill bit running straight.

Now clamp this second piece back onto the first, run the drill down the holes, and drill into the first piece about 1/4 inch just to mark the spots. Take off the top piece, clamp your little straightedge next to each place you want the hole, and drill on down through to the carlin.

You can make the bolts out of regular galvanized rod, available at any steel dealer. You can also use cadmium-plated threaded rod from a hardware store, since these bolts will always be out of the weather—theoretically. Just in case, you might want to paint them with epoxy, or at least run a little tar down the hole.

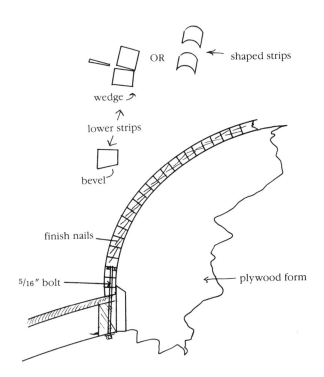

OR

shaped strips

wedge ↗

lower strips

bevel

finish nails

5/16″ bolt

plywood form

Figure 10/5.
You can build a deckhouse to practically any shape by laminating it up using strips covered with glass cloth and epoxy. This can make a relatively high cabin roof look lower and sleeker. You should have a few heavy bulkheads inside for support. You can bevel or wedge the strips to shape, or use pre-shaped strips cut with a molding cutter.

Countersink each bolt hole in the top piece an inch or so. You want enough depth so you can bevel the top for the roof without hitting the nut. Countersinking will probably plug up the smaller hole, so run the bit through from the other end and clean 'em out.

Now clamp the top board back in place, measure the length for each bolt, cut the bolts to size, and start them an inch or so into the hole. Remember, if you rub soap on the bolts they'll drive more easily.

Remove the board, drive the bolts down so that one is sticking out about 1/2 inch and the others are just peeking out, spread glue on the two boards' meeting faces, position the second board, drive the bolts through, and cinch 'em down. Use bar clamps to force the piece down tight, screw the ends to the cornerpost, and you got it. Do the same business on the ends, and you're done.

Pretty slick, huh? Most of us can drill an 8-inch hole using the straightedge and have it come out OK, but drilling a 16-inch hole through 1½-inch stock is a different story. If, God forbid, you *do* drill through the side of the board, don't worry: Just fill the hole with a dowel and try again.

By the time you're halfway into this it probably will dawn on you how much easier it would have been simply to raise the freeboard a bit in the cabin area and make a raised-sheer house. You're right; it would have been. But to many eyes the normal coach-roof-style house looks better; the real side decks and handholds attached to the cabin make moving around on deck easier; and a house is nice to sit on or lean against when laying about.

Finally, if you can't find suitable wide boards but don't want to use plywood (see below), there's no reason you can't strip-build the walls, much like the strip-built bulwarks described earlier. I'd use maybe 2×2s, glued and edge-nailed for maybe half the layers, then drill through them for bolts. I'd glue and nail down the following layers, making sure not to nail into the bolt holes, then I'd drill the rest of the hole from the inside out.

Plywood house walls

The simplest house is just a box made from a few pieces of plywood screwed to the carlins. Years back, when I wasn't as cautious (or maybe as chicken) as I am now, I built a boat with a house made from 3/4-inch AC plywood bolted to the carlins, with no supporting interior bulkheads. I stepped a mast on top of it, and spent several years sailing the thing to Mexico and Honolulu. I never went through any hurricanes, but it had hard use and never gave me any trouble. In fact, the next owner *did* sail it through a hurricane when the boat was 10 years old, now that I think of it. Still, I think it was a bit lightweight, and here's how I did it last time.

Figure 10/6.
Plywood house wall. This is the simplest system, and plenty strong enough for most uses.

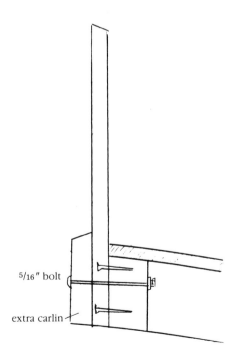

5/16″ bolt

extra carlin

My current boat has a 16-foot-long plywood deckhouse. I started with the same plywood angle guide described for erecting the cornerposts for plank-on-edge houses, held them in place along the deck, and planed the carlins until a straightedge laid against the guide and the carlin was more or less straight.

For some reason I made rabbeted cornerposts. I don't know why; just a whim. On the other ply cabin I made, I didn't bother. I erected the plywood, then screwed cornerposts in *after* the ply was up. This time, because they were rabbeted, I put up the cornerposts first, then erected the house sides.

Next I nailed a 2-foot-wide piece of 1/2-inch MDO single-sided overlay to the carlin, smooth side out, with *lots* of bedding compound behind it. After I had this on all the way around, I glued a second layer on, using epoxy and lots of little 3/4-inch stainless screws to hold it together until the glue set up. Then I glued (with Weldwood Construction Adhesive) some 5/16- by 3-inch beaded tongue and groove knotty pine all the way around the inside. When it's oiled and varnished, this stuff looks real slick; kinda like a mountain cabin. It's pretty reasonably priced, too, and available in most larger lumberyards. Finally, I bolted a 2×6 all the way around, through the plywood and against the carlins and deck beams, to make the inner carlin already described.

This was a pretty easy way to build a house, and I think it's plenty strong, too, although perhaps not as strong as a plank wall well bolted down. The interior has several big plywood bulkheads attached firmly to the bottom and side frames, the house walls itself, and the cabin roof beams. Once the roof is on I'll probably cover the whole thing with glass cloth and epoxy resin, which should strengthen it even more, and leak-proof it to boot.

I used two layers of plywood for this house because it was longer than a normal sheet of plywood, and it would have been hard to bend the curved sides with a heavy single sheet. On a short, straight house, I think you could just buy a sheet of 1 1/8-inch underlayment ply-

A

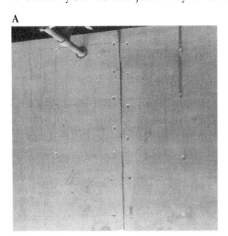

B

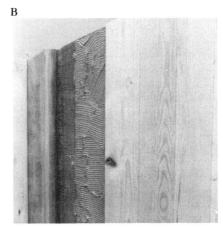

Figure 10/7.
(A) House wall made from two layers of plywood. The first layer is screwed to the carlins; the second layer is glued and screwed over the first. (B) Beaded T & G pine glued to inside of house walls with Weldwood Construction Adhesive. (Note rabbeted corner post.)

Hatches and Houses

wood, the kind they use for subfloors on houses. It's good, reasonably priced stuff, and it would be plenty strong enough.

You can also use plywood to make a plank-on-edge, bolted-down house wall. This might be the strongest way to go, and if the walls have a lot of curve, it's probably the simplest. Basically this will be a three-layer plywood sandwich, with spaces left in the inner layer for the bolts. Use MDO or marine ply for the outer layers, and maybe plain T1-11 for the middle layer.

First, install the carlin with the 2-inch lip above deck and put up the cornerpost forms, just as described for the plank-on-edge wall. Scribe a piece of $3/8$- or $1/2$-inch ply to the deck, fit it, then bed and nail it to the carlin lip, with a few very small, wire finish nails driven into the forms to hold it in position. Now run a long, $1/4$- or $3/8$-inch drill bit down the side (*not* through it) of this first piece of plywood, and drill holes on 14- to 18-inch centers through the main carlin.

Draw a pencil line on the plywood where the bolt will go, then glue on pieces of plywood the same thickness as the bolts between each pencil line. If you have some deep-throated clamps you won't need to use screws. Bring these filler pieces up almost to the line, but be sure you leave enough gap for the bolts. You could even install the bolts first, and glue the plywood fillers around them.

Glue on a final outer layer of plywood to cover everything, and you'll have a solid plywood plank-on-edge house wall, through-bolted to the deck. After all the glue has set up, cinch up the nuts below the carlin to get some tension on the walls.

High deckhouses

If you're building a tall deckhouse, like a wheelhouse or a powerboat cabin, think about how you'll be using the boat. As mentioned before, the deckhouse is generally the most vulnerable part of the boat, and the taller it is the more easily it can be knocked off.

If you're using the boat in protected waters there's no reason to get carried away. I'd just screw sheets of $3/4$-inch ply to the carlins. If the cabin is long or curved, use two layers of $3/8$- or $1/2$-inch ply, as described earlier. A bulkhead or two inside will stiffen things up, as will the roof.

If you're going into open water with a high house, you'll want to give it more thought and try to build something that will stand up to a blow.

The most common system is similar to shoreside house construction, with a sill, plate, and studs on maybe 2-foot centers. The studs may be around $1 1/2$ by $2 1/2$ inches (rip a 2×6 in half). The outside used to be made from 1×4 tongue and groove, but today it will probably consist of plywood covered with glass cloth and epoxy. The inside will be finished off with paneling, like the $5/16$-inch beaded

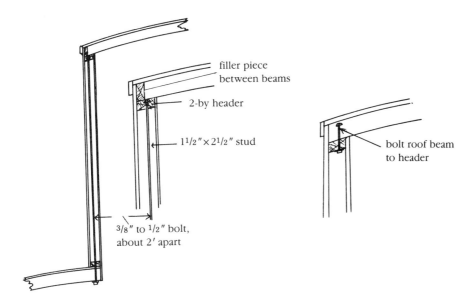

filler piece
between beams

2-by header

$1\frac{1}{2}'' \times 2\frac{1}{2}''$ stud

bolt roof beam
to header

$\frac{3}{8}''$ to $\frac{1}{2}''$ bolt,
about 2' apart

Figure 10/8.
Rugged high deckhouse or wheelhouse construction for offshore use. Use non-magnetic fasteners near any compass. You can fill the void between the inner and outer panel with insulation if you're in a cooler climate.

T & G in Figure 10-7B. The roof beams will be bolted to the plate, or cap.

Unlike in a shore house, this style of wall will be held down to the sill by through-bolts on 2-foot or so centers. And these bolts, at least in the front of the house, *must* be made from some sort of non-magnetic material, like brass or stainless, or you'll never get the compass adjusted. There's something about a vertical steel rod that raises hell with a compass, more so than a steel house for some reason.

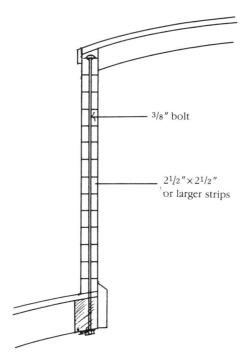

$\frac{3}{8}''$ bolt

$2\frac{1}{2}'' \times 2\frac{1}{2}''$ or larger strips

Figure 10/9.
Extra-rugged high deck-house built with heavy strips through-bolted into the carlins. Again, the through-bolts should be non-magnetic anywhere near the compass.

Hatches and Houses

I think the stoutest high house I've ever seen was built by my friend Paul Svornich. He strip-planked the whole thing up with 2½-by 3-inch strips, then through-bolted that to the deck. Rugged.

HOUSE ROOF

Although I suggest you leave the roof off until you're through with *everything* inside, this seems like the time to talk about it, at least. As always, there are several approaches to take.

Roof with beams

Building a traditional plank-on-beam house roof is a lot like laying a deck: First you make the beams, then you cover them with plywood planking. As with the deck, using the same crown throughout simplifies things.

Make a form just as you did for the deck beams, and laminate up as many roof beams as you need. For small boats and those with low-crowned cabin roofs, you can use sawn beams. Sawn beams will be simplest, too, if you have a fancy roof that changes its crown. If you laminate the beams, you'll have to make a form for each one. Of course, sawing them out is the same as making a form, now that I think about it, but at least you eliminate the laminating business.

If a 2 × 12 isn't wide enough for sawn beams, you can widen it with a glued-on extension; the roof, made from multiple layers of ply,

Figure 10/10.
Cabin roof framing is like a miniature version of deck framing.

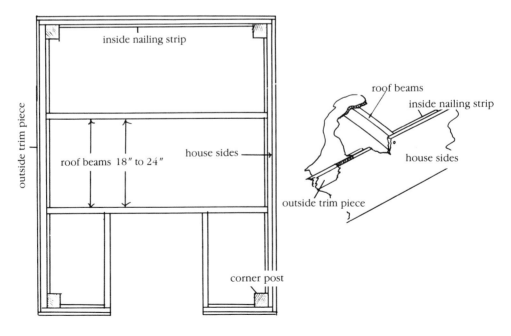

is strong enough for house roof purposes even without the beams. If you want beams thicker than 2-by, glue a piece of 1-by or another 2-by to the first one. This gets rather wasteful with the wood, and I'd suggest laminating the beams to a "Constant Camber," to borrow a phrase.

To get the shape for each beam, set a nail in the center top edge of each of the house ends, then set in others on 8-inch centers, radiating out from the center one. Starting at one end, lay a 2 × 4 across the house sides where a beam will go, lay a long straightedge running the length of the cabin against the centerline nails, and measure the distance from the *bottom* of the crosspiece to the straightedge. Stand a framing square on the crosspiece and you'll be able to measure exactly straight up.

Now move the straightedge to the next pair of nails and measure down to the crosspiece with the framing square. On and on. Draw a centerline on a piece of pattern stock, draw 8-inch ticks out from the centerline, transfer the measurements taken with the framing square to the pattern, connect those dots with a batten, draw it in, and cut it out.

How closely should you space the beams? Depends on how you're building the roof. If the total opening is less than 8 feet wide, the simplest approach is to run the plywood right across. I did this on a roof with beams spaced on 2-foot centers, however, and the plywood sagged between the beams. I don't think this would have happened if I had run the plywood fore and aft, but there would have been a seam down the middle of the cabin roof to deal with.

I could have spaced the beams more closely together, but beams spaced 2 feet apart look nice. I'm working on a roof now with the beams spaced on 2-foot centers, but I'm putting down a layer of that 5/16-inch beaded T & G stuff I keep mentioning first, topped with three or four layers of 1/4-inch plywood. I think the layer of T & G will keep the ply from sagging, so I should be able just to nail it on "across" the opening. There's a pretty heavy crown to the roof, and it may be a bitch to wrap the plywood over. If so, I'll put it on lengthwise, and the T & G will hide the butt.

Also, it isn't carved in stone that the beams have to be evenly spaced. In fact, since my current house is rather long, I positioned several roof beams so I could nail them into several heavy bulkheads that are fastened to the hull framing. This will make it a lot harder to lose the house.

When you get your beams sawn or laminated to shape, whichever, clamp a beam to both the front and back walls to find the proper shape for the ends, draw a line, and saw the ends to fit. Fitting the intermediate beams looks trickier than it is. The beams are butted against the house wall and spiked or screwed in, although some people will notch the wall a bit to hold the end of the beam. With the plywood roof fastened to the house wall, I think it's plenty strong just to butt the beams, and certainly simpler. If for some reason

Figure 10/11. Mounting cabin roof beams. (A) Find top with level. (B) Get angle, transfer to mark found with level. (C) Hold beam end up with L-shaped holder made from plywood scrap. (D) Nail the beam in place.

A

B

C

D

you're building a planked roof, then you'd best notch in the beams, and make a shelf underneath to hold them up. Better yet, use plywood. As with the deck, it's the strongest and simplest way to go, as well as being the only *really* watertight one.

To fit the intermediate beams, stretch a centerline string down the house opening and lay a beam across the house where you want it, with its center lined up with the string. (I always start off on the widest beam in case I cut it too short.) Lay a short straightedge against the inside house wall and the beam, draw a line on the beam showing the angle of the house wall, and set a bevel gauge to this angle. Draw the house side's curve on the bottom of the beam.

Now, stand a level on top of the house wall and mark on the *top* of the beam a point exactly vertical from the inside edge of the wall. Take the bevel gauge, put it against the mark you made with the level, and draw in the cutting angle for the end of the beam. Repeat the operation for the other side.

Figure 10/12 (left). Hanging knees at the mast partners or other points of stress strengthen things and look great. Use epoxy mixed with sawdust if your fits ain't the best; bolt the knee in place after the glue sets up.

Figure 10/13 (right). Roof beams all installed. Position your beams to hit main bulkheads or support other interior joinery. Roof beams needn't be evenly spaced, especially with ply roofs.

Make an **L**-shaped support from a piece of ¼-inch plywood to hold up the beam while you position it for fastening. The bottom of the **L** holds up the beam, and you can move the thing up and down, holding it with a small **C**-clamp to the house wall. Just as you did with the deck beams, you want to position the beam so that a saw blade lying flat on it just touches the *outer* corner of the wall. Spike or screw the beam to the wall when it's positioned.

I like a hanging knee or two inside the house to support the beam, especially if a mast is going through the house. It's a bitch to saw these to fit the wall and the beam perfectly, but epoxy has solved that problem. Make the knee and fit it as well as patience allows. Then mix up some epoxy loaded with enough sawdust to give it the consistency of bread dough. Spread this goop on the face that meets the beam, since it's the curved one and probably doesn't fit perfectly, spread regular epoxy on the face that meets the wall, and clamp the knee in place. After the epoxy sets, drill the knee and put in a few bolts.

After all the beams are up, frame in the hatch opening and cut out the back wall for the entrance, if you're going to have one there. A sliding hatch opening should be at least 26 inches long by 28 inches wide. When you cut out the opening in the wall, leave it a good 6 inches above the deck to keep water out of the house. Glue and screw in 1-by cleats between the beams to back up the top edge of the house when you nail down the plywood roof. (Nails don't hold for beans in the end grain of plywood.)

Once you've completed the roof framing, lay out the plywood just as you did for the deck. Since the top edge of the house is probably a bit rough, I like to glue the first layer of ply to the wall with a tube-type construction adhesive, like the stuff house framers use to glue down subfloors. This works better than a thin glue in this case, but I use a powder glue for the plywood laminations, just like the deck.

Hatches and Houses

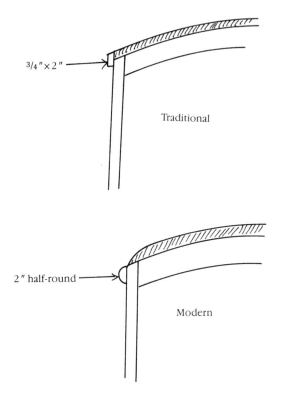

3/4″ × 2″

Traditional

2″ half-round

Modern

BEAMLESS ROOF

Plenty of people like "beamless" cabin roofs. They do give you extra headroom, but I don't care for them. Most boats are constructed the way they are because it's traditional. As new materials or methods are discovered, some pioneers begin using them, and after a while those methods become traditional, too. For instance, the supporting structure for a plywood roof and deck is a compromise between old-time traditional planked decking and what is really needed to support the plywood. The beamless roof is the technically correct approach, because curved, laminated plywood is incredibly strong and doesn't really need added support from deck beams. Not for me, though! I love traditional construction. Looking at frames, beams, bolts, and whatnot is one of the things that make owning a wood boat special. If you believe in glue, want more headroom, or just want the smooth look for some reason, however, a beamless roof is fairly easy to build, and quite strong.

First, glue and nail a 1 × 2 nailer around the top inside, just like the nailers that you put between the beams. The traditional way to go is to put up a few molds running across the cabin, maybe on 2-foot centers, sawn from 2-by material to the crown you want. After you have these forms up, plane off the edge of the house wall so that the plywood roofing will flow smoothly over the edge. An alternative is to run 2×6s fore and aft on 12-inch centers, spiked into the house walls at the ends, and maybe propped off the keel in the middle. This would save the labor of cutting curved forms.

The roof will be laminated from three or more layers of thin plywood. I always use $1/4$-inch ply on a roof because I like lots of crown, and bending anything thicker is a pain. Bend over a sheet, fasten it with ring nails and a tube-type flooring adhesive to the side wall, and tack it with small finish nails to the forms. Spread glue on this plywood and another sheet, nail it down around the edges, and nail it to the form.

Drive the nails into the form through a small block so you can pull them out easily. An option that will save you some hole filling in the bottom layer is fastening the second layer down with $7/16$-inch screws. Also, you might consider weighting this second layer down with sand bags.

After this glue is dry, pull out the nails, if you used them, in this second layer, and glue and nail down a third layer. This time you'll have enough thickness so you can nail down the third layer all over with $5/8$-inch ring nails.

After the glue is dry, remove the forms on the inside, pull the finish nails through with a pair of pliers, and you're done. You'll cover the roof with glass cloth and Arabol or epoxy, just like the deck.

CHAPTER 11

MECHANICAL STUFF

ENGINES

Although I described engine installation back in Chapter 6, I never did go on *about* engines. Powerboat folks, please excuse what might sound like sailboat talk; some of the following applies to you, too.

If you're building on a real budget you might not have bought your engine yet; if you're building a sailboat and are broke or hopelessly romantic you might even be planning to forget about engines altogether.

That's OK. You're letting yourself in for a lot of grief, but you'll learn. When I was 20 and heading out in my little cutter I had the world by the short hairs, knew everything, and was going *sailing*. Engines? Sheeee-it. Besides, I was earning about three bucks an hour and wasn't patient enough to save up for an engine.

Over the next two years I *sailed*—a leisurely trip down into Mexico, eventually ending up in Honolulu. *Sailing*. Sometimes drifting; sometimes not going where I wanted; sometimes taking days to travel short distances (3 days for 15 miles once). I learned a lot of real seamanship skills, like sailing anchors out on what suddenly has become a lee shore with a rising wind; keeping the anchor ready to drop instantly when in close quarters or entering a strange harbor; tacking way before you have to when you're approaching a lee shore; standing off till tides change; remembering that in the afternoon the breeze usually will push you towards shore, and at dawn the breeze will blow you out to sea; thinking through a new situation while hove to; and thinking way ahead in general. As I learned, those who anticipate are those who don't come to grief.

I didn't mind all this. Not once did I miss not having an engine. I didn't feel self-righteous or mystical about it, I simply never gave it a thought. I was *sailing*, which is the only thing I had wanted to do since my sainted mother gave me a Little Golden Book called *Scuppers the Sailor Dog*.

So listen: I've done it, and I know what I'm talking about. Sailing without an engine is a lot of crap. You *can* do it, a few people *are* doing it, some even make money *writing* about doing it—but what's the point?

If you're a punk kid and full of energy, go ahead: You'll be OK. If you're a middle-aged guy suddenly scared about your gut and out to prove something, you'll be OK, too, until you become miserable enough to quit. A good solid marine engine makes cruising a completely different experience. Me? I wouldn't consider cruising without one, even if all I could afford was a lawn mower engine hooked to the shaft with a V-belt.

The problem is finding a *real* marine engine. While most of the engines made today are pretty good, few are "real" marine engines. The new engines are powerful, compact, and lightweight, but that's just the problem: they're *too* refined. I don't think any of them offer the trouble-free long life of the old thumpers.

The ideal engine for a sailboat or displacement powerboat is a diesel. Not because of the lower risk of explosion, although that's certainly a consideration, but because diesels can run without electricity. Maintaining electrical systems in a salt-air environment is a constant hassle.

Also, diesel engines are more efficient. My friend Dave Millihol-land tells me that a gallon of gas delivers roughly 10 h.p. per hour while a gallon of diesel will produce 20 h.p. per hour. For example, a GMC 6V-53 running at 2500 r.p.m. will produce about 160 h.p. and use 8 gallons an hour. A Chrysler Crown 6-cylinder gas engine running at 3200 r.p.m. will develop 110 h.p. and burn about 10 gallons an hour.

Gas engines have some advantages, however. Easthope, an old-time and now-defunct marine engine builder in Canada, said they prefer their heavy, slow-turning gas engines to diesels because their lower compression ratios make them last longer. And like the old John Deere tractors, the Easthopes used a carburetor that preferred gasoline, but would run on many other things. They had a letter from a man who ran out of gas and made it home by pouring a case of beer into his tank. Whiskey and kerosene would work too, they said.

Gas engines are smoother and quieter than diesels, and cost considerably less. Nowadays, with so many people afraid of gas on board, there's always good buys on used gas engines. My friend Vern picked up a nice air-cooled 2-cylinder 18-h.p. Wisconsin with a transmission for only $750. A comparable new diesel of similar power would be around $3,500. You can buy a lot of gasoline for the $2,750 difference in price.

Of course, any engine decision depends on how you intend to use it. A compact, lightweight little engine will work fine for weekending or vacation use. But for a workboat or a cruising power or sailboat, I want as solid and reliable engine as I can get, and I always hunt out a "real" marine engine.

What constitutes a "real" marine engine? For one, seawater cooling. Of course, salt water will rust out anything, but a heavy, cast-iron block running at low temperatures can stand up to it for years. For instance, the 10-h.p., saltwater-cooled Sabb diesel in my last boat probably has thousands of hours on it after 12 years of heavy use. Recently it was torn down just to see what was happening, and there was no sign of deterioration. Listers, older-model Volvos, and several other makes will perform just as well.

Now it's no *great* hassle to rig up freshwater cooling, but it does require an extra pump and more plumbing, and it takes up space. Probably the simplest way to go is a keel cooler, yet even here you'll need the second pump system if you want to watercool the exhaust. It just seems simpler to own an engine that can stand up to the salt and cool it directly with seawater. Most people disagree with me on this, but I suspect it's because few new engines will stand it, and the few still on the market that will usually cost as much as 50 percent more than "modern," more delicate engines. What you get for the extra bucks is a heavy, all-iron, simple, low-temperature, unsophisticated engine that generally will last forever.

One way around the cooling problem is to use an air-cooled engine. They aren't popular for propulsion in the States, but air-cooled engines work very well and don't have the cooling hassle, unless you want to cool the exhaust, in which case you'll need a sea-water pump. Lister and Deutz make excellent, long-lived air-cooled diesel engines, and there are several good gas ones available, too. True, air-cooled engines are noisier than water-cooled ones, and they require air ducting, but last they do. I owned one that ran for years without hassle. I've seen many others, too, including one that was rigged to blow the hot air from the engine compartment into the cockpit to warm the helmsman's feet.

A real marine engine will crank start. This means you need compression releases on each cylinder, and a big flywheel heavy enough to build up sufficient momentum to get her to kick. On multicylinder engines you get the flywheel spinning, close one release to get the engine running on one cylinder, then close the others. The power of the first cylinder will kick the others into action.

Few new engines will crank start because they have lightweight flywheels and no compression releases, not to mention no provisions for a hand crank. A few years ago I was powering down the coast of Brazil, delivering a boat with a new, marinized tractor diesel that ran beautifully. There was no wind and the boat was on autopilot. The woman along with me was sick and getting sicker, and announced very calmly one morning that she expected to die if she didn't get off the goddam boat soon. As she was a veterinarian, I thought she just might know what she was talking about, so we headed for a town.

About then I noticed the engine was overheating. I shut it down, found a broken belt to the cooling water pump, and fixed it, but now the engine wouldn't start. This same belt also turned the alternator, you see. Running the autopilot all night had worn down the battery to where it couldn't turn over the engine, so there we sat, with no way to hand-crank the engine. There was just enough breeze to sail us close enough to shore for a fishboat to find us and tow us in, but it was a hassle. The vet caught the next bus south, by the way.

A friend of mine had the same problem in Alaska. He wore his batteries down while up some fjord, and didn't have the juice to start his 6-cylinder gas engine. Well, he drained the oil into a saucepan and heated it up on the stove, then refilled the engine. He put a pipe wrench on the flywheel and turned the engine to get #1 piston just before top dead center, pulled the sparkplugs, and shot some propane into each cylinder from his stove tank. Then he hit the starter and the engine caught. If it hadn't he'd probably still be sitting there, because he was way up the creek.

Of course both of these situations could have been avoided if the boats had been equipped with two separate battery systems. I expect my Brazilian Experience might have happened anyway, since boats with double-battery setups often are rigged so both are charging when the engine is running, thus both are subject to draining if the alternator fails and an autopilot or something is pulling power. By comparison, my last boat's Sabb engine crank-started so easily that I didn't even *have* an electrical system on the boat for the first three years. After my Brazilian Experience, I wouldn't own an engine I couldn't crank, at least on a cruising boat.

For large boats, big, hand-starting engines are hard to find. An option is the double battery system for the main engine, with the addition of a small, crank-startable engine chain-driving the shaft. If the main engine won't start, crank up the backup engine, which will drive the boat and recharge the batteries, too.

This backup engine should be something like an air-cooled Lister, which is virtually bulletproof. I think if there's one thing in this imperfect world you can always count on, it's that an air-cooled Lister, with a fuel filter in the line, will *always* start. I know of one with *100,000* continuous unattended hours on it. It's interesting to note that the same country that makes Lister engines also makes Jaguar cars, but that's another story. Regrettably, Lister redesigned its engines recently, thinking to compete with the Japanese. Fortunately there are still plenty of older Listers around.

Lister, Volvo, Farrymann, Sabb, and several other companies built these ''real'' marine engines I'm talking about. Unfortunately, the average production boatbuilder didn't buy them. These ''real'' marine engines were big and heavy and expensive. Price is important to a corporate boat factory, weight is crucial on most dinghy-hulled new designs, and many of today's designers and builders think space is better devoted to guest bedrooms than a decent engine installation.

As usual, the Japanese saw the market and built products to meet it. The engines they send to the States are compact, lightweight, and reliable. But the larger ones don't crank easily, because there isn't much of a flywheel; they use a lot of aluminum, so you better not raw-water cool them—they aren't the same thing at all.

In my opinion, a solid marine-quality engine is an absolute must on a cruising boat. Since most of the old-style engines aren't made these days, if I wanted an engine for an offshore boat, quite frankly, I would find an old one and have her rebuilt. If you'll forgive my bragging, in 1986 I bought the last of the old-design water-cooled Listers available new in the States, from Kansas of all places. It's a 34-h.p., 3-cylinder job with a 3-to-1 gear, and it weighs 1,100 pounds. It has a big flywheel and compression releases on each cylinder, and I'm going to keep it the rest of my life. When I'm ready to sell whatever boat it's in, I'll pull the engine and install some throw-away new one.

Now I don't mean to suggest that if you can't have a "real" marine engine you shouldn't bother with one at all. I just wouldn't spend a lot of money for one that ain't "real." Instead, I'd rig up something cheap—a junkyard 4- or 6-cylinder Chevy, or a lawnmower engine hooked to the shaft with V-belts—until I could find a good "real" marine engine. Even if you have to have the "real" engine rebuilt, it'll still cost less than buying one of those new ones, and you'll have a better engine to boot. Even though I'm not in the market, I keep my ears open, and at the moment I know where there's a 2-cylinder, old-style Volvo for $750, a water-cooled Lister that needs rebuilding for $400, a disassembled 30-h.p. Sabb for a grand, and an 8-h.p. Sabb for $1,500.

If you come across a used engine that suits your purposes, give the guy a hundred bucks to hold it for a week, drain off a pint of oil into a clean bottle, find an oil testing lab in your phone book (every large city has at least one), and have the oil analyzed. The report will tell you all the trace metals in the oil, with a printout that tells how much wear is on the crank, bearings, rings, cylinder walls, pistons, and whatnot. Really! Cheap, too. In Seattle it costs 11 bucks. There's no way to hide, either. As long as the engine has been started and warmed up once, even fresh oil will show the traces. I learned about this when I sold an old Mercedes car. A guy came, took samples from the engine, transmission, and rear end, and had them tested. The results changed the deal. I gave him the car and $400 for an old Dodge van, instead of selling him the car for $1,500, which was the original plan.

How much power do you need? Here in the States the tendency is to have lots of power, more than is really needed. Of course, if you're working the boat, you might need reserve power to plow into it, but for cruising you don't need a great deal of power.

Displacement hull boats can't get up on the water and scoot. When you try to drive them past their hull speed they start to sink, looking for more length. I'm sure you've read about this in old sailing books, where some crazy captain stands by the wheel holding a pistol, saying he'll shoot the man who douses sail, and the ship suddenly drives underwater with nary a trace. I always thought this was just literary effect until I was sailing off California downwind in a gale and didn't reef. The boat actually did drive underwater in a gust. There was a good inch of water over the whole deck! I reefed.

A boat's hull speed is generally thought to be the square root of the waterline length multiplied by 1.25 to 1.34. I figure 1.25 myself, just so the boat will go faster than I thought she would. It doesn't take much power at all to go hull speed in calm water. If you're powering into a strong wind or heavy seas you need extra push, of course, but how much depends on how you're using the boat and what kind of propeller you're using. Here's some examples for a 22,000-pound boat with a 30-foot waterline and different types of propellers. The term *speed/length ratio* means the square root of the waterline length multiplied by something.

Speed/Length Ratio	Knots	H.P.	Prop Efficiency
1	5.48	4	normal aux. sail 3-blade
1.25	6.85	13.2	"
1.35	7.39	24.4	"
1.5	8.22	66.8	"
1	5.48	6.7	folding 2-blade
1.25	6.85	22.1	"
1.35	7.39	40.7	"
1.5	8.22	111.4	"
1	5.48	3.2	normal power 3-blade
1.25	6.85	10.5	"
1.35	7.39	19.4	"
1.5	8.22	53.0	"

The normal 3-blade prop is the way to go for a cruising sailboat. The reduced drag of the folding prop might help you a little in sailboat racing, but it isn't very efficient and so needs almost twice the h.p. to push the same boat to its hull speed. The full powerboat prop is more efficient, but it creates even more drag for a sailboat. It might be a good thing to carry a spare powerboat prop, just in case you wanted to motor up the canals in Europe or something.

Just to show you how length and speed relate, here's the numbers for a 50-foot-waterline boat that weighs 60,000 pounds, using a 3-blade auxiliary sailboat-type prop. Compare these to the 30-foot-waterline model that weighs one-third as much.

Speed/Length Ratio	Knots	H.P.
1	7.07	14.2
1.25	8.84	46.6
1.5	10.61	235.2

Now these figures are all well and good, but what exactly *is* horsepower? The dictionary says it's the amount of force one horse exerts in pulling, or 745.7 watts, or 33,000 foot-pounds per minute. I don't know. I do know that there's horsepower and then there's horsepower. My motorcycle's 2-cylinder engine develops over 50 h.p. at close to 8,000 r.p.m. and weighs maybe 200 pounds. My boat's 34-h.p. diesel weighs about five times that and develops 34 h.p. at 2,000 r.p.m.. There's h.p. that develops because of r.p.m., and h.p. that develops from low-speed torque, and in a displacement hull it's *torque* h.p. you're after.

Tow a heavy barge with a little tug powered by a 200-h.p. engine with a good reduction gear, swinging a real prop, and she'll go right along. Mount a 200-h.p. outboard on the same barge and it won't do much but beat the water to a froth. The outboard needs to turn at high r.p.m. to develop 200 h.p. but when it does, the prop blades just cavitate because the hull isn't moving fast enough to give the prop "clean" water to chew, if that makes sense.

I'm sure there's all sorts of complicated rules to use in figuring all this out, but I just use my eyes. If it's a big hunk of iron that turns less than 2,000 at max-rated h.p.—that's horsepower.

OFFSET ENGINE INSTALLATION

Even if you weren't planning on installing an engine, I hope you built the keel with a shaft hole, just in case. But if not, or if you want to install two engines, you can mount the engine(s) off to one side or on an angle, and run the shaft through a strut.

Offset single engine installations aren't seen too often anymore, but they used to be fairly common. Proponents say that the prop, out in clear water beside the hull, will be more efficient than one tucked in behind the deadwood. L. Francis Herreshoff wrote that boats so equipped also sailed better than those with a propeller aperture cut in the sternpost and rudder. That may be, but I learned that it also makes the prop more vulnerable to damage. I backed mine into a log once, and it bent the shaft and really messed up the prop. A centerline prop would have been undamaged because it would have been protected by the rudder. The rudder is built heavy enough to hit logs, you see. Not so with props.

Figure 11/1.
An offset prop shaft is one way of retrofitting an engineless boat without massive backbone surgery. The prop shaft runs inside a piece of heavy stainless pipe, supported at its forward end by a heavy plate bolted to the planking, and at its aft end by a triangular strut. Note the zinc on the strut for electrolysis control.

Figure 11-1 shows a strut we made for *Juno*. Her engine was off-set because I was a purist when I started building her; I wasn't going to install an engine, and I was too stupid to prepare a shaft log just in case I changed my mind or sold the boat. If you don't find any other reason to prepare the keel for a shaft log, figure that a larger sailboat without an engine is worth 40 percent less than one with an engine.

The offset shaft is an option, however. It does offer a bit more freedom in the engine installation, because you can install any engine you want and fit the strut to match its position. It simplifies keel construction because you don't have the shaft hole, but that's balanced out by the need to make the strut. And it's a way to install an engine later on, after you get the romance of engineless cruising out of your system.

Before you get started on this offset engine installation, you might want to re-read what I wrote about engine installations back in Chapter 5. I went into some detail about schematic charts, figuring out mount placements, and making the mount. You'll need that information here.

Sit in the bilge and figure out the best possible spot for the engine, one that keeps it level, gets it far out of the way of the accommodation, and gets the prop deep. Remember, mounting most engines on much more than a 10-degree angle means the bearings won't get oiled properly, and it can be difficult to get the prop low enough so that it stays underwater while keeping the engine semi-level, unless you mount the thing in the middle of the hull. Also, it's said that the engine should be positioned so the top of the prop turns outboard from the keel.

After you figure where the thing will sit, drill a hole about 1/2 inch larger than the shaft diameter through the planking and whatever floor timbers are in the way of the shaft. Run a string through the hole to represent the shaft, nail a brace off the back of the deadwood about where you think the shaft should run, and tie the string to it about where you think the middle of the prop should be. (Call a propeller shop and ask them what size prop you'll need for your boat and engine combination.)

Position the shaft so the prop will have several inches of clearance from the side of the keel. Nail up another brace inside the hull forward of where the engine will sit, and tie the string to it. If the string is rubbing on wood, move the braces around or drill bigger holes. The outside position is the important one, so I'd play with the inside brace the most.

Engine mounts were described in Chapter 5. I think a steel mount is almost essential for the offset prop installation because of the angle of the mount. It could be difficult to fasten wood bearers securely down where they'll need to be, but then I think *any* engine mount should be steel. Lay a piece of plywood between whatever floor timbers the engine will be sitting between and mark the string line (shaft angle) on it. Figure out how high and wide the mount has to be from the shaft line and draw the shape of the top view of the mount on this piece of plywood. Make another pattern showing the angle of the mount in relation to the shaft, the width between the floor timbers the mount will be bolted to, and the height. Again, this was described back in Chapter 5. Remember to make the pattern for the mount about 1/2 inch low so you can shim up the engine. It's easier to do that than to discover the mount is too high and has to be rebuilt.

After you finish building the pattern, wait until you have the propeller shaft strut in hand before having the engine mount built. If the strut doesn't come out just like its pattern you'll need to redo the engine-mount pattern, but you want to make the pattern first so you'll *know* the engine will fit. I think non-pros have to take a cautious tack in things like this because we don't do this stuff often enough to stay familiar with it, and it's so easy to screw up.

Outside the hull, the shaft turns inside a piece of heavy-wall stainless pipe. This pipe runs through a good-sized plate bolted to the planks, and is supported at the outboard end by a triangular brace bolted to the deadwood.

For *Juno*'s strut I used 3/8-inch wall thickness #316 stainless pipe about 1 inch larger inside than the shaft diameter, a 1/4- by 12- by 20-inch plate against the hull, and 1/2- by 4-inch plate for the triangular brace. This is a very strong strut, but it paid off because *Juno* banged on the rocks one night in Alaska and the strut survived.

The pipe must extend through the mounting plate and into the hull far enough to attach the stuffing box. You'll have to weld on a flange on the inboard end to bolt the stuffing box to. The outside treatment depends on what sort of prop you're using. If you're using a normal fixed prop, you could simply insert a *cutless bearing* (a bronze tube that holds a grooved, water-lubricated rubber bearing) in the outer end. Drill two small holes near the end so you can screw in set screws to hold the bearing in place. I used the variable pitch prop that comes with Sabb diesels on *Juno*, so I welded a flange on the outer end to take the prop's hub. Whatever, drill a hole in the pipe just behind the stuffing box flange so you can install a Zerk fitting to keep the tube filled with grease.

After the strut is made up, bolt it to the hull with lots of bedding compound around the hole through the hull. Run the string back through (or the shaft, for that matter), position it exactly in the center of the pipe at each end, and check the engine mount pattern. Adjust it if needed, then take it to a metal shop and have the mount made. I'd use 3/8-inch plate for the front and back, and 3/8 inch by 3- or 4-inch angle for the engine base. Remember to position the angle iron so that the lip faces inboard.

Use 3/8- to 1/2-inch bolts to hold the mount to the floor timbers. As you do with all metal fittings, drill the holes 1/16 inch oversize so the bolt will go through easily. Paint the mount with rust-resistant paint, slop lots of bedding compound and preservative on the floors where the mount will be, then bolt her in.

Now's the time to stick the engine on the mount, which is easier said than done, by the way. I've made elaborate ramps and hoisting systems, bought cases of beer and had lots of people to help, and psychologically prepared myself for dropping the engine through the bottom of the boat. The last time I did it I cut a hole in the roof of the shop over the engine's location and hired a hydraulic boom truck from the local cement company. It took 10 minutes to pick up the engine and lower it onto the mount, and it cost less than the materials to make the ramps and hoists and buy booze for the crew. And the truck is insured. If the engine goes through the hull it's their problem.

Regardless, once the engine is in place, run a stick through the stern tube to the engine to see how long a shaft you'll need. A normal fixed-blade prop shaft requires 1/2 to 3/4 inch of shaft extending out from the stern tube in front of the prop, the thickness of the hub of the prop, and several inches for the prop nut. Get the shaft made, have the coupling machined to be perfectly square to the shaft, and install it.

Line up the engine as close as you can to the coupling on the shaft, then drill holes through the engine mount for the hold-down bolts. I C-clamp the engine in position, remove a clamp to drill a hole, then drop in a bolt before removing the next clamp. After all the holes are drilled, check and fine-tune the alignment. It shouldn't be out more than .003 inch, and .002 inch isn't worth bragging about.

ON ALIGNING ENGINES

There are few things as frustrating and irritating as trying to align the shaft and engine. I did an alignment in 20 minutes once. I gave up on another at .003 after three days. I hope you've done a decent engine installation and allowed lots of access all around. On one 30-foot production boat billed as a cruising boat, the engine and shaft are hooked up before the deck is attached. It's impossible to get to the coupling without a chain saw. Although a proper engine installation might take away interior living area, you'll appreciate it every time you do any maintenance work on the engine, starting right now as you try to align the goddam thing. Before beginning, pour a stiff drink, put some pleasant music on the blaster, and reflect on this: "The hardest thing for a man to do is to fall down upon the ice when it is slippery, and get up and praise the Lord."

Anyhow, with the couplings touching, stick a feeler gauge in the top of the joint. If it reads .009, say, remember this, then check the bottom. If the bottom reads .003, then you are .006 inch out and the front of the engine must drop. Of course, it might be that if you drop the front of the engine the couplings won't be in line. Maybe you'll have to raise the back of the engine. Check the sides. Are you crooked? Do you pull the front or push the back? Do you kick the side or bash the top? Sometimes you're out diagonally, and must tilt the engine a hair.

Thin aluminum makes good shim stock for engine alignment because it's easy to cut and drill. A good hardware store will have shim stock; house roof flashing or, in a pinch, beer cans work too. Once you think you're on, bolt the sucker down good. Turn the shaft a full 360 degrees and check it everywhere. Some people tear a sheet of paper into little strips, stick them in the shaft coupling at 90-degree intervals, and turn the shaft. If it's out of alignment, strips will fall out as you turn it.

I aligned one engine that would change alignment after the hold-down bolts were cinched. I had to bolt her down each time I wanted to check the new position, then loosen it again to move it. Remember, .003 inch is the farthest out of alignment you should be. Leave the couplings unbolted until the boat is transported to the launch site. Check the alignment again a week after launching.

OTHER WAYS

I've described pretty much standard engine mounting stuff, but occasionally you see other systems that work, too. I'm no mechanic, so I won't try to spec out details. If you understand mechanical stuff you can figure them out yourself. If you're not a mechanic, either find one or stick to the standard stuff.

Belt drive

Although a transmission is certainly handy, it isn't essential. A real "budget survivalist" sort of engine installation would be an air-cooled Lister, or an iron block gas engine like a Wisconsin or a Briggs & Stratton, mounted above the shaft and hooked to it with V-belts. In fact, you could install it off to the side, too. I'd use two or three belts to cut down on slip. This would work with an engine that has a transmission too, of course.

Universal joints

I've seen several boats that had the engine mounted way forward, with a long drive shaft running back to the actual propeller shaft. The drive shaft sections were hooked together with automotive-type universal joints. In theory these universal joints could allow you to mount the engine offset, like beside a mast, and run a shaft back to the prop with doglegs around obstacles.

This system requires intermediate thrust bearings bolted firmly to the hull to support the shaft sections, but other than that it seems simple enough. These universals (a further refinement might be to use CV—constant velocity—joints from front-wheel-drive cars) also give you a very smooth drive, with no alignment hassle.

Hydraulic drive

I always thought hydraulic drive was the coming thing, and I'm still surprised you don't see it very often. According to Spencer Fluid Power in Seattle, a good hydraulic system has at least the same efficiency and costs about the same as a good mechanical transmission. However, that's where the similarities end.

A hydraulic drive allows you to mount the engine wherever you please, like sideways behind the cockpit, for instance. You can mount the engine on soft pads to eliminate vibration. Hydraulics produce a sort of variable reduction gear, in that shaft speed is independent of engine r.p.m. This allows you always to run the engine at an efficient speed, which should save fuel. For instance, in a flat calm the engine can idle along with the prop turning fast. In heavy going you can speed up the engine and slow down the prop for maximum thrust and power. Pretty slick.

The hydraulic drive system is simple and robust, and you'd think everybody would use them. I was going to use one in my new boat until I found my Lister. It came with the old-time, heavy-duty Lister gearbox, which they've since quit making. Since I like looking at this thing, and know that it will last forever, I used it, even though it's taking up a lot more space than a hydraulic system would need.

You can buy most new engines without transmissions, and you might check out hydraulic drive. The costs will be similar to buying a new transmission. Do-it-yourself freaks could build one themselves from large lobsterpot hauler components. The German Farrymann diesel is available with a hydraulic drive package, ready to go.

V drives

V-drive systems allow you to mount the engine behind the shaft. Several companies make them, and they're well proven and reliable. The only disadvantage is that you have extra gearing to push, and so lose a bit of the engine's power.

Both Volvo and Yanmar sell new engines with angled and V-drive transmissions already in place. They look good, and don't cost much more than the same engines with their normal transmissions. The only concern I'd have in using them is that if you build them in, you're committed, and you can't easily repower the boat with something else.

SHAFTS AND PROPS

Prop shafts are usually made from stainless steel, although bronze and Monel are used, too. Stainless is the least expensive, although there are plenty of used bronze ones around. Bronze shafts should be 1/4 inch larger in diameter than stainless, because bronze isn't as stiff. What diameter shaft should you use? There really aren't any hard and fast rules other than what looks right.

Of course, the size of the prop you'll be swinging needs to be considered. A very rough guide to sizing stainless shafts for slow-turning engines pushing larger props might be: Use 1 inch up to 20 h.p.; use 1 1/4 inch up to 30 h.p.; use 1 1/2 inch up to 50 h.p.; use 1 3/4 inch up to 75 h.p. For larger engines, ask the dealer.

The larger the prop and the higher the reduction gear ratio, the bigger the shaft you'll need. For instance, a 3:1 gear on a 30-h.p. engine probably should use a 1 1/2- to 1 3/4-inch shaft, while the same engine with a 2:1 gear could get by with 1 or 1 1/4 inch. Go heavy. It doesn't cost much more and will pay off in the long run. High-speed boats don't need such big shafts. My old fishing boat, a lapstrake Chris, has a Chevy 283 V-8 and a 1-inch shaft.

I've mentioned this stuff before, but this seems like a good place to elaborate. The shaft hole will have a bearing at the outer end and a watertight bearing on the inboard end. These days shafts are normally fitted outboard with a cutless bearing. The shaft must be long enough to go from the engine coupling back 1/2 to 3/4 inch past the cutless bearing, plus the distance through the prop, plus enough for the hold-on nut. It's easy to measure for shaft length: Just shove a

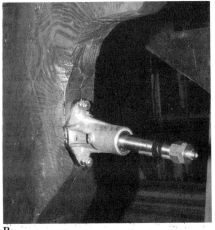

A   B

Figure 11/2.
(A) Inboard, the prop shaft is supported by the stuffing box, which contains rings of oil-soaked flax packing to keep out the water. (B) Outboard, the prop shaft is supported by the cutless bearing, a grooved, water-lubricated sleeve secured within the (usually) bronze fitting lagged to the deadwood.

small stick up the hole to the engine, then add the extra length mentioned above.

The inner and outer bearings must be lined up absolutely square to the shaft hole, which will take some doing. Insert the shaft, slide the inner and outer bearings on, and drill holes for their bolts. Push the bearings in place, bed the inner one, and cinch the lags up snug. Go out and try snugging up the lags for the outer bearing. If the outer bearing is square, parallel to the inner one, the shaft will turn easily. If it ain't, it won't.

It probably won't, so back off the lags and shave off some wood with a coarse rasp. You can tell where by loosening a bolt. If you loosen one and the shaft turns, it means that you must shave off wood opposite this bolt. Not too much! Try it again. When you get things pretty straight, bed the outer bearing well and cinch her down. As you tighten the lags, turn the shaft to see what's happening. You'll probably find that you'll have to leave one bolt just a hair looser than another to keep things in line.

Choosing a prop seems to require a séance or something, as there don't seem to be any hard and fast rules. There are some general guidelines, however. First, do you want a two-blade or three-blade prop? Do you want it folding or fixed? I've already given you numbers that show how the different types of props stack up. As the numbers showed, a folding prop requires about twice the horsepower of a fixed three-blade prop. In other words, a folding prop is useless for anybody who'll be using the engine a lot.

Both power and sailboat people in Europe usually use either variable-pitch props or big two-blade props. Variable pitch props are really nice for power or sailing boats because you can adjust the pitch of the blades to match the conditions. The engine can run at an efficient speed all the time. Also, you get more power in reverse, and some of them will feather down when sailing, which causes less drag. However, they're expensive and more fragile than a fixed prop. The

Mechanical Stuff

big two-blade props can reduce sailing drag by being aligned parallel with the keel when the engine is off, hiding the blades, so to speak, but they're hard to find in the States and expensive, so I use fixed three-blade props.

There seems to be no general agreement on prop sizing. For example, recently I had to pick a prop for my boat. My calculations said I needed one 30 inches in diameter by 20-inch pitch. A local prop shop said I needed a 26- by 26-inch wheel; another one said I needed a 24- by 16-inch one. So who knows? I suppose the thing to do is to average out several companies' recommendations and try it. If you're not achieving hull speed at rated r.p.m. (prop too small or not enough pitch) or the engine won't turn to its full r.p.m. (prop too big or too much pitch) try another one, have it repitched, or cut it down.

Start prop shopping early. There's lots of used props out there, and they sell for maybe 15 percent of the price of a new one. You can use a prop with as much as a 1/4-inch bigger hole than your shaft diameter by shimming the shaft with the sleeves available at prop shops. Plastic sleeves are cheap and make the prop easy to remove, but since the prop is isolated from the shaft and won't be bonded by your zincs, electrolysis can be a problem. Bronze sleeves are preferable, although they'll cost around 60 bucks or so.

SIMPLE EXHAUST SYSTEMS

The theory behind exhaust systems is to get the gas away from the engine with as little resistance as possible. The harder the engine has to push the exhaust, the less power you'll have to turn the prop. So when planning the system, try to run the pipe as straight and short as possible.

Practically all sailboats and many smaller powerboats use a wet exhaust system because it really is simpler when you have a water-cooled engine. Although a dry stack has some advantages, particularly for powerboats, you still have to push the cooling water out of the hull somehow, and it's often easier to mix the exhaust and the water and let them use the same pipe.

Figures 11-3 through 11-6 show various exhaust systems, but as usual I'll add a bit of commentary. Figure 11-3 shows a fairly typical system. Since the engine is close to the waterline, or below it in this case, you must ensure that water can't come back up the pipe into the engine. The illustration shows a *standpipe* installed in the line to serve as a water trap. The standpipe can be welded up from pipe, or various commercial standpipes are available on the market. I use one made of plastic because it will never rust out. However, it's fairly simple to weld up a steel one using a big piece of pipe (say 10-inch I.D. × 14 inches or so), and if you're out in the hinterlands that's

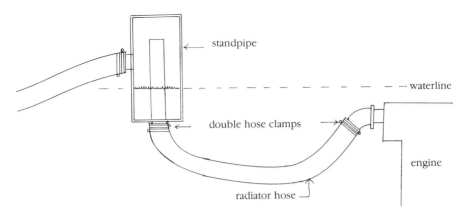

Figure 11/3.
The standard raw-water-cooled exhaust system. The standpipe must be above the waterline to prevent water from being siphoned back into the exhaust system.

probably the way to go. The standpipe is fastened to a bulkhead or something so that a good part of it is above the waterline.

Most newer engines are set up to mix the water into the exhaust right at the manifold, so this system uses wire-reinforced radiator hose for the entire exhaust system. This is nice stuff because it's flexible. You can wrap it around whatever gets in the way and easily line it up with whatever you need to. Normal galvanized iron pipe fittings are used if you have to screw a pipe into something to attach the hose. Although many people (mostly yachtsmen, who like everything to be expensive) disagree, regular mild steel seems better for exhausts than stainless. It deteriorates evenly, you see, rather than looking sound but suddenly getting full of pinholes. And it can be repaired by brazing. You can buy two of everything (for spares) for a mild steel system and still spend far less than a stainless system.

Figure 11-4 shows a system where the cooling water is injected into the exhaust system after the exhaust manifold. You'd do this if you were freshwater-cooling the block, or if your engine didn't mix the water internally for some reason. For instance, if you had an air-cooled engine but wanted a wet exhaust, you'd have a separate pump to pump the cooling seawater into the exhaust.

The water is injected into the system as close to the engine as possible, although lower than the manifold to keep it from getting into the engine. Again, normal galvanized pipe fittings are used, with radiator hose used from there on. Some people use galvanized pipe for the whole system, but radiator hose is far simpler to install.

As mentioned before, you want as little resistance in the system as possible, so the line should be as straight and short as possible. You'll need some curves, of course. For instance, you want to curve the hose up above the waterline so it exits the hull above the waterline. But don't make any short 90-degree turns; make it gentle. If using pipe, hook two 45-degree pieces together with a short, straight piece between them, rather than use a 90-degree elbow.

Mechanical Stuff

Figure 11/4.
Water-injected exhaust
system, used with fresh-
water-cooled blocks or air-
cooled engines.

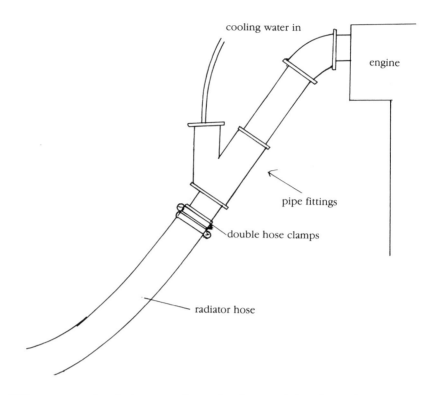

When an engine is mounted too far forward for the exhaust line to reach the transom, some people use the North Sea exhaust, shown in Figure 11-5. The exhaust is T-shaped so that it can go out which-ever side of the hull isn't underwater. Some sort of clamshell vent or rubber flapper is fastened over the through-hulls to keep water from backing up into the system. The North Sea exhaust is common in Europe but seldom seen in the States. The system allows a short exhaust, but it also gets the exhaust out of the hull far ahead of the stern, and if you have an outside steering station, like with a sailboat,

Figure 11/5.
Double-enders or boats
with engines mounted
way forward can use the
North Sea exhaust system
to prevent a long
hose run.

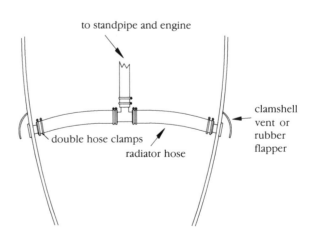

you'll probably get gassed in certain wind conditions. Of course that can happen with any system, but I prefer to run the exhaust as far aft as possible, which helps prevent the exhaust from coming aboard.

Figure 11-6 shows a dry system in a powerboat. This is harder to rig up in a sailboat because there usually isn't a high place to stick the exhaust pipe, although if you have a wheelhouse you can run the pipe up the back wall. I've seen several boats that ran the exhaust up through the mizzen mast.

The dry exhaust really is a simple system, especially if you have an air-cooled engine. It is louder than wet exhaust systems, but a muffler can be installed in the line. Also, the pipe gets hotter than hell, so you should wrap it in some insulating material, at least where it's close to the hull.

I had an air-cooled engine in a boat that ran the exhaust out through the transom and never had any trouble. On the other hand, a friend of mine had one in his boat, and while bucking a current getting into Tahiti its exhaust got so hot that the planking actually started smoldering. This was an unusual situation, because he normally didn't run the engine hard enough to get the exhaust that hot. But in this case he was in a hurry and pushed it. He also burnt an exhaust

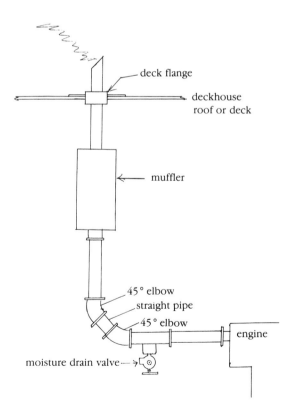

Figure 11/6.
Typical dry exhaust system. This isn't the most elegant solution to exhaust venting, but it's cheap, simple, and works in millions of commercial boats worldwide. All parts are galvanized water pipe except the muffler, which can be a typical discount-store muffler, like a Cherry Bomb.

valve, so he was pushing a bit much. Although burning the valve was a drag, the experience was good for us because he learned how to deal with the exhaust. He moved the place where it exited the hull right down to the waterline so that when under power, the ocean washed over the exhaust flange and kept the area cool.

The very simplest, least expensive, and most trouble-free system I've ever seen was used by Gary Webb in his 35-foot sailboat. He has a 2-cylinder, air-cooled Lister, and when he wants to run the engine he simply sticks a 6-foot length of 1¼-inch water pipe out the hatch. It takes only a few seconds to screw it into the manifold, then he just spins the crank and off he goes. It works great, although everybody will burn their hand once before they learn not to use the pipe for a handhold. Obviously this wouldn't be very good for a powerboat, but it works just fine for an auxiliary sailboat, and at the least would serve to get you going on the water. You can always go back later on and build a "real" system if you don't like it.

Finally, the exhaust pipe allows damp air to flow straight up to the engine's valves and whatnot, and although you'll hardly ever see people bother, I like to put a gate valve where the line exits the hull so you can close off the system when you won't be using it for awhile. That might stop someone from getting very far if they try to steal your boat! Another way to deal with it is to pull the hose off the manifold when you're not going to use the engine for a while, and stick an oily rag in the hole.

SIMPLE ENGINE CONTROLS

The throttle is the easiest control to hook up. I like the old-time tractor-type, spring-loaded, ratcheted throttle control, myself. I probably have half a dozen or so I've picked up at various swap meets. All that's involved is getting a piece of throttle cable as long as you need, snaking it down to the engine, and screwing the throttle control lever to a bulkhead or anything else that's handy.

Compared with the throttle control, the shifting system can be a pain. There are various commercial ones on the market, and a lot of people use a single lever, such as the Morse, which handles shifting and throttle together. But that costs bucks. The simplest and most reliable system was specified by Herreshoff. Although he frequently designed yachts for very wealthy people, he always thought about simplicity, and the Herreshoff shifting system is controlled by ropes. I've used it and it works fine. You can use it to get going, and later on go back and put in a fancier one if you feel like it. Figure 11-7 shows how it works.

I had a Sabb diesel with a variable-pitch prop in one boat. This guy had the pitch control in a post that stuck straight up, rather than the side-mounted pull-push of the normal transmission, which of course takes up less space in the cockpit.

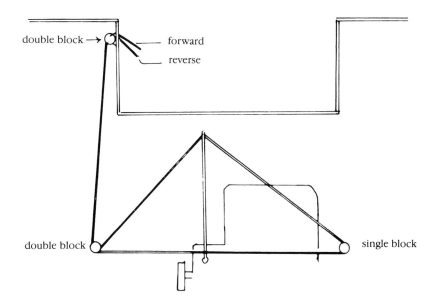

double block →

forward

reverse

double block

single block

Figure 11/7.
A simple rope transmission shifter control—cheap and easily repaired. Use non-stretch Dacron line.

The swing was more than 180 degrees, so we needed a solid linkage. I suppose some sort of cable-driven circular thing would have worked, but I didn't think of that at the time. Instead, I took a piece of wire-reinforced radiator hose the same I.D. as the post on the engine, stuck a wood plug about 8 inches up it, stuck it over the post

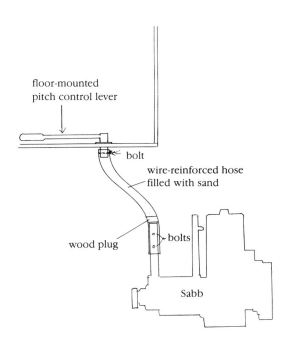

floor-mounted pitch control lever

bolt

wire-reinforced hose filled with sand

wood plug

bolts

Sabb

Figure 11/8.
A simple, homemade variable pitch control for Sabb and other diesels with top-mounted rotary controls.

Mechanical Stuff

and bolted it through, then filled the top of the hose with sand. The hose was flexible enough to bend around obstacles. The plug kept the sand from leaking out; the sand kept the hose from collapsing when it was twisted. I connected the top to a crank sticking through the cockpit floor. It worked perfectly.

Again, if you're not a tinkerer by nature, any marine store will be happy to set you up with a store-bought system. But these home-brew jobs work, they're reliable, and they're cheap.

FUEL TANKS

Fuel tank capacity depends on how you're using your boat. As I mentioned before, one gallon of gas is supposed to produce 10 h.p. for one hour, and one gallon of diesel will produce 20 h.p. for one hour. You can use this as a rough gauge for figuring out how much tankage you'll need.

If you're building a powerboat, you need plenty of tankage, so put in as much as you have room for. For instance, when Commander Beebe (author of *Voyaging Under Power*, Seven Seas Press, 1984) built his 50-foot power cruiser *Passagemaker* for motoring around the world, he installed 1,200 gallons of tankage, which gave him a safe range of 2,400 miles.

A sailboat doesn't need to carry so much fuel, of course. When Eric Hiscock set off across the Atlantic in his first engine-equipped sailboat, he carried an extra 5-gallon can to back up the 3-gallon built-in tank. But then he was British, which often explains a lot, and a sea-man of the old school, and his little 4-h.p. Stuart Turner wasn't exactly a gas hog.

I have 100 gallons of fuel capacity built into my new boat because I got two used tanks cheap, and I had the room to install them without sacrificing something else. Still, I must say that I feel rather decadent with all that fuel capacity.

Custom-built stainless or aluminum tanks, formed to fit into some odd corner, are the best fuel tanks going. My current boat has a nice 70-gallon tank shaped perfectly to sit on the floor timbers aft of the engine and flared to match the deadrise of the bottom frames exactly. It was easy to install and takes up very little room. I like it, but I'm using it mostly because I found it for 10 bucks at a swap meet. I doubt I would have spent the bucks for a new one custom built. My 30-gallon auxiliary fuel tank is one of those neoprene or whatever tanks—basically just a rubber bag that forms itself into whatever area it's stuck in.

As with everything else, if money isn't an issue use the best. Make plywood patterns of the hull shape where you want tanks, and have them custom-built by a specialist from type 316 stainless. Nothing wrong with that if you can afford it! If you're on a budget, there are other ways, although many of them are ''not recommended'' or "illegal," which is why I'm not specifically recommending you use them, you see.

If you're going to be cruising outside the States you'll frequently be in places without dockside gas pumps, so you'll have to carry fuel to the boat by hand. You can extend your tankage by keeping several 5-gallon plastic jerry jugs aboard, and use them to ferry fuel aboard in out-of-the-way places. My last boat had an 11-gallon tank, backed up by two 5-gallon jerry jugs, which gave us probably 35 hours of motoring.

The tank on this boat was interesting. It was installed on a bulkhead over the engine so the fuel would flow by gravity, which meant I didn't need a fuel pump. Although commercial fishboats and yachts used them for years, gravity-feed fuel systems are flatly illegal today and will be written up by a Coast Guard inspector, although these days they're probably too busy looking for dope to notice it.

A gravity-feed tank has its advantages, though. The tank has a sort of cup welded to its bottom, with the line to the engine and a drain installed in it. This setup allows you to drain off any water that condenses inside the tank. Fuel floats on water, you see, and the heavier water collects in the cup. I used to drain off a half pint before I started the engine. Between that and keeping the filters clean, I never had fuel problems. As long as you pay attention to the fittings and connections and *immediately* fix any leaks that develop (I never had any), it's perfectly safe. (I should note that it's a lot safer with diesel than with gasoline. It only takes a few drops of gas in your bilge and an inopportune spark, and you can kiss your tail goodbye as you watch it fly past your face after the explosion. Gasoline systems are safe if carefully handled. Just don't be casual with it.)

This is just one example of a potentially dangerous thing that's simpler, cheaper, more reliable, and more convenient than the cautious, conventional approach. Strictly illegal in the U.S. of A., of course.

Propane is another example. Propane is heavier than air and tends to collect in the bilge. To live with propane cooking and lighting devices, you have to stay aware of them and maintain them. That's a small tradeoff for what you get in return. Yachting author Don Street said he'd rather be blown up by propane than die a slow death trying to keep kerosene and alcohol stoves going. I would have said it first if I had thought of it! The problem is that so many people these days walk around with their heads up their ass that the Coast Guard, and the insurance business, now expect high-tech, no-brain systems for everything. It's unfortunate that they place such faith in high-tech systems. My experience has been that a properly installed *simple* system is inherently more reliable, because there's nothing to go wrong.

At any rate, I like gravity-feed systems on small engines because the lack of a fuel pump means there's one less thing to go wrong. I picked up a nice 10-gallon beer keg at a swap meet, and after Brekke the Welder puts a cup on the bottom for the drain and fuel feed, I'll be installing it on a bulkhead higher than the engine so it can be my "day tank." I'll pump fuel from the big tank to it, where it can flow down to the engine.

This is the simplest system for a diesel-powered sailboat: A 10-gallon or so beer keg, bulkhead mounted, with another 10 to 20 gallons of fuel in plastic containers stored around the boat.

Plenty of people use larger tanks made from 30- to 55-gallon oil drums. I remember Fred and Mary aboard the troller *George Shima* had six or eight 55-gallon drums, hooked in series. This is cheap and simple and works fine. The only problem is that eventually the thin steel drums likely will rust out. You could extend their lives by painting them with epoxy or something. Just be sure to mount them in a place where you can get them out without having to destroy half the boat. Then you can change them if you ever need to, and keep a sharp eye out for leaks.

Another source of tanks is an airplane scrap yard. Apparently many planes use those neoprene tanks, and I've heard you can pick used ones up cheap at an airplane joint. Because fuel leaks can be dangerous, you might want to backstop a used tank by building watertight bulkheads around it to confine the leakage.

Don't use a galvanized tank, like an outboard motor tank, with diesel. Diesel eats the galvanizing, and the system will clog up. Black iron, type 316 stainless, or fiberglass (according to some) work better.

Use 1½-inch fill lines, ½-inch minimum air vent lines that go outside the hull, and whatever size fuel line the engine company calls for. I like the outside fill opening to be on the deck centerline area rather than off to the side or on the cockpit floor, since it seems to keep the area around it cleaner and dryer. I run the vent line up the inside of the house and out near the roof, or up the inside of the cockpit wall and out the side near the deck. I wouldn't run it through the side of the hull, on a sailboat at least. It's too easy for water to get into the system when the boat is heeled.

Fasten the tanks down solidly! Regular galvanized plumbers tape, available at any hardware store, and a turnbuckle or two will hold a tank tightly anywhere you want it. If it's a big tank, make some sort of cradle to support the bottom. Rubber tanks obviously need a smooth place where they won't chafe on anything. And finally, if you're building in large tanks, pay some attention to weight distribution. Don't install them in the very ends, and try to put similarly sized tanks on each side of the centerline. Install the tanks as low as you can, too, but don't cover up the entire keel area because you'll want to be able to get to it for inside ballasting. If you're putting in big tanks, try to leave maybe two feet between them for access to the keel area.

And if you're deviating from the no-brainer, more-or-less foolproof Coast Guard specifications, take the responsibility for it. Commercial boat people around the world have done this stuff for years with great success, as long as they paid attention to detail, knew what they were doing, and kept their eyes open. The ones who didn't? Natural selection. Like the dinosaurs, they ain't around anymore.

12

INTERIORS

I'm not going to go too deeply into how to build interior cabinetry. What I want to do instead is talk about the *philosophy* of interiors. If you want to read details about how to build cabinetry I suggest you get some basic cabinetmaking books from the library, because interior joinery is a whole subject unto itself. I will mention a few points that I haven't seen emphasized in the books I've read.

This book is mostly about cruising boats, *offshore* boats. Aside from its design of course, the things that make a boat suitable for offshore use are that the hull can be subjected to adversity more or less safely, and the interior can be lived in comfortably at sea.

I hope you've noticed that I've been emphasizing brute strength throughout this book, because when push comes to shove, there's nothing like plain old massive construction, period. I know, I know. This attitude is considered archaic and unhip by the new breed of designers and engineering types. But I tell ya, I'd be willing to play chicken for pink slips with my boat against any "modern" engineered boat of similar displacement, in shallow enough water to salvage the loser. I'm pretty sure mine will be the one floating after the collision.

Interiors are unique, because not only do you have to think about strength, you have to think about what's good for living in. But let's deal with strength first. Back in the early 1980s a heavy wind hit Cabo San Lucas, Mexico, where a lot of cruising folks in plastic boats were anchored out. It was a disaster. The majority of them didn't have proper anchoring gear or didn't know what they were doing and so were swept up on the beach, and here's where it gets funny— as an observer, of course. When the boats started banging away on the beach, their interiors came loose and became kindling in the bilge. After that, many of the hulls, unsupported by their lightweight interiors, broke up, too. So it goes.

Well, this won't happen to you with the boats in this book. Of course boats built like this can break up; hell, the *Titanic* sank, didn't it? But let me tell you, if my boat goes on the beach in a storm, which is unlikely with all the anchors and ropes I carry with me, I *know* my interior ain't gonna come apart. It's built *solid*. The boat might break in half, God forbid, but the interior won't come loose. The bulkheads are *heavy*. Everything is bolted or spiked in, and glued, too. No prissy, frail little gingerbread trim pieces either. Everything is ruggedly and simply assembled.

Like all other parts of the oceangoing boat, basic strength of the interior assembly is essential, so much so that it should go without saying, so I won't anymore.

Aside from a few details about building the stuff, what I mainly want to talk about is ideas for interior layout. Designing the interior is where many people screw up; as a result, very few boats are set up comfortably for the owner's life aboard.

Go to a boat show. You'll see all sorts of clever interior arrangements. They look catchy, I know, but hold on a minute. Could you live in it? Practically all production boats are set up to handle groups of people. Although I admit I'm no authority on them, I can't think of one I've seen with an interior that looked really comfortable for living in.

I can hear you disagree with that. Why, you saw the ad for the Grandioso 39 just yesterday, and them two double beds, two quarter berths, galley, shower, and chart table look pretty good to you.

Well, look closer. The only way to get all that stuff into a moderate sized boat of reasonable beam and freeboard is to compact everything as much as possible. This is some of what you'll find if you try to live in it:

- No access to the engine. You have to squeeze in a skinny 10-year-old to check the alignment or change the oil.

- No galley workspace. Oh, I know it looks slick, but look closer. There's no counterspace to work on unless you put little boards over the sink, and who wants to bother with that?

- No convenient storage for pots and pans and food in the galley area. For that matter, there's little real storage room for *anything*.

- If there's a shower it's usually in the same space as the toilet, which means that everything in the room (including the toilet paper) will be damp all the time.

- Frequently the extra bunks are 6 feet long, which isn't long enough for real people.

- The seating area is almost always so low you can't see out the windows.

These features are *not* what you want on a liveaboard boat!

Interiors

THE PERSONALIZED INTERIOR

The first thing to do is think clearly about how you plan to use the boat, because the interior needs to be designed for *your* use. Forget what the plans show, by the way. The boat won't float upside down if you change the interior, so set her up the way you want to.

If you're building a boat for weekend use and plan to sail with lots of people all the time, go ahead and cram in as much stuff as you want. If you're not actually living aboard, you can cheerfully put up with poor counterspace, no storage, and cramped bunks. If that's what you want, study the production boats, because there's some really clever interiors out there, ideal for housing groups of people. I'm not knocking this approach. It's a specific use, as valid as any other.

Another specific interior type is used for really continuous sailing, such as an around-the-world race, or maybe a family pressed for time who plan on pushing on when most of us would be lying around the beach or hove to. This type of boat will have really big fuel and water tanks, bunks near the middle, and a big navigation station where charts can be left out.

Sir Francis Chichester's *Gypsy Moth*, in which he tried to beat the clipper ships' time around Cape Horn singlehanded, is a good example of this type of boat, and his book is worth reading if you're into similar stunts. For instance, he had a chair attached to the stove, with the whole business mounted on one gimbal, so he could easily sit and cook when the boat was on its ear. He also had a pressurized beer system, which certainly is worth investigating.

However, this book has been talking about "cruising" boats, not vacation boats or gung ho, against-all-odds, record-setting boats. Cruising boats take a whole different approach. You're going to be living aboard for long periods of time, much of it spent at anchor or dock. Interiors suited for that is what I'm going to talk about.

Also, I'd better say now that I don't have kids, so I always think of interiors designed for a couple. If you have a little darling or two (God forbid), then you'll have to figure out where to house them yourself, or consider trading them off for a good anchor or something. Lots of designers draw boat interiors that will sleep whole crowds of people, and you can adapt those practices if need be. Few designers design for a couple, which is what most cruisers are, so you're getting a unique product here.

A tour of a real cruising interior

Here's a description, along with some photos and drawings, of an interior from a 35-footer I built. I lived aboard for four years, then sold it to a guy who has lived aboard and used it as a traveling doctor's office in Alaska for nine years now. It's so liveable because it was

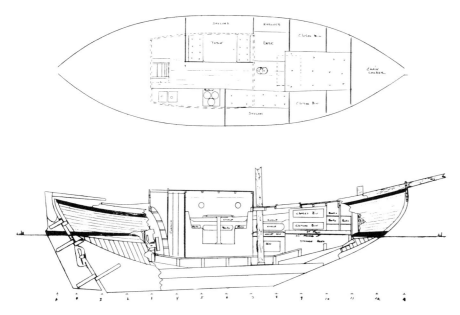

Figure 12/1.
A Little Big Boat. The author's 35-foot cutter *Juno* has a comfortable, liveaboard cruising interior suitable for a couple. Note how the absence of the traditional dropleaf table opens up the interior. Also note the generous storage areas, counter space, and the lounging couch, which can double as a sea berth or a spot for the occasional visitor. The head is curtained-off aft of the dinette. This boat is now being used as a traveling doctor's office.

designed specifically for two people to *live* on, with no compromises made for guests. Yet as it worked out, the dinette drops down to make a spare double bunk, and the couch/seaberth next to the galley can be slept on, so for resale the boat could be said to sleep five. Not on a trip though! If you'll forgive me a little immodesty, I always thought this boat had the best use of space for cruising I'd ever seen in a boat its size.

The first thing a visitor notices is the galley, especially if the visitor is someone who also lives on a boat. The galley is eight feet long, has a three-burner propane stove and oven on one end, a deep double sink on the other, and over three feet of counterspace between them. I placed the stove on the forward end of the galley so I could sit at the dinette and keep an eye on whatever's cooking, as well as for extra heat here in the chilly Pacific Northwest. If you're going to use the boat in hot climates you might consider putting the stove at the aft end so the heat can easily go out the hatch. Of course, then it isn't as easy to cook because you have to get up once in awhile to look, rather than just glancing over. Cruising is about relaxing, after all.

The countertop is 42 inches wide, which gives plenty of room for racks to hold dinnerware, silverware, and canisters of dry foods on top. The canisters are held in place by two pieces of shock cord that run the full length of the counter. Fastened to the base of the house wall over the counter is a four-foot-long narrow shelf that holds a complete variety of spices. Cups, toothbrushes, tea strainers, hot pads, and whatnot all hang from hooks off the beams or house side, over the counter.

There are two pumps at the sink. One goes to a through-hull for seawater, used for washing when you're out in clean water. The other

A

C

B

Figure 12/2.
(A) *Juno's* galley has counter space, storage, and an open feeling seldom seen in sailboats under 40 feet. A real 3-burner stove with oven eases meal preparation and makes even volume canning of windfall mackeral or something into an easy job. Note the twin handpumps for salt and fresh water and the deep double sink. This is a better kitchen than you'll find in many big-city apartments. (B) *Juno's* dinette is elevated to free storage space below and provide an eye-level view out the opening ports. Its location to port doesn't cramp the traffic pattern, unlike the traditional dropleaf table down the centerline, from which you must clear the plates and the jug every time someone wants to go forward. (C) Looking aft from the big double berth, *Juno's* open-plan interior stands in sharp contrast to the typically claustrophobic production-boat interior chopped up into little "staterooms." The decor of simple, white-painted surfaces and natural wood trim makes the interior light, cheery, inexpensive to build, and easy to maintain.

is hooked to the freshwater tanks. Rather than large main tanks, I prefer two smaller ones, maybe 20 gallons apiece, and carry additional water in three-gallon plastic jugs stored all over the boat.

Beneath the counter are shelves and bins. The shelves between the stove and sink are for food used daily. The four boxes on these two shelves keep the food organized. You don't have to bend and rummage around, just pull out the entire box. Running below the lowest shelf are bins for cooking equipment. Battens on top of the frames keep the pots out of any bilge water.

A good galley is essential when living aboard for long periods, which is why I devote so much space to it. In fact, a good galley and a good bunk are the two most important parts of the interior. The bunk is easy to plan, but don't short shaft the galley! I like my galley to be as close as possible to what I'd expect to have in a house.

Directly across from the galley, at the entrance to the cabin, is a small toilet room, or head. This is just a toilet room, and there isn't a sink or shower. There are shelves under the side deck, and raingear is hung on the bulkhead. The room is closed off with a curtain, rather than a door, because the curtain takes up no room, and doesn't interfere with the entrance ladder. The back of the boat is the best place for the head in a moderate-sized chine boat because the hull bottom is sweeping up, and there's less headroom. The head might as well be a bit cramped because it isn't exactly living space. And if the head is aft like this, then the whole forward area can be open living area.

Many boats have heads with a lot of stuff crammed into a tiny room, and it just doesn't work unless you're three feet tall, with weight in proportion. If you want a sink, then there should be a good counter too, which takes room. If you want a shower, it really should have its own stall, otherwise everything will get soaked, or at least damp.

I think the minimum space into which you can squeeze a comfortable shower, toilet, and counter is about 5 by 7 feet—a lot of space on a small boat. I'll do without the frills rather than have an awkward little space I can't turn around in. This really isn't so bad. You can wash up at the galley sink, after all, and for under 20 bucks you can rig up a can with a hose and shower head and hoist it up the mast a few feet (details later). There is no self-contained pressure water system on my boats. Hand pumps work fine, don't require electricity, and normally don't break down.

I like dinette tables and have always built them into my boats. I always raise them up on a platform so you can see out the portlights when sitting down. Underneath the seats is good dry storage for blankets and tools, and below the raised floor is lots of room for water jugs, canned food, and such.

The dinette gets used all the time. I like sitting at it when the boat is sailing. You're out of the weather, you have your coffee close by, and can smoke, read, and look out the ports. It's pleasant! The dinette is always there ready to use, unlike the traditional centerline dropleaf table, which must be put up for meals then dropped down afterwards to allow movement inside.

Larger boats, say 34 feet and up, can have dinettes long enough to convert into double bunks, or seaberths in really nasty weather. I use the dinette even in little boats, and owned one where the dinette was just big enough for two people, one on each side.

The dinette also breaks up the symmetry of the interior. The normal yacht interior with a settee on each side and a folding table in the middle is boring to look at; you can't see out the portlights, and it forces people to sit facing each other, which is no good. When living in a confined space, it's very important for people to have at least the illusion of space around them. You'll even start hating your poor old mother if she's always in front of your face.

With the arrangement shown here, a person can sit at the dinette and read, and another can sit on the couch (I hate that word "settee"), and neither will have the other in their direct line of sight. This may sound like a small, even silly point, but spend a month at sea staring at the same person day in and day out and see how silly a point it actually is.

The macho, gung ho types don't much care for the dinette. They say it's a poor seagoing setup because it's awkward to sit sideways when the boat is heeling much. They're right; it can be awkward when the boat is heeled down. So what? This interior is for *living* in, not for taking care of a race crew. If I can help it, I don't let the boat heel much anyway, because after 15 degrees of heel any boat starts moving sideways a lot, and 90 percent of the time (or more, to be honest) the boat either is anchored, tied in a slip, or in calm water.

Remember, we're talking about living aboard. If you're racing, then you'll want a completely different interior than I'm talking about.

Forward of the dinette there's a permanent chart table. It's big enough to spread out an unfolded chart, and has chart storage below. (Smaller boats can get by without chart tables by using the dinette.) There's shelves around it to hold books, sextant, binoculars, and all that stuff. When you're not using it for navigation, the chart table can become a dresser. I don't use hanging lockers for clothes storage because clothes swing around in them and wear out. I once had a hole worn through the collar of a suit coat (always carry a sport coat or blazer when cruising; it can open doors) after a few months of sailing. You can restrain clothes in a hanging locker with shock cord, which will cut down, but not eliminate the wear, but a hanging locker generally is a waste of space compared to drawers or bins.

Any boat you're going to live and cruise on needs a good bunk, and the logical place for it, except in really large boats, is in the bow, because there isn't room there for anything else. I'll always have a double bunk. You'll read that a double bunk is difficult to sleep in at sea, and that the bow is the worst place for a bunk. Maybe so. However, even Tristan Jones spends 90 percent of his time at anchor or in calm seas. My experience, when cruising even a little boat, was that when it's too uncomfortable to sleep in the bow it will be too uncomfortable to sleep *anywhere* on the boat.

True, in nasty weather two people will be tossed about in a double bunk, but in practice, both of you will rarely be in it at the same

Figure 12/3.
Eschewing the barracks-like atmosphere common to large power cruisers, the 55-foot motorship *A. W. Hudemann* offers plenty of elbow room for a liveaboard couple with occasional overnight guests. The aft stateroom truly merits the name; the pilothouse is huge, and will no doubt be the crew's lounging spot of choice.

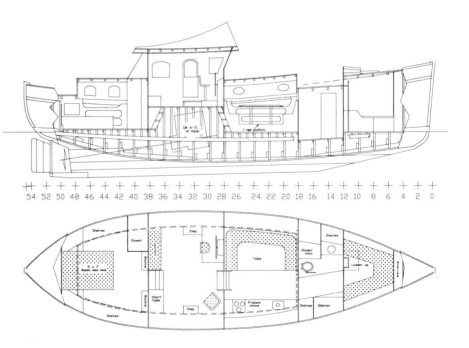

time when cruising because one or the other will be on watch. When you're using it alone, you can wedge duffel bags or something in it to reduce its width. The only times I've had problems with a double in the bow was when we hove to and drifted in bad weather. We found we could still sleep in the bow, although sleeping was sometimes interrupted when the boat was standing on its head. However, in those rare times I found I'd rather be asleep than awake feeling the motion, so could still sleep.

I believe the advantages of a double in the bow, the efficient use of space that has insufficient headroom for just about anything else, and the tremendous storage room below the bunk, far outweigh the rare discomfort you might experience, especially on boats smaller than 40 feet or so.

Finally, the house floor, or *sole* as it's correctly called, is narrow, not over two feet wide. This means that when moving around inside the boat you always have something to lean against, and can't be thrown very far. Many new boats have really wide spaces between each side, and if the boat lurches suddenly, you can be thrown around and hurt. A narrow sole is an important safety feature in an offshore boat.

This interior was very comfortable to live in, and I can't see any way to change it. Of course, if the boat had a longer house maybe the space could have been arranged differently, but I can't see how. Anything else would have made the important things, the bunk, galley, and dinette, smaller, and the longer house would have robbed deck space. Ever notice how few boats, even big boats, have any deck space for a skiff? That comes from trying to make the house too long and provide standing headroom for areas where you're mostly sitting down.

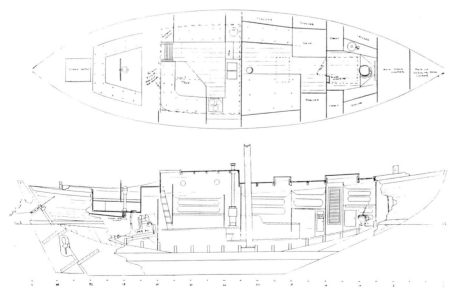

Figure 12/4.
Orpheus, a 50-footer designed for singlehanding, shows the kind of comfortable, spread-out interior ideal for living aboard. Contrast this with typical 50-foot sailboats, which generally pack in enough bunks to sleep a reinforced platoon. For the average cruising couple, all those extra bunks end up piled with spare gear (because there's no real storage), or even worse, with in-laws.

Interiors

The whole interior is open, and you can lay on the bunk and look all the way to the stern. Even the engine sits out in the open. I kept it clean and polished, and find it rather handsome. There's a tremendous feeling of space, and ventilation is good all through the hull. It's an excellent cruising interior layout.

THE PARTICULARS OF INTERIOR CONSTRUCTION

Regardless of how plain or fancy you want it, all boat interiors will need some basic stuff: a stove, sink, windows, tanks, and some sort of basic cabinetry.

But first, a word about interior decor. I do *not* like an interior ceiling—the liner over the frames. I think the entire interior should be as open as possible, both for ventilation, and so I can see all parts of the hull. In practice, most of the frames and planking will be covered up by cabinets and furniture, but if you need to track down a leak or the like, you can still see and get to the inside hull *everywhere* in any boat I build.

Remember, the two things that will kill a wood boat are fresh water inside and a lack of ventilation. Leave things as open as possible. Don't build in any dead air spaces. Saw in lots of air passage holes in closets or doors. As I build in the interior, I fill a garden pump sprayer with green wood preservative and soak down the inside of the hull in the area I'm working, wet on wet, until she's saturated. Some people say they don't like the smell, but I think it disappears after a week or so, although I am a heavy smoker so maybe I can't smell it. It is good for the wood though, and besides, I rather like the smell. If you don't want to use the green stuff, there are clear ones out there. Use *something* though.

Some people paint the inside of the hull planking, which I think is a mistake. I think wood needs to breathe on one side, but plenty of people disagree. If you disagree, fine, go ahead. Be the cause of rot! But don't paint the inside hull until the basic cabinetry is completed, or you'll be unable to glue bulkheads to the frames.

I've always found interiors made of dark, naturally-finished woods oppressive, unlivable, and impractical. The finish work is so pretty that you hate to mess it up by thumb-tacking a pinup to a bulkhead, or discoloring it with tobacco smoke. Besides, they're hard to build, since nothing looks worse than bright-finished work with sloppy fits, so you can't rely on bondo in the not-quite-perfect seams like you can with a painted surface.

I use 3/4-inch plywood for practically everything inside. It's heavy enough not to sag much, so it needs minimal supporting framework. Fir plywood is hard to paint smooth, so if you have some extra money use MDO double density for bulkheads and whatnot where both sides are exposed. As mentioned before, this stuff is made for sign painters and the smooth faces take paint easily. However, if

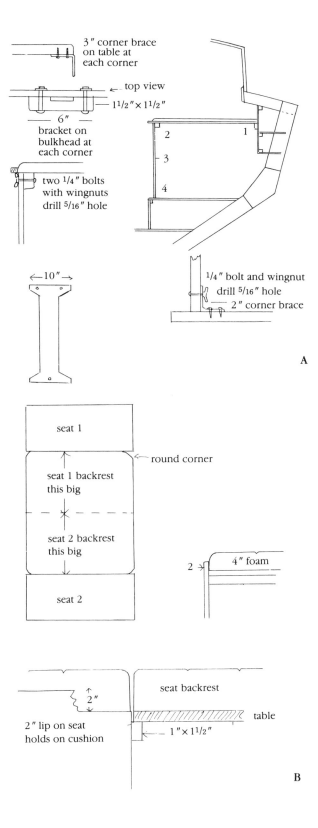

3" corner brace on table at each corner

top view

$1^{1}/_{2}" \times 1^{1}/_{2}"$

6"

bracket on bulkhead at each corner

two $^{1}/_{4}"$ bolts with wingnuts drill $^{5}/_{16}"$ hole

2

1

3

4

←10"→

$^{1}/_{4}"$ bolt and wingnut drill $^{5}/_{16}"$ hole

2" corner brace

A

seat 1

round corner

seat 1 backrest this big

seat 2 backrest this big

seat 2

2

4" foam

seat backrest

2"

table

2" lip on seat holds on cushion

$1" \times 1^{1}/_{2}"$

B

Figure 12/5.
(A) Simple plywood joinery. Here are details for a dinette that drops down to make a double bunk, just in case the in-laws *do* show up. (B) The 4-inch foam cushions make the dinette into a fairly comfortable double. Just remind your guests that Benjamin Franklin said, ''Fish and visitors smell after three days.''

Interiors
207

Figure 12/5 con't.
(C) Put storage hatches
under all seats and bunks.
Use a narrow blade on
your Skilsaw; carefully
"plunge-cut" the open-
ings and use the cut-outs
for doors or lids.

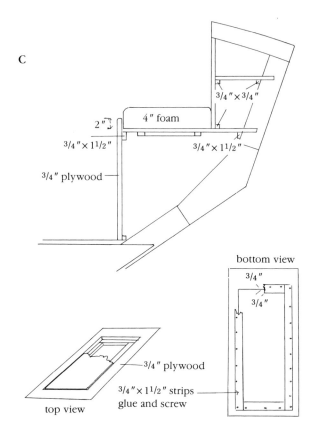

you're going to panel it with something, then AC ply is good enough. I see no reason at all for using marine plywood in boat interiors, regardless of the depth of your pockets.

Building with plywood is easy, fast, and strong. Patterns of $1/4$- by 3-inch strips of plywood make it very simple to fit a plywood bulkhead or shelf. Fasten the bulkhead in with glue and big galvanized nails, and try to attach them to frames. If you can't, because you need room for a bunk or something, then attach cleats across two frames and fasten the bulkhead to that. I suppose you could also attach a cleat directly to the planking, but I don't care for that. Any structural bulkheads must be attached to frames, of course, and I position the house roof beams to be in line with frames wherever a major bulkhead is going to be fitted. By the way, I discussed installing the house roof beams and roof back in Chapter 10, but I hope you didn't do it then. As I said, it's easier to build the interior if there isn't a roof in the way. You can line up the roof beams so that any major bulkheads can be fastened to the hull frame and the roof beam. Uneven beam spacing doesn't make any difference.

I usually use that powdered glue you mix with water for interior construction, but recently I've started using yellow Elmer's Carpen-

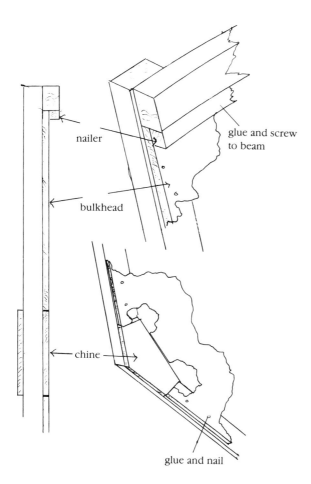

Figure 12/6.
Plywood bulkhead installation details. Glued and nailed both to frames and the deck beams, these bulkheads act as giant gussets, significantly strengthening the hull and tying things together.

nailer

glue and screw to beam

bulkhead

chine

glue and nail

ter's Glue because it comes in a squeeze bottle and is so convenient. There's no need for epoxy for this stuff, although it doesn't hurt anything if you want to use it.

The simplest way to finish off the interior is with white paint. A light-colored interior feels bigger than it really is, and it's easy to clean because you can see at a glance if it's getting dirty. However, as I've mentioned before, I paneled my current boat with that 5/16-inch "beaded" wainscoting sold in packages at larger lumberyards. I used light-colored pine, fastened it to the plywood with Weldwood Construction Adhesive and a couple of finish nails, and finished it off with a gloss Varithane varnish, which, judging from some of the bar tops I've inspected at close range, is strong enough to stand up to a lot of scrubbing. I suspect it'll be even easier to keep clean than paint. As a matter of fact, I've started painting shelves, then Varithaneing over the paint, figuring that will make a surface easier to keep clean. We'll see how it works.

Anyway, this wainscoting isn't all that cheap, but you can create a similar look by rounding the edges of a 2 × 4 with a block plane, then

Figure 12/7.
Three views of a bulkhead
being fitted using patterns
made from 1/4-×3-inch
plywood strips. Fasten
them together with carpet
tacks; use **C**-clamps in
unsupported spots, then
nail them together before
use.

running it through a table saw to rip off a strip 1/4- to 5/16-thick. Round
the 2 × 4's edges again, and saw off another strip. Get the idea? These
strips can be fastened to the bulkheads and will look about as good as
the store-bought stuff, and be considerably cheaper.

This paneling gives an old-time look to the boat, and I think it's
actually less work to do than filling voids and painting the interior

Figure 12/8.
Using patterns to determine cutting schedule for shelf faces. Patterns allow you not only to cut intricate shapes accurately on the first try, but also to fiddle around with things and see how they'll look full size before you cut up a sheet of plywood and find the shelves are too close together to hold your pressure cooker.

with four or five coats. The little pieces go up quickly, and a few coats of varnish makes them look sharp. I got carried away with the stuff on my current boat and have used it everywhere—even over the roof beams before I laminated the plywood over it.

Many commercial builders cover all the interior bulkheads and the underside of the roof with plastic laminates such as Formica. Once you get the hang of installing it, it goes fast, yielding a hard surface that never needs painting and is easy to keep clean. Unfortunately, it looks like a cheap refrigerator, and I rather like seeing wood grain, bolt heads, and whatnot, even when they're painted. Plastic laminates are practical, though, and if you choose one that's a solid color and add some varnished wood trim it looks OK. That wood grain Formica usually looks terrible; I'd stay away from it.

A

B

Figure 12/9.
(A) A 3/4-inch plywood bulkhead installed and ready to finish. (B) Beaded tongue and groove wainscoting installed down to seat top with construction adhesive and a couple of finish nails at top and bottom.

Interiors

I prefer the heavy-duty plastic water tanks available from trailer supply joints. Usually I use two 20-gallon tanks, and carry extra water in 3- to 5-gallon containers. The rest of the water is carried in 3-gallon plastic jugs; 5-gallon jugs weigh too much to carry far, although possibly a folding handtruck could be carried to assist. Eighty gallons of fresh water is plenty for two people for over two months, using seawater for washing.

When you're cruising away from the States, you won't be able to pull up and fill your tanks with a hose, and will generally be anchored out, rowing in with a skiff to carry water. The little jugs allow you to pack the water back to the boat, can be stowed all over the boat, and will make it impossible to lose all your water should there be a plumbing failure. Large tanks take up a good deal of room, and if mounted beneath a bunk make an annoying sloshing sound. Besides, custom-made ones are expensive.

The two 20-gallon tanks give the convenience of having the galley pump, and are kept topped up when at anchor. But when cruising I used to disconnect them, and would fill a 1-gallon container every day. This gave me a measured ration so I could keep track of consumption. One half gallon a day, with a shot or two of hootch in the afternoon, is a comfortable ration per person.

I carried about 80 gallons in my smaller boats, and my 50-footer will have 150 gallons, since I found a good buy on some 25-gallon tanks and have the room to install them. There'll be four of them, and another 50 gallons in portable containers, which will also be used for transporting water to the boat when away from the States.

Mount the tanks on each side of the boat; alongside the cockpit seems the best spot in most boats. Some people fill water tanks from inside the boat rather than using deck fills. This seems like a lot of hassle to me, and is also a good way to splash freshwater around the inside of the hull, which you don't want.

Each tank needs its own fill hose to the deck, and a vent. Clear plastic hose works fine for the lines. Use 1¼ inch minimum for the fill lines, and ³/₈ inch for the vent lines. Run the vent outside the hull, like up the inside of the back cabin wall, and cover the hole with a small clamshell vent. The vents can be put together in a T, but the fills should be separate lines. The lines to the pump should be ³/₈ inch, and these can be joined in a T as well.

I install a shutoff valve on each of the drain (*exhaust* is the proper term) lines, before the T. If you don't, when the boat is on one tack all the water will run to the low side. If you're going to be on one tack for a few days, you can sail on the opposite tack to fill the low-side tank, close its shutoff, then turn to the tack you want. You'll have a bit of water ballast up high, which might make a difference with very small boats. The shutoffs also are a safety system in case you have a plumbing failure.

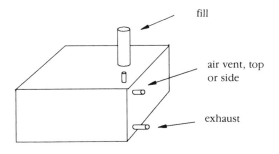

fill

air vent, top or side

exhaust

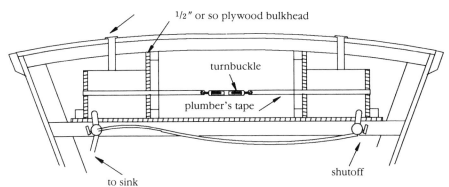

1/2" or so plywood bulkhead

turnbuckle

plumber's tape

to sink

shutoff

Figure 12/10.
Plastic water tanks come in all shapes and sizes at RV suppliers (much cheaper than marine suppliers). Buy the heavy-duty versions! Be sure "exhausts" are on opposite sides so water will drain on any tack. Mount your water tanks solidly. Water is heavy; the water sloshing around in partially filled tanks can rip the whole works loose in rough seas.

Although the heavy-duty plastic trailer tanks work well and are the cheapest way to go, they can fail, so when you install them leave access: you'll probably have to remove them some day. Box them in tightly with plywood to keep them from surging, and be gentle when filling them. They're easily killed when overfilled with a pressure hose, so use a low stream of water. Those "bladder-type" tanks work fine, and custom stainless ones are probably troublefree forever. Again, it all depends on the depth of your pocket.

I like hand- or foot-powered sink pumps, or gravity feed, for that matter. I don't like pressure water systems. The machinery is expensive, and like any other thing electrical in a salt air environment, it fails constantly. Besides, it encourages excessive water use, which you want to avoid on a long trip. If you do decide you want pressure water anyway, there are several inexpensive ways to go about it.

The simplest mechanical system I've seen was on the halibut schooner *Nordby*. The owners just hooked a cheap little 12-volt pump to the waterline; there was a push/pull electric switch to turn it off and on instead of a faucet; and the "nozzle" was a bent piece of tubing sticking out of the counter over the sink.

Another idea is to put a 5- to 10-gallon tank, such as a stainless beer barrel, on the roof over the sink. Pump water into it by hand or pour it in from a jug, then let gravity lead it to the sink. Not much to go wrong here, and the barrel looks rather shippy on deck, even more so if you laminate on thin wood strips to make it look wooden.

Interiors

That's one of the projects you can save for when you're becalmed in the Sargasso Sea.

You can use this same idea for a shower. Showers inside the boat don't work well unless you have a separate stall, for which few small boats have room. Instead, hoist a garden sprayer up the mast or use one of those solar shower things you can buy at the boat store. If you'll be showering in the public eye, you can hoist a shower curtain mounted on a 3-foot diameter ring. This makes a fine, cheap-to-install shower that takes up no room, and will never break down.

If you have a larger boat with room for a shower stall, and you plan to spend some time tied to the dock, you can back up the basic hand-pump cruising system with a normal faucet at the sink and one in the shower, mounted on a bulkhead if you don't have a separate stall. Have a regular garden faucet in the cockpit, piped to the sink and shower for a cold line, and split to run to a small house-trailer/motorhome, 110-volt hot-water tank installed somewhere out of the way, like near the engine.

When tied to the dock, all you have to do is hook the dock water to the faucet, plug a cord into the dock power, and you've got pressure hot and cold water. This system is inexpensive, pretty much troublefree, and gives all the comforts of home when tied to the dock. Then, when you're off using the boat, you use the built-in hand-pump system, with its commensurate water and energy savings and freedom from maintenance.

By the way, if you do install a shower, do *not* let it drain into the bilge. That's a very good way to kill wood boats. Instead, have it drain into a 5-gallon holding tank, which you can either dump over the side, or pump overboard. A bulkhead-mounted pump is the simplest system, with the drain coming through the hull up near the sheer.

The galley

You want a big galley. Give it as wide a countertop as you can, with big bins. I don't bother with drawers—I use boxes instead—but go ahead if you want to bother. Plastic laminate makes a good countertop, but I like the look of ceramic tiles, even though they're slippery and a little harder to keep clean. Put a sea rail along the front of the counter to keep stuff from sliding off. A 3/4- by 1 1/2-inch strip of wood fastened to the front, standing 3/4 inch above the counter, is all you need.

Install a good stove and oven. A gimbaled stove is handy at times but requires extra counterspace, so I don't bother with it. Although there are some beautiful stainless steel marine stoves on the market, they're all expensive, and plenty of people use stoves from a trailer supplier, which cost about a third less—a tenth if you buy a used one.

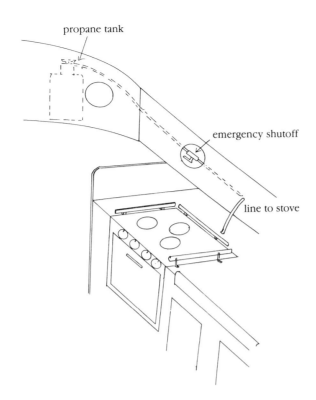

propane tank

emergency shutoff

line to stove

Figure 12/11. Low-tech, nearly fool-proof propane installation. Mount the propane tank on deck, ideally within reach from inside the boat. Mount the emergency shutoff outside an opening port close to, but not directly over, the stove. Have the propane line enter the boat close to the stove. All joints in the line should be *outside*.

They aren't stainless, so they'll rust out after 10 years or so in a salt-air environment, but that's all right. They're cheap enough to replace.

In cold climates a diesel stove probably is the best choice because you can leave the oven on all the time to keep the boat warm and dry. This doesn't work in warm climates, of course, and I personally use propane. A lot of folks are afraid of propane because it can blow you to bits if you ain't careful. If you're *really* careless, maybe propane isn't for you—probably sailing too, for that matter. For normal people, propane's convenience and low cost far outweigh any risk.

Cooking with propane on board is just like using your gas stove at home. You'll have a thermostatically-controlled oven so you can bake pies and bread and stuff. Propane's dirt cheap and available worldwide, if you carry a spare regulator and a few different fill fittings to match varying standards.

The cheapest tanks are the type that stand upright, and you can buy new ones for under 20 bucks at a discount house, far less at a yard sale. I'm a little leery of used ones, especially if they've been painted, because you can't see how rusty they are. This may not be a great place to save money.

The nicest tanks are the ones that lie flat because they have a lower profile, but they cost considerably more. One 5-gallon tank will last a good three months of normal cooking. Two 5-gallon ones are plenty to carry on most cruises, although three might be a good idea if you're really going off to the sticks. That would give you close to nine months of cooking fuel, at a cost of about $15 in the States, far less most other places.

Propane is heavier than air, so if there's a leak it settles into the lowest part of the boat, waiting for a chance to explode. To make this more or less impossible, mount the tanks outside on deck, with the tank's shutoff valve accessible through an opening port. When you light the stove, reach out the port, turn on the tank, *then* light the stove. To shut off the stove, reach out and turn off the *tank*. When the propane burns out of the line, *then* turn off the stove.

Frequently you'll forget to turn off the stove valve, so when you next turn on the tank, raw propane will flow into the boat, which you'll smell right off. Well, you won't blow up instantly. In fact, it takes a fair amount of propane, then a spark. Just turn off the burner, wait a few seconds to clear the gas from the stove top, then light it. No problem. Just remember to turn off the stove next time.

If you have a large boat and don't like looking at propane tanks, you can put them in a recessed box built in somewhere near the stern. This should be sealed off absolutely from the hull, protrude a few inches above the deck, and have an air vent in the top with a vent line leading overboard (minimum 1/2-inch I.D.) from the bottom of the box. This vent line should have no abrupt direction changes in it to trap water, should exit above the waterline at all angles of heel, and should have its outboard end covered by a piece of inner tube or the like for a flapper valve.

If you mount your tanks somewhere inaccessible from a port light, like in the box, you can install a shutoff in the line to the stove. Electric shutoffs are available and generally recommended, but I don't trust them. They work on an electrical impulse, and putting that and a possible spark next to a propane connection worries me. I keep *all* joints in the propane system outside the hull, so if you're running a long line from the stern, I'd route it outside the house and install the shutoff in front of an opening port, then continue the line back through the house wall and down to the stove.

Propane is very simple to hook up, but a few safety features need to be followed. If you aren't familiar with it, go to a propane store, look at some camper trailers, or talk to an RV dealer. Install a pressure gauge at the tank next to the regulator. Use copper tubing for all the lines, and bend it properly around corners with one of them tubing bender things. You can pick up a bender and flaring kit for about 99 cents at a discount tool joint. Attach any long lengths of tubing securely against something solid so it can't vibrate and chafe a hole in the line. Use Teflon tape to seal all connections.

When you get everything hooked up, dab each connection with soapy water, turn on the tank, and see if there are any bubbles. If there are, break down the joint and wrap it again with Teflon tape.

Test the system by watching the pressure gauge. It should hold pressure with the tank turned off for at least a few hours, and lose pressure very slowly, like overnight.

And don't use pilot lights! Not only will they waste propane like crazy, but they can blow out and leak gas. If your stove has one for the top burners, disconnect it. The oven will have a pilot, but it's controlled at the on/off valve. You must light the pilot to light the oven, and when the oven is off, the pilot doesn't get gas. Don't disconnect this one! You need it for baking.

If you're anti-propane, the only other real choice is kerosene. Wood and coal are bulky to stow and too much trouble when all you want is a cup of coffee. Alcohol is useless—it burns cool, it's smelly, hard to light, hard to find, and frighteningly expensive. Kerosene is cheaper, more commonly available, and burns much hotter than alcohol, but it still can't hold a candle to propane.

Despite the fact that they're often chosen because they're "safer," I think both alcohol and kerosene are dangerous, because you have to preheat the burner to get it going. Sterno works well for this, but it's expensive, so most people preheat the little burner cup by filling it with alcohol and touching it off. I've done this in a seaway, had the boat roll, and seen a flaming stream of alcohol suddenly flowing down the counter. No thanks! Use propane.

You'll want a sink in any size boat. I've always liked double sinks, but recently I've begun thinking that a big single sink might be handier. Whatever your personal choice dictates, the seagoing sink should be deep, ideally installed near the centerline so it will drain while the boat is heeled or rolling. This is rarely possible in smaller boats, so carry a plastic dishpan that fits inside, and dump it overboard when you're on the tack the sink doesn't like. In practice, however, you'll keep the boat on its bottom and reef if it starts heeling too much: Cruising heeled way down is just too tiring.

Ideally the bottom of the sink is located well above the waterline so it can simply drain overboard, but if it isn't, which it probably won't be except on larger boats, have it drain into a 5-gallon tank below the sink. You can hook up a hand pump to the tank and pump it overboard. Don't be tempted to use an electric pump. It isn't that hard to pump once in a while, and the hand pump is unlikely to break down. If you install a fairly large one, it could become an extra bilge pump in case of an emergency.

Which gets us to the subject of through-hulls. Some people are afraid of them, figuring they'll fail and sink their boat, and they brag that their boat has none. I was in an anchorage in Mexico with a gringo who had all his through-hulls above the waterline, including the toilet. Man, that was crude. Properly cared for, good through-hulls are as safe as anything else on a boat. A heavy bronze through-hull is probably stronger than the planking, and makes life aboard far easier.

There are some new plastic through-hulls on the market that are supposed to be pretty good, but I don't use them. I've heard of at least one type that deteriorates over the years. One boat that used them almost sank when one broke off. I use bronze, although I suppose you could make your own from galvanized pipe. Bronze through-hulls are cheap enough and well proven, though.

I used to worry about electrolysis with bronze through-hulls in a galvanized-fastened boat. However, it doesn't seem to happen, perhaps because the steel fastenings never touch the bronze through-hull. However, be sure *all* fittings attached to the through-hull are bronze, too. Some cheap gate valves have stainless steel ball valves inside, which could cause problems.

Ideally every through-hull will have a shutoff valve. The best is the old bronze seacock, but they aren't cheap. A lot of people use regular gate valves like you see in houses, but most of them are brass, and brass is eaten up by salt water. (Bronze gate valves supposedly are available, but they're hard to find.) Gate valves probably did a lot to damage the reputation of through-hulls in general, so if you use them, keep them well greased, keep your eye on them, and change them maybe every five years.

If you're building on a real budget, you can get by without the shutoffs. Just make some tapered wood plugs, and leave one on a lanyard next to each through-hull. In the event of trouble you can rip off the hose and shove in the plug. The fact is that with the hoses made today you'll probably never have trouble, but I still use shutoffs anyway. I went cruising on one boat without them, and when I put the boat on the beach to paint the bottom, I forgot that the sink top would now be below the waterline when the tide came up. Sure enough, the tide came up, through the sink, and into the boat. I noticed it wasn't floating, remembered the sink, plugged it and pumped out the boat, and I was OK. A shutoff would have been a lot simpler.

The head

For obvious reasons, you'll want some sort of toilet. The simplest solution is just a toilet seat mounted on a bucket. L. Francis Herreshoff, who designed many huge and expensive yachts, advocated using a cedar bucket, but I think these days anybody who owns a wood boat can in good conscience use a plastic bucket. Sensible solution though the bucket may be, they are a hassle, and almost everyone these days installs a marine toilet, or head, as it's called, with all its officially mandated paraphernalia.

As usual, the politicians have gone after the least offensive and least organized group, and today in the States an overboard discharge toilet is illegal. True, human waste in the water is a national problem, and recreational boaters contribute their share. But the lower section of the Columbia River is radioactive from the nuke plant waste seeping into the ground water; people living in houses built on dredge spoil from the river are dropping dead of leukemia; fish caught in lower Puget Sound are covered with ulcerous sores, and the sludge slick floating around New York City could be the basis for a Japanese horror movie.

Obviously these are problems that won't be the least bit affected by banning overboard discharge from little boats (and not, until very recently, from Navy ships). It does give the politicians the illusion that they're doing something to clean up our environment without offending their political backers, and boaters don't make huge campaign contributions as a block. If you're wondering who is right or wrong, ask a fish which group should be stood against the wall.

Oddly enough, a bucket is a legal marine toilet because "they" assume you won't dump it until you get to land and can flush it into a shore toilet, many of which still are straight-piped right into the ocean. And it isn't illegal *not* to have a toilet, the assumption apparently being that those without toilets never *need* one.

Anyway, if you install a toilet, to be legal it needs to be hooked up to a holding tank. If you're offshore you're still allowed to pump overboard, and there are very few holding tank pumpout stations around, so your toilet drain should be hooked up to a Y-valve so you can pump into the tank when in harbor or alongshore, and directly overboard when out sailing in the open sea. (One anarchist I know has a holding tank and a Y-valve for the Coast Guard to see during inspections. The valve is a phony, and the tank is used to carry gin.)

The tank will need a line running to a deck plate so the tank can be pumped out if you ever actually find a pumpout station, and a vent to release the methane gas generated by the decomposition of your sewage. Methane is very explosive, and I know of one boat that had its holding tank blow up. What a mess.

Another problem is overfilling the holding tank, the first warning of which you'll receive when the toilet either won't flush or the tank blows. So, when you install the tank, also install a water tank for the toilet-flushing water. If the holding tank is, say, 10 gallons, then make the seawater flush tank hold maybe 6 gallons. When you run out of water you can bucket in enough for the "final" flush, and you'll know it's time to pump the holding tank.

There's all sorts of marine toilets on the market in all price ranges. The cheap ones work but the anemic pumps clog up very easily, so I buy a model made for charter boats. My friend Wolf, a very large German, says that if you aren't careful it will suck your testicles off!

Windows

You'll want some windows, port holes, portlights, whatever you want to call them. Fixed windows can be used in some places, but opening ports are essential, at the least on the front of the house.

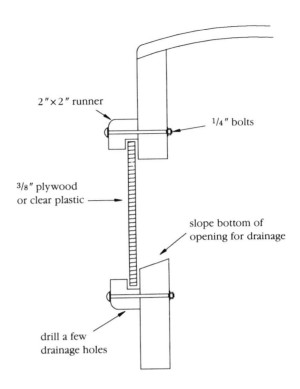

Figure 12/12.
Third-world style opening portlight—just a plywood (or Plexiglas or Lexan) shutter that slides back and forth on a simple wooden track. It works fine, costs almost nothing, and you can always "upgrade" later.

2″×2″ runner

¼″ bolts

³/8″ plywood or clear plastic

slope bottom of opening for drainage

drill a few drainage holes

Bronze marine ports are very pretty but very expensive. A method commonly seen on workboats in "undeveloped" countries is just a hole sawn in the house wall with an outside board, sort of a storm shutter, that slides forward to close off the hole. Fancy ones have a round piece of Plexiglas in the board, or even use Plexiglas for the whole slider.

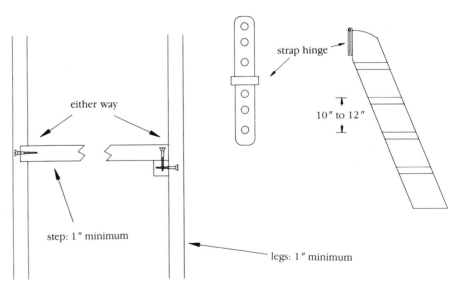

Figure 12/13.
A simple, hinged companionway ladder. The hinges let you raise the ladder for engine maintenance, to gain access to storage, or, when asleep in "hostile" anchorages, to give you extra time to deal with intruders; when raised, the ladder blocks the opening. Use 1- to 1½-inch stock for the sides and steps; space the steps 10 to 12 inches apart.

either way

strap hinge

10″ to 12″

step: 1″ minimum

legs: 1″ minimum

Buehler's Backyard Boatbuilding

If you're building on a real budget you can cut the holes for the ports and use the slider idea until you can afford store-bought ports or turn up some good used ones at a swap meet. Inexpensive ports made of plastic are available and used on many production boats, but they're so ugly I'd use the slider first until I could afford the real thing.

Electrics

Although it's undeniable that they make life easier aboard, electrics aren't really necessary. I cheerfully crank-started my engine and ran my depth sounder off a 12-volt lantern battery for several years before I got around to installing electric start. I *like* kerosene cabin lighting. But nowadays I like the convenience of a reading lamp over the bunk, and kerosene heats up the cabin in warm weather, so a few electric lights are nice. Besides, if you have a simple system you can run your tape player off the engine battery, which is easier than replacing dry cells.

Installing an electrical system is worthy of a book itself, so I'll just touch on it to point out the easiest ways to do things, and to steer you away from some troublespots.

A common error I see is people installing batteries in the bilges. If for some reason the boat gets much water in it you'll have big

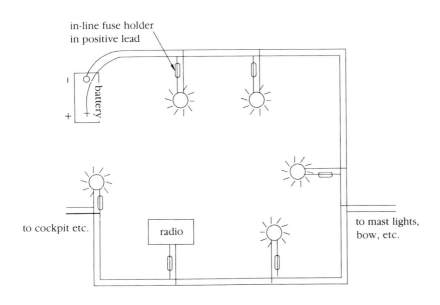

Figure 12/14.
The simplest electrical system—just a pair of heavy wires that circle the boat. Splice in wherever you want power. Put an in-line fuse holder in the positive lead to each fixture.

problems—chlorine gas, for instance, or terrible electrolysis if the positive lead gets into the bilge water and remains undiscovered for a while.

I install batteries in a heavy wood box, mounted as high up as possible. If your engine can't be hand cranked, you should install two batteries, separated by a 3-way switch that allows you to draw from or charge either battery. That way you can run lights off one while keeping the other fully charged for starting the engine.

The simplest system is just to run a pair of heavy wires—#12 to #14 gauge, one for positive and one for negative—from the battery right around the perimeter of the boat. Attach them up under the deck beams as close to the frames as you can, ending on a light fixture or something back next to the battery. This rings the hull with a power source easily accessible everywhere.

Now, wherever you want a light, a radio, or whatever, splice in a set of wires off the main power line and run them to where you want the fixture. You should use different colors for this all around the boat, and be consistent. Standard practice is to use red for the hot lead and black for the return line. Install an inline fuse holder just after the splice where the hot lead hits the power lead. Be sure you don't get the hot line and the ground, or return line, mixed up. That way if the fixture fails, you know the problem can only be in two spots: the fixture itself, or the fuse in the line before it.

This is really a simple system, not nearly as impressive as a fuse panel with little lights and toggle switches and labels and zillions of wires running all over the boat and stuff. It works though. If you want to go whole hog pick up a book on the subject.

Some parting thoughts on interiors

Finally, it's easy to get carried away building an interior, and some people find the temptation overwhelming to pack in a lot of tricky stuff—folding this and sliding that. It don't work. Keep things simple and spacious, at least for now. A fancy interior is harder to build than the boat itself and will take more time and probably more money. I'd suggest you keep things pretty simple. You can always "trick" it out later on after you get bored lying around the beach and drinking. Always keep in mind, Jack, you gotta *get* to the beach before you can lie about on it!

This reminds me of a guy I met years ago. We were both building small boats, under 30 feet. I was going at it hard and fast, he acted like he was building a clock. He kept coming around telling me how sloppy this was and how wasteful that was. Well, I launched and headed south. I never did see him again, but a year later, as I was getting ready to head west from Puerto Vallarta, I sent him a postcard that said, "Having a great time. Heading to the Islands tomorrow; see you there, Melon Farmer." I wonder if he ever did finish.

HUMAN DIMENSIONS

This guy shows the various dimensions you'll need to keep in mind when designing your interior. These are comfortable working clearances, and should be followed as much as possible. Of course it's rarely possible in a small boat to hit them on the nose, but use them as a guide.

Here are some basic interior dimensions that work well:

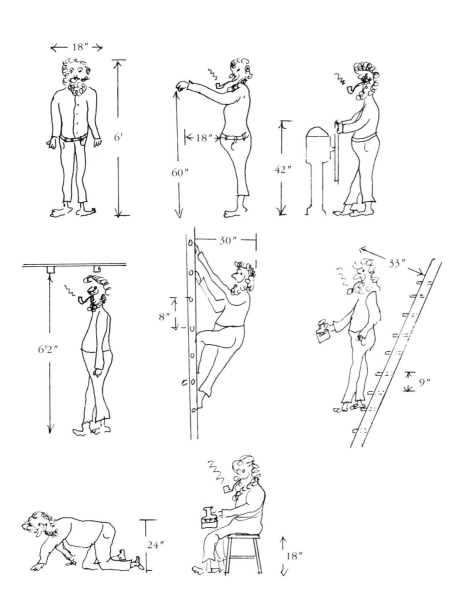

Entrance hatch opening: 30 inches wide by 30 inches long.

Deck hatches: 2 feet by 2 feet, minimum.

Full headroom: 6 feet 2 inches below beams.

Minimum headroom: 4 feet gives sitting headroom over a 12-inch high (minimum) seat.

Headroom over seat: 3 feet minimum.

Height of seat from floor: Maximum 19 inches; average 16 inches; minimum 12 inches. The lower it is, the wider it must be.

Bunks: 6 feet 6 inches long, minimum; 7 feet is ideal; 6 feet don't work. Minimum 21 inches wide at the shoulder, 18 inches at the foot. Double berths need to be 48 inches wide at the head, 28 inches at the foot.

Headroom over bunks: 2 feet minimum.

Seat cushions: 4-inch foam is ideal; 3-inch will work.

Toilet room: 3 by 3 feet, minimum; 3 by 4 feet is more comfortable.

Tables: As big as you can make them. Each person needs about 2 feet of elbow room. Tabletop should be 12 inches above seat cushions.

Galley counter: As wide as possible, 36 inches above the floor, minimum.

Cabin sole (floor) width: As narrow as possible, to allow safe movement inside in bad weather.

MORE BOLT-ONS: COAMINGS, RAILS, COMPANIONWAYS, AND RUDDERS

Things are moving along well now, and the end is in sight! Pretty soon you'll be able to throw the sucker in the water. Perhaps now's the time to start doing a few situps so you'll look good on the beach. Cutting back on the booze will do it, too. A few years ago I spent six months as, among other things, "Acting Shipwright Foreman, Royal Saudi Navy, Western Flotilla," and I knocked off 25 pounds, since there's no hootch over there. (Actually, there *is* hootch available, but a fifth of bourbon costs $175 or so on the black market, and if the cops catch you with it, it means maybe two years in the can.)

COAMINGS

If your boat has a cockpit you'll want *coamings*. I was too lazy to install them on one boat, and it sure made driving uncomfortable: There was nothing to lean against, and when the boat was heeled and rolling much you'd get your tail wet. Even a 6-inch-high coaming will give a bit of support, provide something to lean a cushion against, and keep most of the deck water off you.

The coamings often need to be curved, especially on smaller boats, to leave enough room on deck for comfortable sitting. The easiest way to make them is to laminate them up from strips of wood. First you'll need to make a bending form, very similar to the one you used for deck beams back in Chapter 8. Draw a straight line on each side of the deck from the coaming's starting point (normally flush with the side of the house) to its end, just aft of the cockpit. Connect these two points with a straight line; this will become the baseline for the curved coaming. Now draw a curved line connecting the two points to indicate where the back will go. You can draw this line in

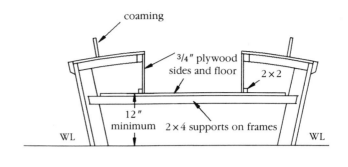

coaming

3/4" plywood
sides and floor

2 × 2

12"
minimum   2 × 4 supports on frames

WL   WL

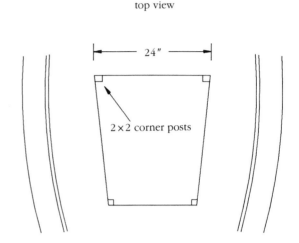

top view

|← 24" →|

2 × 2 corner posts

Figure 13/1.
The basic footwell is the traditional cruising cockpit. Sit right on cushions on deck and lean back against the coamings. Construction is simply a plywood box covered with glass cloth and epoxy. Install a 1½-inch drain leading overboard in the center, or put two drains in the corners if you'd rather. Large cockpits with built-in seating are made the same way but have the coaming extending up from the floor. Note that the cockpit floor extends the full width of the hull to provide added storage or a platform for water or fuel tanks.

freehand, but you'll do a better job if you have a few helpers to hold the front, back, and middle of a flexible batten while you scribe the line.

Measure up from the baseline to the curve on 12- to 16-inch intervals, note the dimensions, then transfer them to the building form, again sweeping in the curve with a batten. Figure 13-2 shows a simple form you can use for laminating the coaming.

If there isn't much curve to the coaming you can make it from two pieces of 1 × 12; saw the top edges to a nice sweeping curve before laminating them together. If you're making a *really* curved coaming, you can glue it up from ⅛-inch plywood "doorskin." This stuff is cheap, very flexible, and holds up well if entombed in epoxy. In fact, if you're into epoxy and tricky curved shapes, doorskin is a good material with which to indulge your fantasies.

Fasten the coamings to the deck with through-bolts, preferably down through deck beams. Screw the forward end into a 2 × 2 attached to the house and lined up so that the outboard side of the coaming and house side flow together on the same line.

Some people make a fancy job of it by attaching a half-round block to the house, and rabbeting the coaming into it. This will add

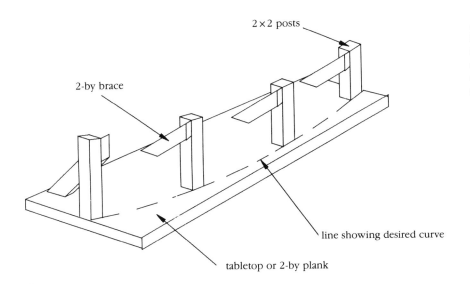

Figure 13/2.
Make a simple form like
this and laminate cockpit
coamings with too much
curve to saw out of 2-by
stock.

2 × 2 posts

2-by brace

line showing desired curve

tabletop or 2-by plank

to the sitting room because the coaming will be farther outboard. I've
never bothered, myself.

Be sure to saw a good notch in the bottom of the coaming where
it hits the house so deck water can flow off and not be trapped against
the house wall, causing it to rot out. Remember our motto: "Think
Ahead, Stupid!"

Stand the coaming in place and prop it up to whatever angle
looks comfortable to you. It probably doesn't fit the deck at all, so
you'll have to scribe a line down each side for trimming. If, for
instance, the coaming is an inch off the deck in the middle, hold a
pencil on a 1¹/₄- or 1¹/₂-inch block set on the deck, and run it all the
way around the coaming, inboard and outboard. Putting the line on
each side makes it easy to plane the bottom edge down to the correct
angle and curve.

If your boat has narrow deck beams and you're nervous about
drilling down through an angled, curved coaming, expecting to hit
the skinny beams dead center, stand the coaming on deck (after it's
fitted of course) and mark the locations for the beams on it. Flip it
over and start drilling from the bottom. That way at least the hole will
be over the center of the beam at the deck, so should make it through
the beam the whole distance. Bolting it to the deck is good enough,
of course, as long as you use plenty of bolts and good backing plates
made from ³/₄-inch plywood behind the nuts. If you're just bolting to
the deck I'd put a bolt about every foot.

If you have trouble drilling straight holes, remember the trick of
sighting along a straightedge clamped to whatever you're drilling.
And if you do drill through the side of the coaming, don't slit your
throat: Just glue a dowel in the hole and try it again.

More Bolt-Ons

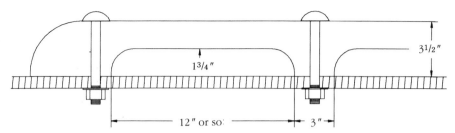

1 3/4 "

3 1/2 "

12 " or so

3 "

HANDRAILS

You want heavy handrails a foot or so in from the edge of the house roof. If you're building a flush-deck boat, you might think about putting one rail down the middle of the deck. There'll be times when you'll want it, let me tell you.

The delicate teak rails sold in marine stores are dangerous and don't belong on a cruising boat. Forgive me, I know how boring "sea stories" can be, but for those of you who've never been out in bad weather in a little boat, let me tell you it can get *hairy*, even for Charles Bronson. At times you'll be using strength you didn't know you had. A handrail *must* be solid enough for you to really hang on to. I make them stout enough to tie spring lines to when docking the boat.

A good piece of fir 2 × 4 makes a fine handrail, and can be cut for comfortable handholds—a 1 3/4-inch cutout is plenty big enough to wrap your fingers around—while leaving enough meat for strength. Fasten the rail down with 5/16-inch bolts through the roof. Backing plates will stand out and look bad, so I use big washers against the roof, with the normal washer and nut over them.

Rails look best when they flow parallel to the side of the house. They're easy to bend to shape: Just pre-drill the bolt holes through the rail, drill through the rail down through the roof for the first bolt, and stick the bolt through. Wrap the rail around parallel to the cabin side until it's in position for the second bolt, drill down through the hole in the rail and insert the next bolt, continuing on until you have them all drilled. Lift the rail up a bit, slip some bedding compound under it, then drive the bolts home and cinch 'em up.

COMPANIONWAY

Basic hatch covers were covered in Chapter 10, and the same idea will work for the main entrance, or *companionway*, as it's called. However, a sliding hatch is more convenient, and is so traditional that it would be almost heretical not to install one. I use one on any roof 4 feet or longer, since that's the minimum length you can make the runners and still have a hatch opening big enough to get through.

The hatch shown in Figure 13-4 is a good one: fairly simple to make, strong enough not to carry away if you capsize, and about as watertight as these things get. It slides on metal runners (normally brass, but aluminum works too), which also hold it down.

You can close off the back wall with drop boards or with a hinged swinging door. In fact, some people don't saw a hole in the back wall at all, figuring it makes it more difficult for green water on

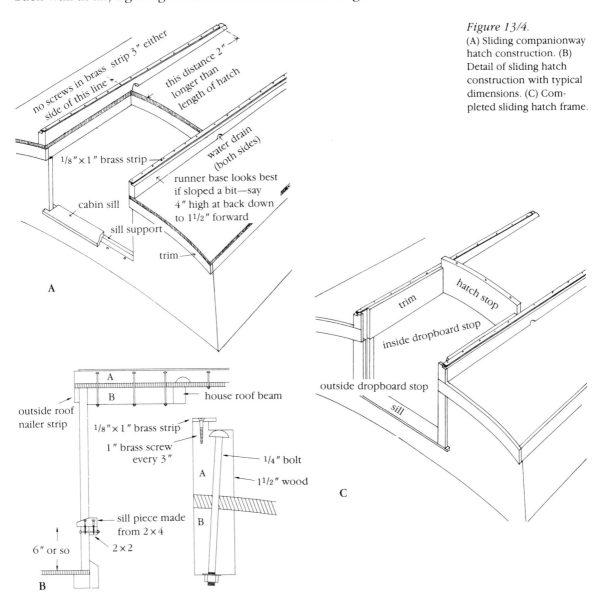

Figure 13/4.
(A) Sliding companionway hatch construction. (B) Detail of sliding hatch construction with typical dimensions. (C) Completed sliding hatch frame.

More Bolt-Ons

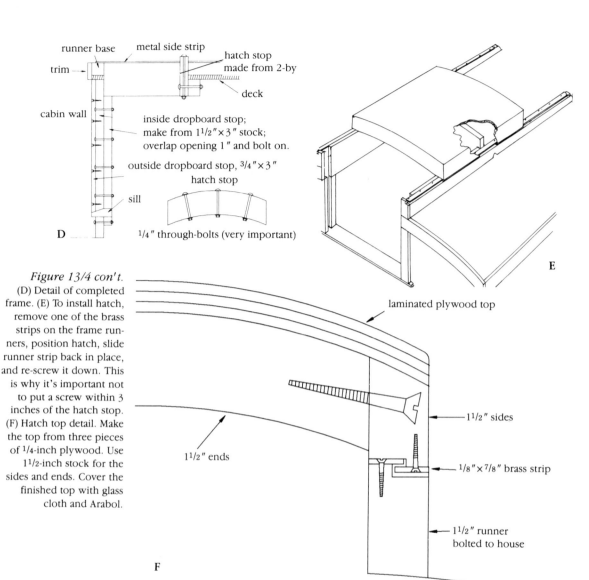

runner base   metal side strip

trim

hatch stop
made from 2-by

deck

cabin wall

inside dropboard stop;
make from $1^{1}/_{2}" \times 3"$ stock;
overlap opening 1" and bolt on.

outside dropboard stop, $^{3}/_{4}" \times 3"$

hatch stop

sill

D

$^{1}/_{4}"$ through-bolts (very important)

E

Figure 13/4 con't.
(D) Detail of completed frame. (E) To install hatch, remove one of the brass strips on the frame runners, position hatch, slide runner strip back in place, and re-screw it down. This is why it's important not to put a screw within 3 inches of the hatch stop. (F) Hatch top detail. Make the top from three pieces of $^{1}/_{4}$-inch plywood. Use $1^{1}/_{2}$-inch stock for the sides and ends. Cover the finished top with glass cloth and Arabol.

laminated plywood top

$1^{1}/_{2}"$ sides

$^{1}/_{8}" \times ^{7}/_{8}"$ brass strip

$1^{1}/_{2}"$ ends

$1^{1}/_{2}"$ runner
bolted to house

F

deck to find its way below, but that makes going below more of a hassle. I like an opening in the wall, and always use drop boards because I think they're stronger than a hinged door, not to mention easier to build.

Make drop boards in two or three pieces so you can leave out one or two for air, yet still have the opening partially closed off. If you cut them on an angle where they join together, any water or condensation will drip into the cockpit, not into the cabin. Some folks also make extra drop boards with the centers cut out and replaced by screening so they can still have air below in buggy areas.

Figure 13-4 should have all the information you need to build a companionway, but I have a few comments just the same. Start off by making the sill that sits on the base of the entrance, and work up from there. A strong and nice-looking job is a 2 × 2 bolted inside the cabin, flush with the opening, with a 2 × 4 sill beveled down to about 3/4 inch screwed down on it, with the bevel facing the cockpit.

Run vertical pieces of 2 × 3 up each inside face of the opening, bolted through the house wall and overlapping the opening by about 1 inch. These form the back of the track for the drop boards, and are stout enough to keep them from being stove in by a wave. You'll also need a lip on the outside to finish off the track, but since there's never much strain in that direction the outer piece can be 3/4-inch thick.

Finally, the hatch will look better if you make the back higher than the front, although it makes no actual difference structurally— just aesthetics. Also, note the through-bolts on the hatch "stop." These are essential: If you don't install them, the sliding hatch eventually will split the top of the stop right off. That's how I learned to install them, by the way.

Forgive my continually repeating this, but when building the hatch, *use glue*. This reminds me of the grade school teacher saying, "and don't forget to flush." My editor thinks you-all are too dumb to have figured out by now that you'll glue things like hatches together when you assemble them. Just to make *sure* you got that, I'll say here, *glue* these pieces of the hatch together as you assemble them; *bed* the hatch runners when you bolt them to the roof.

A

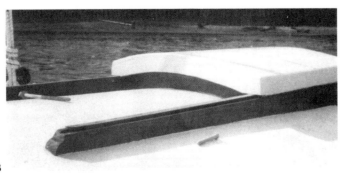

B

Figure 13/5.
(A) Completed sliding companionway hatch. Note the fuel and water vents on port side of hatch opening. (B) Taper the sliding hatch runners and cut an interesting shape into their forward ends for aesthetics' sake.

OUTBOARD RUDDER

An outboard rudder is very simple to build. Some people make a big deal of it and use glass-covered plywood faired carefully into an airfoil. In my opinion they're wasting their time and money, ending up with a weak, poorly shaped rudder.

I make my rudders from heavy planks bolted together edgeways: 2×12s on boats to 24 feet, 3×12s on boats to 30 feet or so, and 4×12s on larger boats. This makes a solid, heavy rudder. If it gets hit by a water skier, as a friend of mine's did, the skier will break, not the rudder.

Lots of boats suffer from poor rudder design, drawn to look rakish on the study plans rather than for what actually works well at sea. If your plans show a suspiciously artistic rudder, you might consider changing it. A good rudder slopes up on the bottom so it won't be damaged if the boat runs aground or is hauled out on a railway. I keep the forward end at least 4 inches above the keel and the aft end at least 8 inches above the keel.

Although it flies in the face of currently accepted wisdom, I don't shape my rudders to an airfoil, either. Instead, I leave them rectangular, with hard, sharp corners at the trailing edge. This seems to cause eddies when the boat is moving, which forces the water into a circular pattern as it flows past, resulting in the water itself taking on the airfoil shape and effectively enlarging the rudder. The faster you go the better this works! If you don't believe me, fine; but try it anyway. It's easy to build a rudder like I'm describing, and you can always go back and trick it out if you think it's not working well. You won't, though; take my word for it. If you need any further convincing, take a peek at the trailing edges of rudders on big wood fishboats.

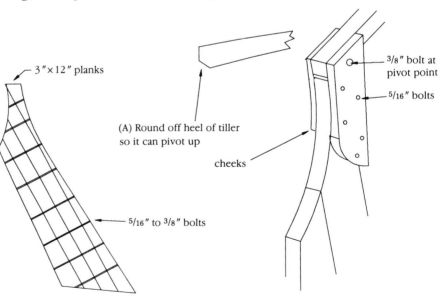

Figure 13/6.
Outboard rudder construction. Rudder made from 12-inch-wide planks—3-by for smaller boats, 4-by for bigger ones. Tiller sits on top of rudder, held in place by "cheeks" made from 3-by or 1/4-inch steel plate (2-by cheeks are OK for smaller boats).

3″×12″ planks

(A) Round off heel of tiller so it can pivot up

cheeks

3/8″ bolt at pivot point

5/16″ bolts

5/16″ to 3/8″ bolts

I like steering with a tiller, and tillers should be mounted so they can pivot up and down. This means the top of the rudder must stick up about 6 inches higher than the stern. The tiller, made from a piece of wood the same thickness as the rudder, with its aft lower edge rounded so it can pivot up, sits on top between a pair of "cheeks" bolted to the rudder. These are made from 2-by in smaller boats, or 3-by or 1/4-inch steel on larger ones, and should stick up as high as the top of the rudder.

Connect the tiller and rudder with a pivot bolt run through the cheeks and tiller.

Leave the rudder high like this even if you're planning on wheel steering. It'll make it easier to hook up an emergency tiller if you need one and, as will be mentioned later, the steering lines from the wheel can simply be hooked to the tiller, avoiding the need for a quadrant and holes through the hull.

As usual, make a plywood pattern of the rudder, clamp your rudder material edgeways with some sliding bar clamps, lay the pattern on it, and scribe it around. Unclamp it and saw out the pieces. Clamp them back together and drill them for the through-bolts that hold the rudder together. You'll need a bolt about every 12 to 14 inches. You can make them from 20-foot lengths of galvanized rod, cut to the lengths required. Use 1/2-inch rod in 4-by, 3/8-inch rod in 3-by.

If you're worried about drilling long holes in this stuff, use the same methods you used for the house sides: Drill through the middle piece first (if the rudder is made from three or more pieces), then clamp it to the joining piece and start the holes to mark the spot. Countersink both ends of the bolt. Bed the pieces well before clamping them together, drive through the bolts, and cinch 'em up. Nothing to it, but remember not to put a bolt in the way of the prop aperture if there is one.

A stout rudder must be mounted very stoutly to the boat, and Figure 13-7 shows simple, inexpensive fittings you can have welded up that will take the strain. I use mild steel for these rather than stainless. I don't like stainless much under water; it corrodes funny and it's hard to weld. Mild steel is the next best thing to wood, and although it can rust, it won't if it's protected. These fittings will last as long as the boat.

Rust, by the way, is interesting stuff. It needs oxygen to get started, so steel that's underwater all the time rusts very slowly, the only air around being what's dissolved in the water. And rust itself is a protector! It isn't as good as galvanizing, of course, but after surface rust forms it doesn't penetrate very fast, because the surface rust excludes oxygen from the rest of the metal, if that makes sense. I still suggest galvanizing them, or at the least painting them with epoxy.

I hate unnecessary maintenance, so rather than fit the *pintles* (the male part of the fitting) into close tolerance *gudgeons* (the female part), I use very heavy pieces with a sloppy fit. That way there are no bearings to wear out, and the steel is heavy enough to wear for life.

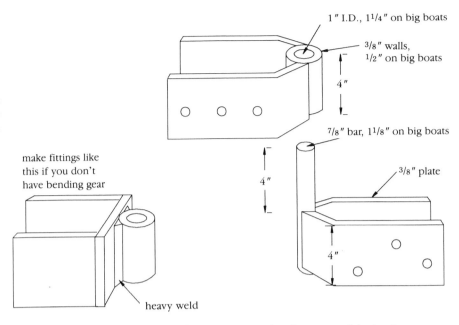

make fittings like this if you don't have bending gear

heavy weld

1" I.D., 1¼" on big boats

³/₈" walls, ¹/₂" on big boats

4"

⁷/₈" bar, 1¹/₈" on big boats

³/₈" plate

4"

4"

The gudgeon should have an inside diameter ¹/₈ inch greater than the pintle. On boats 40 feet or longer I like gudgeons made from 1¹/₄-inch I.D., ¹/₂-inch-wall thickness pipe, with 1¹/₈-inch bar pintles. The straps should be ³/₈ by 4 inches. Make the straps long. The ones on the rudder can be as long as the rudder is wide. The top two on the hull will be blocked by the planks, but the lowest one generally can be 24 inches or longer.

You can use the same size straps on smaller boats, although you can use ³/₈-inch wall thickness gudgeons and 1-inch pintles on boats in the range of 30 to 40 feet, and maybe ¹/₄-inch-wall pipe on smaller boats if you want. But what the hell, the parts are cheap, and heavy fittings even on a little boat won't hurt anything, so make 'em stout. The heavy wall thickness pipe is available at specialty pipe outlets, which you'll find in any city.

With an outboard rudder, the top pintle will be an inch or so longer than the gudgeon, with a hole drilled through it near the top to receive a ¹/₄-inch bolt, which will lock the rudder in place and keep it from lifting out of the pintles. You can also thread this upper pintle and use a big nut to hold down the rudder, which maybe looks a bit neater, but it doesn't really matter: In practice the rudder doesn't try to lift anyway.

I always mount the pintles on the boat and the gudgeons on the rudder, using three sets of fittings. The top one won't have much meat to fasten to since the stem is probably only 3 to 4 inches out from the rabbet, so I run a ¹/₂-inch-diameter bolt edgeways right through the stem where the top fitting runs before I mount the top fitting. This makes it impossible for the rudder to split off the sternpost if it's hit hard by something. Not that it would, because the lower two fittings will hold it on, but what the hell. The bolt won't hurt, and someday you might need it.

Remember the movie *The Guns Of Navarone*? Anthony Quinn played a guerilla soldier who was asked how he had stayed alive so long doing the things he did. I never forgot his answer: "I'm alive because I'm afraid of everything, so I worry about everything, and am prepared for anything." *That* explains why I do things like put bolts through the top part of the stem. You don't need to, of course. People go to sea in practically everything, from plywood trimarans to production boats designed by those slick marketing types. Me and Anthony Quinn, though, have the imagination to think ahead and say, "What if . . ."

I fasten the fittings to the boat with lag bolts, so I drill staggered holes in the straps so the lags from the other side don't interfere. I use through-bolts to hold the straps to the rudder. People concerned with drag rivet the ends of these bolts rather than use a nut, but I don't bother.

These fittings are just hinges, and as on a door, hinges must be lined up straight or they won't work. Position the gudgeons on the rudder and insert a broom handle through them to line them up. Mark their position, slide them off and bed them, then put them back on. Put the broom handle through again, then put the bolts through.

Bed the pintles and stick them on the hull. Hold them in what looks like the correct position with a nail through two holes. You can

Figure 13/8.
Rudder details. Note the heavy tiller cheeks through-bolted to the rudder head, the hold-down bolt on the top pintle, and how the rudder stops short of the keel shoe to protect it from grounding damage.

More Bolt-Ons

tack a straightedge to the side to sight along. Stand the rudder up and drop it down onto the pintles.

The rudder is gonna be really heavy, and you'll need a few people to help. I ended up rigging an **A**-frame out of two 2 × 6s for my last boat, and hoisted up the rudder with a come-a-long. Put some blocking below the rudder's bottom forward corner to support the weight until you have the pintles fastened securely in place.

If your Karma is good the rudder will drop right on. If you're like most of us, you'll need to tilt the pintles up or down to get them to fit in the gudgeons. This isn't so bad, because the rudder is supported by the blocking and held up by friends or ropes. Once the pintles are in the holes, bang on the pintles to lift them so that the gudgeons bear on all of them, then lag them in position.

A couple of points: I always mount a rudder about three inches back from the keel so I can get bottom paint in there. Also, these types of fittings leave a slot between the bottom of the keel and the bottom of the rudder. Although the odds are it won't happen to you, I snagged a crab pot line there once and had to jump in the water to free it, not long after *hearing* about *Jaws*! That's one movie I'll *never* watch! I like being *on* the water, not in it. To keep you from snagging kelp or ropes and stuff, screw on a short piece of wood or steel to the bottom of the rudder, round off its face, and position it really close, say 1/8 inch or so, to the keel.

INBOARD RUDDER

I've yet to see a production boat that didn't have a rudder stock made from a long bar running from the bottom of the keel up through the hull to the deck or quadrant. This really is poor design. It's impossible to remove the rudder without either lifting the boat with a crane or digging a hole deep enough to drop the shaft and rudder down into. You'd never be able to remove the rudder between tide changes, for instance, and since many boats simply have a stuffing box where the shaft comes through, you can't drop the rudder out in the water or the boat will sink. The rudder shaft *must* be made in two pieces, joined together with flanges, so you can remove the rudder if you have to.

Many designs show inboard rudders with the top of the shaft ending below a stern bunk or something. This is poor design, too, because there's no way to attach an emergency tiller if the steering system breaks down, which it will some day, probably just when you're in a tight spot.

Do *not* sacrifice safety or maintenance concerns for an interior layout! Some day you'll regret it. I like the shaft to run clear up to the deck, or failing that, up into a cockpit locker or something so I can quickly and easily hook up a tiller in an emergency. I think if some of the production boat designers were sentenced to a lifetime of maintenance on their designs, like removing the rudder or aligning the engine, you'd see a few more user-friendly ideas in their designs. They should spend a little more time looking at workboats to see how things are supposed to be done.

If your boat will have an inboard rudder, you should have drilled the hole for the shaft way back when you were making the keel. If you didn't, do it now, and pray you don't run into any drift bolts or something. Nail a long straightedge parallel to the back of the keel to use as a sight gauge, and hang a plumb-bob off the keel, too. If you have a helper standing a few feet back, he'll be able to keep an eye on the drill and the plumb-bob and tell you if you get off. Use a *long* drill bit. It's easier to sight along.

Figure 13-9 shows the setup "far better than my poor power to

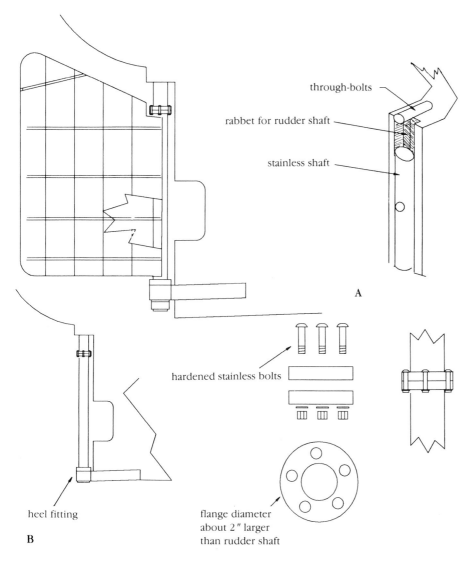

through-bolts

rabbet for rudder shaft

stainless shaft

A

hardened stainless bolts

heel fitting

flange diameter
about 2″ larger
than rudder shaft

B

Figure 13/9.
(A) Inboard rudder construction (fittings similar to outboard rudder are often used, too). Use 3-by planks for medium-sized boats; 4-by for big boats. Note that the rudder shaft is in two pieces. Although most production boats don't, all workboats do this to simplify maintenance. The alternative is digging a deep hole under the rudder if you need to remove it. (B) Detail of rudder shaft coupling. Make the distance from the top of the flange to the bottom of the boat 1/2 inch longer than the depth of the heel fitting.

Figure 13/9 con't.
(C) Detail of inboard rudder through-hull. The strongest and most trouble-free method is to run a heavy-wall pipe right through to the deck. Alternatively, or if you're using belowdecks steering gear, use a conventional stuffing box mounted on a flattened spot on the keel. To reduce wear on the stuffing box, consider extending the shaft up to a bearing mounted beneath the deck. (D) You need some way to keep the rudder from floating out of its heel fitting. Two methods are shown here; there are many others that work, too.

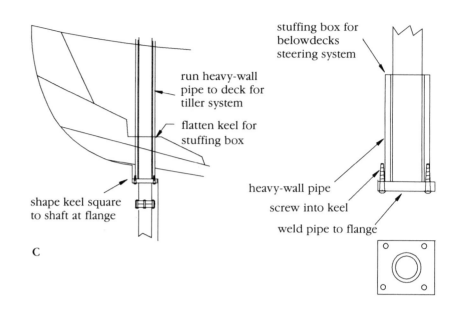

run heavy-wall pipe to deck for tiller system

flatten keel for stuffing box

shape keel square to shaft at flange

C

stuffing box for belowdecks steering system

heavy-wall pipe

screw into keel

weld pipe to flange

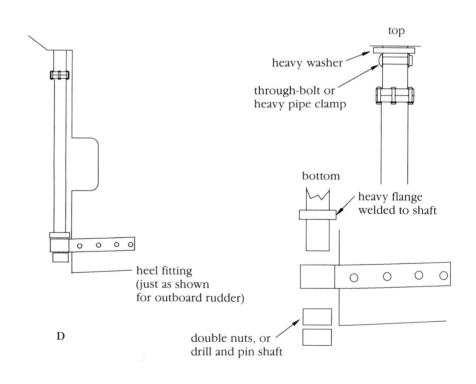

heel fitting (just as shown for outboard rudder)

D

top

heavy washer

through-bolt or heavy pipe clamp

bottom

heavy flange welded to shaft

double nuts, or drill and pin shaft

add or detract,'' but there are a couple of points worth mentioning. The shaft itself is in two pieces, joined together by flanges welded to each end. Make the top shaft long enough so that when you uncouple it from the lower shaft flange and draw it up against the hull, you have enough room to lift the rudder straight up and remove it from its heel fitting. The heel fitting, by the way, is just a piece of heavy-wall pipe strapped to the keel, just like the gudgeon on the outboard rudder. The rudder is held to the shaft, as the illustrations show, with through-bolts. These are the same bolts that hold the rudder pieces together. Rabbet the first piece of the rudder so that it covers maybe 50 percent of the rudder post. No need to round it out, but put lots of tar in the groove before you bolt the rudder to the post.

Since it wouldn't do to have the rudder lift out of the heel fitting when you don't want it to, you'll need a "hold-down" system. This can be a bolt inserted through a hole in the upper shaft just below the keel with a big washer on the shaft above it, or a split pipe coupling of some sort bolted together above the top flange. Probably the strongest way is to extend the lower shaft down through the heel fitting an inch, and drill it there for a bolt. If you do it that way, weld a heavy collar to the shaft to serve as a bearing surface against the heel fitting.

Although a stuffing box is the most common thing used where the shaft enters the boat, I like the idea of a heavy-wall pipe running from the bottom of the boat right through to the deck; I think it's a lot stronger and less likely to leak. This pipe should have a plate

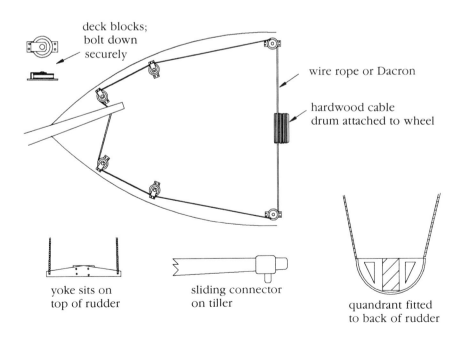

deck blocks;
bolt down
securely

wire rope or Dacron

hardwood cable
drum attached to wheel

yoke sits on
top of rudder

sliding connector
on tiller

quandrant fitted
to back of rudder

Figure 13/10.
Tiller steering works fine and is as low-maintenance a system as you can find. Wheel steering has its advantages of course, but store-bought wheel steering systems are expensive. Fortunately it's easy to make your own. Just run wire rope or low-stretch Dacron around deck blocks (some people run the cable through bent pipe instead) from the rudder to a hardwood cable drum attached to the wheel. Laminate your own wheel from plywood or go to a truck or bus salvage yard and find a wheel that suits your sense of aesthetics. The three most common methods of attaching the cables to the rudder are a hardwood or metal yoke atop the rudder, a metal or hardwood quadrant attached to the rudder's back, or a sliding connector on the tiller. Steering ropes can be snapped on when needed, such as for an auxiliary inside steering station.

More Bolt-Ons

welded to one end to fit against the outside of the keel. Like the outboard rudder's gudgeons, this pipe can be a hair larger in diameter than the shaft, or you can make it big enough to take a cutless bearing in the bottom to keep the shaft from moving. That might be a good idea, but it's up to you.

The full 1/8-inch slop used on the outside rudder's fittings might be annoying to some people because the rudder can make a bumping sound if you're anchored and the rudder is held immobile. It's no problem with a tiller system because you can just let the rudder swing free, but a wheel steering system might hold it too tight to move much. I don't know. Frankly, I've never owned a wheel-steered boat, although my new one is gonna have *two*! I picked up the systems for next to nothing at a swap meet, you see. Anyway, if you want a closer fit you can use a shaft the same diameter as the pipe, but have it turned down 1/16 inch by a metal shop. That would fit closely enough to eliminate most vibration.

Mild galvanized steel should work fine for all this, especially if you're just running the shaft through a pipe, but if you're using a cutless bearing or stuffing box, you should use stainless because the galvanizing would tear the bearing up.

Figure 13/11.
Two-station wheel steering system. Edson—the steering gear people—recommends attaching two quadrants to the rudder shaft and running two separate steering systems. This would make a complete steering failure unlikely. The system shown here is simpler and cheaper. You can always slip an emergency tiller over the rudder shaft head where it passes through the deck. This system uses chain sprockets at the wheels driving a short chain connected to the ends of the wire steering rope. The middle "junction" is a heavy shaft mounted on pillow blocks, bolted to something solid. Use large blocks for this type of system to reduce friction.

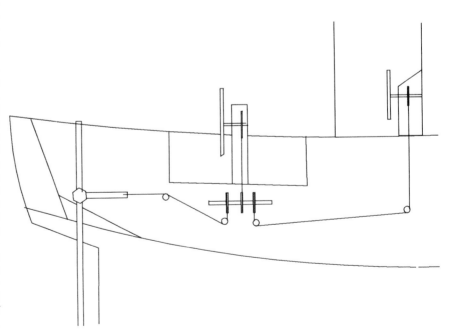

Since I worry about strains and stuff on everything, I don't care for the normal inside rudder setup: the shaft is supported only at the keel and where it enters the hull. In addition to this, I'd use two pintles and gudgeons on the rudder to really hold it with no strain on the through-hull part. If I had to remove the rudder, I'd unbolt the pintles from the keel. This would work fine, because in practice you hardly ever need to remove the rudder. It's just that if you don't plan on having to do it some day, you'll almost certainly need to, and then, as they say, "Shame on you!"

CHAPTER 14

THE FINISH: PAINTS, VARNISH, AND OILS

You have to cover the wood with something oily to protect it, and you have a choice of paint, varnish, or oil. Each has its good and bad sides, and all will be used somewhere.

The image of the shining natural-wood boat appeals to many folks, but stop and think about the maintenance it takes to keep it up. Aside from that, a varnished or oiled finish requires really top-quality woodwork—tight fits and no bondo—or it looks shoddy. Nothing looks worse than an almost-perfect joint, beautifully varnished. It may be perfectly strong, but if it isn't perfectly fitted it will stand out like a sore thumb to anybody who knows anything about woodworking. Paint the same area with a dab of trowel cement to fill the unevenness, and it will look perfect.

Although an oil finish is the easiest to keep up because it never cracks or peels, I always paint the hull. Oil needs to be applied fairly frequently to stay shiny; you can get by with painting once a year. Besides, I like to use bright colors, and the green wood preservative I slop around inside the hull generally has come through many of the caulking seams. Actually, that green looks pretty good, and after applying several coats of it to the outside of the hull I've thought more than once about leaving it as the finish. Never have, though.

Give a lot of thought to the color scheme. Earl Barlow, a wonderful marine artist in East Boothbay, Maine, built several cardboard models of his new boat and painted each side of each model in a different scheme so he could compare them. He ended up choosing bright yellow for the hull, with black trim. Sounds awful, I know, but oddly enough it looked great. Yellow with black trim, by the way, was a combination particularly favored for all sorts of working craft in Colonial days—even early vessels of the Continental Navy—so there's historical precedent behind his choice.

Light colors make the hull look bigger and don't show off plane marks or other irregularities as much as dark colors. Light colors on a deck seem to look cleaner than dark colors, too, and don't heat up the surface as much. It's hard enough to walk barefoot on a light deck in hot weather; impossible on a dark one.

A bright band of glossy color at the sheer and above the water-line will make the hull look lower and sleeker. Boats with a poor sheer can have a sprightly one painted on and will look great. Boats with excessive freeboard will look lower if given a wide band of color at the sheer.

A bright boottop the same color as the sheer band, which on my boats will be on the bulwark and rubrail, looks great. In fact, a boat without it always looks sort of sad to me, like it's missing something. Start the boottop 8 to 10 inches or so above the waterline at the bow, sweep it to about 3 inches above the waterline aft of the midsection about 15 percent of the length or so back, then up to about 6 inches above the waterline at the stern. If you have an outboard rudder, con-tinue this stripe right onto it.

If the house sides are the same color as the hull and the house roof the same color as the deck, the house looks lower, or at least that's the theory. In practice, I like a white-painted house side, no matter what color the hull happens to be. I've seen boats with a red hull and house sides to match, and it just didn't look right. So let's put it this way: The house sides should be white (or natural if you like) and the roof the same color as the deck.

A bit of natural wood on the outside really sets things off. I've about given up on varnish, at least on the exterior, because it's just too much trouble. Instead, I use an oil finish, and oil the handrails, house trim, tiller, spars, bowsprit, and whatnot. It is true that nothing looks quite like 6 or 7 coats of varnish, and I'll cheerfully use it on an old Chris-Craft I'm restoring, even though it will need more mainte-nance than an oil finish. I'd never bother with varnish on a work or cruising boat, though, although plenty of people do.

Some people varnish the house sides and trim, then put a coat of paint on top. The idea is to seal the wood grain with varnish to keep the paint out of the pores of the wood. People who do this have the low upkeep of a painted surface, but if they want to sell the boat or ''dress it up'' for some reason, it's easy to strip off the paint with paint stripper or a heat gun, and a simple matter to get the varnish looking good. Again, I've never bothered.

At the risk of being redundant, I suggest you give a lot of thought to your exterior decorating. Nothing is sadder than a pretty design burdened down with an unimaginative or inappropriate color scheme. Even a very plain design can look good with the proper col-ors and use of stripes to create lines that the designer was too dull to draw. And a boat that is well proportioned to begin with will really look great.

PAINT

Like everything else connected with ''yachting,'' marine paints are priced out of this world. I never thought there was a real difference between marine and house paints, so I usually use house paints, like porch and deck enamel. The color selection is better, and they're half the price.

Somebody who knows told me I'm "misstook," however, and marine paints hold up better. I don't know. I do know that house paint lasts a long time, and that marine paints often have driers and whatnot in them to make them faster-setting and easier to use in commercial yards, which seems to me should make the paints more brittle.

Use what you like. I'll stick with exterior oil house paint for the most part. A lot of commercial fishermen swear by exterior latex paint, but I've never tried it. The oil in traditional oil-based paint is good for the wood, I think.

If you like a really high-gloss finish then you'll probably have to buy marine paints. A kitchen enamel might work as well, but so far I've seen nothing quite as shiny as the top-grade marine paints. In fact, Interlux makes a white that is *so* white it looks blue. Although I begrudge the price I can't help but like it, and I've used it on hulls and interiors more than once.

On my current boat I've gone in completely the opposite direction. This boat is 100 percent cruiser, which is the same as a workboat, you know. I wanted a durable finish, and the very best is Atco Carbon Elastic, less glamorously known as "gutter paint." This stuff comes only in black, and it's full of oil and tar.

When you paint it on the hull you're committed, because it will bleed through anything if it gets warm, although I'm hoping four coats of epoxy paint on the boottop, which is low enough to the water to stay cool, might work.

It's really shiny, but never completely sets up, so it will raise hell with fenders if you worry about that stuff. It's very good for the wood, though, gives some protection from worms (bugs really prefer not to eat oil) when you're heeled on one tack for a month, the tarry finish fills little cracks and seams, and it's cheap. It's often used on barges, tugs, and fishboats, even below the waterline under the bottom paint, so I painted the entire hull and keel with it. However, as a topside finish it definitely ain't yachty, and using it is bound to have some effect on resale value, if you care about that.

Epoxy paints are really durable, but that very durability is a problem. "Only the rocks live forever," and any paint is going to break down eventually and need to be stripped and refinished. Oil paints don't last as long as epoxy, but they're easier to work with.

I've been buying a two-part epoxy paint from a surplus place for 10 bucks a gallon, and it's pretty good stuff. So far my carbon elastic hasn't bled through the boottop, and a friend who painted his pickup canopy with it says it still looks pretty good six years later. The color selection isn't the best, though. It comes in drab white and nauseating green. Charlie buys the white, then tints it with normal oil paint. This seems to work, and it doesn't appear to affect the stuff's setting-up or lasting qualities—so far. Universal tints, available at most larger paint stores, will work with epoxy, too. Perhaps other brands have more color choice, but I like the price of this surplus stuff.

Anyway, painting is pretty basic stuff, and with a bit of practice anybody can do a good enough job. I don't spray paint. I don't like breathing the stuff or getting it in my eyes, and that super smooth sprayed finish is possible, but not probable, with an inexperienced person manning the spray gun. Besides, spraying requires expensive equipment; a $50 airless won't do it. Spraying is much harder to learn than brushing, and takes hours of prep time in masking off stuff.

VARNISH

Varnishing is difficult to do well. Anybody can paint it on, but a true varnish job, flawless up close, requires experience, period.

Flow it on. Not too much, but not too little, either. Use a very good quality brush. Sand with 180- to 220-grit paper between coats. Don't varnish in direct or hot sun. Put on at least six coats.

Still, after all this, six weeks of Latin sun will start blistering it and you'll have to put on another coat, because once you let it start to slip it looks like hell.

I don't use any of the "super" varnishes like Varithane or epoxy on the exterior. I'm sure they work well, but when they need stripping, which they all will eventually, they're really hard to remove.

They'll last forever inside the boat, however, and I use them there because they stand up to scrubbing longer than normal varnish. As a matter of fact, I've started putting on super varnish over painted shelves, figuring it would make them easier to scrub and keep clean.

Many varnish artists are really compulsive and first stain the wood to make it all uniform in color. This has its place, I suppose, but I don't like it. I like looking at various wood grains and stuff. In fact, inside the boat I use a lot of weathered wood, which I hit a bit with a disc sander, then varnish. It makes all sorts of interesting colors to look at.

OILS

Oils are the simplest and easiest finishes, and probably best for the wood. Oil's wonderful stuff to use, since all you need do is slop it on with a brush or rag. It doesn't need sanding between coats, and it doesn't leave brush marks.

No oil finish retains its gloss very long in the weather so you'll end up having to re-oil everything every couple months or so, but it's so easy to do that I've never minded.

Since spilling some kerosene on bare wood and observing the result I've suspected that most oil finishes may be little more than odorless kerosene. Standard Oil sells one called "Pearl Oil," which is highly refined and the best you can get for lamps and stoves, and I've been tempted to try it sometime. I never have, since I seem to be a sucker for a boat on the label, but some day I'm gonna.

FINISHING FIR PLYWOOD

Never sand fir plywood before it's painted because its surface grain is made up of hard and soft areas (the grain lines are hard). If you sand it when bare you'll get a washboard effect that's impossible to smooth up. Just wipe off the dust and put on the first primer coat. *Lightly* sand that, being careful not to sand all the way through it. Do this four times, then put on two coats of finish paint.

Varnished fir plywood rarely looks very good except maybe for a tabletop. Many yards use mahogany-faced plywood for bulkheads because it's much easier to paint smooth. MDO is even easier to paint smooth, costs less, and is probably a better grade, although it's a bit late now if you didn't already use it.

PAINTING THE BOAT

The smoother the surface the smoother the job, so do a bit of sanding before you start to paint. Use 100-grit paper, which is plenty fine enough for a hull. You can use one of those little ''jitterbug'' reciprocating sanders or a rotary sander with a soft pad. High-quality yacht yards don't allow power sanders near the boat, but the fact is that a soft pad on a machine won't leave sanding marks if you keep it moving.

After you've smoothed the hull, wipe off the dust. A rag with some thinner on it works well. Then I suggest soaking the hull down wet on wet with wood preservative, but that's up to you. After that dries, you'll need about four coats of primer to keep the green from bleeding through.

Before you really get started painting, though, you'll have to find the designed waterline. This is the line the designer drew in from which to figure all his displacement calculations. The chances are the boat won't float on that line when launched—in fact, let's hope it doesn't because you want to be able to load the boat down with provisions and whatnot without putting it below its lines. That's why the waterline's correct name is *Load Water Line*.

First, find where the designed waterline hits the ends of the boat. Maybe you marked this when assembling the keel, but if not, scale the plans to get the distance from the bow and stern to the waterline, and mark on the bow and stern where the waterline hits. There's two ways to go from here, although you should check and make sure the hull is still sitting level.

To do this, put a straightedge across the hull in front of the house or somewhere. Put equal sized blocks on each side at the sheer to raise the straightedge off the deck, and sit a level on the straightedge. If it doesn't read level, then jack the boat or use wedges to shore it level. Of course the risk is that one side is higher than the other, so by wedging it over you might actually be making the hull lean. You can check this by hanging a plumb-bob off the bow and stern to see if they hang parallel with the centerline. If you squared things up well when you first put up the frames everything probably is still OK. Now there are a couple of ways you can go from here.

For the parallel strings method, nail a horizontal board, about 4 feet wider than the boat at the widest part of the waterline, to each end. The boards' top edges should be even with the waterline mark. Brace them solidly to the ground.

Stretch two strings about a foot apart down each side of the boat, fastening them to the horizontal boards just mentioned with a couple of nails. Have a helper hold a pencil against the hull while you stand back and sight over the strings; it's easy to see if the pencil point is in line with the two strings. When it is, tell your helper to make a mark. Do this every couple of feet or so, the whole distance, down each side of the boat.

Lightly nail a thin batten to the hull along the pencil marks, then scratch in the waterline with a 16d nail or a file handle ground down to a chisel edge. Make this groove about 1/16 inch deep or so. I've done this alone by making a mark, then sighting over the strings to check, then making it again, but it's a hell of a lot easier with a helper.

The other way to mark a waterline is with a water level. You'll need two people for this, too, but it's a pretty accurate way to do things. The idea behind the water level is that water always flows until it reaches a level spot. I mean, did you ever see a waterfall not fall? Or a stream not stream? A water level is the same thing. If you fill a 100-foot hose with water and hold up each end, the water level will be exactly the same in each end, hence the name water level.

Make the hose from cheap, 1/2- or 5/8-inch garden hose, about 10 feet longer than the boat. Stick a piece of clear plastic tube about 12 inches long in one end and cable-clamp the hose down tight to it. Do the same to the other end after you fill the hose with water. Make two cylindrical plugs to stop up the ends of the tubes.

Filling the hose is easier with a tapered fitting because the hose has to be really full to avoid air pockets. You can do it without the tapered thing, but it takes longer to work the air out. Just let the water run through until it flows out freely. Insert the other clear tube, and top up the level with a jug so there's maybe 6 inches of space left in the tubes, then plug them.

The plugs must come out before the thing will work. Have an assistant stand at one end, holding the clear tube to the WL mark. If the waterline doesn't come out at the stern where the lofting says it should, it means the hull isn't sitting on the correct line, so you'll have to jack up the low end until the water level reads level with the front end.

Starting 2 feet or so away from the end, hold your end of the hose against the hull. Your assistant will yell "up" or "down" until you've moved your end to the position that brings the water level at his end even with the waterline mark. When he says it's right, make a mark on the hull even with the water level, go on down the hull another 2 feet or so, and make another mark.

If the water is bouncing up and down, put your finger over the end for a moment and it'll stop. If your assistant isn't paying attention, lift up your end high really fast and the water will shoot out his end; if you're lucky, you'll get him in the face. Of course then you'll have to add water to the hose. I keep a gallon jug handy to deal with this. With practice you'll learn to keep a finger over the ends until you're ready to use the water level.

Anyway, once the marks are all on, nail on the light batten and scratch in the waterline, as described earlier.

The third method is simply to launch the sucker and wade around it, marking the waterline right from the water. Add 3 or 4 inches for the weight of gear and provisions, and if she looks much higher than the plans, add another 4 to 6 inches or so for inside ballast. This ain't scientific, but some people do it this way.

Next, scratch in the boottop. The boat won't float upside down if you don't do this, but you'll really be hurting her appearance. I'm probably as lazy as the next guy, but I *always* do a boottop.

Draw a boottop on your plans (if the designer didn't) and scale it off. The forward part should be a good 6 or 8 inches or more higher than the waterline, it should taper to a low point *aft* of the midsection, maybe 2/3 of the way back, then rise up to the stern. You don't need many reference points; if you use a long batten you can eyeball it pretty well. Do the first side, then measure its height every 4 feet or so from the waterline and duplicate it on the other side.

Now, paint a coat of primer on the topsides. No need to be really compulsive about staying above the waterline, because bottom paint sticks to primer fine. If you have a planked hull, however, give some thought to painting the underwater area with carbon elastic. If you're doing that, paint that first because you want this stuff on the wood, not on the primer paint.

After the first coat of primer is on, go around the hull and fill any nicks and scratches with trowel cement, then sand the whole thing gently with 100-grit paper, being careful not to sand through the paint. Wipe off the dust and repeat this for at least three coats of primer, then put on two or three coats of finish paint. If the bulwark and rail are a different color than the hull, and the boat will look far better if they're the same color as the boottop I hope you put on, then paint them before the final coat on the hull.

By the way, you only need to go through all this priming and sanding when you're starting with bare wood. In the following years all you need to do is sand the hull and repaint it with one coat of finish. Eventually it builds up so thick it starts cracking, and you'll have to burn it off with a torch and go through the whole process again.

The common wisdom goes, "don't put on the finish coat too thick," but the best boat painter I've ever seen laid the stuff down about 1/16-inch thick and the finish looked wonderful. He always worked in hot sun with a professional-grade marine paint, which is probably how he avoided runs.

You and I *will* get runs if we put it on thick, so don't do it. Always paint with the grain. If you see a run, brush it out. If you see brush marks your brush is too coarse. Although professional painters would rather be shot than do it, you'll be better off if you use masking tape to help paint a straight line. Regular masking tape works fine, but if you leave it on more than a day it's very hard to remove. I pull it when the paint is tacky enough not to run. Plastic electrical tape costs more but can be left on a day or so and still come off, although it might leave glue residue. The best thing to do is just pull the tape as soon as you're done painting.

Now it's time to paint the bottom, but first, a keel made up from heavy timbers is almost certain to have some checks in it, maybe a deep knot, or some other flaw. You can fill the checks if you want to, but they'll probably swell up and spit out the filler. Use a soft putty, like roof patch, which can squeeze out of the checks. Knots and holes should be filled with something hard. A boat without an engine can use Bondo autobody filler, but vibration from an engine will separate it from the wood eventually, and polyester really doesn't seem to stick that hot to wood anyway. Personally, I use a dough made of epoxy and sawdust from the table saw. This seems pretty permanent, and costs little or no more than Bondo.

Although there are numerous fancy bottom paints out there, I just use a soft "fishboat" grade. Buy by poison content, not price. Oddly enough, some of the cheap off-brands have a higher poison content than the low-end, big-name brands.

Get the bottom paint shook-up well at the store, because it's a bitch to hand stir it if the pigment and poisons are lumped up. I had a welder make me a paint stirrer for an electric drill. This is an 18-inch piece of 3/8-inch rod with a couple of short pieces of 1/8- by 1- by 4-inch plates welded to it on different angles. This stirs paint well, but I still have the store shake it up first.

Just put on one or two coats of bottom paint for now. The soft paints, which are all you need for a displacement boat, need to go into the water within about eight hours after application, so don't put on the final coat until just before launching.

The house sides, coamings, hatch tops, and interior are painted just like the hull, but the decks and house roof need a nonslip surface. Never use varnish on deck! That sounds obvious, but I've seen it done.

I first lay strips of 2-inch masking tape around the outer edge of the deck, around hatch bases, handrails, the bowsprit, where cleats will go, and so on. Then I buy a 100-pound bag of fine sand at a lumberyard. Paint about 2 square feet with undercoat paint, then sprinkle on sand until the paint is completely covered. Do the whole deck and house roof this way. Give the paint a couple of days to really set up, then broom off the excess sand. Pull up the masking tape, and you have a deck similar to a sheet of 80-grit sandpaper, with neat molded-looking lines around the deck fittings. Paint the whole thing with maybe two coats of primer, then two coats of finish paint. I always use a porch-grade enamel here.

Once I mixed sand into the paint before applying it. What a mess. It was hard to spread, the grit wasn't even, and the whole thing didn't look very good when done. I wouldn't do it that way if I were you.

Finally, here are a few general painting tips which I've probably mentioned before here and there, but which ought to be put together.

- Be sure to put all paint on an electric shaker for 3 minutes; 5 minutes for bottom paint.

- Use good-quality brushes if you want a smooth finish. Some people swear by those cheap foam brushes, especially for smoothly brushing epoxy or varnish, but I've never tried one.

- Gasoline, diesel, and kerosene all make good brush cleaners, but use paint thinner for a final cleaning, then wash the brush in water before storing it. I have old, natural-bristle brushes from a long-dead house painter. They're still in good shape, kept in a wood box filled with cedar shavings.

- If for some reason you let paint dry in a brush, paint remover will soften it up.

- Regular vinegar will cut wet epoxy resin, and is the best thing to use to clean epoxy from your skin because it's non-toxic.

- Paint rollers are the best way to put on bottom paint, although you'll still need to brush the seams.

- If fresh, damp paint is exposed to frost or dew it will lose its gloss, so if you're painting without cover don't start in the late afternoon.

Some wood butcher's friends are:

- Hard putty like Plastic Wood, Famowood, etc. Use them for filling scratches and nail holes in wood to be finished natural. Most come in various colors that are supposed to match wood species. Remove the lid just long enough to dip your putty knife, then put it back. These things dry out really quickly.

- Interlux Trowel Cement. This stuff is used to fill scratches and things like bung holes that aren't perfect. It's easy to work, sands well, but shouldn't be used to fill very deep holes.

- Epoxy resin mixed with sawdust. Make this up to the consistency of bread dough. You can fill deep scratches, bolt holes, and so on. It sticks very well.

- Autobody plastic (Bondo). This works, especially on boats without engines. But you have to watch it down the line because it will start to separate eventually, which can be bad news. If you get a slight crack behind it, a teredo worm might get into the keel, which you don't want to happen. Epoxy and sawdust works better.

- Tube caulks, like bathtub caulk. I use a brand called Polyseamseal. This is good stuff for boats with engines because vibration doesn't seem to affect it. It's easy to use: Simply squirt it on, then dampen a finger and run it along the seam to push the stuff in. Wipe off the excess with a damp cloth.

THE LAUNCH

You've fiddled around in your backyard long enough. You might as well drag the thing to the water now. I've already described the cradle and I assume you've built one, unless you found a local transport outfit that doesn't need it.

Every state has different laws regarding what you can transport legally. If you're going to move the boat yourself, check with the cops about local restrictions on beam and height. Smaller boats, like *Hagar*, can be transported on a rented equipment trailer, pulled easily by a pickup or a big car, like a '74 Buick. The problem isn't so much pulling, it's *stopping* you want to be concerned about! Check the trailer brakes.

A big boat will probably require a professional boat mover. I suggest you check the local laws on oversize loads and see what the permits to move a boat like yours cost, even if you're hiring it done. I've heard of at least one transport company that charges customers a lot more for the permits than they actually cost.

For that matter, check all the options you can think of. When I lived in Maine (I left; too many bugs. I'm afraid I'm a West-Coast kinda guy), Bald Mountain Boat Works in Camden dragged a new boat down to the water behind a team of oxen!

Most people take the boat to a marina where there's a travel lift for launching. This makes sense, because if you have some problem, like a big leak, the machine can get you back out of the water immediately. Be aware that it will cost you, however.

If you live in an area with a tide range greater than the draft of your boat, you can have the truck offload the boat when the tide is out, and she'll float when the tide comes in. If you do this, either weight the cradle down with rocks, or better yet, disassemble it and prop the hull up with shores; otherwise the cradle will float when the boat does and will stay attached to the hull—a drag. If you launch off the beach, set an anchor 100 feet behind the boat so you can pull her out into deep water when she floats.

And stay cool! Even if you have a major leak the boat ain't gonna sink immediately, so when the boat actually floats, stand back and take a look at it. You deserve it! This has been a big job, and even the hippest boatbuilder will feel a justifiable sense of pride. After you've had your eyeful, *then* go aboard and look to see if you're sinking.

Almost all boats leak at the launch. Relax! Things most likely will tighten up by the next day. The way wood swells is really something.

I've seen boats that leaked like a pasta strainer swell tight within 24 hours, so don't worry too much if yours leaks a lot, too. Still, it doesn't hurt to have a big pump or two handy, especially if you're launching off a beach. Check any through-hull fittings, too, and especially check the prop stuffing box, because it's possible you left off a hose clamp or forgot to pack the stuffing into the box.

Various ceremonies are usually expected by the onlookers at a boat launching, and they can be fun. At the best launch I've ever seen, the owner blasted off a miniature cannon, then had a blaster play the "Star Spangled Banner." The Vikings used to roll the boat to the water on logs, with a few slaves thrown in for lubrication. Other cultures would ice a maiden or two, and animal sacrifices are still done here and there.

Here in the States a lot of people break a bottle of wine over the bow. Few, I'm sure, realize the symbolism of this. In case you haven't caught on yet, the broken wine bottle represents BLOOD! DEATH! PAGAN CEREMONY!

How crude. It's also ecologically unsound to pour chemical-laden wine into the sea. Me, I pour a shot of good Bourbon over the bow for the boat, pour a shot into the sea for Neptune, and pour the rest down me 'cause, "it's mah party an' I'll do what I wanna."

Finally, the odds are pretty good that the boat will float way high above the waterline. Not only that, but it's probably going to be really tippy, too. Don't worry. Stay happy! Read on and you'll find out all about inside ballast, which will fix that.

Have a good launching party. Again, you deserve it. Regardless of how beautiful or sloppy a job you've done on the boat, *you* still *built* it, which is a helluva lot more than most folks ever do.

INSIDE BALLAST

Inside ballast isn't very popular these days. The new production boats are carefully engineered, and generally float pretty close to their load waterline at launch without the need to add inside ballast.

On the surface that sounds ideal, but just hold on. Needing inside ballast isn't always the sign of sloppy engineering by the designer, depending on the type of boat. Obviously a racing sailboat should be designed to float at its waterline, and as much weight as possible needs to be put as low as possible to help the boat stay on her feet when pointing. But a cruising boat is designed to different criteria; although the ability to stand up to wind is a consideration, it isn't the main emphasis.

As I mentioned earlier in this book, inside ballast has several advantages for cruising boats: it raises the center of gravity, which helps dampen the roll; and movable inside ballast can lend reserve buoyancy and allow a cruising boat's weight to be adjusted according to its use.

Any cruising boat must be able to carry weight, and in varying amounts. If you're just weekending and daysailing, you won't have a lot of provisions and gear aboard, and a cruising boat designed to handle added weight might float high on her marks; you might want to add some inside ballast to bring her back down. If you decide to head south for some extended cruising, you'll be loading up with lots of extra provisions, water, clothing, books, scuba gear—what have you. If the boat is floating near its waterline when empty you won't have much margin left. But if you have some inside ballast, you can take it ashore or pitch it overboard, and load her right up.

Of course you can, like many people, simply repaint the waterline a few inches higher and probably not hurt anything. But most boat design elements—the section shapes, the shape of the ends, and especially transom shape—are planned around a particular waterline. For optimum performance, the boat should float on or near it.

Fixed inside ballast

Inside ballast can be either fixed, movable, or a mixture of the two. The best and most common permanent inside ballast is junk metal held in place with concrete poured directly into the bilge. This system is used a lot on workboats, and has a long and honorable history with a number of advantages.

A bilge full of concrete ballast can actually protect deep hulls. A friend's boat ran aground and banged on the rocks for a while. Six months later when it was hauled, he found that the planking had been crushed in a few places, but the concrete poured in the bilge had kept her watertight. The boat probably would have been lost without the concrete inside.

Concrete even appears to preserve the wood beneath it. I've known people who've bought old boats and were worried about the condition of the hull below the concrete ballast. After days of chipping the stuff out they learned that the hull was in better shape below the concrete than it was above.

Of course there are disadvantages to using concrete. The boat won't be as stiff as one with outside ballast, there won't be as much room below the floorboards, and purists say it will hurt the resale value. But that's alright; I use it anyway. A concrete ballast casting combined with inside concrete ballast is the simplest and least expensive way of building a ballasted boat, and that alone makes it worth considering.

You'll pour your inside ballast after launching. The longer you wait the better, because the wood will absorb a lot of moisture during the first few weeks after launching, which will cause the boat to settle gradually in the water.

It's debatable whether or not concrete should be poured right onto bare wood. A little wood preservative first can't hurt anything,

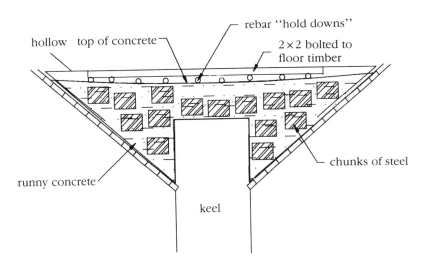

hollow   top of concrete

rebar "hold downs"

2 × 2 bolted to
floor timber

runny concrete

chunks of steel

keel

Figure 15/1.
Permanent inside ballast,
consisting of chunks of
scrap steel encased in
concrete, has a long and
honorable tradition in
workboats. Be sure to
sculpt the final pour of
concrete so that any water
drains away from the
planking and toward the
bilge pump. Use 3/8- or 1/2-
inch rebar "hold downs"
held in place with 2 × 2s
bolted to floor timbers to
keep the ballast from
getting adrift in a knockdown.

but it's up to you. If you use it, give it a few days to dry well, round up
some scrap metal, then go rent a cement mixer.

Mix up a batch of really runny cement—not watery, more like
good loose mud. Ask a kid into mud pies to show you how thick it
should be. I start off working between about the middle three floor
timbers. Fill this area right up to the top of the keel, unless it's really
deep, making sure the cement flows into any little cracks and whatnot. Now start packing in steel, as closely together as you can, encas-
ing it in cement as you go. Try not to let any steel actually touch
wood.

Keep packing steel and adding cement until you get about 3 1/2
inches below the top of the floor timber. As you work, walk about
100 feet away from the boat occasionally and eyeball things. You
want to ballast it so that she's sitting level. (Some small boats are ballasted to ride bow-down at anchor to compensate for the crew's
weight in the cockpit.) If you need more weight, fill in between
another few floor timbers. Try not to ballast the very ends; a boat
with light ends lifts better in a seaway, but sometimes you have no
choice. Ballast her down to within several inches of the waterline.
You want to leave enough reserve buoyancy to carry all your junk,
you know.

When she looks right, mix up a firmer batch of cement, pour it
about 1/2-inch deep, and shape it so that it's lower in the middle. This
will keep water from being trapped against the hull, which will rot
out the planking.

After you finish, let the cement dry for awhile, then go in and
drill a limber hole or two through every floor timber so bilge water
can get back to the pump. Although your boat isn't supposed to leak,
she might sometime. It's easier to drill limbers that pass water to a
central pump than having to bail between each set of frames.

The Launch

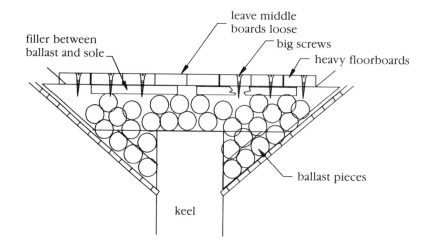

Figure 15/2.
Loose inside ballast can allow the hull's weight to be adjusted according to use. For weekending and short cruises, you'll want more ballast aboard than you would if you're heading South. It's possible to mix permanent and loose inside ballast by pouring a cement/scrap mixture flush with the top of the keel and using loose ballast from there up. Each piece of loose ballast should weigh no more than 50 pounds (big rebar is ideal if you can find it cheap), or you may have trouble getting rid of it in an emergency.

filler between ballast and sole

leave middle boards loose

big screws

heavy floorboards

ballast pieces

keel

Loose inside ballast

Poured concrete ballast makes the neatest looking interior, but it has one big disadvantage: You can't get rid of it without a jackhammer. Normally that's what you want, but if you're cruising in isolated areas and run aground, it's possible the only way you'll be able to free the boat is by lightening her up. All that food and water weighs plenty, but removing a few tons of ballast might make all the difference.

With that possibility in mind, I now mostly use loose inside ballast. I still like the idea of filling in the area between the planks and the top of the keel (again, unless it's really deep) with runny cement. Over that I use chunks of steel packed in as tightly as I can. If you worry about the steel rusting, paint it first.

If you have plenty of room you can cast steel into blocks of concrete. Try not to use anything that weighs much over about 50 pounds so you can handle it fairly easily. This type of ballast can be pitched over in a hurry if you need to.

Finally, whichever type of ballast you use, you want to do something to hold it down in case you get knocked over. The concrete in the bilge grips the wood pretty well, but you should lock it down just the same. One way is to lay a few pieces of 3/8- or 1/2-inch rebar between the floors, then bolt a 2×2 through the floors to hold the rebar in place.

I lay a few pieces of wood on top of loose ballast—enough to fill the area between the ballast and the cabin floor, then screw down the floor tightly to its supports with heavy screws. Leave the middle floorboard loose so you can lift it quickly in an emergency.

I should mention that some people really don't like concrete, and instead hold loose ballast in place with melted pitch. This works fine, but melting pitch is a lot more trouble than pouring concrete, and the pitch adds no weight of its own. I've never used it, nor shall I, but some people think it's better. To each his own.

THE RIG

Some if not all of this chapter might sound rather radical to a few of you, but if you haven't tossed out this book yet then maybe you're open-minded enough at least to think about what the chapter says before you place an order at the yacht rigger's. The ideas discussed here can save you literally thousands of dollars over what the poor SOBs who buy production boats spend on their rigs, and I think you'll get a stouter and more seamanlike rig to boot.

Excuse me, but I always get a kick out of that word "radical." In a Capitalist society the word refers to a melon farmer who doesn't like corporations; in a socialist society it refers to a melon farmer who doesn't like the State. I suppose a strict definition of "radical" would be an idea that differs from the accepted norm. But just *who* defines "the accepted norm?" I've never been polled by anybody, so how does Gallup *know* what the majority of Americans give a hoot about?

I've spent time in democracies, dictatorships, even a theocracy. And you know what? Regardless of a society's philosophical basis, the opinions of the "common-man" majority are formed through straight propaganda, be it political, religious, or consumer advertising. The Yachting Society is no different, and the "average guy" is brainwashed when it comes to boat rigging.

The rigging is the least understood and frequently the most overdone part of the whole boat. If you want to see the accepted norm for rigging just go to any marina or read the yachting press. Of course many elements of yacht design are based purely on fad, but the rig in particular seems to be the most affected.

The main concern of many designers is avoiding weight aloft. Weight certainly has an effect, but there's other things to consider, too. The fact is that weight aloft isn't such a bad thing for a cruising boat. In fact, the higher center of gravity makes the boat a lot more comfortable. It may roll more, but it rolls more slowly. Many of the newer designs have such an abrupt and jerky rolling motion that movement aboard actually can be dangerous, and a long passage would be too uncomfortable even to consider. I spent a week on one of those boats and was seasick the whole time.

Wind resistance aloft can cause more problems than weight aloft. A big box-section mast with several sets of spreaders causes a *lot* of drag. The effects of windage can be seen on a breezy day in any marina, as some boats start rolling wildly in flat water when the afternoon sea breeze kicks up.

I've always thought that the mast should have enough strength of its own and should be stepped securely enough so that if a wire lets go, the mast won't break in half or fall. That sounds pretty reasonable, but it isn't usually the case these days: one wire snaps and the whole thing comes down.

About now you're probably saying to yourself that, although you suspected it before, now you *know* I'm full of crap. If these modern rigs ain't so hot, then why do we see so many of them?

Well, there are several reasons, but one stands out: Most of today's boats come from factories. The big problem in factories is labor. Skilled labor is hard to find, and insists on being paid a living wage. As a result, production boats use as many machine-made items as possible. This isn't at all unique to the boating industry, just part of the trend.

With a factory and wages and executives and insurance and depreciation and advertising, boats is big biz! Look at the prices. The normal 30-foot production boat costs more than most houses. A discount mail-order place in 1988 was asking $3,500 for the mast and booms for a 36-foot cutter and $2,000 for the rigging wire, or $5,500 for the whole package—exclusive of all the fittings. In 1990 I can put up the same rig for under $500, and it will be stronger and I think better looking. One rig of my design was hit by a seaplane. The plane was destroyed, but the rig wasn't hurt. What do you think would have happened to the factory rig, where one snapped wire can spell disaster?

The gist of this socioeconomic tirade is that you can approach the rig in one of two ways: expensively or inexpensively. I'm only going to tell you how to put up an inexpensive rig, because I happen to think that even though it may cost less than 10 percent of the price of the production-boat version, it's a lot better rig, and far more suitable for a cruising boat.

As is the case with most everything else in this book, let me make clear that *nothing* I say in this chapter is original with me. I've learned how to do this stuff by hanging around the commercial waterfront and reading and meeting a few of the old-time cruising people. These rigging ideas I'm writing about have been done for many years by commercial boat owners. Of course costs are always a consideration to these fellas, but not drowning is a bigger one. Although a workboat owner may keep unneeded frills off his boat, he will never install a system that won't do the job. The rig I'm describing is about as reliable as possible, but it just doesn't have that dime store brightness that fans of Taiwan Baroque boats go for. I think it looks *better*.

SOLID MASTS

An evergreen tree—fir, pine, or spruce—will make a first-class mast. Its naturally round, tapered shape offers minimal wind resistance. The inherent strength and fatigue resistance of wood (wood is the *only* material that can flex continuously and not fatigue) means it doesn't need the support of elaborate rigging to keep it standing. Fittings and sailtrack are easily attached. It doesn't make that annoying clanking sound when hit by halyards. It's warm to the touch, and when finished with oil it's very good looking. It doesn't even weigh that much more than a metal mast. We cut a mast for a 36-foot boat and it was all eight people could do to lift it. A year later, after it had seasoned, we found that two of us could carry it, even with all the rigging attached.

Some people make a big deal out of converting a tree into a mast. One book published recently talks about first bowing to Mecca, removing the bark, carefully shaping the tree into four sides, tapering it, then shaping it into eight sides, then 16, then rounding it.

Go through all that if you want. Me, I'll just cut a tree that's about the same size as the mast I want. After removing the bark, 45 minutes with a power planer had the last mast I made ready for rigging. Up close it isn't as smooth as the traditionally tapered and rounded mast, but it's smooth enough and probably stronger. I leave on the sapwood, you see. A tug captain told me that a piling with sapwood takes more abuse than one that was turned down. The sapwood does tend to check more than the inner wood, but the checks don't hurt anything, and a well-seasoned pole kept well oiled doesn't check all that much anyway.

Like all lumber, a mast is best cut in the middle of the winter, when the sap isn't flowing. Spend a bit of time looking for a good one, because there's many trees out there that seem born to be masts. They live in thick stands of trees where the light doesn't penetrate, which forces the tree to grow straight up with very little taper.

I pick one about an inch larger in diameter than I want for my mast. After barking, it will be close to the right size. If you want to carve it down in the old yachting fashion, pick one at least 4 or 5 inches larger. Actually, the diameter of a mast isn't carved in stone, and if you're within 1/2 inch or so of what the plans call for you'll be fine. Most people make masts heavier than they really need to be.

You want to cut a tree that's 20 to 30 feet longer than you want your mast so it will be thick enough at the top. Measuring is fairly easy. Make a mark on the tree where you want to cut it, then another one 5 feet higher up. Now get a string several feet long with a weight, such as a 3/8-inch nut or something, tied to the end. Walk 100 feet or so away from the tree.

Hold up the string at arm's length and adjust its length so that the top of the string is in line with the top of the tree and the weight is in

line with where you want to cut. Tie a knot or something at the spot marking the top of the tree. Grab the string with your free hand, in line with the 5-foot mark you made on the tree. The distance from the weight to your free hand equals 5 feet, and you want to find out how many of those 5-foot intervals there are in the length of string between the weight and the knot marking the top of the tree. Fold up the string in coils equal to the distance between the weight and the 5-foot mark, right up the string to the knot marking the top of the tree. Multiply by 5, and that's approximately how tall your tree is. Ten folds times 5 feet equals a 50-foot tree.

After you drop the tree, trim off the branches. I bark it then, too, because it's much easier to remove bark while the tree is still alive. On the other hand, the bark protects the wood from the drying effects of the sun, which keeps down checking. I keep the mast covered with a tarp, which reduces checking as well as bark, but doesn't harbor mold and insects.

After you get the mast back to the shop, build a rack or put blocks on the ground to support the mast and keep it straight. Paint the ends with tar or thick paint, and oil the whole thing. I use a mix made from old crankcase oil and diesel fuel, which seems to work well. It does darken the wood, but you'll be removing the dark layer when you plane the tree to smooth it up.

I roll the mast a half turn and slop on the oil about every six months, keeping it covered with a tarp. This keeps the mast pretty straight, but if it does develop a slight kink don't worry about it. When you assemble the parts you can position things so the kink is to the back, and the headstays will probably pull it straight. If they don't, well, nobody will notice.

If you do want to work down a heavy pole, or if you find a perfect tree that is an inch or two thicker than what you want, there's an easier way to work it down to size than the traditional way. After it's seasoned, smooth it up fairly well with a power plane, set a Skilsaw to *half* the depth you want to take off the pole, and run the saw all over the pole. Make cuts *everywhere*, as close together as you can, the more the better. Now you can take a drawknife or a big chisel and work it down quickly to the saw marks, which give you a built-in gauge for how deep to cut. This ain't a very traditional way of doing it, but it should be a hell of a lot quicker than going through that 4-, 8-, and 16-sided stuff, maybe cutting off your foot with an axe while you're at it. The Old Boys didn't have power tools, you see, which is why you don't see many of the traditional methods anymore.

Whether you're using the tree as it comes or working it down, the quickest way to smooth it up is with a power plane. Go ahead and finish it with a hand plane and sandpaper if you want, but many people don't bother.

The plans should tell you how long the mast should be. I prefer a measurement taken from the sheer rather than from the mast step, because the odds are that the boat is a bit different from the plans: The deck crown's a little more or less, the freeboard is off, the stems are on a slightly different angle, the keel top is higher or lower— there'll be something. A measurement made from the sheer to the mast top will get you the correct height, then you can add on the difference from the sheer to the step off your own boat rather than from the plans. This will ensure the wire lengths on the plans will fit, assuming the designer measured correctly. I'd check those lengths before ordering wire, if I were you.

So, scale the distance from the sheer to the top off the plans. Lay a straightedge across the boat where the mast goes, and put a level on it. When you have it level, have somebody measure from the edge of the deck to the base of the straightedge, which tells you the deck crown. Measure down from the mast partner (the hole in the deck) to the mast step, subtract the deck crown, add the distance from the sheer to the masthead, and that's the mast's length.

Figure 16/2.
Juno's rigging plan shows where everything goes and how long it should be. Study it (and the other plans in Appendix B) to familiarize yourself with rigging stuff.

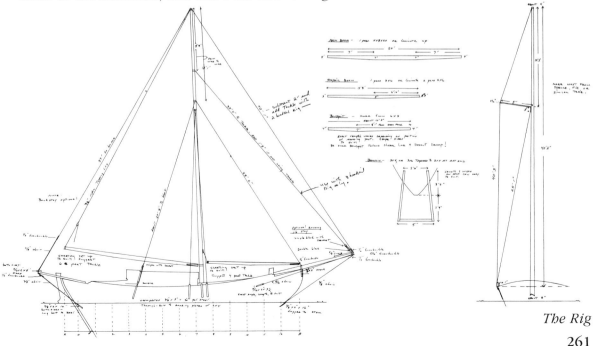

The Rig

The mast step

The mast step is pretty simple. It must be *extremely* secure, and I think the steel version shown in Figure 16-3 is the best way to go about it. Bed it well, lag-bolt it to the keel, and through-bolt it to at least one of the floor timbers.

I prefer a mast stepped on the keel because it's stronger than a deck-stepped mast. Granted, a deck-stepped mast is stronger in theory, because the shorter the pole the stronger it is for a given diameter, but that assumes it can't bend and the wires don't let go.

In practice, a flexible wood mast, stepped on the keel, wedged well at the partners, and loosely stayed, will take far more abuse than a deck-stepped mast, and is far less likely to fall if you lose some rigging.

All this assumes the keel-stepped mast is stepped through the *deck*, not the house, because a keel-stepped mast could take the house with it if you get knocked down. This is why some people prefer a deck-stepped mast if it's located on a house. I've used both, and nowadays prefer keel-stepped ones, even if they do go through a house. I put big heavy bulkheads near the mast and big knees inside to brace it, which messes up the interior, but I'm still not especially comfortable with it.

I just saw the results of an international cruising boat design contest, and one of the three winning designs was a boat with an

Figure 16/3.
A steel mast step is probably the strongest system to use. Square off the lower part of the mast to fit into the 2-inch steel lips. Bed the step well, and be sure to put a silver dollar below the mast butt in case you need to pay Charon to ferry you across the river Styx into Hades.

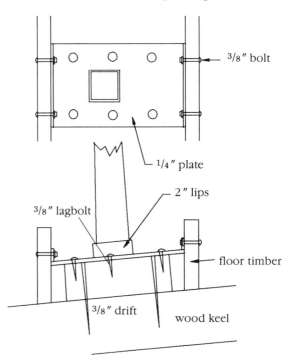

3/8″ bolt

1/4″ plate

2″ lips

3/8″ lagbolt

floor timber

3/8″ drift

wood keel

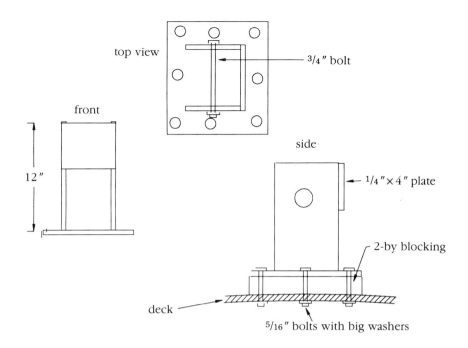

top view

front

12"

3/4" bolt

side

1/4" × 4" plate

2-by blocking

deck

5/16" bolts with big washers

Figure 16/4.
This deck-mounted mast step, or tabernacle, allows you to raise and lower your mast more or less unaided, and can open up cruising grounds denied most sailboaters. This one is suitable for boats to around 30 feet. Make it from 1/4-inch galvanized steel. Saw off the heel of the mast at an angle so it clears the tabernacle's front plate, then drive in wedges to hold the mast steady when erect.

unstayed mast that went right through a big deckhouse that was mostly windows. I'm really curious to see how long that stays up. I'm constantly amazed by how many boat designers have no feeling for structural integrity or respect for the forces to which an oceangoing boat will be exposed.

Anyway, if you're going to step the mast on deck, Figure 16-4 shows a simple way to make the mount. Since you've stepped the mast on deck, you might as well make it capable of folding, so my deck step actually is a tabernacle.

In Holland you see huge gaff-rigged boats with tabernacles. These rigs are stepped on the keel, with the mast sawed off at an angle above the deck and a heavy hinge attached. I didn't trust this deal until I spent some time over there looking at them. It seems to work fine, and has done so for hundreds of years. Still, I feel more comfortable with a solid pole running from keel to masthead; I'd do it that way unless you need to lower your mast frequently.

Be sure to position a heavy post running from the keel to the deck directly below this tabernacle. You'll have to round off the back edge of the mast butt or cut it off on maybe a 45-degree angle so the mast can rotate as it is lowered. I think cutting it at an angle is better than rounding it because you can easily insert a wedge in the space when the mast is up, which will get the strain on the wood, not the bolt, and should cut down any tendency for the mast to move around.

The Rig

263

Figure 16/5. Hollow mast construction, as done by a Famous Maine Boatyard. Use a good grade of fir, spruce, or equivalent. Top and bottom can be 2-by; 1-by on smaller boats. Inner layers can be 1½-inch square, but The Method is to saw out a slot from one or more wide boards. Leave solid areas where tangs and spreaders are attached. Stagger splices well (better than in the drawing), and make them at a 6- or 8-to-1 slope. Drill drain holes in solid blocking to release condensation.

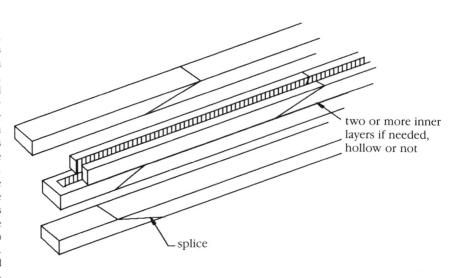

two or more inner layers if needed, hollow or not

splice

BUILT-UP MASTS

If you live somewhere with no suitable trees for masts, you can always laminate one up. The box-section hollow mast is the traditional built-up yacht mast, but they're difficult to build. I swept the floor and butchered wood years back for a Famous Yacht Builder in Maine, and Figure 16-5 shows how they make masts. I like this system better than the traditional box-section mast; I think it's both stronger and easier to do. You can make it hollow, as the drawing shows, or solid.

Hollow masts are lighter, but I prefer solid ones; they're more reassuring somehow. If you do make it hollow, leave it solid in places where any spreaders or tangs will be attached (check your rigging plans). Be sure to drill drain holes in these solid areas so any condensation inside the mast can drain down to the step, otherwise the mast will rot from the inside out. Along with this, drill a good hole in the side at the bottom to let out accumulated moisture.

Some people install electrical wire for spreader and masthead lights inside the mast before assembling it, but I prefer wire attached outside so I can get to it easily. The new rage among production boats is internal halyards. I never would do that: I want to be able to keep an eye on the condition of all the parts of my rig.

Obviously for a mast like this, glue is pretty important. I'd use resorcinol or epoxy, and I'd keep the mast varnished or painted to protect the glue from moisture.

Although this is a good way to build them, I still don't like laminated masts and wouldn't own one. My first boat had one. I remember once sailing down the Maine coast with no engine, the wind rising, and a fog bank headed my way. I looked up and saw that my laminated mast was coming apart. I had to climb the mast while the boat was sailing, hanging on with one hand while driving in wood screws with the other, all the while swinging in great arcs as the god-dam boat rolled and pitched. No thanks. If I lived in a place with no trees I'd launch the boat and motor it someplace that *had* trees.

UNSTAYED MASTS

One of the latest pitches from the hypesters is unstayed masts, the angle being that when coupled with a simple sail design it makes a boat easier to handle. I agree when comparing the handling ease of an unstayed rig to the typical production-boat rig, which usually is borderline raceboat, but I don't think it holds true when compared with a good cruising-type rig.

Unstayed masts are nothing new. They were used on large boats several hundred years ago, not for simplicity's sake, but because a fisherman was too cheap to buy rigging and so used an oversize mast that wouldn't need it. Unstayed masts were also used on boats that weren't self-righting, the idea being that the bending of the mast would spill the wind. In a last resort, the mast would break (that's right, break) if the boat was hit by a squall.

A solid-grown mast has the strength and flexibility to stand unstayed, but a few rigging wires will make the rig much stronger, and the mast will be braced well enough to take a knockdown at least, and maybe even a capsize. As I've mentioned before, I know of one rigging-supported grown mast on a 42-foot cutter (*Olga*, plans shown in the back of this book) that swatted a small airplane out of the sky without damaging her rig. I doubt an unstayed pole could have done that.

If you want to use an unstayed mast you should have planned for it back in the deck construction, because the mast should be a bit oversize, and be braced by very heavy partners at the deck. I'd also put tie-rods down to the keel. I know you see some designs with unstayed masts going through a deckhouse, but that's asking for disaster: When the mast goes (and go it will), the deckhouse will go with it.

I know of two boats with unstayed masts that were knocked down, one custom and the other a production boat. Both lost their masts. I wouldn't have one on a seagoing boat, myself.

THE SAIL TRACK

Whatever mast you decide on, once you get it worked to shape it's time to start installing the hardware. I start off by laying out the sail track. This should run from a point about 18 inches down from the top of the mast to about 12 inches above the boom. You'll likely need to scale the distance from the boom to the mast top off the plans,

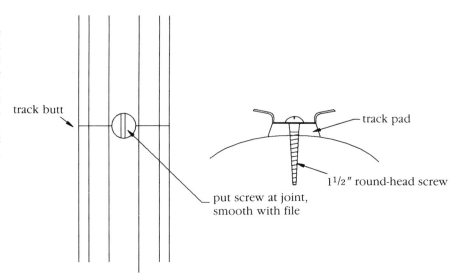

Figure 16/6.
Sail track details. The
wood pad between track
and mast is optional, but it
looks neat and keeps the
track free of paint or oil.
Locate the track now, but
don't install it perma-
nently until the tangs,
spreaders, and other mast
fittings are in place.

track butt

track pad

1½″ round-head screw

put screw at joint,
smooth with file

since few designers seem to remember to give that dimension. It's the little things like this that show you which of them has ever built a boat!

Most people mount the sail track on a ¼- to ³/₈-inch-thick pad. This keeps it away from the mast and makes it easier to paint or varnish the mast without getting paint on the track, which interferes with the slides. You don't need this pad with an oiled mast, but I put it on anyway because it looks neat.

Prop the mast up level at a comfortable working height. Roll it to see if it's straight. If it isn't, decide where you want the kink. I've always put it in back, although you could put it to one side and pull out the kink with the side stays. That might put the mast under more stress, however, so I'll probably keep putting it to the back. Once you decide which face is the back, nail blocks beside the mast to keep it from rolling.

Snap a chalk line down the middle, then tack down the track pad with a few small finish nails so that one side follows the chalk line. The top of the pad should be as wide as the base of the sail track. Once that's on, roll the mast a hair to get the pad sitting level.

I don't actually put on the track itself until the tangs and the spreaders are on, but by drawing the line and tacking on the track pad I've established a "top" on the mast which makes it easy to attach the other parts evenly on each side.

STANDING RIGGING

Rigging wire is just wire rope, or cable. Cable comes in a variety of fashions depending on the way it's made. The common types used for rigging are 1×19, 6×7, and 7×7. These numbers refer to the number of wires per strand times the number of strands. So, 1×19 means each strand is one wire, and 19 of them are twisted together to make the cable; 6×7 means there's 6 wires per strand, and 7 strands are twisted together to make the cable. I suppose rod rigging could be called 1×1.

The normal yacht rigging wire is 1×19, 300 series stainless. It's used because it doesn't rust, it's stiff, low stretch, and a bit stronger than the other "weaves" for its diameter.

I don't use it. I can hear you sigh, but see here: In my opinion going out on the ocean in a small vessel is serious business. Throughout this book I've emphasized simplicity and economy, but not out of recklessness. I am concerned with costs, but I'm not suicidal, and I don't compromise on the basic integrity of any part of a boat to save a buck.

To me the appeal of ocean cruising is that I am totally dependent on my own skills. I don't believe in hollering into a radio for help if something goes wrong. If I can't deal with it, then "*C'est la vie, Melon Farmer.*" If everyone—mountain climbers, sailors, whatever— had to pay back every dime it cost to launch a full search and rescue mission to save their silly tails when they no-brained themselves into a corner, the world would be a better place.

The rig is probably the most fragile part of the whole boat, but I'll make mine as stout as I can, and just as important, make it so that I can maintain and repair every part of it without needing a machine shop. Visit any cruising port around the world and you'll see broken down production boats, often with pathetic and plaintive "For Sale" signs nailed to their sorry sides. The electrics go first, of course, because electricity and salt air don't mix. Next goes the fancy stuff— the roller furling, the pressed fittings, the miracle goops. If these people had gone for simplicity and strength instead of glitz and flash they might still be cruising.

Oh well, I'll spare you any more of this tirade and get on with it. But let me say for a final time that nothing I've said anywhere in this book is original with me. It's just commonsense workboat stuff that used to be *common* until big biz got mixed up with boats. It was common because it works, it's cheap, and you can fix it on the spot with simple tools, easily carried spares, and whatever happens to be lying around.

Anyway, I don't like stainless wire. It's too expensive, too brittle, and the individual strands in 1×19 have a habit of breaking and sticking out, becoming "meathooks" to shred your hand when you grab hold.

Because 1×19 is too stiff to be wrapped around a rigging eye, all the rigging terminals have to be swaged or glued on. Aside from costing lots, I don't like these terminals because you can't see what their condition is until they fail.

I know that machine-pressed swages are very strong, as are some of the new glue-on or screw-on fittings. But they do sometimes fail, and in the end you're relying entirely on faith. For instance, I knew a guy who used those epoxy-filled end fittings. He jibed the main in strong wind; when the boom reached the end of its swing the shock jerked all the wires on the weather side out of their $30 terminals and the deck-stepped mast fell right over.

I prefer flexible galvanized wire, like 6×7. It's about a third the price of stainless and it's flexible enough so you can wrap the ends around an eye and "seize" it, have it spliced, or even use cable clamps.

Compared with a swaged fitting at $20, or screw-ons or glue-ons for $30, a splice in 3/8-inch 6×7 at the local wire rope shop costs about $8, cable clamps cost about $3 per end, and seizing is about a buck. All three systems hold very well, and are preferable for a cruising boat because they aren't prone to sudden failure and you can see the condition of the ends at a glance. If an end is starting to slip, which I've yet to see by the way, you can patch it on the spot.

Cable clamps look awkward, but you can cover them with a canvas boot, which looks rather shippy, or with a split section of garden hose running about 6 feet up the wire. This isn't a bad idea regardless of fittings because it makes the wire easier to grab, yet the hose can easily be opened once in a while so you can inspect the condition of the ends.

Galvanized wire can rust, but with very basic care it lasts almost forever. It's common to see galvanized headstays, rubbed hundreds of times by jib hanks as the sail is raised and lowered, lasting 20 years. I rub galvanized rigging down once a year with a rag soaked in oil, but some people serve and parcel (covering it with oiled marline and spiraled strips of cloth or tape) the entire wire, which protects it indefinitely. I don't care for that, preferring to oil it yearly, for the same reason I don't like ceiling inside the boat. I want to be able to see what's going on *everywhere*.

True, compared with 1×19 stainless, 6×7 galvanized wire will stretch a bit, but so what? There's no need for bar-taut headstays unless you're racing, and since wood masts can flex a bit without harm, I think a little stretch to the wire serves as a shock absorber and eases strains on the boat. Besides, any stretch can be taken up with the turnbuckles.

So, other than saying something about rod rigging—it has no place on a cruising boat, period—that's what I think about rigging wire. If you want to buy 1×19 wire with swaged ends, be my guest. If you want to save money and rig your boat with something you can both prepare and repair yourself, here's how to get started on the stays.

Making the stays

I buy one long piece of wire and make my own stays and shrouds. (Stays hold up the mast fore and aft; shrouds from side to side.) You'll need a 12- to 18-inch overlap on each end of each stay, so add the lengths of all the stays and shrouds together, add $3^1/2$ or 4 feet to each one, subtract the length of a *half-open* turnbuckle from each wire, and you'll know how long a piece to order.

By the way, I use open galvanized steel turnbuckles, about double the size of the wire. On $^3/_8$-inch wire I'll use $^1/_2$- or $^3/_4$-inch turnbuckles. These cost about $25 for galvanized, compared with $75 to $90 for stainless.

I don't know if there's any set rule governing what size wire to use. If your plans don't specify it, look around and see what other people are using. However, I never use wire under $^1/_4$ inch, even on small boats, because $^1/_4$ inch is the smallest you can grab without hurting your hand. I fell off a boat when singlehanding once, and caught the backstay. The adrenalin rush gave me the strength to swing myself back aboard, one handed. It hurt, though, and I wouldn't want to have to try that with wire smaller than $^1/_4$ inch. That little experience taught me to wear a harness.

Wire rope is a bitch to cut. Buy a very good hacksaw blade, and set up two vises in line and close together on a bench. Clamp the wire in both vises, which will hold it pretty steady, and wrap a few layers of tape around the place you want to cut to keep it from unraveling.

I've never learned wire splicing, so I have a choice between cable clamps and seizing the ends, or of course hiring someone to do the splicing. I use cable clamps most of the time because they're so handy. I figure when I get bored with lying around drinking on the beach I might go back and seize the ends. So far I never have, so rather than tell you what I've read about seizing, I suggest you pick up a rigging book and read direct from the horse's mouth how to do it.

Cable clamps will get you going and they work fine. Wrap the wire around an eye, or *thimble*, as they're also called, then clamp it. The rule is "never saddle a dead horse," so install the clamp with the saddle, which is the flattish piece that the U-bolt goes through, on the long length of wire; the U-bolt goes around the short piece.

Some people splice one end of the wire stay around a thimble and attach it to the mast. The other end, with a good 12 inches or so extra for overlap, is left alone until the mast is erected. The mast is held in position by the halyards, the wire stays attached to the turnbuckles, and the lengths adjusted so that the turnbuckle "eyes" are all on the same line. Then the stays are clamped or seized. This looks really sharp and ship-like. A pipe or bar can be inserted through a row of turnbuckles done this way to keep them from gradually opening on their own.

Although many designers don't specify them, I always put running backstays on the mast. These are attached behind the staysail (at the masthead on a mizzen), one on each side, and run down to about 4 feet off the deck. They're set up and tensioned with a simple tackle, consisting of a single block with a becket on the wire end and a double block on the chainplate. You should have enough rope (forgive

Figure 16/7.
A boomkin extends the
staying base aft and gets
the backstay out of the
way of the boom. Hulls
with inboard rudders can
use a pole boomkin. This
is particularly common on
British designs.

me, *line*, to be properly nautical) rove through the blocks to allow the
runner to be slacked off and left tied to the side rigging, where they'll
stay about 99 percent of the time.

Someday when you're hove to in nasty weather or running off in
strong wind you'll look at your mast, think of the strains on it, and
cringe. Then you'll be really happy that you can unhook the runners
and cinch them up.

A mizzen doesn't need a tackle on the runner. Some people just
use a pelican hook. Even a line that can be tied off at a cleat would
serve.

Most boats these days use standing backstays, even though until
recently it was "common knowledge" that this was a bad idea for sail
shape. However, the convenience offered by the permanent backstay
offsets that. Before standing backstays, you had to cast off and reten-
sion the runners each time you tacked.

Sometimes the permanent backstay requires special treatment.
Double-enders with outboard rudders come to mind, and any boat
with a long boom. The backstay has to more than clear the boom. It
has to be far enough back so the end of the boom can lift 45 degrees
or more, which it will in a jibe, and not hit the stay. Lots of boats are
dangerous because the boom can hit the stay in a jibe, which could
break the boom or knock off the wire.

The backstay can be extended aft by using a *boomkin*. Normally
the boomkin comes together in a point at the outer end, but I prefer
using one that's rectangular, as Figure 16-8 shows. This style can be
stayed more securely because the chain hold-downs can go to chainplates lagged into the keel on each side of the rudder without interfer-
ing with the rudder's swing.

Pointed boomkins need their chainplates positioned farther forward to clear the rudder (on boats with outboard rudders) so the
plates have to be bolted into the planking, which isn't as strong. Also,

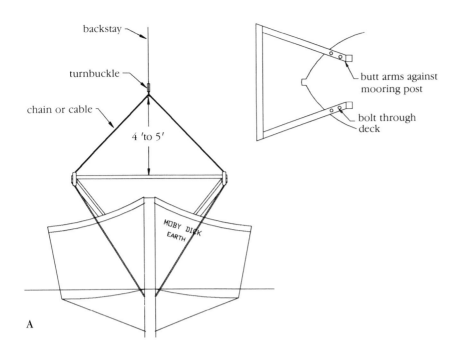

backstay

turnbuckle

chain or cable

4 'to 5'

butt arms against mooring post

bolt through deck

MOBY DICK
EARTH

A

Figure 16/8.
(A) Although most boomkins are pointed, a rectangular one like this is sturdier and provides additional storage space. Make the arms from 2 × 4s in smaller boats, 3 × 4s in big boats. The crosspiece can be as wide as you like, but about 3 feet works well. (B) Boomkin details.

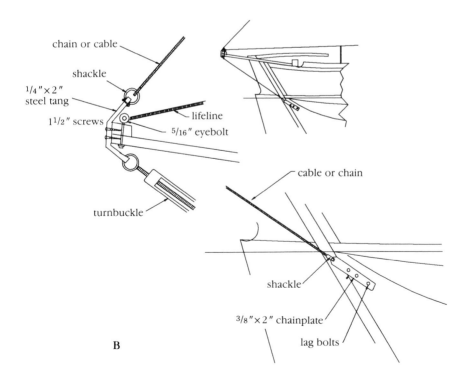

chain or cable

shackle

1/4″ × 2″ steel tang

1 1/2″ screws

lifeline

5/16″ eyebolt

turnbuckle

cable or chain

shackle

3/8″ × 2″ chainplate

lag bolts

B

The Rig

271

Figure 16/9.
Backstay chainplate for a double-ender with a short boom and an outboard rudder. Find the exact dimensions off your boat. Use heavy steel, 3/8-×3-inch minimum. Attach the backstay to the wire yoke about 6 feet above the deck.

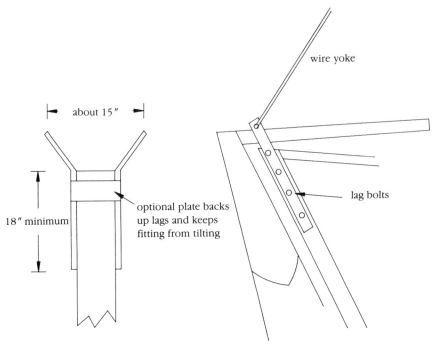

about 15"

18" minimum

optional plate backs up lags and keeps fitting from tilting

wire yoke

lag bolts

Figure 16/10.
Bowsprit details. (A) Stay-sail chainplate and 'sprit "hold-em-down-Tony." Use 3/16- to 1/4-inch steel. (B) Chainplates, 1/4×2-inch×12 inches or so. The lower one on the stem can be longer, and is lagged into the keel. (C) Commercial "4-eye" fitting, or weld four eyes onto a piece of pipe large enough to slip over the bowsprit. Use heavy chain for the bobstay—3/8-inch minimum on 30- to 35-foot boats; heavier for larger boats.

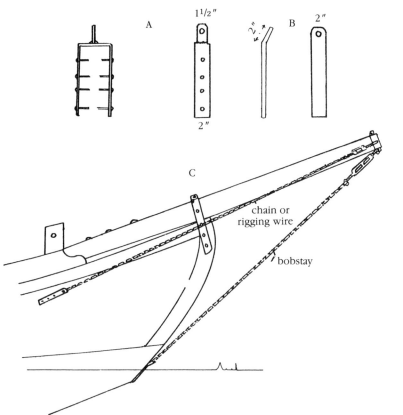

A

1 1/2"

2"

B

2"

2"

C

chain or rigging wire

bobstay

the rectangular boomkin is a handy place to lash an outboard engine or a basket of stores, anchor warp, oranges—whatever. Less genteel types use it for a toilet seat.

The boomkin's arms can be made from 1½- by 3-inch stuff on up to mid-30-footers, and maybe 2½- by 4-inch stuff in bigger boats. Note that the inboard ends butt against mooring posts for strength. There'll be a good deal of strain on these things at times, so note how the stay is attached by a tang that wraps around the outer end (see Figure 16-8B). I tried it once with a through-bolt and the boomkin arm split.

If you're building a double-ender with a boom short enough not to need a boomkin, you can make a chainplate like the one in Figure 16-9. These arms sticking up separate the stay so the tiller can swing between it. This fitting is for a 50-footer, and is made from ½-inch steel. On the other end of the boat, the bowsprit needs some standing rigging to support the forestay. Figure 16-10 shows how to do it.

Attaching the wires to the mast

The old way of attaching stays was splicing the wire right around the mast before installing the sail track. This is the simplest and least expensive way to go, but it makes removing a wire next to impossible. I prefer to attach the wires to metal tangs, or to a mast collar with welded-on eyes.

Tangs are easy to make. I use stainless, and attach them to the mast with one through-bolt and plenty of screws. The bolt isn't the best idea because it weakens the mast a bit, but I'm afraid to rely entirely on screws.

Carry a small magnet when stainless-shopping at the junkyard,

Figure 16/11.
By first making a plywood pattern of what you want, you can get all kinds of metal rigging fittings made at local metal shops, from stainless or mild steel (have it galvanized after fabrication).

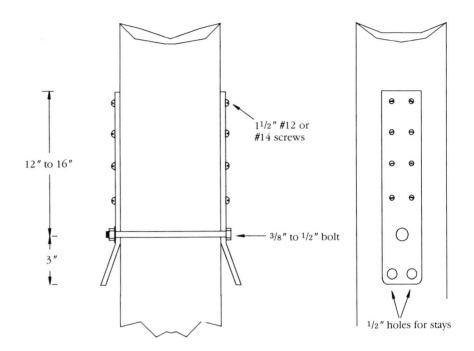

Figure 16/12.
Attach homemade tangs (use stainless or galvanized steel) to the mast with a through-bolt and many screws.

12" to 16"

1½" #12 or #14 screws

3"

3/8" to ½" bolt

½" holes for stays

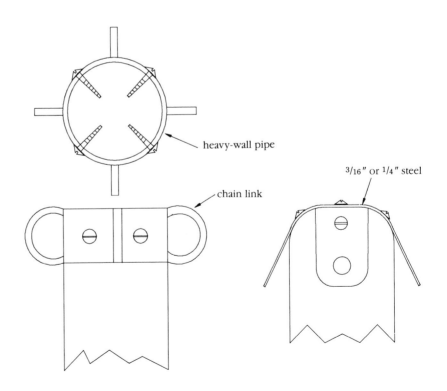

Figure 16/13.
Two approaches for mast-head fittings. Use heavy-wall pipe with four chain links or heavy-duty washers welded on (notch a shoulder into mast top to hold up fitting). Alternatively, make a "cross" over the mast top from 3/16- or ¼-inch stock (or use several stacked thin layers of stainless), screwed to mast.

heavy-wall pipe

chain link

3/16" or ¼" steel

Buehler's Backyard Boatbuilding

because the marine grades are non-magnetic. If you're buying it new, get 304 grade. It's softer, not quite as brittle, and easier to work than the harder grades, like 316.

If you don't have a good drill press, start drilling stainless with a small bit, then redrill the hole with a bigger one until you get to the size you need. Drill all holes 1/16 inch oversize.

The collar might actually be the best way to go since it doesn't need a through-bolt, although they're a bit tricky to install. To keep from notching (and thus weakening) the mast, collars need to be very close to the right diameter. The simplest way to make them is in two pieces that bolt together, with the stays attached at the bolts and a few screws through the collar into the mast to hold it in position. A collar will need to be installed before the sail track.

Spreaders

Most rigs need spreaders on the mast. Any wire that would run at less than a 10-degree angle from the mast to the chainplate needs to run through a spreader to increase the angle. At less than 10 degrees, a shroud doesn't have a wide enough "stance" to support a mast.

The lower part of the mast will be supported by the lower shrouds, which run from the chainplates to tangs about halfway up the mast. Just above the tangs are the spreaders, with the upper shrouds that support the top part of the mast running from the chainplates, over the end of the spreader, and to the masthead. This gives the upper shrouds about the same angle from the tip of the spreaders to the masthead as the lowers take from the rail to the spreaders. Very tall rigs might use two sets of spreaders, but one is usually plenty on a normal cruising rig, especially with a grown mast.

Figure 16-14 shows the spreader in detail. They're made from a plank the same width as the mast's diameter—one spreader on each side of the mast, held together with a strip of stainless screwed into both spreaders and into the mast. A spreader doesn't need to be very heavy, really, and even 50-foot boats will have spreaders made from 2-by. A very rough guide might be 3/4-inch stock in boats to 26 feet; 1-inch stock in boats to 33 feet; and 1 1/2-inch stock in larger boats.

A common mistake is making the spreader too long. I like a spreader to be maybe a foot shorter than half the beam at the mast. This allows the shroud to lean inboard a bit. If the spreader is as long as half the beam or longer, you can't bring the boat against a tall dock or raft against other sailboats.

Again, this is a very common mistake, so if your plans call for a long spreader, you might want to shorten it. However, *if* you shorten it, remember you must keep a minimum 10-degree angle from the spreader tip to the masthead—the more the better. Raise the spreader (and the lower shrouds, since the two are always mounted together) if you need to. In practice you shouldn't. Few designers would draw a spreader wider than the beam. All I'm saying is be sure yours is nar-

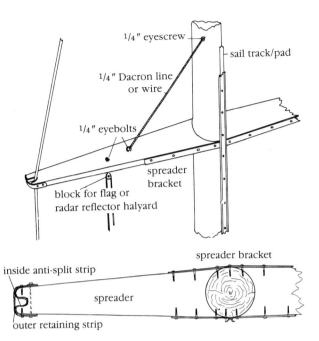

Figure 16/14.
Spreader details. Spreader is held to mast with the 1/8- × 30-inch stainless bracket, mounted on both sides of spreader with 1 1/4-inch screws. Note how the sail track/pad goes *over* the spreader bracket. Make the spreader from 1-inch-thick stock on small boats; 1 1/2-stock on big boats. Bed it well where it intersects the mast, and keep it well painted or varnished—particularly the upper side, where rot will start. The inside strip on the spreader tip keeps the stay from splitting the wood; make it from 3/32-inch stainless—the same for the outer strip, which holds the stay in the spreader notch. The short lanyard from the spreader to the mast keeps the spreader from drooping; don't leave it off.

rower than the beam! You can easily see this stuff by using a protractor on your rigging plan.

The attachment system shown in Figure 16-14 is simple and very stout. Note the Dacron line which prevents the spreader from drooping. This is very important, although many boats don't use it. You use it! I learned its importance when I had a boat with a deck-stepped mast. Because the spreaders weren't held securely in position, they would droop slowly over time, loosening the stay and putting the mast in danger. I fixed that with the little rope shown.

Note the details showing the spreader's outer ends. Although some people attach the stay rigidly to the spreader end, I think it's better to allow the stay to float a bit. At least in theory this keeps the strains on the chainplate, where they belong. The notch in the spreader tip is lined with lightweight stainless to keep the stay from splitting the wood, and another light piece is screwed around the outside after the wire is installed to keep the wire from flopping out. Be sure to bed all parts to keep moisture out of the joints.

Hang a small block off an eyebolt in the middle of each spreader for flags and radar reflectors and whatnot. Wrap the spreader ends and the tangs with scraps of "earth tone" shag carpet. From a distance this looks exactly like old-time baggywrinkle, and protects the sail from chafing on the metal.

Once the spreaders are on you can install the sail track. The track is held down with 1 1/2-inch round-head screws, or 2-inch if you used the pad. Don't bed it, or you'll goof up the slides. When you install the track, keep a sail slide on it. This makes it easier to line up two pieces. Get them *perfectly* aligned, or the slides can jam.

After you've fastened down two meeting pieces, drill and put in a screw right in the middle of the joint, then smooth up the butt with a file so the slide passes easily over the joint. I drill a hole for a ⁵/₁₆- by 1-inch lag bolt just above and another just below the track. The upper one serves as a ''stop'' when hoisting the sail, and the lower one is screwed in after the sail is attached to the mast to keep the slides from falling off the track when the sail is furled.

A

B

C

D

Figure 16/15.
(A) Simple, rough-and-ready mast and rigging displays workboat ancestry. This mast and all its rigging cost less than the wire alone for a Regulation Yacht-Finish Rig. Note the spreader support lines, carpet baggywrinkle, and the halyards for flag and radar reflector. (B) Big galvanized turnbuckles like these cost a quarter as much as stainless yacht turnbuckles of similar strength. (C) Spreader details . . . (D) . . . and tang details. Note the cable clamps covered with electrical tape, and shackles wired closed.

The Rig

RUNNING RIGGING

The running rigging is all the stuff that moves. Halyards hoist the sails and sheets pull in the sails. There'll also be topping lifts and lazyjacks and reefing lines and downhauls and outhauls. You can get seasick just reciting the names.

The rope (or line, pardon me again) for all this, except the topping lift and lazyjacks, where it doesn't matter, should be as low stretch as possible. Solid-core braided Dacron is best, but it's expensive, and 3-strand Dacron works fine.

Once, when building on a really tight budget, I used polypropylene. This stuff rots in the sun, it's hard to handle, and it doesn't hold knots very well. However, it's non-stretch and very inexpensive, and if you're having a cash flow problem it will work—for a while. Lots of people will sneer at it, but so what? I'm not recommending it, but as I said, it will work and get you going if you're low on bucks.

Because wire halyards stretch less than Dacron, they are used on many yachts. Not by me, though. I had a boat with wire halyards once. I lost the winch handle overboard, and I can tell you hoisting a sail while pulling on a 1/8-inch wire is no fun.

Some people use rope-to-wire splices, the theory being that the lower stretch wire is all aloft and the easier-to-handle rope tail, which doesn't need a special winch like wire, is down where you can handle it. This custom came around in the very early 1900s, before the advent of low-stretch synthetic rope. Today, it just doesn't make any sense, at least to me. I use rope halyards, period. Dacron rope stretches only a little more than wire, and is so much easier to handle, aside from costing less to install, that it's the only thing that makes sense on a cruising boat.

I think all halyards and sheets should be 1/2 inch in diameter; smaller line is hard to grasp or pull on. Larger sails will be a lot easier to hoist if you rig the halyards as a two-part tackle. If you need to go aloft you can hook a bosun's chair to the tackle and pull yourself right up the mast.

Although you see them all the time, I don't like pulley sheaves for the halyards installed in the mast; instead, I run all halyards through blocks attached to the mast. There's one less place for rot to start and nothing can get snagged. Ideally, the blocks should be attached to the tangs holding the wire stays. If you have to put a block where there is no tang, install one just as you did for the wires.

Some people lead all halyards back to the cockpit, thinking this makes the boat easier to handle. I don't like this: The cockpit becomes enough of a rat's nest with the sheets; the halyards just add to the confusion. You can get to them at the mast in about one second if you need to, and they'll always be out of the way, unable to tangle up in anything else.

Cleats on the mast are the most common system for belaying the halyards, but I rather like pinrails, as shown in Figure 16-16. These

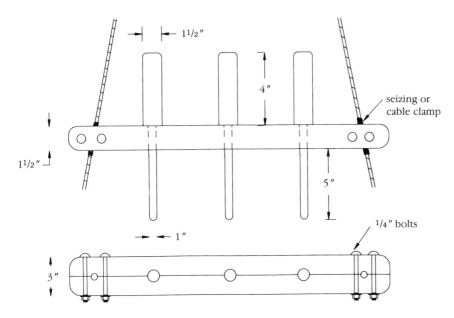

Figure 16/16.
Belaying pins and pinrails are suitably shippy places to make fast halyards and the like. Make the pins from 2 × 2s turned on a lathe, or peel them round with a drawknife and spokeshave (or use a power plane). Make the pinrails from two pieces of 2 × 2 bolted together around the rigging. Hold it in place with cable clamps or seize it. Sizes shown are for a 35-foot or so boat.

Labels in figure: 1¹/₂″, 4″, seizing or cable clamp, 1¹/₂″, 5″, ¹/₄″ bolts, 1″, 3″

hold the halyards well away from the mast so they don't slap against it, and look slick on most boats. They can be awkward to get to if the boat is heeling much, but you get used to that.

Be sure to rig a topping lift. This is essential to keeping the boom under control. Some production boats use a short wire attached to the backstay instead. The wire is hooked to the boom during reefing or when lowering the sail. Try that in strong weather sometime!

The topping lift supports the boom when you're handling the sail and avoids the need for a fixed boom crutch. When anchored you can pull the back end of the boom up on a 45-degree angle, which looks jaunty and gets it out of the way. When running off the wind you can tighten the topping lift and lift the boom, which turns the sail into a nice bag for catching the wind. I put a topping lift on all booms, including the staysail.

Make the topping lift from 3/8-inch nylon (because it's a little stretchy), run it to a block at the top of the mast, then down to the pinrail or a cleat on the mast. On larger boats the boom will be easier to handle if the lift has a tackle built in, as Figure 16-17 shows.

The sheeting arrangement might require some experimentation. A sail on a boom is easy to deal with. All you need to do is figure out how many parts you want the tackle to have. (The more parts a tackle has, the easier, and slower, it is to pull in.) But a boomless, or "flying sail," needs just the right angle on its sheet or it doesn't work right.

Generally this angle is about 90 degrees off the stay the sail is hanked to. You can approximate the location of the padeye for the sheet block by drawing a 90-degree line on the plans back from the stay to the deck, in line with where the sheet hooks to the sail. The safest thing to do, however, is take the boat for a sail before

The Rig

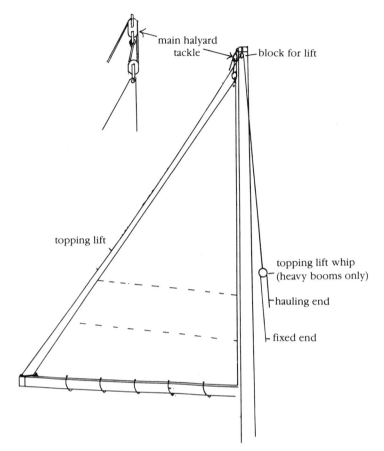

Figure 16/17.
Details of mainsail halyard and topping lift. A 2-to-1 main halyard tackle means you won't need a winch to tighten the sail's luff; in addition, you can hoist yourself unaided to the masthead in a bosun's chair. Make the topping lift from 3/8-inch nylon (it's stretchy, you see) rove through a block fastened to the side of the mast top at the stay. For heavy booms, rig a whip on the end of the topping lift to make things easier. Attach the topping lift to a single block about 8 feet above deck; attach one end of a piece of line permanently to a cleat or chainplate, run it through the block, and haul on the free end.

installing the padeyes on deck to hold the blocks. Hoist the sails and have somebody stand on the sheet in different places. It's pretty noticeable when the sail is pulling well and when it isn't. Mark the place and bolt down a padeye with a backing plate.

When fastening this stuff down try to keep the deck as uncluttered as you can. Since a few inches left or right won't kill the sail's efficiency, mount the pads off to the side a bit so you don't trip over them some dark night.

There's a number of quick-release jam cleats on the market designed to make sheets easy to cast off in an emergency. They're all rather expensive for what you get, and a normal cleat works fine, taking only milliseconds longer to cast off. You can make your own cleats out of hardwood for next to nothing. It's best to mount cleats at about a 45-degree angle to the strain.

Winches assist in pulling in the sheets of boomless sails. The cockpits of raceboats are literally covered with them. They're handy all right, but they're expensive and not truly essential. To harden in a sheet, all you need do is luff the sail, which means point the nose of the boat into the wind a bit so the sail flops, and you can pull it in as tight as you want.

Some people buy one big winch and lead all sheets to it through individual jam cleats placed between the winch and the load. You winch in a sheet until you get it where you want it, then latch the jam cleat and cast off the sheet, freeing the winch for another one. It's a good way to spread an expensive winch around, but I think I'd put a real cleat nearby and put a turn on it. I don't trust jam cleats. I'd hate to be leaning against the jib sheet spying on a fish and have the thing slip.

Personally I have a lot of winches. What's not on the boat are bookends and paper weights and whatnot. I buy them at swap meets for pennies on the dollar! So many people want the New Thing, and the New Thing in winches is self-tailing, which sounds vaguely obscene, doesn't it? Before self-tailing, the New Thing was quiet bearings, and before that chromed finish. As a result, there's a lot of perfectly good old bronze, clanky sounding, trouble-free winches out there available *cheap*. God Bless the power of advertising. Let us pray The Suckers keep breeding.

BOOMS

It's easy to make a boom from a small tree, but a shaped one looks more finished. I like them tapered from a wide point in the middle to maybe 1 inch narrower at each end. Make the boom maybe 8 inches longer than the foot of the sail so you have plenty of room to tie the outer end down and hook on the end fittings.

I don't bother with sail track on booms. I let the staysail fly loose-footed, just attached at the outer end, and I lace the mainsail to its boom. Of course there's no reason not to use track if you want; install it just as you did on the mast.

I like heavy booms, so I use solid ones, but you can make a hollow boom just as described for the mast. It's hard to find *goosenecks* for wood booms, but Figure 16-18 shows how to make them yourself. The wood jaws on the main boom work fine, by the way. The simple chain attachment on the staysail boom (Figure 16-20) works well, too.

The booms need some rigging too, and I think all the drawings show enough details for you to puzzle it out. Put a topping lift on the staysail boom. Jiffy reefing on the mainsail boom is really handy and makes shorthanded sailing far simpler. *Lazyjacks* simplify sail handling because they keep the sail from flopping around when it's being raised and lowered. They can cause chafe, so if you don't baggywrinkle them, keep a good eye on the sail for wear.

I keep a rope tied permanently to the end of the main boom, long enough to tie the boom down tightly to a chainplate when running off the wind. The proper name for this is a *boom vang*, and it holds the sail out tight in light weather and keeps the boom from lifting if the boat is rolling. I do a similar deal on staysail booms with

Figure 16/18.
(A) Goosenecks attach the boom to the mast. This is the simplest one; it worked fine in Nelson's navy and it works fine now if you protect the mast from chafe with thin stainless (bed under it well) or epoxy and cloth. Support the boom when the sail is furled with blocks fastened around the mast (traditional), or hang it from a rope (easy). (B) A slightly more elaborate gooseneck. All parts are made from common galvanized pipe. Straps are 3/16-inch flatbar. Note that the long eyebolt holds boom to mast as well as securing the sail's tack.

A

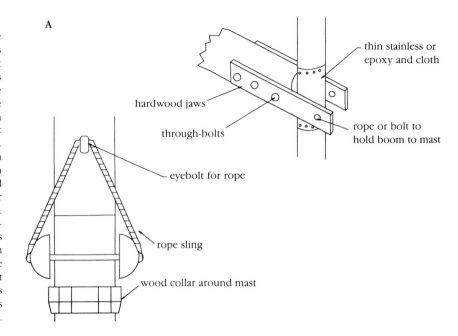

thin stainless or epoxy and cloth

hardwood jaws

through-bolts

rope or bolt to hold boom to mast

eyebolt for rope

rope sling

wood collar around mast

B

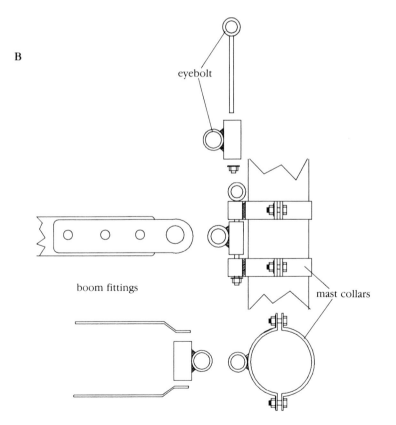

eyebolt

boom fittings

mast collars

boats that have 'sprits, although since it has to be shifted around the staysail stay depending on the tack, I leave the end coiled on deck, attached to the mooring post, when not in use. When in use it runs from the mooring post, out to a block on the end of the sprit, and back to the aft end of the staysail boom.

Figure 16-25 shows a reefing headstay system for boats with bowsprits. This idea works perfectly, and makes sail handling much safer because you don't need to go out on the 'sprit. I suggest you use it. Cut the wire 18 inches short and attach a single block with a becket. The block should be able to take 1/2-inch rope. I'll get into this a little more when I talk about running rigging.

There's all sorts of rigging things you can do, most of which will become obvious as you use the boat and can be added at your leisure. It's odd that people with production boats pay thousands more for their rig than I do, yet mine's handier. Their rigs usually don't have the things that make life easy: multiple reef points, boomed staysail, bits of rope here and there to tie things off.

Speaking of boomed staysails, there's nothing better. You might get hit once by the boom, but then you'll know it's there. A boomed staysail is such a convenience. You can reef the sail; it's self-tending, so there's no Chinese fire drill when you're short-tacking up a river or something; it can be sheeted in without winches because it has a tackle; and in light weather it can be tied out to keep the sail working. I wouldn't have a boat without one.

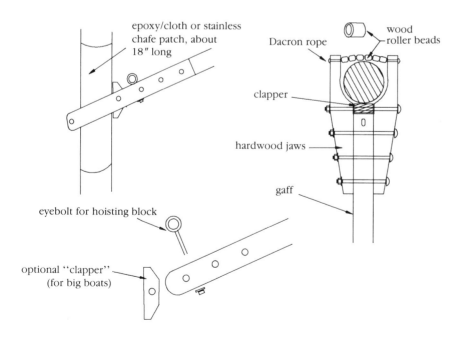

Figure 16/19.
Gaff rigs have a lot to offer. They're better off the wind than marconi rigs (although they're marginally inferior to windward), sail shape is less critical, and to some eyes they look better. Gaff sails need another small boom, called, oddly enough, a gaff, to hold up the head of the sail. Some new boats use heavy sail track for the gaff and sail. This is the old way.

Figure 16/20.
A simple staysail goose-neck that works fine and costs next to nothing to make. Watch out for chafe at bolt and shackle.

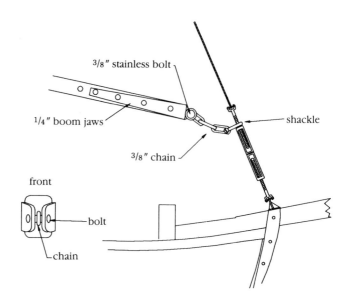

3/8″ stainless bolt

1/4″ boom jaws

3/8″ chain

shackle

front

bolt

chain

Figure 16/21.
(A) The simplest boomed sail sheeting system. On big sails, add extra parts to the tackle to reduce hauling effort. (B) Boomed sail sheet using a traveler. I don't like this system because some night you'll trip over it. Some people use heavy sail track as a traveler. I don't like that either!

A

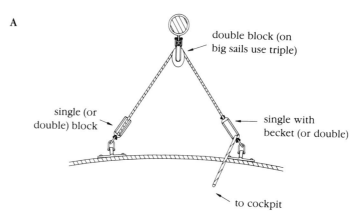

double block (on big sails use triple)

single (or double) block

single with becket (or double)

to cockpit

B

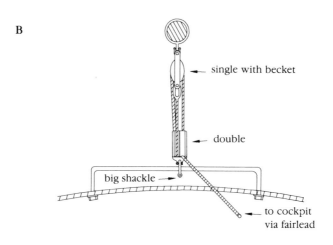

single with becket

double

big shackle

to cockpit via fairlead

Buehler's Backyard Boatbuilding

C

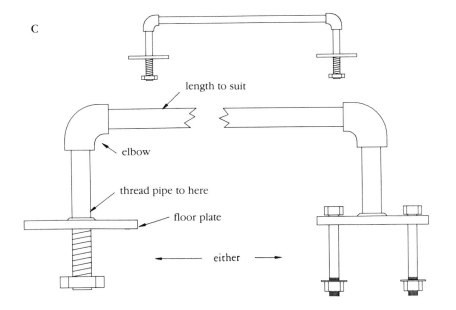

length to suit

elbow

thread pipe to here

floor plate

← either →

Figure 16/21 con't.
(C) Details of a homemade traveler. All parts common galvanized pipe fittings.

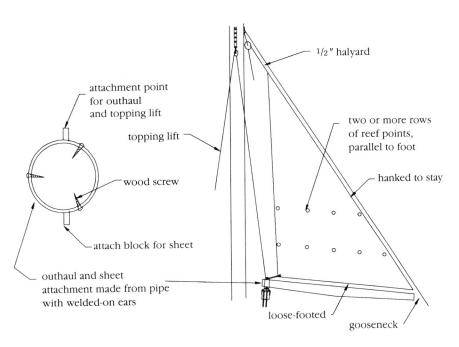

attachment point
for outhaul
and topping lift

topping lift

wood screw

attach block for sheet

outhaul and sheet
attachment made from pipe
with welded-on ears

1/2″ halyard

two or more rows
of reef points,
parallel to foot

hanked to stay

loose-footed

gooseneck

Figure 16/22.
Staysail details. See Figure 16-20 for details of staysail gooseneck.

The Rig

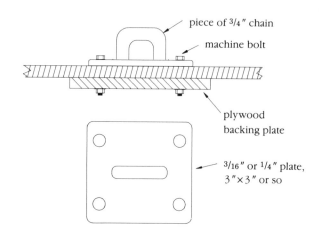

Figure 16/23.
You'll need a number of deck padeyes scattered around the boat for attaching various sheets, vangs, preventers, and whatnot. You can buy them for around $15, or make them for $1.50.

piece of ³/4" chain

machine bolt

plywood backing plate

³/16" or ¹/4" plate, 3"×3" or so

Figure 16/24.
Using the method shown here, you can put in a reef quickly and easily right at the mast. Just ease the sheet a bit until the sail is almost luffing, take up on the topping lift, slack off on the halyard a bit, haul down the reefing line at the luff (E) and belay it at the cleat (F), then haul down the reefing line at the leech (A), and belay it at the cleat (D). Now tighten up the halyard and slack off on the topping lift and you're ready to go. You can tie up the bunt of the reefed sail with the reefing nettles as time permits. This is all harder to describe than it is to do. Make the reefing line (A) from ³/8-inch Dacron, tie off at (C), go up through hole in sail at reef point, back down to (B), then out to cleat (D).

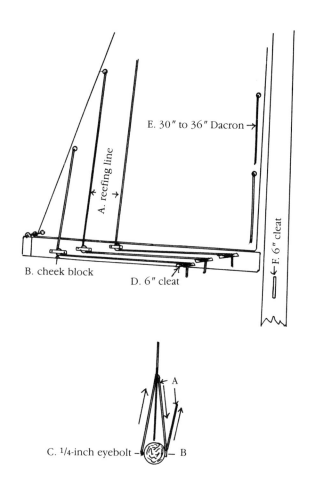

E. 30" to 36" Dacron →

A. reefing line

B. cheek block

D. 6" cleat

F. 6" cleat

A

C. ¹/4-inch eyebolt

B

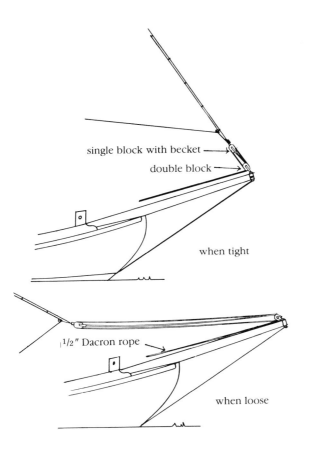

single block with becket

double block

when tight

$1/2''$ Dacron rope

when loose

Figure 16/25.
In the old days they called bowsprits *widow makers* because so many seamen were lost trying to get in the outer jib. That's why many of the later fishing schooners were 'spritless, or *bald-headed*, which is a pretty accurate description of a boat without a bowsprit. Rather than climb out on the 'sprit to deal with your jib (or even worse, eschew a bowsprit altogether), cut your headstay about 2 feet short and end it on a tackle between the stay and 'sprit. Cleat the tackle either to the mooring post or to a big cleat mounted on the 'sprit. When you want to lower the jib, loosen the tackle and bring stay, sail, and all, right into the deck. When you want to raise it, just haul on the tackle. This simple, safe, and reliable system works well, and takes all the danger out of long bowsprits.

Figure 16/26.
Here's a nicely done 'sprit. Note the pulpit, walkway, lifelines, and the safety netting—all designed to make it safer to go out on the 'sprit and get in the outer jib. The running headstay, however, makes the trip unnecessary, which is the safest solution of all.

The Rig

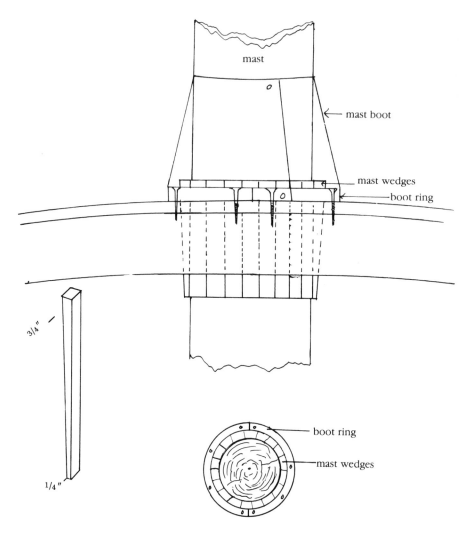

Figure 16/27.
Mast wedges and boot. The wedges fix the mast firmly in place at the mast partners. The boot keeps out the weather. Make the wedges about 18 inches long with very gradual taper; saw them off to length after installation. Make the boot from canvas painted with Arabol, tacked to the mast with one carpet tack. Tack the bottom to a 3/4-inch square-section ring screwed to the deck.

mast

mast boot

mast wedges

boot ring

3/4"

1/4"

boot ring

mast wedges

MAST ERECTIONS

Once you've made your rig you have to stand it up. Nowadays there's usually a crane available for this stuff, but once in Ellsworth, Maine, when I didn't have the cash to hire a boom truck, we floated the mast out to a bridge, dangled a come-a-long from the bridge, hoisted up the mast, and lowered her in. It was a real production, both from the booze that always seems to flow at these sort of deals and because the current in the river was going like hell and the boat didn't want to stand still long enough to drop the mast down.

However you get the sucker up, assuming it's a keel-stepped job, attach the stays, then wedge the mast tightly in the partners as shown in Figure 16-27. Make these wedges long with a gradual taper, and trim them off after you have them all in. Cover the opening with a canvas boot, then paint it with Arabol and you're done.

OUTFITTING

The subject of outfitting is worthy of a whole book, and there's a few out there now. Be wary of the new books because they often stress buying out the chandlery. I hear to be hip nowadays you gotta carry a satnav and watermaker and a four-cycle outboard for your rigid-bottom inflatable skiff. Phooey! Read things by folks like Tristan Jones, Bill Robinson, David Lewis, the Hiscocks, John Guzzwell, and others who cruised and wrote before the early 70s. These were all regular guys, so to speak, living on normal incomes, not checkbook cruisers.

Don't go overboard. If you pay attention to the marine press you'll spend thousands of dollars on stuff that I promise you is going to fail eventually. Elaborate furling systems, electronics—they all break down if used much or exposed to a salt-air environment. The guy who keeps things simple is the guy who in the long run has the least hassles. Most of you won't believe me here, I suppose. That's alright. See for yourself.

I've always had a depth sounder, but that's it for electronic stuff, aside from my blaster, of course. European cassette machines have shortwave bands instead of AM/FM, which is nice. I might get a VHF some day. I've thought one would be handy ever since I was passed by a cruise ship one night. If I had the radio I could have asked them to toss over a bottle of hootch. I don't think I'd bother with satnavs, ham, watermakers, loran, or radar. Radar would be handy, but a friend who had one told me that when it failed one night he was terrified because he had become so used to it.

Anyway, you want a good compass, a couple of anchors, and a fire extinguisher or two. Some sort of skiff is handy, as is *lots* of rope. I always carry a good smoking jacket and pair of slacks so I can pass for normal in a yacht club.

Here's a list of "necessities" for a 1,500-mile, singlehanded winter cruise from New York to North Carolina and back in a 23-foot catboat. This excerpt from C.P. Kunhardt's *Small Yachts, Their Design and Construction*, is just about as pertinent today as it was when first published in 1885. (Forest and Stream Publishing, 1891. Reprinted and abridged by *WoodenBoat*, 1985.)

1. Shore Clothing & Toilet
Suit of clothes, pair of shoes, felt hat, neckties, umbrella, gloves, soap, shaving soap, razor, razor strop, shaving brush, looking

glass, blacking brush, hair brush, toothbrush, thin socks, underclothing, white shirts, collars, cuffs, handkerchiefs, collar and cuff buttons, tooth powder, towels, scissors, needles and silk, buttons etc., pins, whisp broom.

2. Yachting Togs
Two pair trousers, two jerseys, two neckerchiefs, buckskin gloves, pea jacket, canvas shoes, leather slippers, leggings, worsted cap, cloth cap, old vest, oilskin coat, southwester, rubber sea boots, insoles for same, rubber gauntlets, suit overalls, woollen drawers, woollen undershirts, thick socks, cheap handkerchiefs, jack-knife.

3. Cooking Gear
Oil stove, oil, wick, stew pot, pan, coffee pot, ladle, griddle, kettle, tin cans, dipper, market basket, water breaker, cake boxes, knife tray.

4. Cabin Table
3 cups, 3 saucers, 3 plates, 3 dishes, 3 tumblers, 1 pitcher, 3 knives, 3 forks, 3 tablespoons, 3 teaspoons, can opener, corkscrew, dish towels.

5. Cabin Furniture
Cabin lamp, clock, mattress, pillow, blanket, brackets, wire baskets, mats, photos, pictures, chintz curtains, camp chair, foot stool, oilcloth, screw hooks, picture tacks, oilcloth covers.

6. Navigation
Compass, barometer, anchor light, lantern, thermometer, binoculars, lead & line, fog horn, charts, frame, parallel rule, dividers, log book, flare up, burgee.

7. Boatswain's Stores
Bucket, scrub brush, salt-water soap, swabs, broom, 25-lb. anchor, 30-lb. anchor, skiff, 6-ft. oars, rowlocks, luff tackle, sponge, spare rope, ball marlin, palm and needles, twine and wax, cotton, old canvas, leather, shackle, eyebolts, thimbles, etc.

8. Carpenter's Chest
Hatchet, scraper, sandpaper, rasp, draw-knife, screwdriver, chisel, gimlets, saw, vise, brace and bits, compass saw, putty, nails, screws, tacks.

9. Medicine Chest
Quinine, cathartic pills, opium pills, sticking plaster, glycerine, liniment.

In addition,

10. Sketching & writing materials

11. Library

12. Stores

13. Photography equipment.

"As it is next to impossible to keep a small boat dry inside," wrote Kunhardt, "such articles as would be damaged were enveloped in pliable oilcloth. The charts were cut into sections and the one in use inserted for the time being in a common glass-covered picture frame. This enabled it to be set up in the cockpit and preserved from the wet."

This seems like a pretty complete description of outfitting for a cruise. Dampness inside isn't such a problem for a wood boat with a plywood deck, although of course the damp air can't be avoided. I'd add only a few items, such as an extra place setting so I could feed four people, a plastic sextant, a short-wave receiving radio for time signals, and a cassette tape player. I carry a few life jackets too, along with fishing equipment.

I've always carried a sheet of 1/4-inch plywood cut into various sizes, from 12 inches square up to maybe 12 by 36 inches, whatever will store conveniently. I start a few nails in the edges, in case I need to make a patch in a hurry. Along with this goes two 1-gallon cans of roof-patch tar plus a few cable clamps that fit the rigging.

I wouldn't carry a gun. I've been in some real ratholes in my time and never had problems that weren't quickly ended by me staying friendly. The only places you really need a gun it's illegal to carry one, and the "authorities" will give you far more hassle than the local bad guys if they find the thing. Besides, in a pinch you can blast a melon farmer with your flare gun. If you insist on carrying a piece, I'd make it a single-shot 12-gauge. You can buy a used one for 50 bucks, it doesn't look as serious to a cop as a hogleg or an assault rifle, there's not much that can go wrong with it, and it's absolutely deadly close in, which is why police use them for riot control. Tell the cops you use it for killing sharks.

This isn't a cheerful subject, but a problem with carrying weapons is if you're paranoid and break it out, then what do you do? A bad situation can become very bad in a hurry. Besides, the type of guys you need the gun against probably know far more about the subject than you do. I've been told by people from the Caribbean, where problems do happen, that big, shiny, production boats are far more of a target for bad guys than our wood boats. All you have to do is change the name on a production boat and nobody is the wiser. But boats like we own, well, bad guys know they can't steal ours, because the boats are one of a kind. If our boat pulls in, somebody will surely notice, and wonder why we aren't on it.

Since Mr. Kunhardt outfitted his boat, opium tablets have become illegal. I think carrying a good pain killer is wise, and most physicians will give you a prescription if they believe it's for a Ship's Medicine Chest. It's all over-the-counter in Mexico if you can't get it here, but I'd first talk to the U.S. Customs Service about it. This "zero tolerance" stuff is a pain in the tail, and it would be a shame if some zealous DEA guy took your boat because he didn't like the looks of your medicine chest.

A good dinghy is essential. I like wood ones, because the inflatables are fragile, don't row worth a hoot, and always get stolen. Even *Hagar* can carry a plywood skiff. I make them boxy, with a sheer that will fit the deck crown of the sailboat, and I carry the skiff crossways on deck. I had one 5 feet 6 inches long and it floated two people OK. Make it out of 1/4-inch plywood, and epoxy and glass the outside.

You'll read more details in the books on the subject of outfitting, but one thing rarely mentioned is cable for anchoring. Many commercial boats use wire rope for the anchor, because it has better chafe resistance than rope, stores easily on a drum (unlike chain), and isn't very expensive. Something to think about.

Regarding anchors, whatever pattern you use, carry big ones and lots of line. Many people use an anchor that looks like a plow, and I hear it's very good. I could never use it myself, after reading L.F. Herreshoff's comment on it: "Mankind spent centuries developing the most efficient shape for plowing the soil, and what happens; some con man comes along and sells it for an anchor!"

Finally, carry lots of paperback books. When you arrive in a new harbor lots of skiffs will head out to see you, and the first time it happens you'll think they're all being friendly. Most are of course, but they *also* want to trade books!

Well, that's all I have to say about that—for now, anyhow. Remember, as Tristan Jones says; "When in Danger or in Doubt, hoist your sails and Bugger Off Out!"

BOAT PLANS

Here are some plans for cruising boats that have worked well for other backyard builders. These boats are economical and relatively easy to build, assuming you follow the directions laboriously spelled out in this book. In some ways that's the hard part, and you may lose a few friends along the way.

These days, too many folks are content to sit around talking about what they're *gonna* do someday. If you actually get up and *do* it, you become a threat. And if you do it in a way unendorsed by your particular peer group—in this case, the boating set—then you're an absolute menace.

Few of your friends are apt to have much of a background in the old-time workboat ways this book has been talking about; seeing you build your boat this way will drive some of them wild. They've read all the new books that stress sewing and miracle goops and nonferrous metals and séances, they *know* you're doing it wrong, and they won't hesitate to tell you. Under this kind of peer pressure, it's hard to keep on track.

A case in point is a fellow building a *Juno*. He started off OK, but he was building in a marina where there were lots of other guys working on boats, all of whom knew as much as he, which was zilch. Rather than follow the plans, he got brainwashed by advice from people whose ideas are based on the currently hip crop of advertiser-supported magazine articles. So far he's spent more on epoxy alone than I spent for my entire hull. The last I heard he was talking about a double-spreader rig.

I've said this right along and I'll say it again: Very little of the information in this book is original with me. What's new is a boat-building philosophy that combines the best of traditional-workboat wood boatbuilding with a West Coast counterculture outlook based on both a love of tradition and an awareness of life in a Target Area.

Building a cruising boat, even a little guy like *Hagar*, takes time and, yes, some money. More than a few relationships have soured when one member takes on a project like this, and it's always sad to see a boat sold because of a divorce. So, if you're living with somebody, involve your spouse in the deal. Although it's still typical that the male is the driving force behind building a boat, times and roles are changing. One of the nicest boats I know was built by a couple, and Diana learned carpentry and did more than half the work by herself.

Anyway, these plans are all feasible projects for you backyard builders. The boats all are likely to float rightside up, and can be built for a reasonable amount of money—as long as you don't mind bucking the Accepted Wisdom of the Yachting Purists Party Line.

These drawings are the complete plans for the boats. Since they're rather small and maybe awkward to read, I've written out the specs after the drawings, which, along with the book, is really all you need. Some people feel more comfortable with large-scale plans, however. If you want 'em for some reason, they're available from me: George Buehler, P.O. Box 966, Freeland, WA 98249, U.S. of A. I generally keep an ad in the classified pages of some of the yachting mags, so if I've moved, and assuming I'm still kicking, you can get the current address that way.

The dimensions given for the materials are minimums. Go heavier if you want. Also, when I write 4-by I mean a lumberyard 4-by, which is probably 3½ inches. When I write ¾ inch, however, I mean just that. Note that all plans show Sabb diesels. These are great engines, but hard to find in the U.S. nowadays. You can substitute any solid marine engine, like Lister or Volvo.

The sail areas shown are small by current standards. This is because I've just drawn in the basic working sails, rather than including the full "fore-triangle," on the theory that your sail plan should be efficient and handy for general use. You can always buy a large genoa if you want. Don't let a sailmaker talk you out of the multiple reefs. Some will try!

HAGAR

LOD: 28'
Beam: 8'
Draft: 4' 6"
Displacement: 8,000 lbs.

For me, boats are personal things. If my boat has a masculine name I call it *He*—never mind umpteen centuries of boating tradition. With that in mind, although *he* is 28 feet long, there's less interior room than commonly seen in production boats this size. In *Hagar*'s favor, he's seaworthy, easy to build, and inexpensive. This is a trimmed-up version of a boat I built for $3,500 in 1972 and cruised slowly to Puerto Vallarta, Mexico, then to Hawaii, where I sold it. Last I heard it was still there. I had no engine, polypropylene halyards, and minimal everything else, and you know what? It didn't bother me in the least. Funny how being broke doesn't bother you when you're young.

I designed this boat right after the trip, and it incorporates a number of refinements that suggested themselves along the way. I sold lots of plans for *Hagar*, and they've been built all over: Yugoslavia, Guatemala, Canada, Australia, and America. One fellow took seven years, one less than two months. Several were built for around $5,000 (without engine); one cost $20,000. Some have stayed around the coast, some have gone cruising, and so far nobody got drownded that I know of. The only complaint I've heard is that she's initially tender, so make the ballast as heavy as you can. That tenderness is part of the design, since the idea was to have comfortable motion at sea.

Over the years I've done several versions for different people, and all are included here. The canoe stern is an added hassle to build, but it looks good. I don't care for the round bow shown with the canoe stern lines, and suggest you use the straighter one. I also don't like the raised sheer house, and would change that to a normal deckhouse with 10-inch minimum side decks.

I got a letter from one builder which I'll share parts of with you-all.

> *George:*
> *We've lived aboard* Raisuli *for four years now . . . . We've been as far north as Desolation Sound, Canada, and as far south as San Diego. We gunkholed down the whole West Coast . . . . The worst ride was crossing the Columbia Bar in a full gale. The best has been in southern California with warm reaching breezes and 6-plus knots for mile after mile . . . . The lobster on Catalina Island aren't bad either!*
> *Matt & Karen Mathews*

If you have short pockets but want a boat to go to sea in, *Hagar* will do the job.

Keel:	6-by minimum
Floor timbers:	3-by
Frames:	2×4
Gussets:	$3/4''$ plywood
Chine:	2 pieces $3/4''$
Stringers:	2 pieces $3/4'' \times 2^{1/2}''$
Planking:	$3/4''$ minimum or two layers $3/8''$ plywood
Deck beams:	$1^{1/2}'' \times 3''$
Deck:	2 layers $3/8''$ plywood

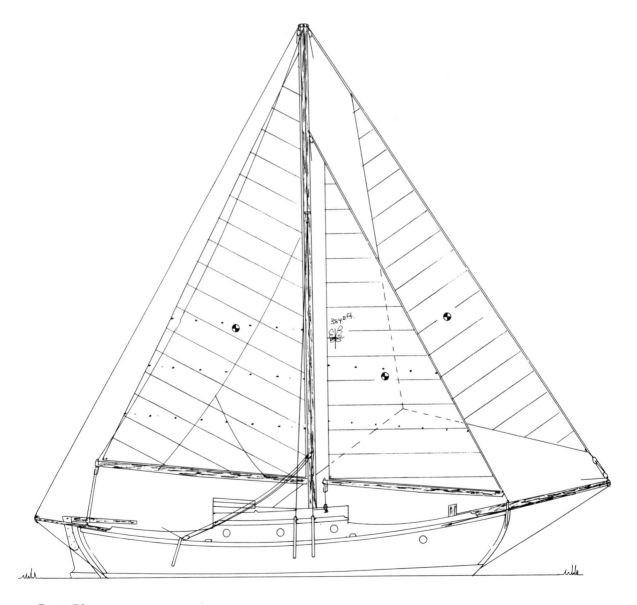

Boat Plans

296

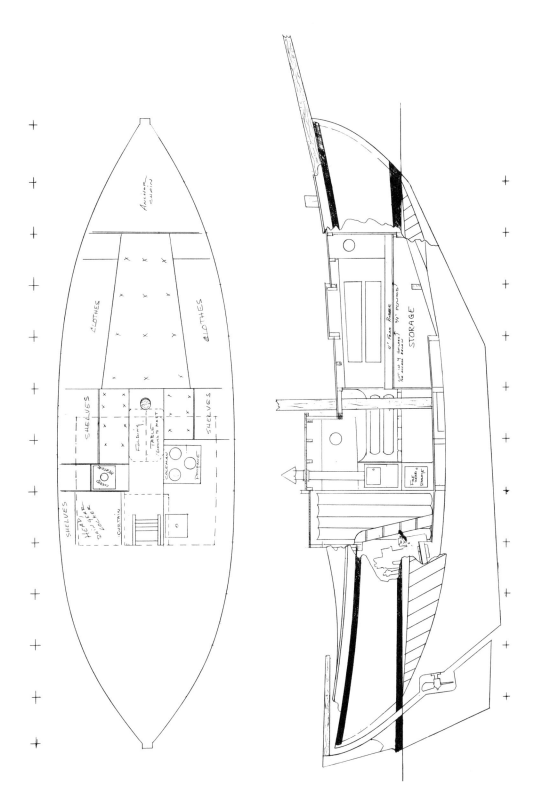

Hagar

TABLE OF OFF-SETS

"HAGAR" for "HAGAR OF THE NORTH"

Design by George Buehler
Box 10274 Bainbridge Isl. WA 98110

HEIGHTS

	A	0	½	2	3	4	5	6	7	8	9	10	B
SHEER	7-5-2+	7-1-2	6-9-5	6-7-9	6-5-9	6-5-6	6-4-3	6-8-0	6-10-2	7-1-4	7-5-6	7-10-7	6-4-0
CHINE		4-6-0	4-3-3	4-1-7	4-0-6	4-0-1	4-0-0	4-0-4	4-1-1	4-2-2+	4-3-6	4-6-0	
RABBET		4-6-0	3-5-1	2-9-1	2-5-0	2-3-3	2-3-4	2-4-3	2-6-3	2-10-5	3-6-2+	4-6-0	
KEEL	3-11-0		1-1-2	0-1-1	— STRAIGHT —		0-7-0	0-7-0	0-10-6	— STRAIGHT —			4-2-0

HALF WIDTHS

	A	0	½	2	3	4	5	6	7	8	9	10	B
SHEER	0-3-0	1-9-1	2-11-4	3-7-1	3-10-7	3-11-4	3-7-6+	3-11-0+	3-3-7	3-4-7	0-9-2	1-9-1	0-3-0
CHINE	0-3-0	0-3-0	1-6-2	2-5-5	3-0-4+	3-4-4	3-5-3	3-3-2	2-10-5	2-2-7	4-0-1	0-3-0	0-3-0
RABBET	0-3-0		— STRAIGHT —										0-3-0

- ALL MEASUREMENTS IN FT-INCHES — 1/8 S (EIGHTHS) INCHES
- STATION SPACING 27"
- WL TO BASELINE — 4'6"
- LENGTH BETWEEN PERPENDICULARS 27'
- BEAM — ABOUT 8'
- DRAFT — 4'6"
- DISPLACEMENT — ABOUT 8,500 POUNDS

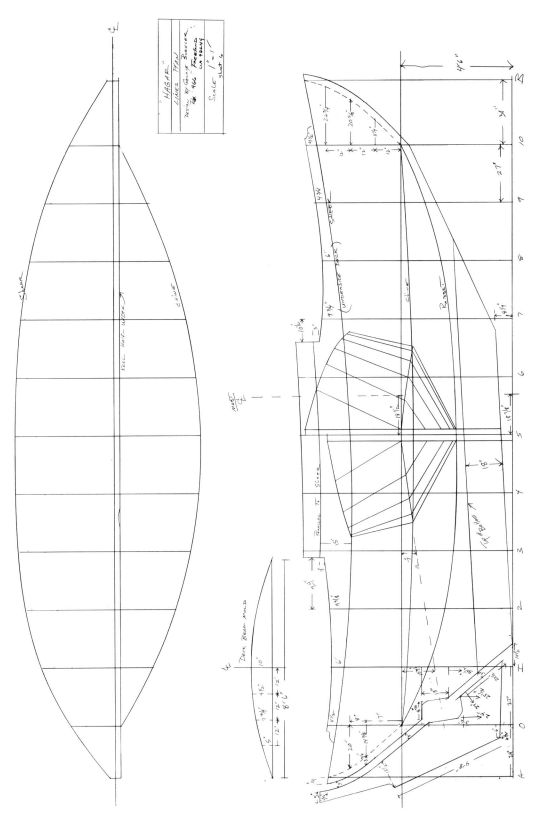

Hagar

299

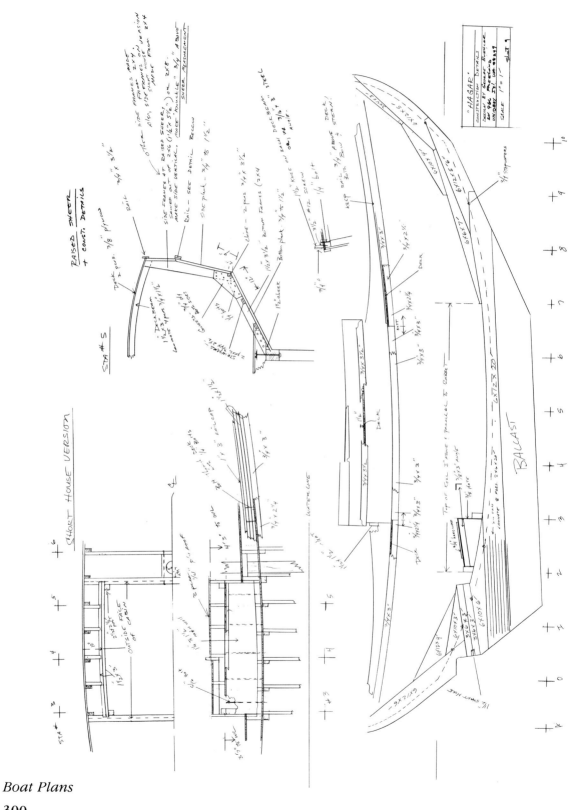

Boat Plans

300

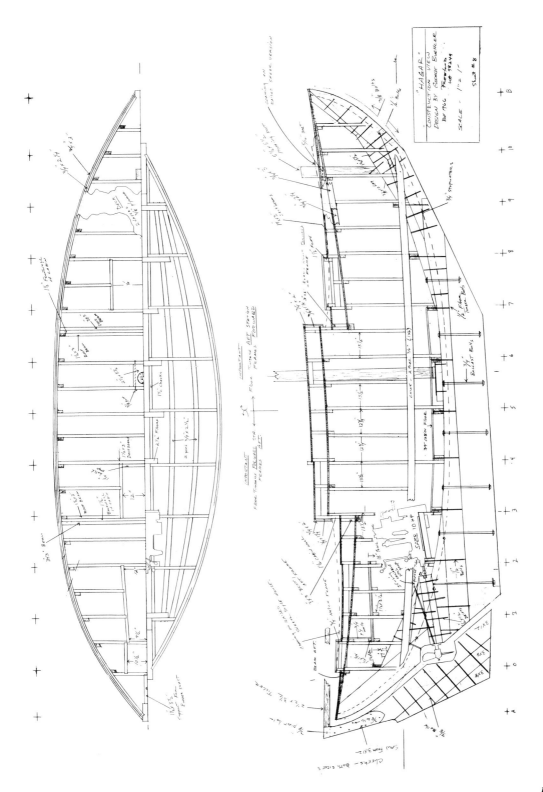

Hagar

301

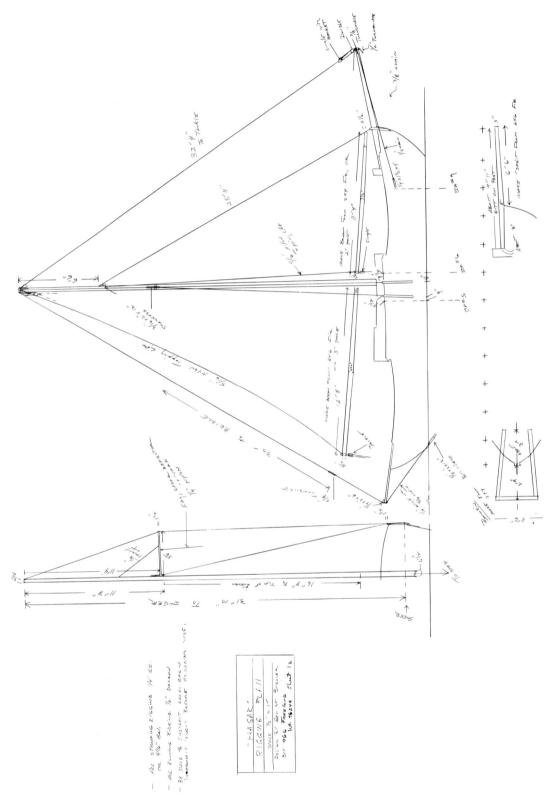

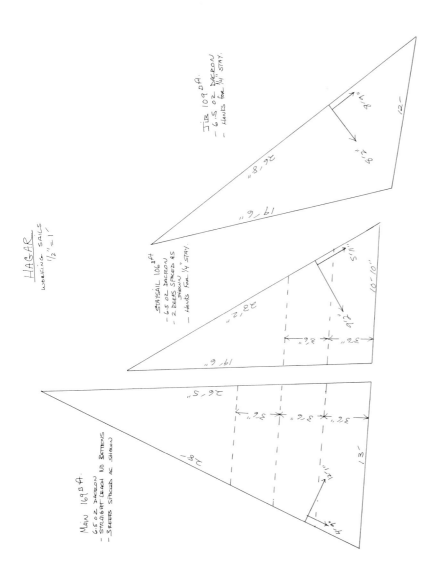

HAGAR
WORKING SAILS
1/2" = 1'

JIB 109□Ą
- 6.5 OZ DACRON
- HANKS FOR 1/4 STAY.

26'8"

19'6"

9'2"

8'4"

12'

STAYSAIL 106□Ą
- 6.5 OZ DACRON
- 2 REEFS SPACED AS SHOWN
- HANKS FOR 1/4 STAY

23'2"

19'6"

3'6"

3'6"

9'2"

5'11"

10'10"

MAIN 169□Ą
- 6.5 OZ DACRON / NO BATTENS
- STRAIGHT LEACH
- 3 REEFS SPACED AS SHOWN

26'5"

3'6"

3'6"

3'6"

3'6"

12'11"

4'6"

13'

JUNO

LOD:	35' 6"
Beam:	10' 7"
Draft:	5' 6"
Displacement:	22,500 lbs.

I built this boat for myself and we lived aboard for four years. I got bogged down doing stuff and never really cruised her seriously, but Len Feldman, her current owner, has used her as a traveling doctor's office in remote parts of Alaska for nine years now.

Juno worked out just great. She sails well and handles so nicely that, going due downwind in a steady breeze, you can just tie off the tiller and she'll steer herself. She's comfortable for two to live on, and a great seaboat. Like *Hagar*, she's a bit tender for her size, but it's all a tradeoff. Gary Webb sailed his down the coast and wrote saying she rides like a '53 Buick.

The plan shows 3 headsails. Try it! It doesn't cost much extra, and if you don't like it you can always toss the middle wire and buy the other jib shown on the plan. But the three headsails are a lot of fun to play with, and really look good. For instance, once I was tagging along at a schooner meet, and was invited to sail along. I said something like; "Oh, I can't. I don't have a schooner." They said, "*Juno* is a schooner!"

Keel:	8-by minimum
Floor timbers:	4-by
Frames:	2×6
Gussets:	3/4" or 1" plywood
Chine:	3 pieces 3/4"
Stringers:	2 pieces 1½"×3"
Planking:	1" minimum or 3 layers 3/8" plywood
Deck beams:	1½"×3"
Deck:	3 layers 3/8" plywood

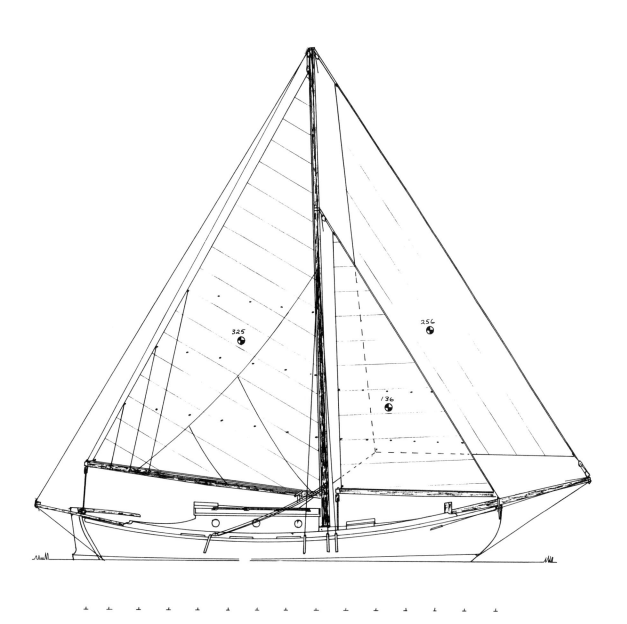

Juno

305

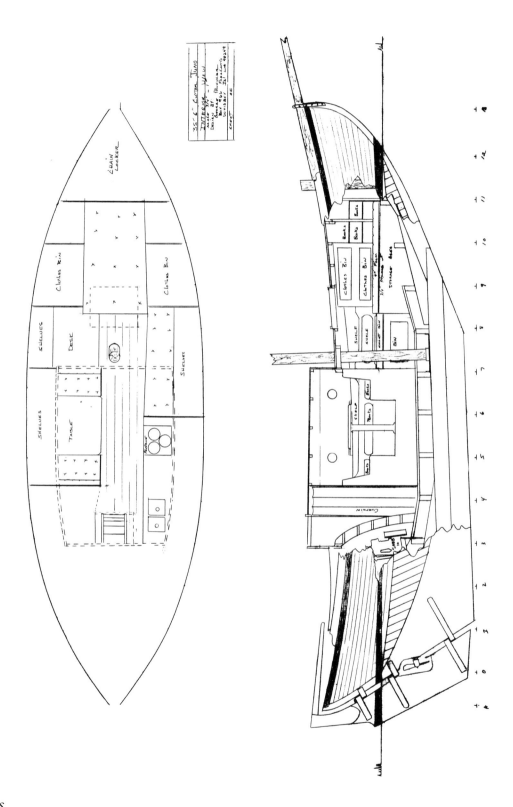

TABLE OF OFFSETS

35'6" Cutter "JUNO"

HEIGHTS ABOVE BASE

STA #	A	0	1	2	3	4	5	6	7	8	9	10	11	12	B
SHEER	8-10-5	8-5-4	8-0-2	7-8-3	7-5-4	7-4-0	7-3-4	7-4-3	7-5-6	7-8-2	8-0-0	8-4-4	8-10-4	9-4-7	10-1-5
CHINE	5-6-0	5-6-0	5-2-2	4-11-4	4-9-5	4-8-1	4-7-5	4-7-6	4-8-3	4-4-1	4-0-4	5-0-6	5-3-0	5-6-0	
RABBET	4-11-3⁺		3-5-0	2-8-0	2-2-4	1-11-4	2-0-5	2-4-4				3-6-4	3-9-6	4-10-6	
KEEL		4-9-3													

HALF-WIDTHS

STA #	A	0	1	2	3	4	5	6	7	8	9	10	11	12	B
SHEER	0-3-6	1-8-5	3-2-3	4-2-4	4-10-1	5-2-3	5-3-6	5-3-5	5-3-4		4-10-1	4-3-4	3-4-2	2-0-5	0-3-6
CHINE		0-3-6	1-6-2	2-6-7	3-4-0	3-10-0	4-1-3	4-2-4	4-1-2	3-9-5	3-3-3	2-6-1	1-6-5	0-3-6	0-3-6
RABBET/KEEL	0-3-6				← STRAIGHT LINE →										0-3-6

WL TO BASELINE — 5'6"
COMMON STA SPACING — 2'9"

	10	11	12
WL - #1	3-3-6	3-10-0	0-11-2
WL - #2	3-10-0	2-9-7	1-5-6
WL - #3	—	3-3-0	1-10-4

Juno

307

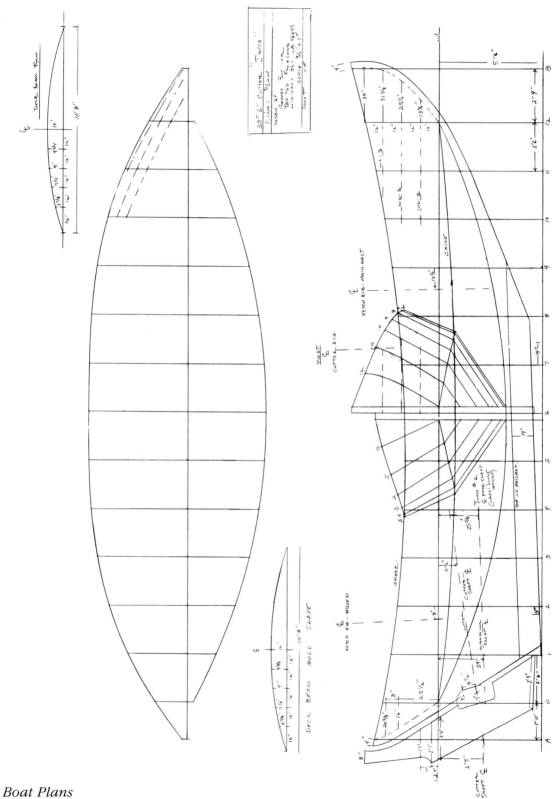

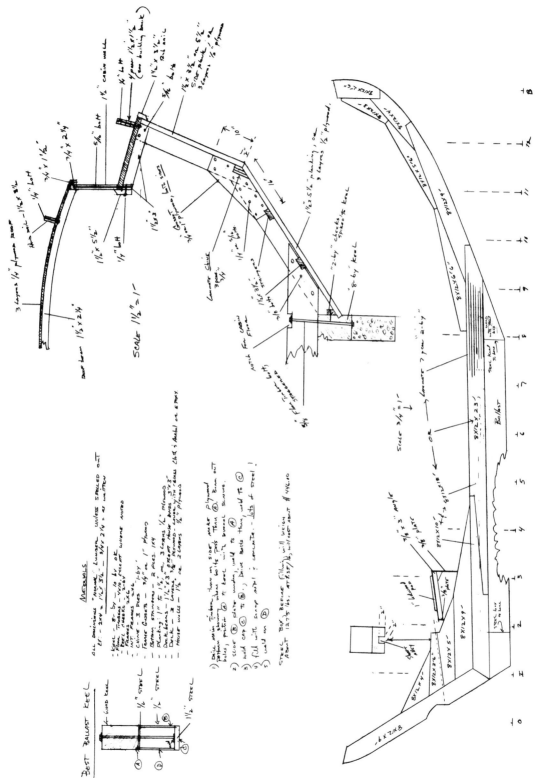

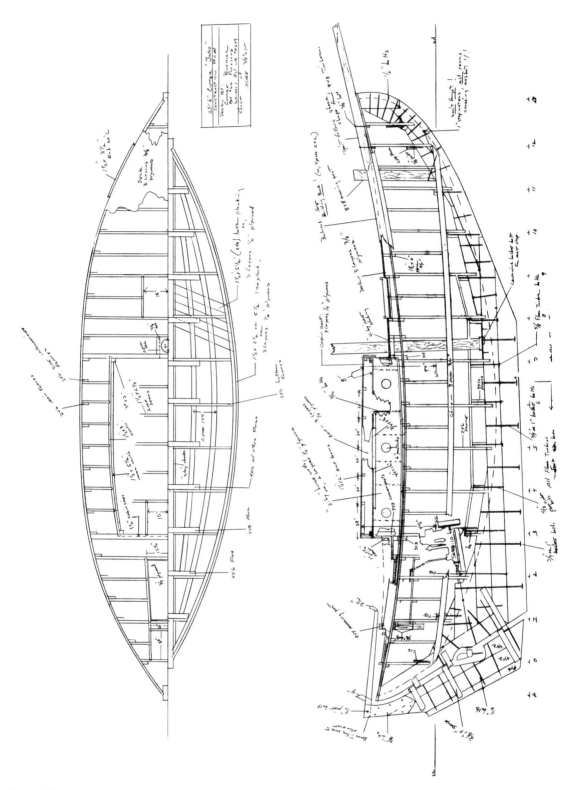

Boat Plans

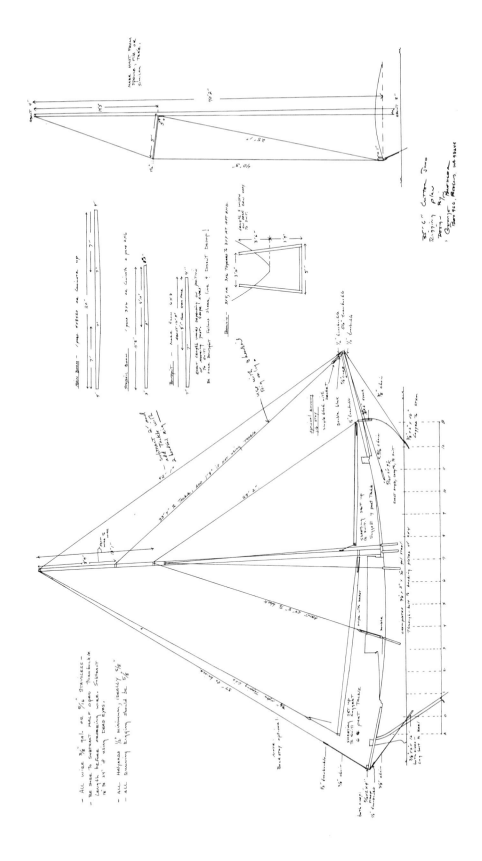

Juno

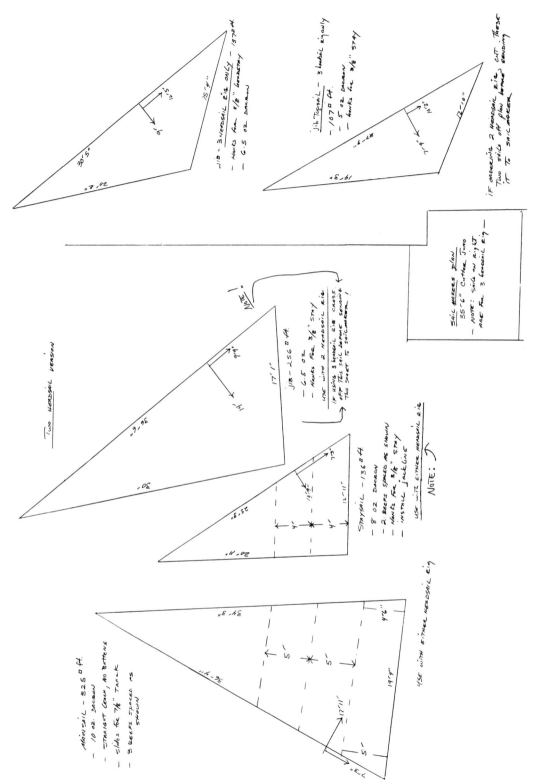

JIB - 3HEADSAIL RIG ONLY - 137□ ft
- HANKS FOR 5/8" HEADSTAY
- 6.5 OZ DACRON

JIB TOPSAIL - 3 RADIAL RIG ONLY
- 107□ ft
- 5 OZ DACRON
- HANKS FOR 3/8" STAY

IF ORDERING A HEADSAIL RIG, CUT THESE
TWO SAILS OFF PLAN BEFORE SENDING
IT TO SAILMAKER.

SAIL AREAS PLAN
35'6" CUTTER JUNO
- NOTE: SAILS ON RIGHT
ARE FOR 3 HEADSAIL RIG

TWO HEADSAIL VERSION

JIB - 256 □ ft
- 6.5 OZ FOR 3/8" STAY
- HANKS WITH 2 HEADSAIL RIG
IF USING 3 HEADSAIL RIG CROSS
OFF THIS SAIL BEFORE SENDING
THIS SHEET TO SAILMAKER.

Note:

STAYSAIL - 136 □ ft
- 8 OZ DACRON
- 2 REEFS SPACED AS SHOWN
- HANKS FOR 3/8" STAY
- INSTALL JACKLINE
USE WITH EITHER HEADSAIL RIG

NOTE:

MAINSAIL - 825 □ ft
- 10 OZ. DACRON
- STRAIGHT LEACH, NO BATTENS
- SLIDES FOR 7/8" TRACK
- 3 REEFS SPACED AS SHOWN

USE WITH EITHER HEADSAIL RIG

ARCHIMEDES

LOD: 43'
Beam: 13' 6"
Draft: 6'
Displacement: 42,000 lbs.

I think this boat would be a *lot* of fun. It has a definite traditional look about it, almost too much, maybe. But I think a wood boat can look like this and pull it off. A plastic boat looks phony if it tries to look shippy.

This guy has an interior that will house a couple, but there's also a wheelhouse and a small hold area. Steering is rope, hooked to the tiller. The engine is in the hold and can have "bin-boards" around it so you can pack stuff in there, too—motorbikes, crab traps—all sorts of stuff.

You could leave off the wheelhouse and have a great big cockpit, which is nice in warm climates, or use a **V**-drive on the engine and move it aft, which would let you build another low cabin or a wheelhouse where the engine now sits.

If you're building in plywood, make the forward frames and the stem rabbet straight lines and shape the stem face to look "clipper." The alternative is to diagonally strip the bow as described in Chapter 7 under Plywood Planking.

Keel:	8-by minimum, suggest 10- or 12-by
Floor Tim-	
bers:	4-by
Frames:	2×6 OK, 3×6 better
Gussets:	1" plywood
Chine:	4 pieces 3/4"
Stringers:	2 pieces 3/4"
Planking:	1½" or 3 layers ½" plywood
Deck Beams:	2¼"×4½" (Note: with plywood deck, deck beams can be on main frames alone)
Deck:	1½"×2½" fir planking, or 3 layers ½" plywood

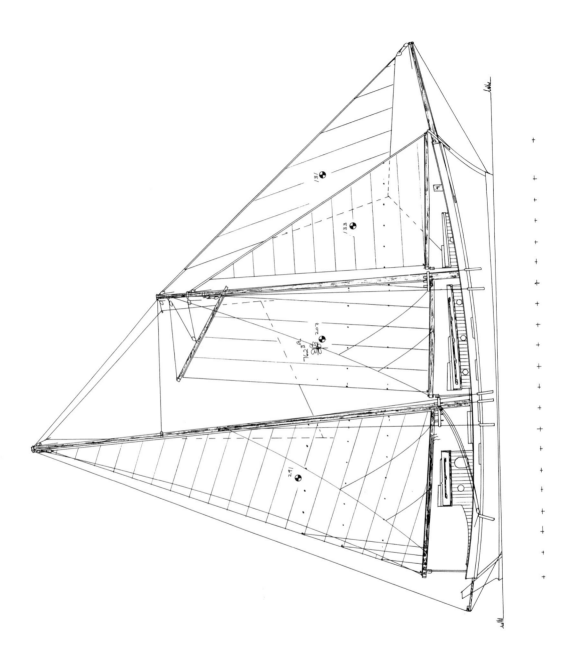

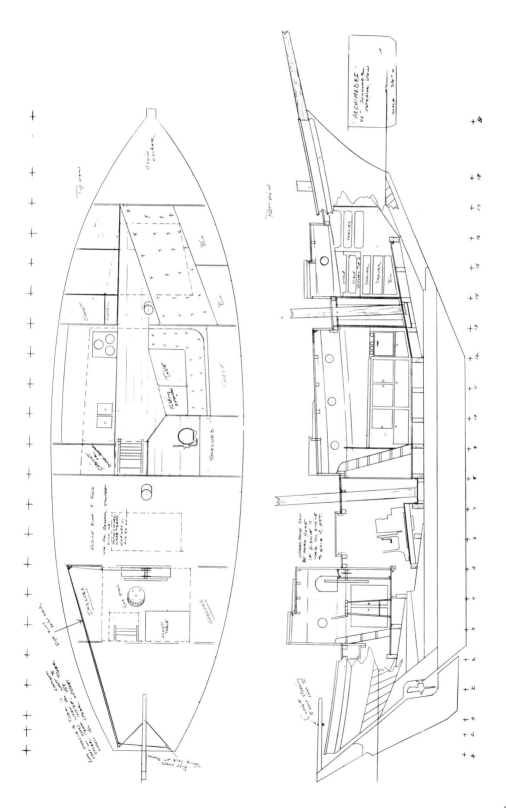

Archimedes

315

LEIGHTS (Heights)

	A	C	0	1	2	3	4	5	6	7	8	9	10	11	12	13	14	15	16	17	18	B
Sheer	8-10-3	8-5-5	8-3-0⁻	8-1-0⁻	7-11-5	7-10-6⁺	7-10-3	7-10-3	7-10-7	7-11-3⁺	8-0-4	8-1-7	8-3-7	8-6-0	8-8-4	8-11-4	9-3-0⁻	9-7-0	9-11-3	10-4-4⁻	11-2-4⁻	
Chine		7-2-7	6-1-6⁺	6-7-0	6-3-2	6-0-0	5-9-6	5-7-6	5-6-0	5-4-5	5-3-6	5-3-1	5-3-2⁻	5-3-4	5-5-0	5-5-1	5-6-1	5-7-4	5-2-4	5-4-0	5-10-5	6-0-0	6-0-0
Rabbet			6-0-0	5-1-3⁺	4-4-4	3-9-4⁺	3-4-0	3-0-0	2-7-3	2-6-3	2-6-1	2-6-4⁻	2-7-5⁻	2-4-3	3-0-1	3-4-0	3-9-4	4-4-6	5-1-5	6-0-0		
Keel				1-1-4	0-0-2⁺			0-0-4	←— STRAIGHT —→						←— STRAIGHT —→				5-8-0⁺			

HALF-WIDTHS

	A	C	0	1	2	3	4	5	6	7	8	9	10	11	12	13	14	15	16	17	18	B
Sheer	2-1-6	3-3-4⁺	4-4-4	4-9-7	5-4-4	5-9-4	6-1-1	6-3-3⁺	6-4-6	6-5-6	6-6-3	6-6-2	6-5-4	6-5-7	6-3-7	6-1-4	5-9-7	5-4-3	4-9-0	3-11-4	2-11-0	0-3-6
Chine	1-8-1	2-3-0	3-3-0	4-0-5	4-8-3	5-2-0⁻	5-5-7	5-8-4⁺	5-9-3	5-8-5	5-7-3	5-4-7	5-1-4				4-8-4	4-0-4	3-0-6	1-10-0⁺	0-3-6	
Rabbet			0-3-6					←— STRAIGHT —→											0-3-6			
WL #1																	4-6-1	3-6-0	2-3-0⁻	0-7-6		
WL #2																	4-10-6⁻	3-1-0⁻	2-8-3	1-1-7		
WL #3																	5-3-0⁺	4-4-5	3-3-0	1-9-3		
WL #4																				2-6-4		

— ARCHIMEDES —

43' CARGO SCHOONER 2/81

TABLE OF OFF-SETS

DESIGN BY GEORGE BUEHLER
BOX 10274 BAINBRIDGE ISL. WA 98110

— ALL MEASUREMENTS IN FEET-INCHES-⅛ INCHES.
— COMMON STATION SPACING 2'0".
— WL TO BASELINE — 6'0".

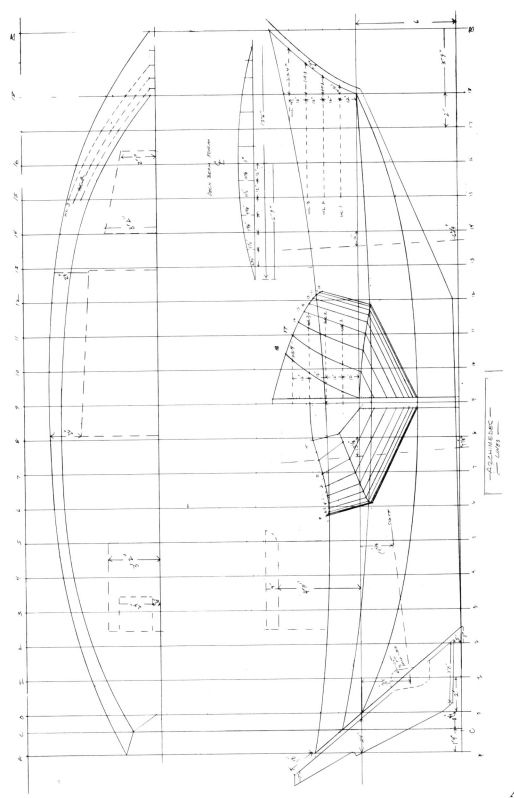

Archimedes

317

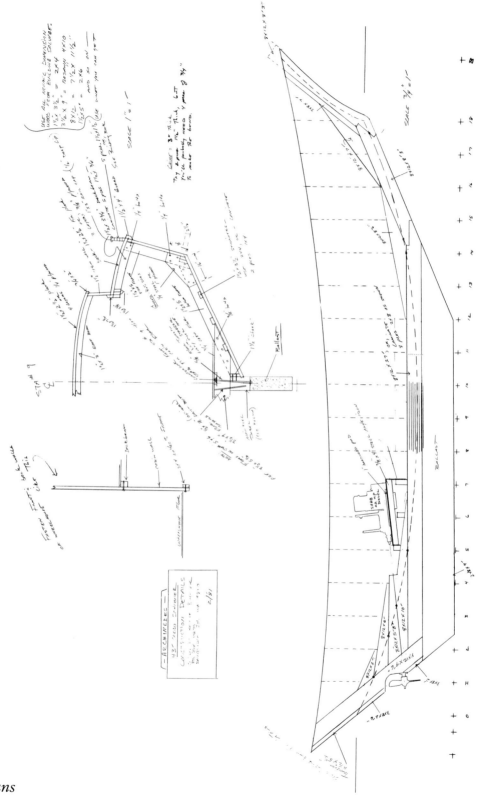

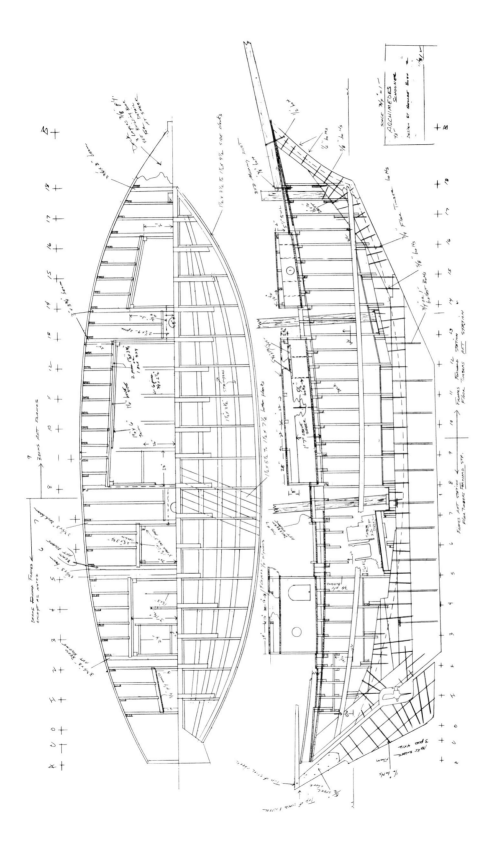

Archimedes

319

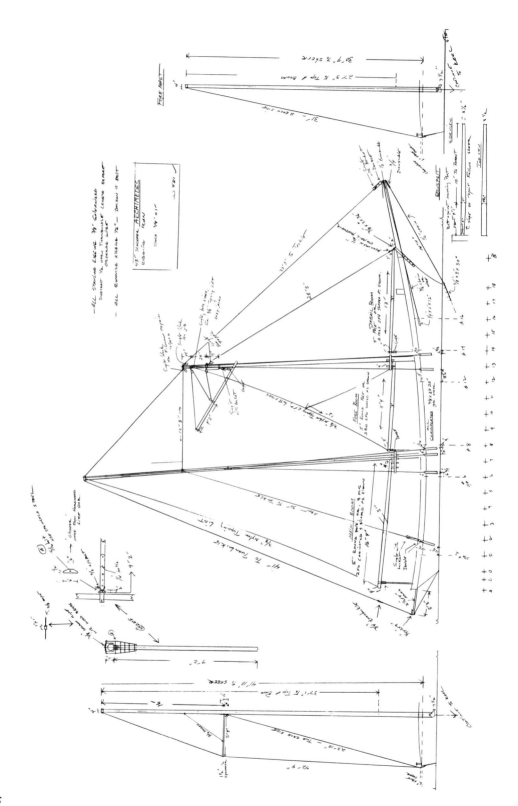

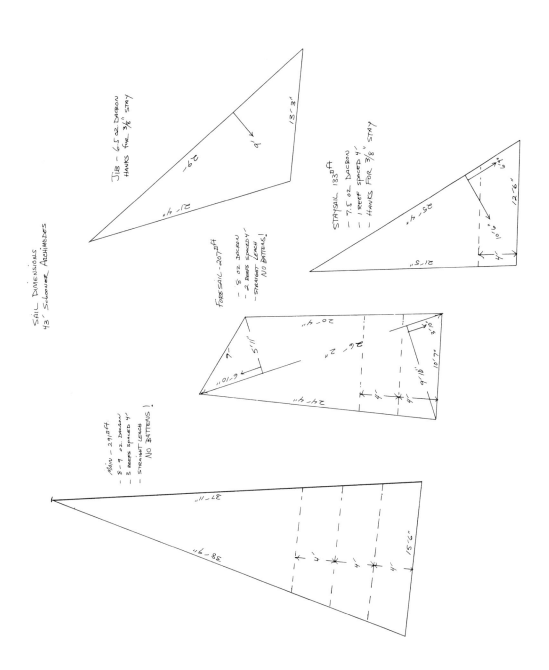

SAIL DIMENSIONS
43' SCHOONER ARCHIMEDES

JIB – 6.5 OZ DACRON
HANKS FOR 3/8" STAY

13' 3"

9'

29'

21'-4"

STAYSAIL 130 ☐ft
– 7.5 OZ DACRON
– 1 REEF SPACED 4'
– HANKS FOR 3/8" STAY

9' 4"

12'6"

25'-4"

10'6"

4'

21'-5"

FORESAIL – 207 ☐ft
– 8 OZ DACRON
– 2 REEFS SPACED 4'
– STRAIGHT LEACH
NO BATTENS!

20'-4"

9'

5'11"

6'10"

26'-2"

3'10"

10'7"

9'10"

24'-4"

4'

4'

4'

MAIN – 297 ☐ft
– 8 – 7 OZ DACRON
– 3 REEFS SPACED 4'
– STRAIGHT LEACH
NO BATTENS!

37'-11"

38'-9"

4'

4'

4'

15'6"

Archimedes

321

OLGA

LOD: 42′
Beam: 12′ 2″
Draft: 7′
Displacement: 46,000 lbs.

This boat generated a bit of criticism because of the extreme dead-rise, which is supposed to be no good. However, the design was a joint effort between myself and Doug Gilson, who built the first one, and neither of us could understand why a round-bilge boat like a Block Island Cow Horn could have so much deadrise while a chine hull couldn't.

I mentioned earlier the static you'll get as you build, from people who've read everything and know you're doing it wrong. This boat was built near Pt. Townsend, Washington, which has become a sort of Mecca of woodboat and aspiring woodboat people, and a lot of these folks did *not* like this boat. The further along Doug got the more he heard how poor the design was, and I even got several letters, quoting dead gurus like Chapelle and Herreshoff, caustically demanding to know why such and such was so and so. Eventually even I started doubting the design, so it must have been very hard for Doug to keep up the morale, but he did, and did a beautiful job of building her.

When I heard the launch date was set I wasn't gonna go and was off at a travel agent finding out about Brazil, but when I returned I found a note on my shop saying even *death* wasn't a good enough excuse not to be there. So, with thoughts about going into the beach cabin business, I went to the launching, and was relieved to see the boat float rightside up. And a few months later when she was rigged, as a marconi cutter, I was relieved to see she sailed forwards rather than backwards. Doug and Suzi went on a shakedown cruise to Hawaii and back, then a year later took off to the South Pacific, where they still are.

The boat sails quite well, although she's initially tender for her size. Doug says she heels over, then seems to start to lift, and the faster she goes the more she lifts, which is interesting. Although certainly not a raceboat, she once beat an aluminum "performance boat" by an hour from Maui to Honolulu. The weather was breezy, and she has the weight to carry through chop. But then Doug is pretty gung ho about sailing, and I've heard he's even taken the boat sailing/surfing off Waikiki beach, to the total disbelief of guys on surfboards around him. And me, too, when I heard about it.

This gaff ketch version was designed for a guy in Norway. Apparently logs from Siberian log booms wash up on his beach, and he wanted a big simple boat in the Scandahoovian tradition in which to salvage them. This design was a natural because she's very simple, and certainly big and heavy. The hull form is so buoyant that you could really pack in a lot of stuff before you get her down to her waterline. Man, I'd love to hear the comments this hull must be generating from the "Old Boys" up that fjord! The scantlings for *Olga* are the same as for *Archimedes*.

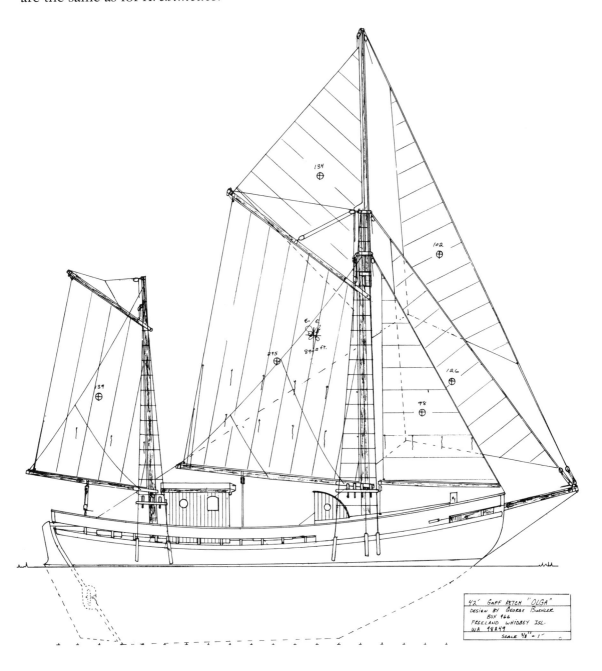

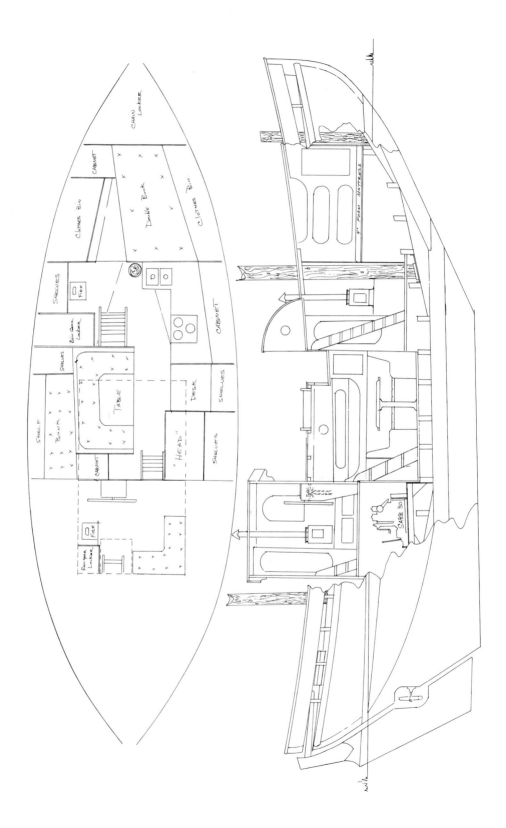

Boat Plans

324

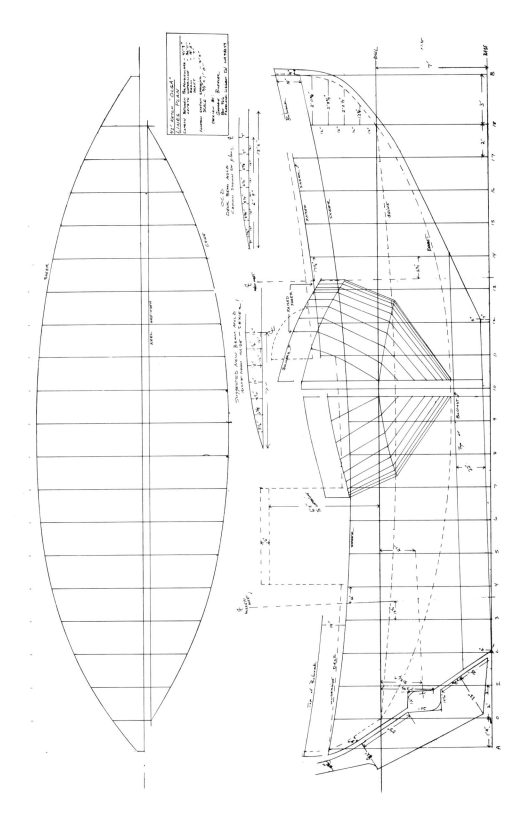

Olga

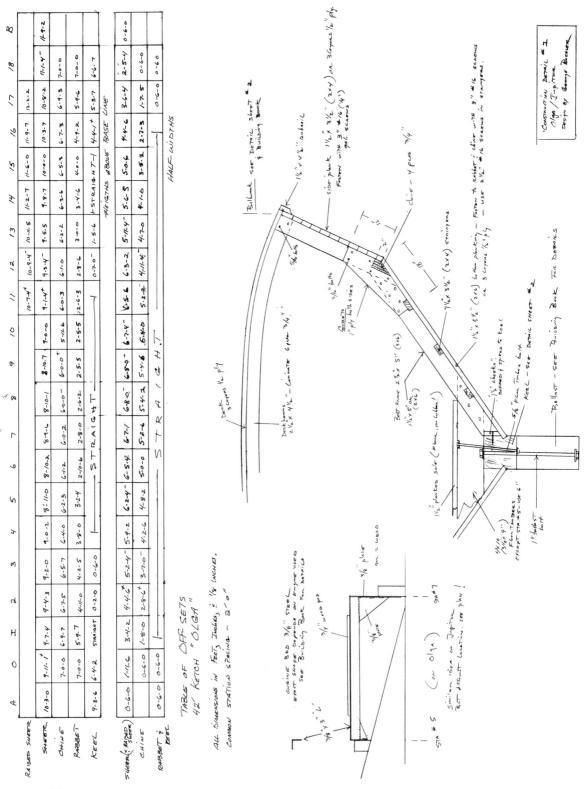

TABLE OF OFFSETS
42' KETCH "OLGA"

ALL DIMENSIONS IN FEET, INCHES, & ⅛ INCHES.
COMMON STATION SPACING — 2'-0"

HEIGHTS ABOVE BASE LINE

	A	O	1	2	3	4	5	6	7	8	9	10	11	12	13	14	15	16	17	18	B
RAISED SHEER												10-7-4	9-1-4	9-3-4	9-5-5	9-7-7	10-0-0	10-3-7	10-5-2	11-1-4	11-4-2
SHEER	10-3-0	7-11-1	9-4-3	9-2-0	7-0-2	8-11-0	8-10-2	8-10-2	8-9-6	8-10-1	8-10-7	7-0-0	7-1-4	9-3-4	9-5-5	9-7-7	10-0-0	10-3-7	10-5-2	11-1-4	11-4-2
CHINE	7-0-0	6-9-7	6-5-7	6-4-0	6-2-5	6-2-3	6-2-4	6-0-2	6-0-0	6-0-0	5-4-6	6-0-3	6-1-0	6-2-2	6-2-6	6-3-6	6-5-3	6-7-3	6-9-3	7-0-0	7-0-0
RABBET	7-0-0	5-9-7	4-4-0	3-9-0	3-2-4	2-0-6	2-8-2	2-5-5	2-5-5	2-6-3	2-8-6	3-0-0	3-4-6	4-2-1	4-4-7	5-4-6	5-7-6	6-6-7			
KEEL	6-4-2	STRAIGHT				← STRAIGHT →						1-5-6	0-7-0		STRAIGHT						

HALF-WIDTHS

	A	O	1	2	3	4	5	6	7	8	9	10	11	12	13	14	15	16	17	18	B
SHEER (RAISED SHEER)	0-6-0	1-4-6	3-4-2	5-2-4	5-9-4	6-2-4	6-5-4	6-7-1	6-8-0	6-8-0	6-2-4	6-5-6	6-3-2	5-4-4	5-6-5	5-0-6	4-4-6	3-6-4	2-5-4	0-6-0	
CHINE	0-6-0	1-8-0	2-8-6	3-7-0	4-2-6	4-8-2	5-0-0	5-2-6	5-4-4	5-4-6	5-4-6	5-2-0	4-7-0	4-4-2	4-1-0	4-1-6	3-6-2	2-2-3	1-7-5	0-6-0	
RABBET & KEEL	0-6-0	0-6-0					STRAIGHT					0-6-0	0-6-0								

Construction drawing labels:

Bulwark — see detail sheet #2 & building book

Side plank 1½" × 3½" (2×4) on 3 layers ½" ply. Fasten with 3" #16 screws (4½"). 9½" × 4½" bubinch

Deck beams 1½" × 5" laminate 6 per 3/4"

Deck ½" ply 3 layers ½" ply

5/16" bolts

Gussets 1" ply both sides

Chine — 4 pcs ¾"

1½" × 3½" (2×4) stringers

1½" × 3½" (2×4) bottom planking — fasten to rabbet, glue with 3" #16 screws (4½") — use 3 layers ½" ply

Boat frame 2½" × 5" (2×6)
1½" × 5" (2×6)

1½" planked sole (from 2×6 lumber)

1½" cleats, bolted & spiked to keel

5/16" frun timber bolt

Keel — see building book for details

Ballast — see building book for details

Engine bed ⅜" steel. Exact shape depends on engine used. See building book for details.

⅜" plate

¾" wood pad

STA #5 (or Olga)

Similar idea on Jupiter but different location. See plan!

4×10 (3½×9) frun timbers except STA #5 — use 6"

1¼" fore timber bolt

1½" keel bolt

CONSTRUCTION DETAIL #1
Olga/Jupiter
Design by George Buehler

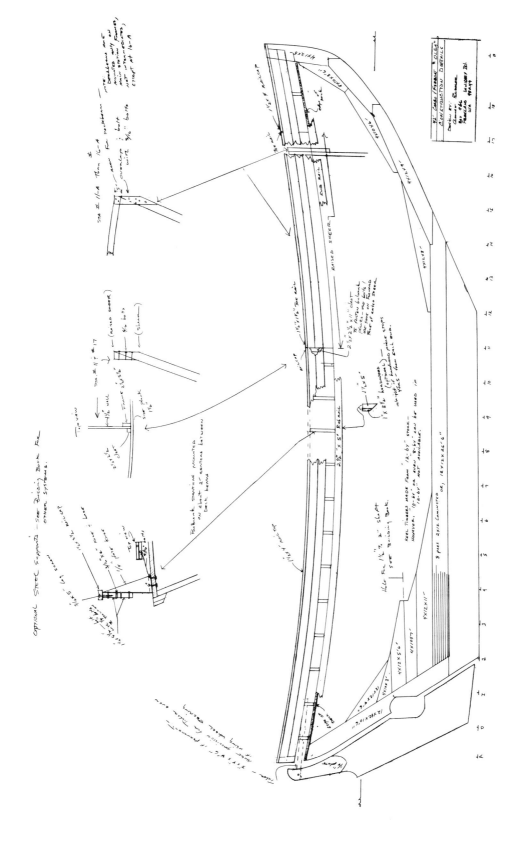

Olga

327

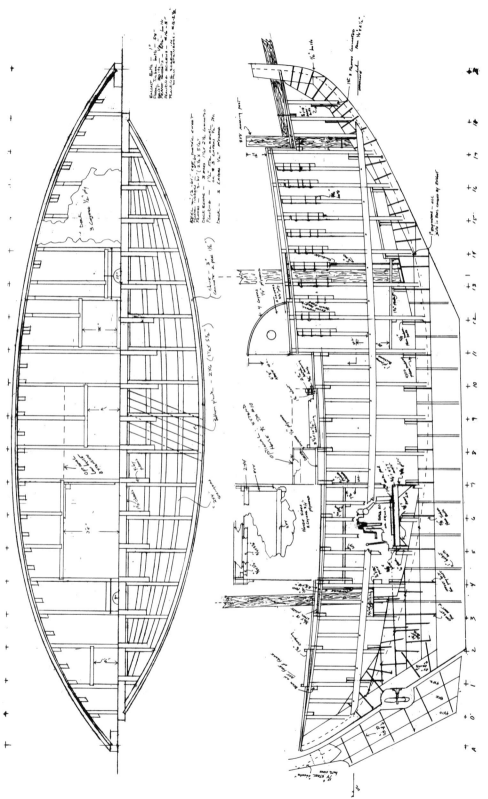

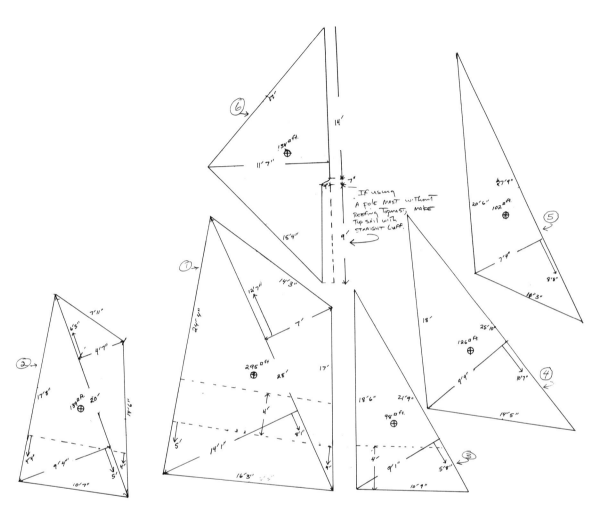

① **Mainsail**
295 SQ. FT. — 10 OZ DACRON
STRAIGHT LEACH - NO BATTENS
½" DIAMETER GROMMETS IN LUFF
FOR LACEING TO MAST.
SPACE REEFS AS SHOWN.

② **Mizzen**
139 □ FT. — 10 OZ DACRON
STRAIGHT LEACH — NO BATTENS
½" DIAMETER GROMMETS IN LUFF
FOR LACEING TO MAST
SPACE REEF AS SHOWN

③ **Staysail**
98' SQ. FT. — 10. OZ DACRON
HANKS FOR 3/8" STAY.
SPACE REEF AS SHOWN.

④ **Jib**
186 SQ. FT. — 8 OZ. DACRON
HANKS FOR 3/8" STAY.

⑤ **Jib Topsail**
102 SQ FT. — 6 OZ. DACRON
HANKS FOR 3/8" STAY.

⑥ **Main Topsail**
134 SQ. FT. — 6 OZ. DACRON
½" GROMMETS IN LUFF FOR
LACEING TO TOPMAST.

SAILMAKER'S PLAN SHEET
42' GAFF KETCH "OLGA"
DESIGN BY:
GEORGE BUEHLER
BOX 966 FREELAND WHIDBEY ISL. WA 98249
SCALE 3/8" = 1'

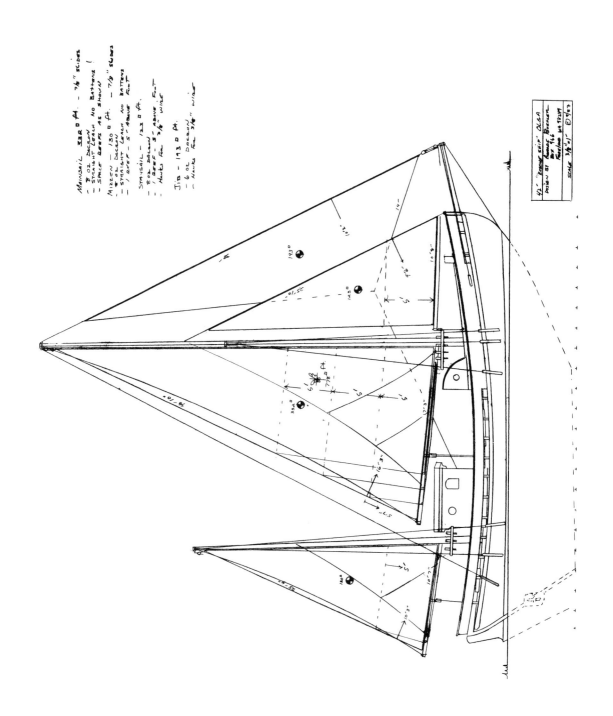

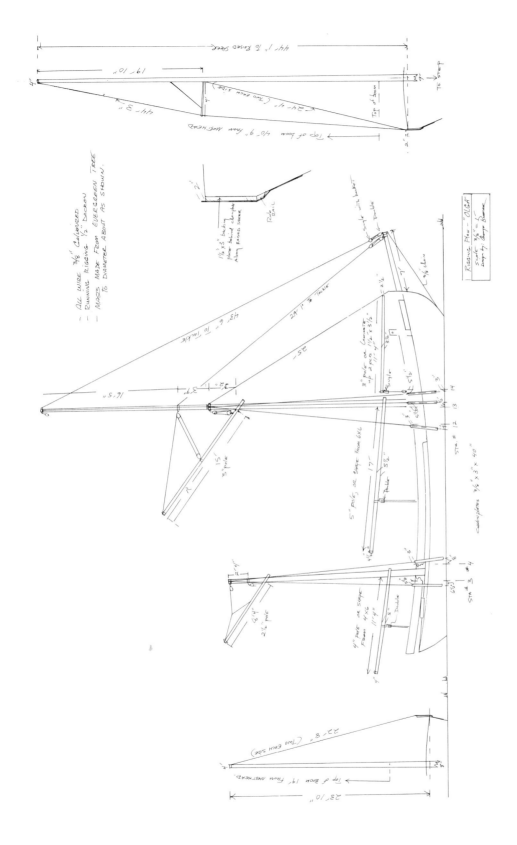

Olga

331

ALASKA

LOD: 34'
Beam: 11'
Draft: 3'6"

This is your basic powerboat, suitable for just messing around in or for small-time commercial fishing. If you wanted it as a pleasure boat you could lengthen the house, but as drawn I think it would be pretty nice for "serious" sportfishing and recreation. The house is big enough for weekend use, and there's lots of deck space for folding chairs. The hold could carry crab traps and whatnot. One good change, for recreational use, might be to drop the back deck to maybe 18 inches below the sheer so you'd feel like you were inside the boat when back there. If you do that, make it watertight and self draining.

Power shown is a 4-71 GMC, which is bigger than needed unless you're going to do some sort of work, in which case extra power is often handy. Any engine will serve, however, from a junkyard 6-banger on. There's plenty of room.

Keel:	8-by minimum
Floor Timbers:	4-by
Frames:	2×6, 3×6 OK
Gussets:	3/4" or 1" plywood
Chine:	4 pieces 3/4"
Stringers:	2 pieces 3/4"×3"
Planking:	1/2" or 3 layers 1/2" plywood
Deck beams:	2 1/4"×4 1/2"
Deck:	3 layers 1/2" plywood

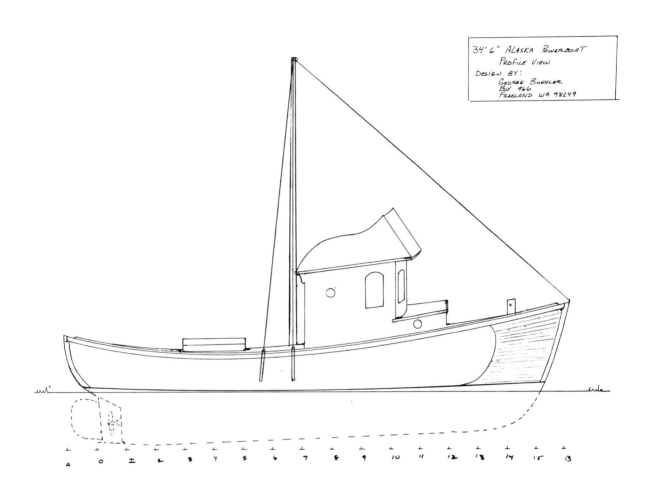

34' 6" ALASKA POWERBOAT
PROFILE VIEW
DESIGN BY:
George Buehler
Box 966
Freeland WA 98249

A   O   I   L   2   3   4   5   6   7   8   9   10   11   12   13   14   15   13

Alaska

333

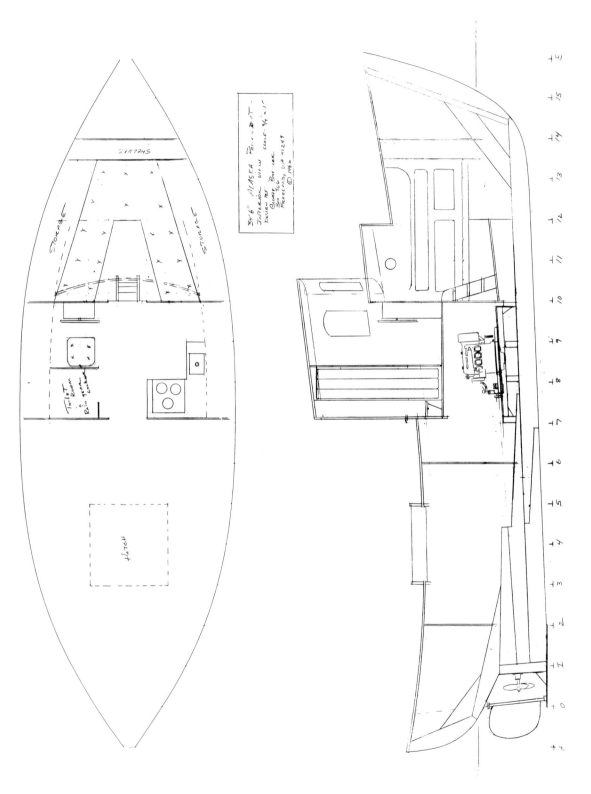

Within the drawing, handwritten labels include:

SHELVES

STORAGE

STORAGE

Toilet Room
Fresh
Water Tank

HATCH

34'6" ALASKA POWER BOAT
INTERIOR VIEW   SCALE 3/4" = 1'
DESIGN BY: BRUCE LEEK
George Buehler
Box 91760
Freeland, WA 98249
FREELAND 1980

34'-6" Alaska Powerboat
TABLE OF OFF-SETS

	A	O	1	2	3	4	5	6	7	8	9	10	11	12	13	14	15	B
SHEER	7-0-6	6-8-0	6-4-0	6-1-0	5-1-4	5-10-4	5-10-4	5-11-4-	6-1-3	6-4-0	6-7-0	6-10-5	7-2-4-	7-6-3	7-11-0	8-3-7	8-8-7	9-2-0
CHINE		3-4-0+	3-6-0	3-0-5	2-11-0+	2-10-0	2-10-0	2-7-3	2-7-0	2-9-3	2-10-0	2-11-0	3-0-0	3-0-3	3-2-0	3-3-7	3-6-0	
RABBET	3-6-0	2-10-7	2-4-2	1-11-0	1-7-0	1-4-3	1-2-3+	1-4-	1-1-0	1-0-7+	1-1-0	1-1-3	1-1-6	1-2-7	1-6-3		3-6+	2-10-2
KEEL	3-2-4	0-0-4	0-0-0	← STRAIGHT LINE →											0-10-7-	1-2-1		

	A	O	1	2	3	4	5	6	7	8	9	10	11	12	13	14	15	B
SHEER	0-3-6	2-11-0+	3-10-6	4-7-0	5-0-6	5-4-6+	5-6-0	5-6-4	5-6-4	5-5-4	5-3-4-	4-11-3	4-5-1+	3-8-0	2-8-2	1-6-4	0-3-6	
CHINE	0-3-6	1-5-3+	2-3-6	2-4-7	3-6-3	3-10-7	4-1-6	4-3-3	4-3-2	4-1-2	3-8-7	3-2-7	2-7-3	1-10-7	1-1-4	0-3-6		
KEEL	0-3-6			← STRAIGHT LINE →													0-3-6	
WL #1	0-11-6	2-0-5	3-0-3															
WL #2	1-4-6	2-6-3	3-6-3															

COMMON STATION SPACING - 2'-0"

WL TO BASELINE - 3'-6"

Alaska

335

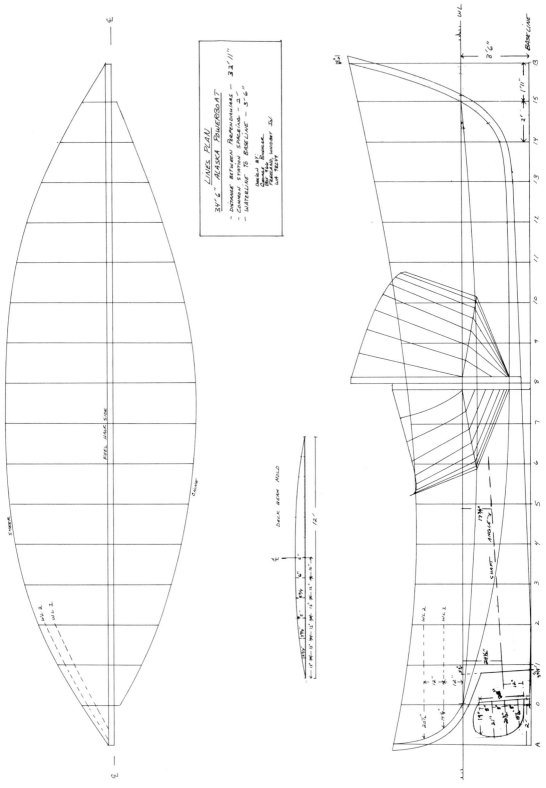

LINES PLAN
34' 6" ALASKA POWERBOAT

- DISTANCE BETWEEN PERPENDICULARS - 32' 11"
- COMMON STATION SPACEING - 2'
- WATERLINE TO BASELINE - 3' 6"

DRAWN BY:
CONRAD BUCHHOLZ
BOX 466
FREELAND, WHIDBEY ISL
WA 98249

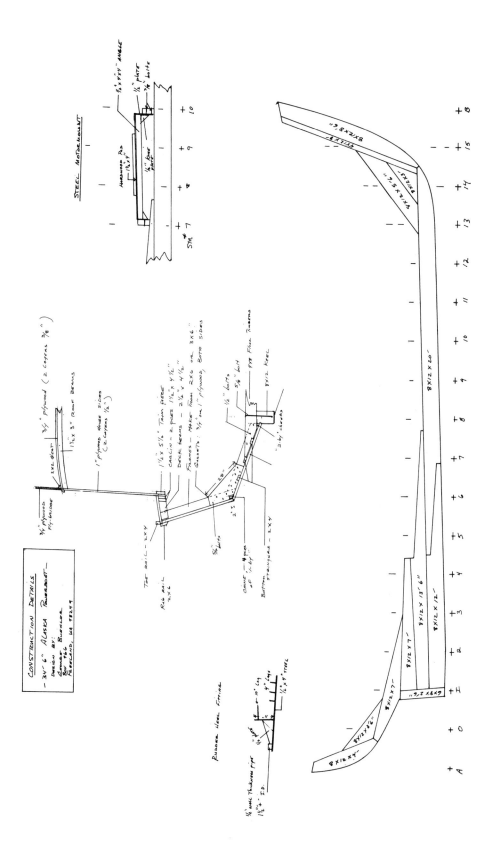

Alaska
337

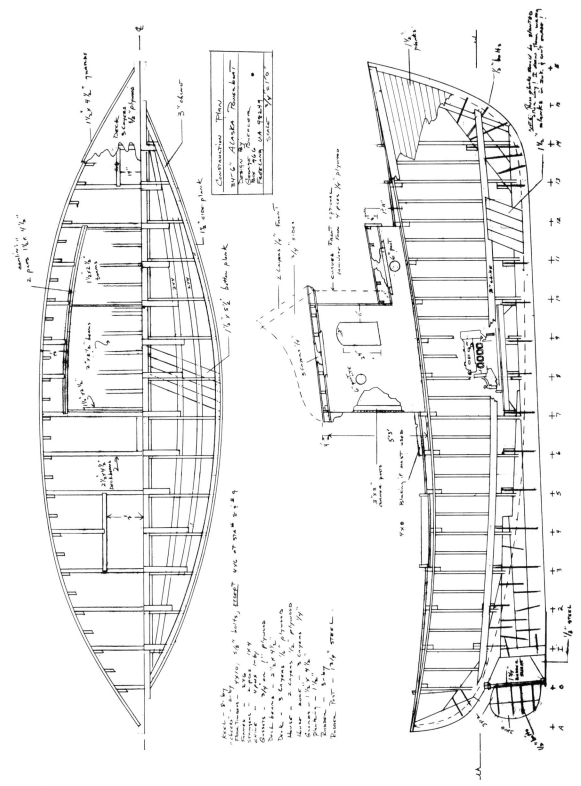

Construction Plan

34'-6" Alaska Powerboat

Design By
George Spencer
Box 966
Freeland WA 98249
Scale 3/4"=1'-0"

Keel — 8×8
"cheeks" — 2-by 4×10, 5/8" bolts, EXCEPT 4×4 at Sta's 8 & 9
Stem/Timbers —
Frames — 2×4's
Stringers — 2 pcs 1×4
Chine — 4 pcs 1-by
Gussets — 3/4" or 1" plywood
Deck beams — 2½"×4½"
House — 3 layers ½" plywood
Deck — 2 layers ½" plywood
Guards — 1½×4½
Planking — 1½
Rudder — 3-by
Rudder post — 1¾" steel.

JULLIAN ADDERLY

LOD: 30′ 4″
Beam: 10′ 3″
Draft: 3′ 6″

This is a very basic powerboat with a bigger interior than *Alaska*. *Jullian* is the sort of powerboat you hardly ever see any more; just a basic boat. Nowadays it seems almost all the boats come from the factories so pimped out it would kill a guy to actually cut a little bait on the side deck, or drag a fish over the stern. In fact, yesterday a 34-foot glass powerboat burnt up in Seattle. The radio said it was a $140,000 loss. Wow. How in the world can a 34-foot production powerboat cost that kinda bucks, and where in the world did the dealer find a guy who'd buy it? As they say: "There's a sucker born every minute," and "Nobody ever went broke underestimating the intelligence of the public."

A boat like *Jullian* probably offers the most fun for the buck of any boat. It's cheap and simple to build, just big enough to be safe in semi-protected water, rugged enough to be used hard, and roomy enough to house a few people on overnight trips. Power requirements are low because this hull wouldn't plane with a PT Boat engine, so any small engine will do the job. Although a 30- to 50-h.p. diesel would be ideal, a junkyard 6-banger will serve.

Keel:	6-by
Frames:	2×6 bottom, 2×4 side
Gussets:	3/4″ plywood
Chine:	2 pieces 3/4″
Stringers:	2 pieces 3/4″
Planking:	1 1/2″ or 3 layers 1/2″ plywood
Deck beams:	2″×3″
Deck:	2 layers 3/8″ plywood.

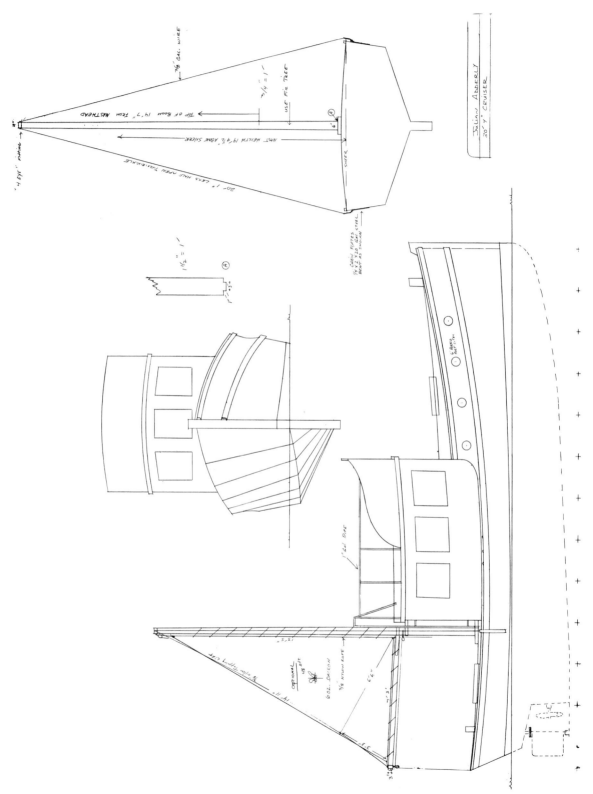

Jullian Adderly

HEIGHTS

	T	d	0	H	2	3	4	5	6	7	8	9	10	11	B
SHEER	5-8-5	—	5-7-0	5-4-3+	5-2-4	5-1-3	5-1-2	5-1-6	5-3-4	6-11-5	7-2-7+	7-7-2	8-0-4	8-6-5	9-1-2
CHINE	3-2-3	—	3-2-1	3-0-3	2-11-1	2-10-1	2-10-0	2-10-0	2-10-0	2-10-0	2-10-6	3-0-0	3-1-4	3-3-4	3-6-0
RABBET	—	—	2-9-4	2-2-7	1-9-1	1-4-3	1-0-5	0-10-5	0-10-2	1-0-3	1-7-2	1-3-0?	1-7-2	2-1-2	3-6-0
KEEL	—	—	2-9-4	2-2-7	0-0-0	STRAIGHT →					0-8-2	0-11-0	1-3-2	1-9-2	2-8-2

HALF-WIDTHS

	T	d	0	H	2	3	4	5	6	7	8	9	10	11	B
SHEER	3-11-3	—	4-2-0	4-6-0	4-9-0	4-10-7+	5-0-1	5-0-5	5-0-2	5-2-6	4-11-2	4-5-4	3-7-4	2-3-6	0-3-0
CHINE	—	3-7-6	3-8-0	4-0-5	4-4-3	4-7-0	4-9-0+	4-9-1	4-7-0	4-2-6	3-8-4	2-11-4	2-1-3	1-2-5	0-3-0
RABBET	—	—	0-3-0	←	STRAIGHT	→									0-3-0

ALL MEASUREMENTS TO OUTSIDE OF PLANKING ¢ WRITTEN IN FEET-INCHES — 1/8's INCHES
"+" OR "—" MEANS 1/16

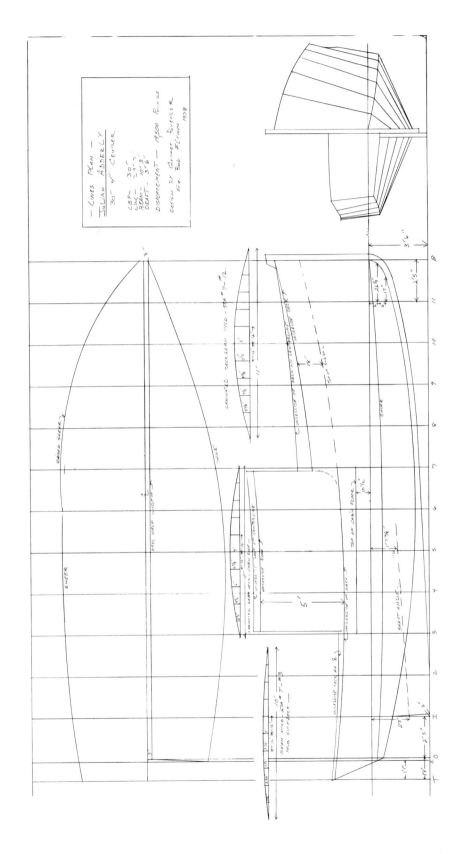

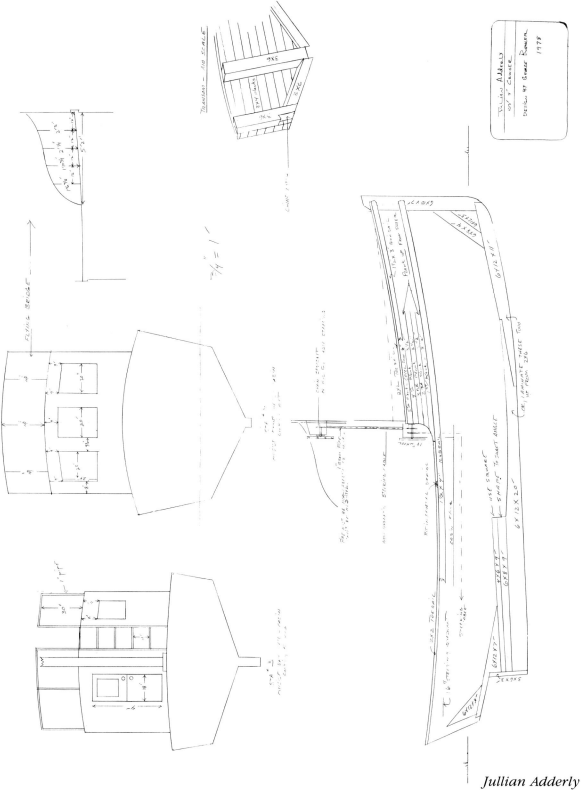

Jullian Adderly

343

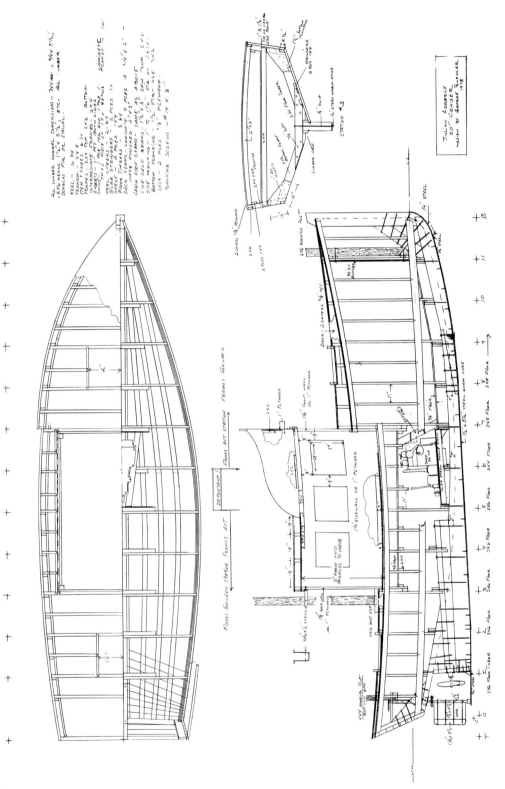

DRAGONFLY

LOD: 50'
Beam: 11' 6"
Draft: 6'
Displacement: 36,000 lbs.

Dragonfly is a good example of a Little Big Boat. Many of the photos in the book are of her. The idea was to create a singlehander that had room inside. You see, 30 feet is plenty big enough for a cruising boat, but there's no storage or elbow room. So with *Dragonfly*, I took the beam and freeboard of a fat 30-footer and added 20 feet. Now I have room for two people to be comfortable and lots of storage space. She's built like a tank, too. She's 6¹/₂ inches thick every 9 inches (the frame spacing), but because she's so, well, graceful, she still has a Displacement/Length ratio of 217, which is quite low. And because she's so trim, she doesn't need much sail area to move, so she can still be handled by one guy. Clever, huh?

Actually this isn't an original concept at all, although you don't see it very often. It also isn't an idea that will appeal to all, but it is valid, and since plans for this sort of boat are few and far between, I thought I'd include these here.

You'll see there are several sail plans, and two interior and deckhouse versions. I started off thinking of the three-master because it's so pretty. In fact, I've heard several were built this way. However, *Dragonfly*'s just too small for this rig to be very efficient, and it costs extra, too. It would make a beautiful motorsailer though. Anyway, practicality took hold, and I reduced her to one mast right in the middle. This is the most practical rig, but rather boring, I admit.

Next I decided I'd make one long house with a short wheelhouse attached, so I took the chain saw to the long deck and changed that. Now, the area which had been the aft cabin/wheelhouse is a 6-foot cockpit, which will be real pleasant laying about in, while anchored somewhere. Then I picked up some big anchors at a swap meet, and suddenly realized that I'm getting too fat and lazy to haul them up over the side, so I added the bowsprit. With a roller out on the 'sprit, I can haul the anchor up to that and never need to hoist it on deck. That's sort of sad though, because this boat's long overhanging "Indian Head" bow is really beautiful, and the 'sprit hides that. I might remove it yet, and have Brekke the Welder make me a real hawsepipe through the side planks like the Big Boys do. But as drawn, the 'sprit can be used to hold a huge roller-furling drifter. I picked up a furling system at another swap meet, you see.

The scantlings are the same as for *Archimedes* and *Olga*, although 3×6 for the frames is better, if you can find some. If not, use 2×6.

Boat Plans

346

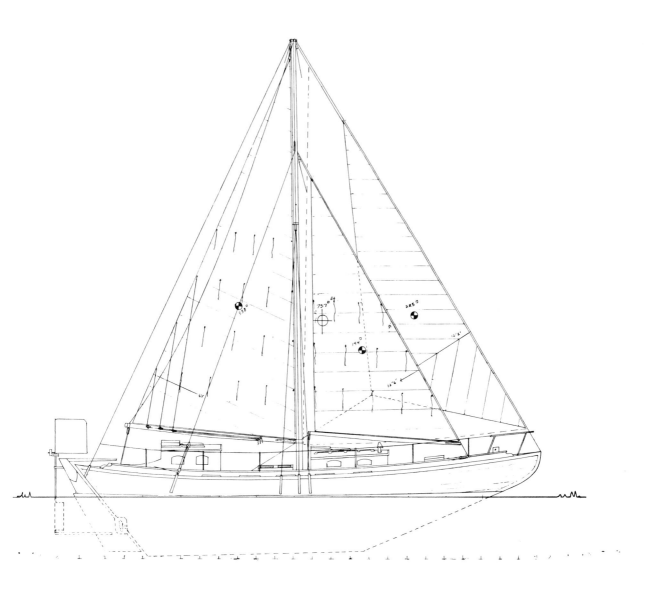

Dragonfly

347

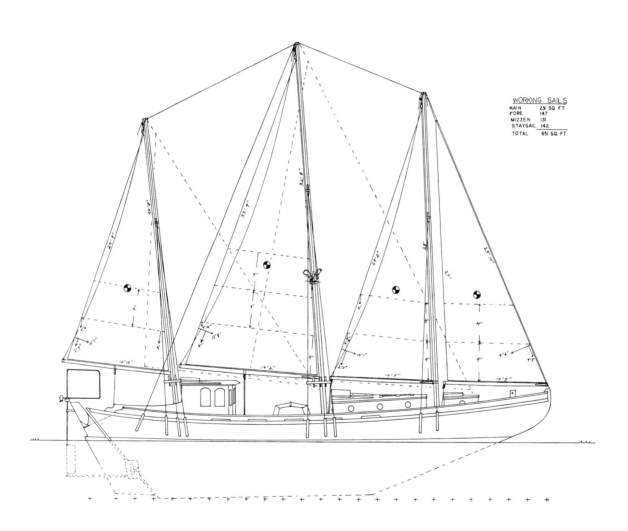

WORKING SAILS
MAIN   231 SQ. FT.
FORE   147
MIZZEN   131
STAYSAIL 142
TOTAL   651 SQ. FT.

Boat Plans

348

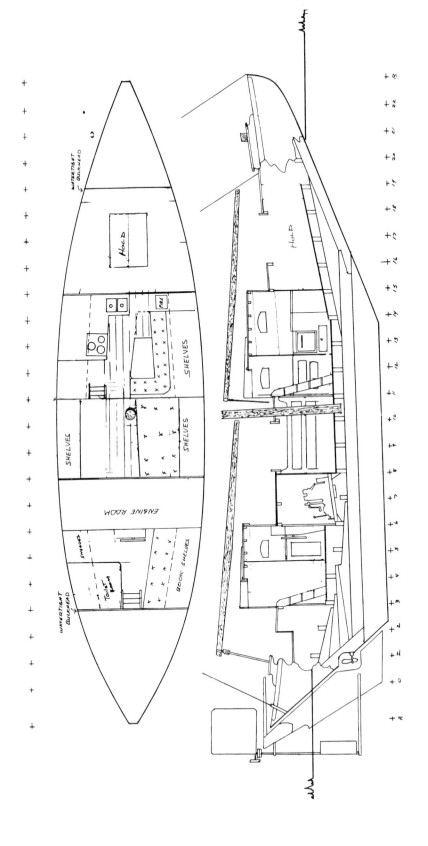

Dragonfly
349

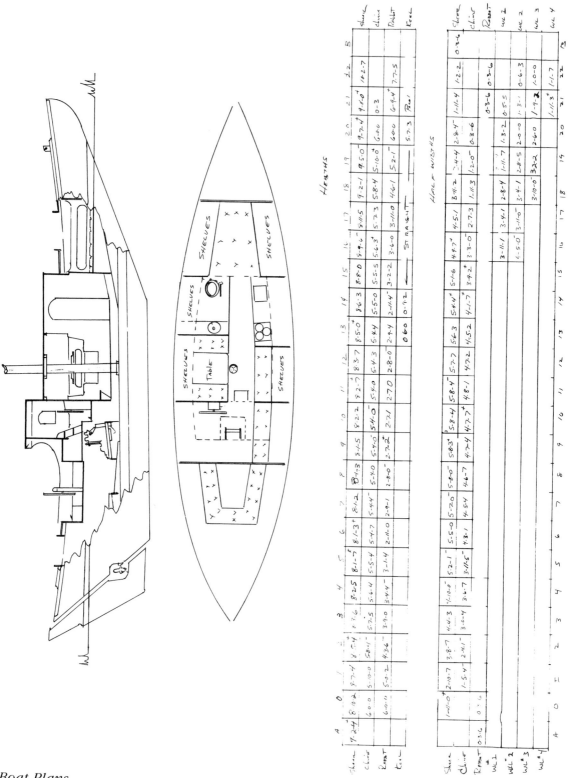

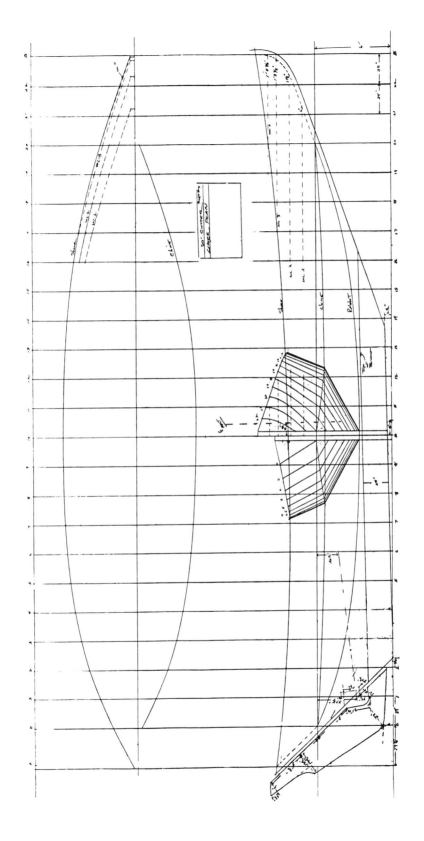

Dragonfly

351

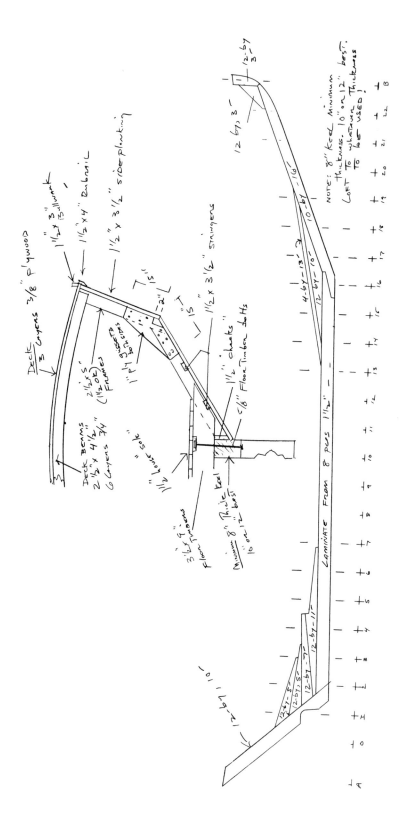

Deck Covers 3/8" Plywood

1½ x 3" Bulwark

1½ x 4" Rubrail

1½ x 3½" Side Planking

Deck Beams
2½" x 4½" x 24"
6 Layers 3/4

2½ x 5"
(1½ OK)
Frames

15"

2"

"T"
15"

1½ x 3½" Stringers

1"Ply Gussets
to insides

1½" cheeks
5/8 Floor Timber to H's

1½" house Sole

3½ x 6"
Floor Timbers

Minimum 8" Thick keel
10 or 12 best

12-67, 3'

12-67, 3'

NOTE: 8" Keel Minimum
thickness. 10" or 12" best.
LOFT To whatever Thickness
To be used!

B
12 21
22

4-67-13'-3"
12-67 10'

10-67 10'

Laminate From 8 pcs 1½"

12-67 1'-10'

2-67, 5'   12-67-11"
12-67-7'

0 1 2 3 4 5 6 7 8 9 10 11 12 13 14 15 16 17 18 19 20 21 22

H

A

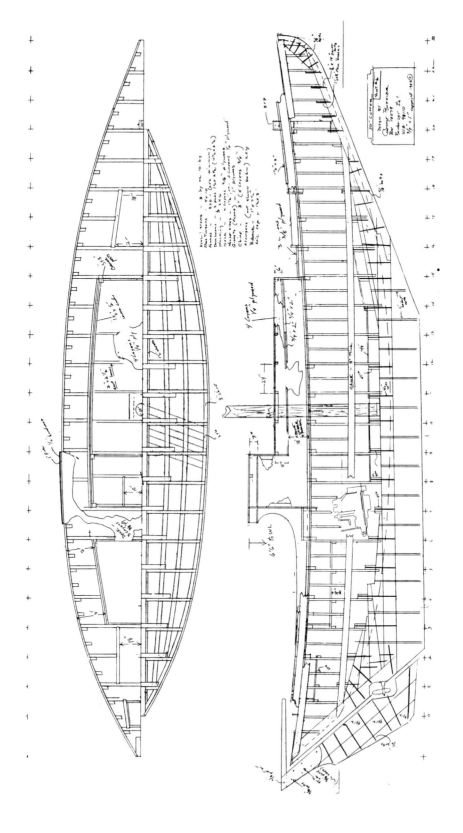

Dragonfly

353

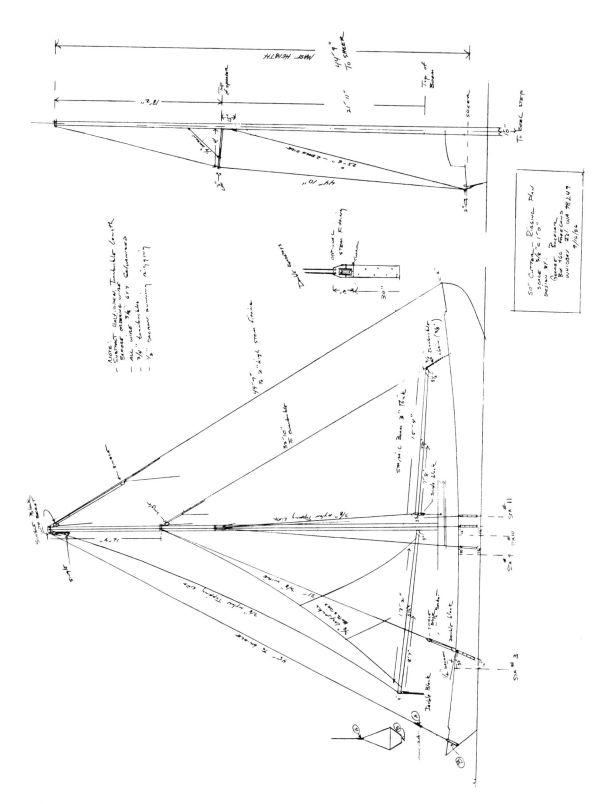

A.W. HUDEMANN

LOD:	55' 4"
LWL:	53' 7"
Beam:	15' 6"
Draft:	6'
Displacement:	73,600 lbs.

This big boat is very similar to the northern European fishboats, with one huge difference: The chine hull makes him easy to build. I would love to own this boat. I could easily get used to cruising under power.

AW's engine room is big, and a GM 4-71 is sketched in because that's an easy engine to find secondhand. But if I was building him, I'd use a Deutz 4- or 6-cylinder aircooled diesel. These things are rugged and fuel efficient. As mentioned back in the book, aircooled engines need air ducting, but you could route it to blow hot air into the wheelhouse during cold weather, which makes all that ductwork worth the effort.

I'd also change the interior. I'd remove the two bunks in the bow and put the head there. The area where the head is now would become part of the main cabin. The whole area behind the wheelhouse is devoted to the owner's bedroom, with a 5- by 7-foot walkaround double bed. I suppose the galley and table could be moved there, but I like the idea of a real bedroom in a boat. Sounds luxurious.

Scantlings are the same as the big sailboats, although the frames this time are 3 by 6. Although 1½-inch planking is enough, I'd consider gluing and nailing another two layers of ½-inch plywood over it, as described back in Chapter 7. This would give you a 2-inch skin. As this is a big and heavy boat, she needs to be built hefty.

Put in as much fuel tankage as you want. I'd build in maybe 800 gallons minimum, in 50- to 100-gallon tanks hooked in series. Oh yes, this guy will have *two* hawsepipes through the planking for anchors!

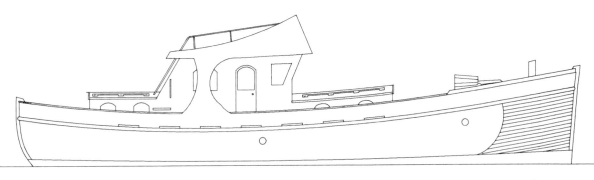

A.W. Hudemann

Table of Offsets

55' motorship A.W. Hudemann

Design by George Buehler

Distances from Water Line

	0	2	4	6	8	10	12	14	16	18	20	22	24	26	28	30	32	34	36	38	40	42	44	46	48	50	52	54	54'-8 5/16'
Raised sheer	8-8-1+	8-3-7+	7-11-6	7-7-5	7-3-8	7-0-0	6-8-3+																						
Sheer	7-2-4+	6-10-2	6-6-0+	6-1-7	5-9-7	5-6-0+	5-2-3+	4-11-1	4-8-1+	4-5-2+	4-2-6+	4-0-4+	3-10-4	3-8-7	3-7-4	3-6-3	3-5-1	3-5-0	3-4-6	3-4-6	3-5-1	3-5-6+	3-6-6	3-8-1+	3-10-0	4-0-2	4-2-7+	4-5-7+	4-7-0-
Chine			0-0-7	0-0-3+	0-3-7+	0-5-2	0-6-5	0-7-6	0-8-6	0-9-5	0-10-2	0-10-7	0-11-5	0-11-6	0-11-7	0-11-6	0-11-5	0-11-2	0-10-6	0-10-0	0-9-1	0-8-0+	0-6-6+	0-5-3	0-3-7	0-2-3	0-0-6		
Rabbet			1-9-5	2-0-6	2-3-6	2-6-6	2-9-5	3-0-3	3-2-7	3-5-1	3-7-1	3-8-6	3-10-1	3-11-0	3-11-6	4-0-0	4-0-0	3-11-4	3-10-5	3-9-2	3-7-3	3-4-6	3-1-4	2-9-1	2-3-5	1-9-0	1-1-6	0-6-0	
Keel																													

Keel profile dimensions are given on Lines Plan

Half-Widths

	0	2	4	6	8	10	12	14	16	18	20	22	24	26	28	30	32	34	36	38	40	42	44	46	48	50	52	54
Sheer	0-3-6	1-2-1	2-1-2	3-0-0	3-10-1	4-7-2	5-3-4	5-10-4	6-4-2	6-9-0	7-0-6	7-3-4	7-5-5	7-7-1	7-8-1	7-8-7	7-9-1	7-8-7	7-8-0	7-6-4	7-4-1	7-0-5	6-7-3	6-0-1	5-2-3	4-1-3	2-8-7	
Chine		0-8-4	1-4-2	1-11-7	2-7-3	3-2-6	3-9-7	4-4-6	4-11-1	5-5-1	5-10-5	6-3-4	6-7-5	6-10-7	7-1-2	7-2-6	7-3-1	7-3-1	7-0-5	6-9-5	6-5-4	5-11-5	5-3-6	4-5-1	3-4-4	2-2-2	0-11-1	
Rabbet																												
WL 2'																							5-4-7		4-5-6+	3-4-2	2-0-2	

Keel half-width is 0-3-6 the entire lenght

PARTICULARS

Lenght between Perpendiculars: 54'-8 5/16"
Lenght Water Line: 53'-8"
Length on Deck: 55'-4 5/16"
Draft: 6'-0"
Beam: 15'-6"
Loaded Displacement: 73,601 pounds.

Note: All heights are based off waterline, so, CHINE and RABBET dimensions are BELOW waterline. Common station spacing 2'-0"

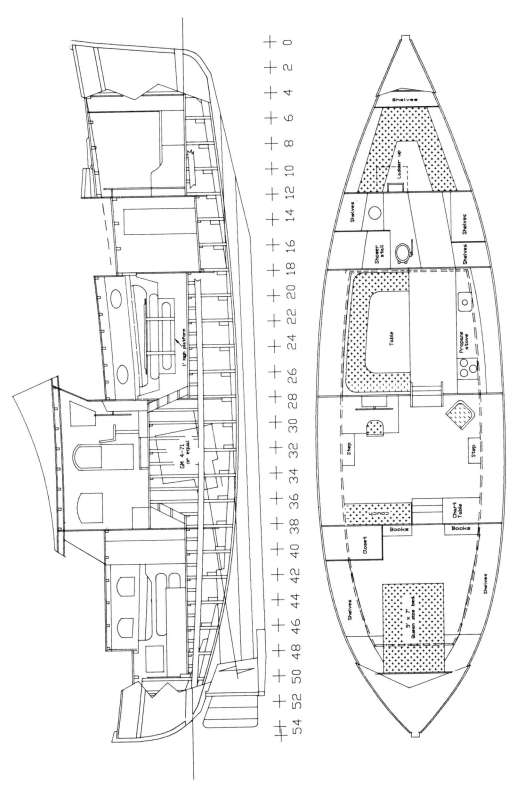

A.W. Hudemann

357

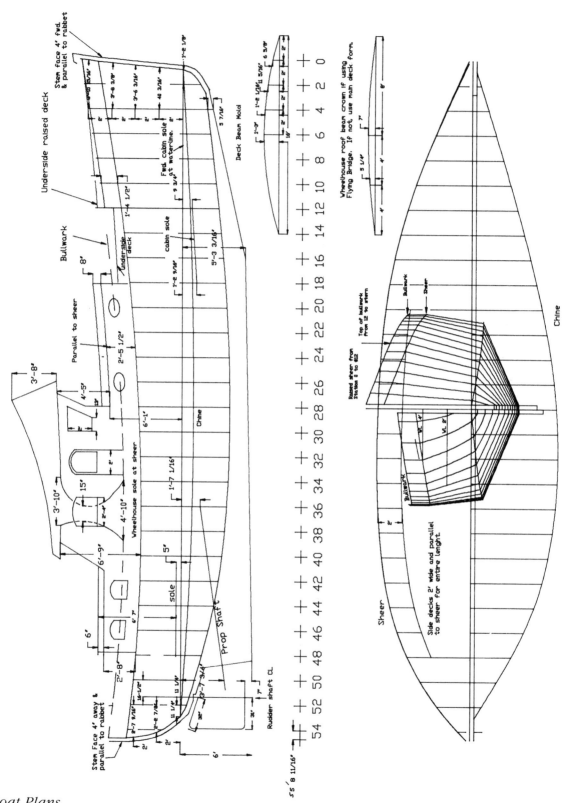

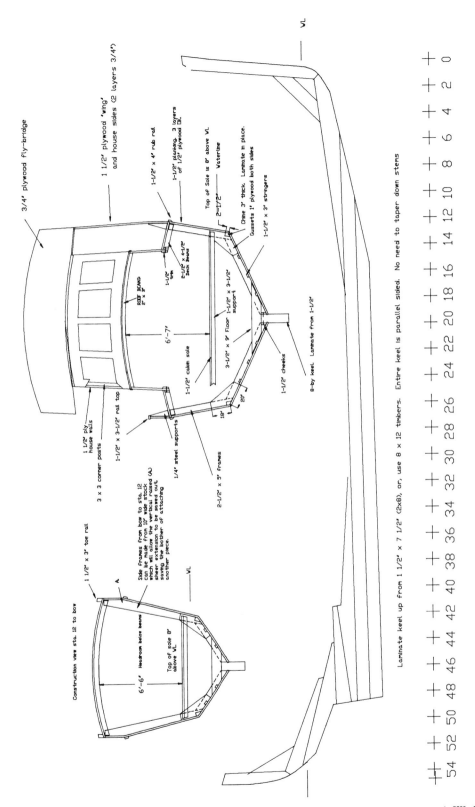

3/4" plywood fly-bridge

1 1/2" plywood 'wing' and house sides (2 layers 3/4")

1-1/2" x 4" rub rail

1-1/2" planking, 3 layers of 1/2" plywood Dk.

Top of Sole is 8' above VL   Waterline

2-1/2"

Chine 3" thick. Laminate in place.

Gussets 1" plywood both sides

1-1/2" x 3" stringers

2-1/2" x 4-1/2" Deck Beams

1-1/2" trim

ROOF BEAMS 2" x 3"

3-1/2" x 3-1/2" support

6'-7"

1-1/2" cabin sole

3-1/2" x 9" Floor

1-1/2" cheeks

8-by keel. Laminate from 1-1/2"

1 1/2" ply house walls

3 x 3 corner posts

1-1/2" x 3-1/2" rail top

1/4" steel supports

2-1/2" x 5" frames

18"

20"

Construction view sta. 12 to bow

1 1/2" x 3" toe rail

A

Side frames from bow to sta. 12 can be made from 10" wide stock which will allow the vertical raised (A) sheer extension to be sawed out, saving the bother of attaching another piece.

A

Headroom below beams

6'-6"

Top of sole 8' above VL

VL

Laminate keel up from 1 1/2" x 7 1/2" (2x8), or, use 8 x 12 timbers. Entire keel is parallel sided. No need to taper down stems

VL

54 52 50 48 46 44 42 40 38 36 34 32 30 28 26 24 22 20 18 16 14 12 10 8 6 4 2 0

VL

A.W. Hudemann

359

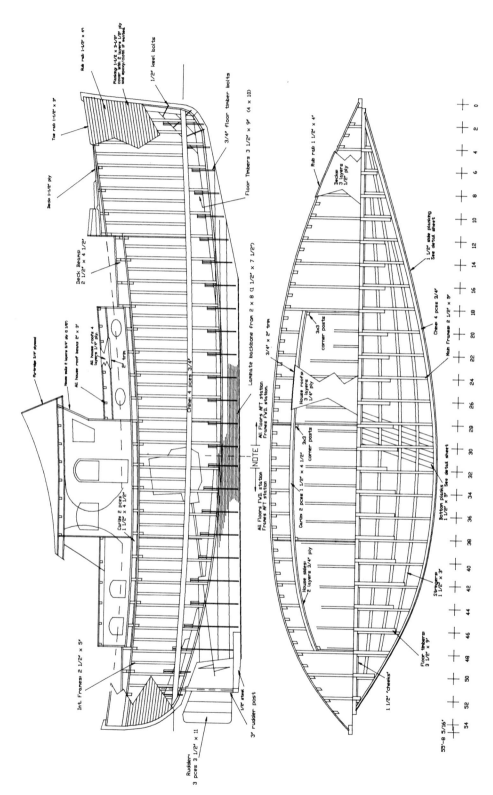

CHANGING A DESIGN

Some designers act as though Divine Guidance moved their pen along the paper. I happen to be a designer, too, and maybe it's my life-style, but the fact is I just draw what I like. I suspect that's all the others in the business do, too. This being the case, there's no reason why you shouldn't change a design if you want. Maybe you're a different denomination.

This becomes more of a problem than just dogma-diddling when a guy who knows nothing about boats starts making changes. The most common mistake is raising a boat's freeboard, and one of the saddest boats I've ever seen was a Chapelle schooner built by a dirt farmer who raised the freeboard 18 inches. He killed the boat, and its bowsprit drooped with shame.

But, if you see a design that's very close to what you want, and if you have some feel for boats and a little experience using them, the odds are your ideas will make the boat even better, or at least easier to build and no worse. This is especially true these days, when many of the current designers have no building experience and so draw shapes that are hard to build for no particular reason other than aesthetics: a round cabin front, for instance, or a curved transom.

Using my own plans as an example, you'll note that the wheelhouses and cabins are ''square,'' not round. I could have made the drawing a lot flashier-looking by showing round houses and transoms, inboard rudders, or fuller sterns on the double-enders. However, the odds are a beginner or an average guy couldn't have built it. If you're a crackerjack craftsman with a lot of confidence, by all means give *Olga, Jullian*, or *Archimedes* a round face to the wheelhouse. It will look great.

In fact, *Olga's* plans could be changed a fair amount without hurting her. For instance, you see how the top of the bulwark isn't a continuation of the side? Well, you could make it a straight line from the chine to the railtop and raise the deck to the top of it, which would make her more comfortable inside because the floor (sole) would be 18 inches higher, and so wider. Of course, she wouldn't look so neat, but everything's a tradeoff.

You could change her rig to a marconi, or throw away the wheelhouse. The rabbet line could be raised a good 12 inches or more, which would decrease the displacement and make her stiffer, too. Of course if you do that, you'll have to change the chine width to keep the parallel lines on the bottom frames, which is a good thing. If you do that, be aware that you're doing major surgery; don't do it if you're new to boats.

Cabin shapes are simple to change. So many new designs have raked fronts and backs on the deck houses, which means windows and the entrance hatch can't be open in the rain or you get wet inside. Square them up! As mentioned before, *Hagar* has a raised-sheer house which I'd change to a deck house with 10-inch side decks if I were building it. *Archimedes* has a reverse-curved rabbet on the stem. It won't affect him at all if you make this a straight line, which would make building a little simpler.

The powerboats could have outside rudders. If you do that, straighten out *Alaska's* stern so the sternpost rabbet is a straight line. This will make the planking a bit easier to fit and the rudder simpler to hang. For that matter, the curve to the sterns on all the double-enders was done to make the drawing look better, and the boat will be easier to plank if you make the stern rabbet a straight line.

Changing the interior won't make any difference at all. Build what you want. It's your boat, after all. Let me warn you that most people make interiors too busy. Keep things simple and spacious.

Most boats will be better if stretched. The simplest way to do this is, when lofting, to increase the station spacing and keep the other dimensions the same. Obviously, if you lengthen it then you have to redo the rig, too. I wouldn't stretch *Hagar* since he's already sort of a stretched 24-footer.

Juno has quite a sweep to the sheer, and if you raised it in the middle area you probably wouldn't hurt her. She'd be drier, but she wouldn't look as good. As she is she works beautifully. I've single-handed her in what the radio said was a full gale, and I felt safe and comfortable and never took water over the ends.

What I'm trying to say is that no boat's design is carved in stone and there's no reason why you shouldn't change a plan around *if* you know what you're doing. If you see a design that's close to what you like but not "it," then do what you want. It's your time and money.

Of course, if you change a design and it doesn't work, you have only yourself to blame. Having faith and confidence in yourself and accepting responsibility for your own actions is rare and even socially unacceptable these days. "Da Debble made me do it"; "He was stoned; He had a rough childhood"; we hear all sorts of excuses.

That's one thing rather appealing about Moslem law. They don't care *why* a guy did something, just whether or not he did it. You know, if Lyndon Johnson had simply gone on the tube and said something like: "Ma Fellow Amurkins, ah fugged up. Ah trusted the generals, ah trusted the corporations, ah didn't have the nerve to change Kennedy's policies, and now 50 some-odd-thousand young Amurkins are daid. God alone knows how many of them Vietnamese folks are daid, too. Let's get outa there."

If Lyndon had done that, maybe things would be different today. But then it seems like there are definite spots throughout history where, if only such and such had happened, the whole picture would be different. Imagine how different the world might be today if Lincoln hadn't been shot, Hitler had been accepted into art school, or if Coltrane hadn't died young.

I see I'm getting off the subject again, which was changing a design. Sure, do it if you want, if you think you can do it better. The odds are you can, because there's almost always some little thing that could make a finished design better, at least for you!

SUGGESTED READING

There are a few books that I recommend you read along with this one. I'm sure there are more good ones out there than I'm mentioning, but these are books that I use for reference myself, for whatever that's worth. Most are available in better book stores, or mail order from International Marine Publishing Company, 1-800-822-8158; otherwise, try your local library or used-book store.

Boatbuilding   by Howard Chapelle (W.W. Norton, 1941 and 1969). This book has been called the *Bible* of wood boatbuilding. Anybody building a boat should own it. You'll note a few places where Chapelle says to do something different than I do. There's a reason: my way is simpler, and I started doing it my way after *trying* to do it as Chapelle says.

How To Build A Wooden Boat   by David C. "Bud" McIntosh (WoodenBoat Publications, 1987). This book is both informative *and* fun to read. Although the hull section is about round-bilge boats, all the rest applies to any boat.   You'll enjoy reading it, and will likely find it a handy reference source.

Boatbuilding In Your Own Back Yard   by Sam Rabl (Cornell Maritime Press, 1947 and 1958). I would have found it *impossible* to build my first boat without this book! It's really slanted to home builder types. However, it does leave out a lot of things, which is why I wrote the original version of this book, which was my Shop Manual. Although mine is more complete and more "contemporary," Rabl's book is still worth owning.

The Sailor's Sketchbook   by Bruce Bingham (Seven Seas Press, 1983). I've never met Bruce, but I can tell ya he's one of them guys you love to hate. Too much talent. Anyhow, this book is full of tips and detailed drawings of little things you can do to your boat to make things more comfortable or easier. It's worth owning.

The Rigger's Apprentice by Brian Toss (International Marine Publishing, 1984). If you want to *really* get into rigging and ropework stuff, Brian's book is the one for you. He's a local boy who lives not too far from me, and he knows his stuff.

OK, those books will help you build your boat, in the highly unlikely event you need additional info beyond what *my* book says. The following books will help you get going once you're afloat.

Cruising Under Sail and ***Voyaging Under Sail*** by Eric Hiscock (Oxford University Press, 1959). These two classics went out of print, and were revised and combined into one volume, ***Cruising Under Sail, Third Edition*** (International Marine Publishing, 1981). This is still the best general information about outfitting and sailing that I know of.

The first time I got in a blow while alone on a boat, off Point Sur, California, I had no idea what to do, so I let everything flap, dived into the cabin, and speed-read Hiscock's section on heaving-to. I put on a life jacket and stuck a flare gun in my pocket (for some reason), went outside and did what he said. It worked! When I got things tied down (I didn't have the jiffy reefing described in this book), I looked up and there was a ship, dead in the water, about 100 yards from me! Apparently they saw that I didn't know what was happening, and were all set to rescue me. I waved and they honked their horn and took off! Get Hiscock's books. They're the best.

Ocean Passages For The World published by the Hydrographer of the Royal Navy and available at any good chart store. This book is an updated version of the original, which lists the route to take if you want to go *anywhere* on the planet by water. It's now in two sections—the first half for power-driven ships, and the second half a shortened version of the original, which was for sailing ships. The text warns that, ''routing advice in this section was intended for large sailing vessels able to stand up to, and take advantage of, the heavy weather to be expected on many of these passages.''

For instance, if you want to go from Puget Sound to the South Pacific or Hawaii, the book says: ''Stand seaward to make a safe offing, but keeping as close inshore as prudence dictates, to avoid the heavy seas found further out. Proceed S until within 300 miles of San Francisco, and thence proceed direct to Honolulu. W. of Honolulu the route is seasonal.'' Numerous fold-out color charts come with the book.

World Cruising Routes by Jimmy Cornell (International Marine Publishing Company, 1987). This is more or less the same book as *Ocean Passages*, but without the charts and the power ship routes, and rewritten without the nice formal British English. Personally, I like the original, but Cornell's is perfectly good. I own them both.

Learning how to use a sextant is essential, even if you do carry a satnav! There are numerous books out telling you how to do it, but only two good ones, as far as I'm concerned. The simplest, clearest, most basic "how-to" is **How To Find Where You Are From The Sun**, by Yours Truly. It does *not* teach you astronomy. It just tells step by step how to do it. It's available from me, and from several of the better maritime book stores in the U.S.

Primer Of Navigation   by George W. Mixter (Van Nostrand Reinhold, 1967). This is the best real book on navigation. Mixter was one of those renaissance guys, like Jefferson, who dabbled in many things. Navigation was his hobby, and the book he wrote was so good that it became the standard. It was used as the training manual for many World War II navigators, and has been upgraded several times since his death in 1947 to include whatever new stuff came along, like radar or loran. Unfortunately it's out of print, but so many were printed that it will be easy to find a copy through a used book seller.

INDEX

Index

Index